Islamic Images
and Ideas

Encyclopedia of Islamic Herbal Medicine (McFarland, 2011)

Islamic Images and Ideas

Essays on Sacred Symbolism

Edited by
JOHN ANDREW MORROW

McFarland & Company, Inc., Publishers
Jefferson, North Carolina, and London

Library of Congress Cataloguing-in-Publication Data

Islamic images and ideas : essays on sacred
symbolism / edited by John Andrew Morrow.
p.   cm.
Includes bibliographical references and index.

ISBN 978-0-7864-5848-6

softcover : acid free paper ∞

1. Islamic art and symbolism.   2. Symbolism.
3. Islam.   I. Morrow, John A. (John Andrew), 1971–
BP182.5.I85 2014   297.3—dc23   2013037134

British Library cataloguing data are available

On the cover: Book of Holy Qur'an (iStockphoto/Thinkstock)

Manufactured in the United States of America

*McFarland & Company, Inc., Publishers
Box 611, Jefferson, North Carolina 28640
www.mcfarlandpub.com*

For Ya-Sin and Ta-Ha

Acknowledgments

The image of Islam has suffered greatly since September 11, 2001, thanks not only to some misguided Muslims themselves, but also to the desire of non–Muslims to exploit such tragedies to advance their particular political and economic causes. As a result, there has been a rise in works aimed at undermining Islam and further marginalizing Muslims. In fact, attacking Islam has become a lucrative business for a certain circle of scholars and political pundits. As the contributors in this anthology have shown, however, scholarship need not be destructive; it can be constructive.

While one cannot deny that Islam has been misinterpreted and even misappropriated by particular parties, such a phenomenon is peripheral and does not impinge upon its essence. As the Prophet Muhammad has said, "Allah is beautiful and loves beauty" (Bukhari). As such, the authors of this work, which features studies by both Muslims and non–Muslims, have attempted to bring the beauty of Islam back into the light.

As one can imagine, it was a distinct honor and privilege to direct such a strong team of scholars who embraced my vision of unity as opposed to division, peace as opposed to conflict, and harmony as opposed to discord. As a result of this inclusive approach, we have been able to produce a book which embraces diversity. I thank you all, then, for confirming that differences in interpretation are not detrimental or damaging to Islam and that the inclusion of Sunni, Shi'ite, and Sufi views actually help to enrich it.

Table of Contents

Introduction

John Andrew Morrow

From its earliest days, Islam was viewed as a threat by the Western world. In the minds of many Europeans, Muslims were violent, savage, idolatrous barbarians who sought to destroy Christendom through plunder and pillage. For more than a millennium, the true nature of Islam was hidden behind an iron curtain of ignorance which was rarely pierced by adventurous Europeans in search of knowledge and understanding. As the Islamic world commenced to crumble, and the Western world started to rise in its place, European powers commenced a campaign of conquest and colonization. Although some Westerners learned a great deal about Islam and Muslims in the process, the very nature of imperialism required the continual dehumanization of the conquered subject and a protracted campaign of propaganda aimed at justifying the subjugation and slaughter of the exotic other.

As former subjects of European imperialists slowly regained their apparent independence in the twentieth century, a brief window of opportunity was opened allowing a momentary breeze of information to spread to the Western world. This period of time, however short, produced a large wave of conversions to the Islamic faith in both Western Europe and the Americas and increased understanding between Muslims and non–Muslims around the world. Regrettably, as a result of revolutions, revolts, and rebellions around the Muslim world in the early twenty-first century, public attention has shifted from Islam to Islamism. Due to the detrimental over-emphasis on political Islam, the true legacy of spiritual Islam has suffered significant neglect. For many people in this day and age, Islam is viewed primarily as a perilous political ideology which is determined to destroy democracy. When Western powers conquered or occupied India, China, Southeast Asia, Africa, Oceania, and the Americas, virtually none from these colonial powers described their plunder and exploitation as the work of Christianity. However, whenever Arabs or Muslims engage in imperial endeavors or violent action, the blame always falls on Islam. Consequently, the true nature of Islam, as a spiritually rich, family-based faith with an overriding emphasis on ethics, has eluded many individuals. Misinformed and misled by the mass media, which overemphasizes the unrepresentative actions of a minority of misguided Muslims, many individuals in the West maintain the same sorts of ideas about Islam that once prevailed in Medieval Europe at the height of the Crusades.

As much as Islamism merits serious scholarly study, it should not come at the expense of Islam. Since Islamism is the product of modernity, and a recent innovation in Islam, it cannot, and must not, take precedence over Islam as a world religion and a 1,400-year-old faith that sustains nearly two billion human beings. As a result, and in response to the growing demand for academic works which reveal what Islam truly teaches, I decided to devote a study on Islamic images and ideas to expose readers to the inner dimensions of the Muslim faith. Inevitably, any such studies on Sufism, *tasawwuf*, or Islamic Gnosticism rep-

1

resent an inherent rejection of the literalism and fundamentalism that fuels extremist interpretations of Islam. While my initial intent was to complete this work on my own, I was prevented from doing so as a result of my numerous other academic endeavors. Fortunately, I was not alone in objecting to the over-emphasis on militant Islam instead of mystical Islam. As a result, I soon rounded up a team of outstanding academics from around the world — including Algeria, Azerbaijan, Canada, Egypt, and Iran, as well as Italy, Morocco, Pakistan, and the United States — all of whom were especially eager to expand the Western world's understanding of Islam.

Islamic Images and Ideas: Essays on Sacred Symbolism is a sourcebook for students and scholars seeking a deeper understanding of Islam's spiritual and social side. It is not a book about beliefs (*usul al-din*), does not deal with religious duties (*furu' al-din*), and does not focus solely on jurisprudence (*fiqh*). The work in question falls primarily into the field of '*irfan*, or mysticism, and *tasawwuf*, the science of spirituality, while tackling theological and social issues at the same time. *Islamic Images and Ideas* explores a series of significant symbols found in the Qur'an and the *Sunnah* with each chapter addressing the multifarious manifestations of a single image according to Sunni, Shi'ite and Sufi sources. Each image is analyzed literally and metaphorically from an imaginative, eclectic, innovative, and interdisciplinary approach, which brings together both religious and cultural studies. Consequently, the individual images and ideas are examined exoterically and esoterically, literally and allegorically, as well as theologically and philosophically. Since so much scholarship nowadays is simply based on fundamentally flawed secondary sources, the use of authentic primary sources has been stressed in this study. Rather than rely on the tendentious interpretations of individuals hostile to Islam, the academics involved in this project have based themselves on the Qur'an and Sunnah, namely, the sayings and actions of the Prophet and his Household, as well as a broad range of Qur'anic commentaries, all enriched by the contributions of traditional scholars of Islam whose works have grasped the faith in both its outer and inner dimensions. The end product is an inventory and analysis of the predominant images in the Qur'an and the Sunnah, demonstrating the diversity which exists at the heart of Islamic unity. Rather than impose a modern interpretation of Islam from the outside, the scholars who participated in this project have allowed Islamic sources to speak for themselves and their approach to Islam is totally traditional.

As much as the Qur'an and the Sunnah have been studied in the past, the approaches have almost always been linear or chronological. The Qur'an was interpreted verse by verse and the Sunnah was interpreted saying by saying. The shift towards thematic commentaries of the Qur'an is relatively more recent. The most famous of these works include Sayyid Qutb's (1906–1966) *al-Taswir al-fanni fi al-Qur'an* (*Artistic Imagery in the Qur'an*) (1945), Shaykh Muhammad al-Ghazzali's (1917–1996) *Nahwa tafsir mawdu'i li al-suwar al-Qur'an al-karim* (*Thematic Commentary of the Qur'an*), as well as Ayatullah al-Uzma Nasir Makarim al-Shirazi's (1924–) ten volume *Payam-e Qur'an* (*The Message of the Qur'an*) (1998). With its stress on specific symbols in the Qur'an and Sunnah, *Islamic Images and Ideas* belongs to this new body of scholarship which has taken a radical departure from the age-old sequential approach in which images are examined in isolation. Following in the footsteps of 'Allamah Muhammad Husayn Tabataba'i (1892–1981), who believed in interpreting the Qur'an by the Qur'an, the academics involved in this ambitious project endeavored to expound upon Islamic images based on authentic and authoritative Islamic sources. Considering the coherence and interrelatedness of the Qur'an, its images and ideas interpret themselves.

As much as imagery may seem intangible to the untrained reader, it forms the core of the Qur'an and the center of the Sunnah. An image is the representation of an idea. In literary works, whether of divine or human provenance, images are transmitted via metaphors and allegories. Imagery is thus a pattern of related details in a work. The Arabic word for image is *surah*, which also means shape or form. As a noun, it denotes anything formed, fashioned, figured or shaped after the likeness of any of God's creatures, animate or inanimate. *Surah* also conveys the sense of a mental image or a resemblance of any object, formed or conceived by the mind. It expresses a quality, an attribute or a property. It is a description in the sense of the aggregate of the qualities, attributes or properties of a thing. *Surah* is thus the essence of a thing. It is related to the verb *sawwara*, which means to form, give shape to, and to fashion. In the Qur'an, God Himself is described as *al-Musawwir*, the Fashioner or the Originator (59:24). Allah is not only a literal and physical Creator. As the Creator of the Qur'an, a Book of Signs, Allah is also a Weaver of Images and a Sublime Artist whose masterpiece is creation itself.

Symbolism, like imagery, is the key to comprehending the Qur'an and the Sunnah. A symbol is a token, a watchword, or the outward sign of something. Hence, a symbol means something more than its literal meaning. In this sense, the Qur'an and the Sunnah is simply saturated with symbolism since, in addition to their literal or denotative meanings, their words convey a more complex range of readings. In the Arabic language, symbolism is *ramziyyah*, from the noun *ramz*, which signifies a sign. Another Arabic word for sign is *ayah*, which also means a token or mark by which a person or thing is known. It properly signifies any apparent thing inseparable from a thing not equally apparent so that when a person perceives the former, that individual perceives the latter. Images, symbols, and signs all come together in the Qur'an, a *magnum opus* of multi-layered meanings, which has marveled the most brilliant exegetical minds for nearly a millennium and a half.

While not a complete survey of imagery and symbols found in the Qur'an and Sunnah, which would be an impossible task to accomplish, the work provides an analysis of twenty-four important images and ideas. For the sake of organization, intellectual coherence, and ease of reference, *Islamic Images and Ideas* is divided into four sections: the divine, the spiritual, the physical, and the societal.

The first section, "The Divine," commences with the be all and end all of Islamic belief: "Divine Unity" or *tawhid*. Taking a universal approach to the various theological schools in Islam, I present a panoramic view of the multiple modes of *tawhid*, demonstrating that the degree of commonality between all Muslims far outweighs the differences that have divided them historically. The study on divine unity is followed by Anna Maria Martelli's piece, "Creation," which poses many pertinent questions concerning the world's coming into being. In "Wrath," Amar Sellam shows the severity of the Divinity. Though God is the Avenger in Islam, He is always completely, totally, and utterly just. Hence, Hisham M. Ramadan, a jurist trained in both the Sunni *shar'iah* and Western law, helps complete the profile of the Creator in "Justice."

Having explored issues of faith and theology in the first section, the second section focuses on "The Spiritual." It commences with my study, "The Path," which demonstrates the depth and diversity of Islamic spirituality, thus promoting hermeneutic pluralism as opposed to essentialism and fundamentalism. In "Servitude," Mustapha Naoui Kheir demonstrates that according to Islam, true freedom is solely found through submission, a concept that is quite counter-intuitive to the Western mind. In my study, "Perfection," I explore the Sufi concept of the Perfect Human, a purified person who has become the manifestation of the divine attributes. Anna Maria Martelli's "The Jinn" is a stimulating scholarly survey on the subject of spiritual beings made of smokeless fire. While they are similar to angels and demons in a certain sense, the jinn are interdimensional beings who live within our world and beyond. Like humans, however, they are fallible and are subject to free will. In "Intoxication," Matthew Long provides a meticulous examination of inebriation in all of its dimensions: legal, physical, spiritual, and metaphysical. In the final chapter in the spiritual section, Bridget Blomfield engages in an especially esoteric approach of the Lady of Light, the dignified daughter of the Prophet Muhammad who is much revered by Muslims, particularly those of the Sufi and Shi'ite persuasion. As Blomfield evidences in "Fatimah," Fatimah al-Zahra' is very much the physical embodiment of Islamic spirituality.

The third section, "The Physical," debuts with "Water." In his analysis, Cyrus Ali Zargar provides a profound analysis of water as both physical and spiritual matter. In "The Tree," Said Mentak analyzes another interesting image which many inattentive readers simply pass by when reading the Qur'an. Naglaa Saad M. Hassan's "The Sea" is an expansive examination of oceanic imagery in the Qur'an. In "The Ship," Said Mentak's second study, the scholar showcases the socio-spiritual significance of sea-faring vessels while Naglaa Saad M. Hassan, in what is also her second study, whets the appetite of readers with "Food," a pertinent work that makes a welcome contribution to culinary history. Tackling a touchy topic, Mahdi Tourage's "The Phallus" explores the symbolism of the sexual organ, a work with a firm theoretical foundation. In "Eyebrows," Aida Shahlar Gasimova's shows how Islamic imagery has simply saturated Sufi poetry. In the last piece in this section, Mohamed Elkouche's "The Camel" examines the camel and the needle's eye, in light of both the Bible and the Qur'an.

In the fourth section, the study shifts towards "The Societal." In "The Center," Hamza Zeghlache provides a study on the symbolism of the axis in traditional Islamic architecture and how Islamic images and ideas inspired the physical layout of ancient Muslim cities. This fascinating study is followed by "Ijtihad" by Sayyed Hassan Vahdati Shobeiri, an exploration of a traditional feature of Islam which allows it to adapt and evolve with the times while remaining rooted in immutable Islamic principles. In their study, "Governance," Zahur Ahmed Choudhri and Zahid Shahab Ahmed examine the image of political rule in the Qur'an and Sunnah, an issue which has been of critical concern to the Muslim community since the passing of the Prophet. Mohamed Elkouche's "Otherness" is an especially intelligent exposition of Muslims and their perceived place in the order of society. In "Ashura," Muhammad-Reza Fakhr-Rohani stresses the significance surrounding a tragedy so central to Shi'ism: the tragic slaughter of the Prophet's grandson Husayn in Karbala. Considering the connection between language, culture, and identity, I close this section with "Arabic," an investigation on the importance of Arabic to Islam and Muslims.

Unlike other works on Islam, participants in this project were required to respect their subject and remain rooted in the greater Islamic tradition with its rich diversity. As such, this work very much embraces a broader definition of Islamic orthodoxy which embraces adherents of the four Sunni schools of Islamic jurisprudence — the Hanafi, the Maliki, the Shafi'i and the Hanbali — the two Shi'i schools — the Ja'fari and the Zaydi — as well as the 'Ibadi and Zahiri. Besides recognizing the various legal interpretations of Islam, this work accepts its authentic spiritual and mystical side manifested in the true practices of *tasawwuf* or Sufism. All Muslims agree upon the main elements of their creed and their similarities on fundamentals far outweigh their differences on secondary issues. If fundamentalism, essentialism, and literalism impoverish Islam, divergence of opinion and diversity enrich it.

While each study was subjected to a rigorous process of peer review, inclusion in this volume does not imply approval of each and every idea expressed. Studies were accepted on the basis of a sole criterion: whether or not they made a contribution to scholarship in the field. As such, the scholars featured in this study are solely responsible for the content of their studies and any shortcomings they may contain. Although as editor I may have made modifications for reasons of spelling, syntax, style, and structure, each work remains faithful to the voice and thought of its source. Since the use of diacritical marks exponentially increases the potential for typographical errors, a joint decision was made to suppress them for the sake of simplicity. Diacritics are only of use to specialists who do not need them in the first place. Exceptions have been made, however, with the *ayn* and the *hamzah,* which are generally represented in names and words that have not been Anglicized. Surely, anyone who knows Arabic can identify *sawm* as "fasting" and would be well aware that the "s" in question represents the Arabic letter *sad* as opposed to *sin*. With the exception of specialists, many educated readers find plain print devoid of diacritics to be easier to read as well as easier on the eye.

Since the Qur'an is like an ocean, of which only a small proportion has been explored, this work cannot claim to be complete. As the Prophet professes in the Qur'an, "If the ocean were ink (wherewith to write out) the words of my Lord, sooner would the ocean be exhausted than would the words of my Lord, even if we added another ocean like it, for its aid" (18:109). And yet again: "[I]f all the trees on earth were pens and the ocean (were ink), with seven oceans behind it to add to its (supply), yet would not the words of Allah be exhausted (in the writing): for Allah is Exalted in Power, full of Wisdom" (42:33). While we have only skimmed its surface and scuba-dived to the extent of our physical, intellectual, and spiritual abilities, this exploration will be of value to those who may never have even seen the shores of the sea much less dived into its depths. Even experienced undersea explorers will relish at previously unforeseen perspectives. Considering the treasures it contains, from corals to the most precious of pearls, *Islamic Images and Ideas* provides a panoramic view of many of the major signs and symbols found in the Qur'an and Sunnah. Not only will it illuminate, it may also inspire, serving as a starting point for subsequent studies. One can only hope.

THE DIVINE

Divine Unity[1]

JOHN ANDREW MORROW

"Say He is Allah, the One and Only." (Qur'an 112:1)

Introduction

Despite their doctrinal differences, all Muslim theologians, be they Sunni, Shi'i or Sufi, have listed *tawhid* as the first pillar of Islam. Consequently, the theological mode of *tawhid* is the one which is most familiar to the majority of Muslims. For most Muslims, *tawhid* is the simple profession that "There is no god but Allah," which, in reality, is the lowest level of faith. The theological mode of *tawhid*, however, is far deeper than most Muslims imagine. The very essence of Divine Unity, manifest in the image of the word *Allah*, is the be-all and end-all of Islam: everything originates from it, and everything revolves around it. *Tawhid* is thus the very axis around which Islam revolves: its very *raison d'être*.

The Symbolism of the Shahadah

The profession of faith, *La ilaha illa Allah* or "There is no god but Allah," is not a single statement. In actuality, it contains two components, *La ilaha*, "There is no god," which is followed by *illa Allah* or "but Allah." The first part of the profession is the proclamation that there is no God. There is no God as "God" can be capitalized, it can be written in small caps, it can be made plural as in "gods" and it can be made feminine as in "goddesses." The first part of the proclamation of faith, then, is a negation of God. In other words, before one can believe, one must disbelieve, disbelieve in gods and goddesses, in all shapes in form, spiritual or material. The first part of the *Shahadah* is atheism, in the Western philosophical sense of the destruction of human-made deism that stands in opposition to the Divine.

The second part of the proclamation of faith, *illa Allah* or "but Allah," is an affirmation. Since the second part is dependent on the first, one cannot reach the second unless one has accepted the first. In a spiritual sense, one cannot truly believe in Allah until one has detached oneself from all false deities. These imaginary gods are not only deified cultural heroes, both mythological and historical. These imaginary gods are not merely material wealth, women, and children. As far as Muslim mystics are concerned, anything other than Allah is a false god that must be rejected before one can truly accept the Oneness of Allah.

The belief that "There is no god but Allah," as important as it may be to Muslims, is

8

not sufficient for salvation. If that were so, Iblis or Satan, who was once one of the closest of the Jinns to Allah, would be considered the Best of Believers since he refused to bow to anyone other than Allah. No. In order to be a Believer, one must submit to Allah, something which Satan refused to do out of arrogance and insolence. This obedience towards Allah is specified in the second section of the *shahadah*, "Muhammad is the Messenger of Allah." In order for one to truly believe, one must believe in three things: (1) There is no God, (2) There is only Allah, and (3) Muhammad is the Messenger of Allah. The first part of the *shahadah*, *La ilaha illa Allah*, represents negative energy, while the second part of the *shahadah*, *Muhammadan Rasul Allah*, represents positive energy, without which there would be no light of faith. The union of both is a symbol of *tawhid*, of unity, of oneness, between Allah and His messenger.

In accordance with their interpretation of Islam, the Salafis have attempted to minimize the spiritual might of Muhammad, insisting that he was mere man through whom Allah sent a message. They claim that it is *shirk* or polytheism to place the name of the Prophet next to the name of Allah "as if they were equal." Some have even gone so far as to refuse to recite the salutations to the Prophet in their prayers and the blessings upon the Prophet and his Holy Household, both of which are obligatory according to every school of Islamic jurisprudence. As the Qur'an commands: "Allah and His angels send blessings on the Prophet, O you who believe! Send your blessings on him, and salute him a thorough salutation" (33:56). The Qur'an is emphatic regarding the obligation to obey both Allah and His messenger: "O you who believe! Obey Allah, and obey the Messenger and render not vain your deeds" (47:32) and "He who obeys the Messenger has indeed obeyed Allah" (4:80).

The Multiple Modes of Tawhid

For Sunni Muslims, there are three, and sometimes four, types of *tawhid*: *tawhid al-rububiyyah*, *tawhid al-uluhiyyah*, *tawhid al-asma' wa al-sifat*, and *tawhid al-hakimiyyah*. *Tawhid al-rububiyyah* or the Unity of Lordship means that God is One, the Sole Source of Existence, the Creator and Sustainer of the Universe. *Tawhid al-uluhiyyah*, also known as *'ibadah*, means that all acts of worship belong to Allah alone; and *tawhid al-asma' wa al-sifat* is an affirmation of the attributes of Allah as mentioned in the Qur'an and Sunnah and an assertion that Allah is without similitude. The final form of *tawhid*, *tawhid al-hakimiyyah* or the Unity of Law, is called into question by some Sunnis and some Salafis who claim that it is an innovation. In essence, it means that Allah is All-Law, the sole source of *shari'ah* or legal legislation.

For Twelver Shi'ites, *tawhid* is of three types: *tawhid al-dhat* or the Unity of the Essence, *tawhid al-sifat* or the Unity of Attributes, and *tawhid al-af'al* or the Unity of Action. The Names of the Essence refer to eternal attributes which are specific to Allah alone. The Names of Attributes refer to names whose opposites cannot be applied to God. For example, Alive, Knowing, Powerful, Hearing, and Seeing. The Names of Action refer to names whose opposites can be applied to Allah: Merciful/Wrathful, Gentle/Severe, Beautiful/Majestic, Guider/Misguider, Forgiver/Avenger, Exalter/Abaser, Beneficent/Harmer, Life Giver/Slayer, and Expander/Contractor. One can only become aware of the Unity of Essence if one becomes aware of the Unity of Attributes and the Unity of Action, both of which derive from the Essence from which everything emanates. The Unity of Attributes is manifested prior to creation while the Unity of Action is manifested after creation. *Allah* is the Name of the Essence clothed in all its Attributes. Individual Attributes of Allah, such as *al-Rabb*, represent merely one Aspect of the Essence.

The Positive and Negative Attributes of Allah

In order to better understand Allah, Twelver Shi'ite theologians have described the Divine by means of positive and negative attributes. Just as the profession of faith is composed of both a negative and a positive component, Allah is represented by both negative and positive attributes. The positive attributes of Allah are known as *sifat thubutiyyah* while the negative attributes of Allah are known as *sifat salbiyyah*. The positive attributes of Allah are eight in number and include:

1. *Qadim*: Allah is eternal.
2. *Qadir*: Allah is omnipotent.
3. *'Alim*: Allah is omniscient.
4. *Hayy*: Allah is alive.
5. *Murid*: Allah is independent in action.
6. *Mudrik*: Allah is aware.
7. *Mutakallim*: Allah speaks.
8. *Sadiq*: Allah is Truth.

The negative attributes of Allah are eight in number. They include:

1. *Murakkab*: Allah is not made of material.
2. *Jism*: Allah does not have a body.
3. *Makan*: Allah is not subject to place.
4. *Muhtaj*: Allah is not dependent.
5. *Mar'i*: Allah cannot be seen.
6. *Mahal hawadith*: Allah is not subject to change.
7. *Sharik*: Allah has no partners.
8. *Hulul*: Allah does not incarnate into anything or anybody.

In the place of *sharik*, some scholars list *sifat za'idah* which means that Allah does not have added qualities. In other words, the attributes of Allah are not separate from His being.

The Masculine and Feminine Attributes of Allah

Since it is impossible to understand the essence of Allah — since none knows God but God — the Almighty has revealed attributes through which we may get to know Him. Known as the Ninety-Nine Names or the Most Beautiful Names of Allah, these attributes have been divided into both masculine and feminine attributes by Muslim theologians. The terms "masculine" and "feminine" must not be understood in the sense of male or female as Allah does not have gender. While neither male nor female, Allah unites both the Sacred Masculine and the Sacred Feminine as part of His perfect *tawhid*. It is for this reason that Ibn al-'Arabi says that Allah can be referred to as both *Huwa* (He) and *Hiya* (She). This is also possible because Allah is a genderless noun.

The masculine attributes of Allah, known as the attributes of might and power or *Jalal*, include *al-Malik*, the King; *al-Muhaymin*, the Protector; *al-Jabbar*, the Compeller; *al-Mutakabbir*, the Majestic; *al-Qahhar*, the Subduer; *al-Hasib*, the Reckoner; *al-Qawiyy*, the Strong; *al-Muntaqim*, the Avenger, among many others. Even the Feminine Attributes of Allah are employed in their masculine form.

The feminine attributes of Allah, known as the attributes of beauty or *Jamal*, include *al-Hakim*, or the Wise, derived from *hikmah*, the Arabic word for wisdom, the equivalent of the Greek *Sophia*. The attributes of *al-Rahman* and *al-Rahim* are also feminine attributes, and derive from *rahim*, the Arabic word for womb, matrix or uterus. Most remarkable of all, the word for the Divine Essence itself, *al-Dhat*, is equally feminine. This Divine Essence has been described by Sufi Master Najm al-Din Kubra as "the mother of divine attributes." Although most Muslims employ a masculine pronoun when invoking Allah, following a grammatical tradition in which the masculine takes precedence over the feminine, Ibn al-'Arabi would sometimes employ the feminine pronoun in addressing Allah, keeping in view the Essence. Since Almighty Allah Himself says that "My mercy prevails over My wrath" (*rahmati sabaqat ghadabi*) (Bukhari), the Greatest of Masters is justified in giving precedence to the feminine (*rahmah*) over the masculine (*ghadab*).

The feminine and masculine attributes of Allah exist in opposition to one another, much like the Taoist yin and yang. For example, Allah is the Avenger (*Muntaqim*), the Judge (*Hakam*), and the Just (*'Adil*), but He is also the Gentle (*Halim*), the Oft-Forgiving (*Rahman*), and the Most Merciful (*Rahim*). He is the First (*Awwal*), but He is also the Last (*Akhir*). He is the Creator (*Khaliq*), but He is also the Destroyer (*Mumit*). He is the Giver of Life (*Muhyi*), but He is also the Giver of Death (*Mumit*). He is the Light (*Nur*), but He is also the Hidden One (*Batin*). He is the Abaser (*Khafid*), but He is also Exalter (*Rafi'*). He is the Provider (*Muti'*), but He is also the Withholder (*Mani'*).

Although Islam does not allow Muslims to invoke God as Father or Mother — categorically rejecting the notion that human beings are the children of God — the Feminine and Masculine Attributes of Allah can also be conceived of in terms of the Eternal Paternal and the Eternal Maternal. In a tradition not found in traditional sources, Ibn al-'Arabi cites the Prophet as saying: "The creatures are Allah's family" (*Futuhat* 228.3).

On one occasion, the Prophet and his companions came upon a group of women and children. One woman had lost her child and was looking for him, her breasts flowing with milk. When she found her child, she joyfully placed him in her bosom, and started to nurse him. The Prophet asked his companions: "Do you think that this woman could throw her son in the fire?" They answered "No." He then said: "Allah is more merciful to His servants than this woman to her son" (Bukhari and Muslim).

On another occasion, the Prophet saw a woman running in the hot sun searching for her son. When she found him, she clutched him to her breast saying: "My son! My son!" The companions of the Prophet witnessed this touching scene and wept. Delighted to see their mercy, the Prophet said: "Do you wonder at this woman's mercy [*rahmah*] for her child? By Him in Whose hand is my soul, on the Day of Judgment, Allah shall show more mercy [*rahmah*] toward His believing servant than this woman has shown to her son" (Bukhari).

On yet another occasion, the Prophet said that: "On the day that He created the heavens and the earth, God created a hundred *rahmahs*, each of which is as great as the space which lies between heaven and earth. And He sent one *rahmah* down to earth, by which a mother has *rahmah* for her child" (Muslim). There are also several sayings stressing the symbolism of the womb such as: "I am Allah and I am the All-Merciful. I created the womb and I gave it a name derived from My own name" (Ahmad); "The womb is attached to the Throne" (Muslim) and "The womb is a branch of the All-Merciful" (Bukhari).

Besides the Qur'an and the Sunnah, which offer ample examples of Paternal and Maternal Attributes, images of Allah as both Mother and Father abound in Islamic literature. As Jalal al-Din al-Rumi says: "Even if the mother is all mercy, observe God's mercy in the father's severity" (Rumi. *Diwan* 12409; cf. Schimmel, *Triumphal Sun* 128).

Eternal and Non-Eternal Attributes of Allah

Twelver Shi'ite theologians have also divided the names of Allah into eternal names and non-eternal names, that is, in attributes which existed prior to the Creation, and attributes which manifested themselves after Creation. While Allah was always and will ever be One, He was not always an active Creator. And while Allah was always Merciful, His mercy could only manifest itself after creation; otherwise, there was nothing towards which He could be merciful. As Shaykh al-Saduq explains:

> For example, we say that God was forever Hearing, Seeing, Omniscient, Wise, Omnipotent, Having power, Living, Self-Existent, One and Eternal. And these are His personal attributes. And we do not say that He was from ever Creating, Doing, Intending, pleased, displeased, Giving sustenance, Speaking; because these virtues describe His actions; and they are not eternal; it is not allowed to say that God was doing all these actions from eternity. The reason for this distinction is obvious. Actions need an object. For example, if we say that God was giving sustenance from ever, then we will have to admit the existence of a sustained thing from ever. In other words, we will have to admit that the world was from ever. But it is against our belief that nothing except God is Eternal.

The division of attributes between eternal and non-eternal names is also a symbol of *tawhid*. Muslim theologians, both Sunni and Shi'i, have traditionally divided the most beautiful names of Allah into attributes of incomparability, and attributes of comparability. All divine attributes can be understood in terms of Allah's incomparability. As the Holy Qur'an states: "Nothing is like Him" (42:11) As such, every Attribute of Allah can be used in this sense while professing the *shahadah*: "There is no real but the Real"; "There is no truth but the Truth"; "There is no light but the Light" and so forth.

Transcendence and Immanence

Historically, Muslim theologians have been divided into those who believe in *tanzih* or transcendence and those who believe in *tashbih* or immanence. The proponents of immanence hold that Allah is present in all things while the proponents of transcendence believe that Allah is above His creation. Rather than seeing these positions as contradictory, they can readily be reconciled in the realm of *tawhid*.

The proponents of transcendence or incomparability point to the following verses in their support: "Nothing is like Him" (42:11) and "No vision can grasp Him, but His grasp is over all vision" (6:103). The proponents of immanence or similarity cite the following verses in their support: "And to Allah belong the East and the West. And in whichever direction you turn, there is the Face of Allah. Truly Allah is Vast, All-Knowing" (2:115); "We are nearer to him than the jugular vein" (50:16); "with you where you are" (57:4); "It is not you who slew; it was Allah. When you threw, it was not your act, but Allah's" (8:17). The idea of transcendence is clearly conveyed in the following sacred sayings:

> God the Almighty says: "O man! I was ill, but you did not visit Me." Man says, "My Lord! You are the Lord of all the realms, how can I visit You?" God says, "Do you not know that so-and-so of my servants got ill, but you did not visit him. If you had visited him, you would have found Me with him" [Muslim].
>
> God the Almighty says: "My Servant does not draw near to Me with anything more loved by Me than the religious duties that I have imposed upon him, and My servant continues to draw near to Me with supererogatory works so that I shall love him. When I love him, I am his hearing with which he hears, his seeing with which he sees, his hand with which he strikes, his foot with which he walks..." [Bukhari].

The belief in transcendence is espoused by the followers of exoteric Islam while the belief in immanence is espoused by the followers of esoteric Islam. Although these theological differences have divided Muslims since the dawn of Islam, neither position can be exclusive. The first is associated with Allah's right hand, which symbolizes mercy, and the second is associated with his Left Hand which symbolizes wrath. According to Murata, "God is similar in His incomparability and incomparable in His similarity. Both positions must be maintained if perfect knowledge is to be achieved" (Murata 51–52). Consequently, His transcendence is certainly not in conflict with His immanence. The balance between both positions is what is endorsed by spiritual masters such as Ibn al-'Arabi. As the latter explains in chapter three of his *Fusus al-hikam*: "If you speak of incomparability, you delimit. And if you speak of similarity, you define. If you speak of both, you have hit the mark. You are a leader and a lord in the Gnostic sciences."

Divine Unity, Divine Duality, and Multiplicity of Unity

In trying to articulate the purest form of *tawhid* possible, Isma'ili theologians use the dialect of double negation. They say, for example: He is Merciful, yet He is also not Merciful. He exists, but He also does not exist. The first positive statement affirms that God possesses the attribute while the second negative statement keeps from limiting Him to that particular attribute. For the Isma'ili, unity expresses duality, and duality expresses unity.

The Attributes of Almighty Allah are further subdivided into various categories. Individual names like *Rahman* and *Rahim* express a duality of degree. *Rahman* refers to the fundamental mercy which permeates all things while *Rahim* refers to the secondary mercy which may be held back. *Rahman*, which is stronger than *Rahim*, applies to all of existence. *Rahim* is the mercy which is manifested in heaven and whose opposite, Wrath, is manifested in hell. But the *Rahman* overrides them all. As Allah said: "My Mercy prevails over my Wrath" (Bukhari).

For many Muslim mystics, the concept of Divine Unity embraces a Divine Duality: *ahadiyyat al-ahad*, the Unity of One, and *ahadiyyat al-kathrah*, the Unity of Many. As Murata explains: "In respect to His Self, God possesses the Unity of the One, but in respect of His names, He possesses the Unity of Manyness" (Murata 58–59). This is why Ibn al-'Arabi used to refer to Allah as *al-wahid al-kathir* or the One/Many. Allah is One in Essence, but many in the relationships He has with the cosmos. Muslim mystics also speak of *ahadiyyah*, Allah's Exclusive Unity and *wahidiyyah* or Allah's Inclusive Unity. The Exclusive Unity applies to Allah Himself while the Inclusive Unity or Universality envisages Allah as the Source of Creation. The names of Almighty Allah are also divided into differentiated names or *tafsil* and undifferentiated names or *ijmal*.

For Twelver Shi'ites and Isma'ilis, the concept of *tawhid* is the solution to many theological debates. Take, for example, the question of free will, *qadr*, and predestination, *jabr*, which have divided the majority of the Muslim world. According to the Mu'tazilites, Allah had given guidance to humanity; however, their ultimate destiny depended on themselves. In other words, they had the choice to be guided or misguided, good or bad. According to the Sunni traditionalist, however, the final fate of humanity has been predetermined by Almighty Allah. The solution to the problem was to be found among the Twelver and Sevener Shi'ites who argued in favor of an "intermediate" solution between the absolute predestination of the Ash'ari and the Mu'tazili doctrine of freedom or *tafwid*. Both the Imami and the Isma'ili base their arguments on a famous tradition from Imam Ja'far al-Sadiq which says: *la jabra wa la tafwida bal amrun bayna amrayn*: Neither *jabr* nor *Tafwid*; but something intermediate between the two [extreme] alternatives (Mutahhari). This is just one of many examples in which Shi'ite theologians follow the "middle path" (2:143) of *tawhid* or Divine Unity in finding solutions to doctrinal differences.

Conclusion

Although *tawhid* is typically translated as "oneness," the term derives from the Arabic root *wahhada* which means "to unite, to join, to combine, and to gather." Although Allah is absolutely and utterly One, and Islam adheres to the strictest and purest form of monotheism possible, *Tawhid* literally means "unity" which means "to bring together." As Murata explains, "As soon as we accept the principle of singularity, duality is demanded by Unity and Unity by duality" (58). As the Ikhwan al-Safa' expressed: "God is truly one in every respect and meaning, so it is not permissible that any created and originated thing be truly one. On the contrary, it is necessary that it be a one that is multiple, dual, and paired" (Ikhwan al-Safa'. *Rasa'il* III 201–2). Although Allah is one in essence, He is dual in divine names, and multiple in His manifestations. Allah is that Irresistible Primal Principle to which everything and everyone is drawn. He was the First for He is Allah. He is the Last for He is Allah. Since everything is derived from Allah, and everything will return to Allah, there is truly none other than Allah.

Chapter Note

1. This study was previously published as the preface to the English translation of the *Kitab al-Tawhid* by Shaykh Saduq (See: Saduq, Shaykh. *Kitab al-Tawhid / The Book of Divine Unity*. Trans. Sayyid 'Ali Rizvi. Ed. John Andrew Morrow, Barbara Castleton, and Sayyid 'Ali Rizvi. London and Qum: The Saviour Foundation, 2010) It also appeared in an anthology of my academic articles titled *Islamic Insights* (See: Morrow, John Andrew. *Islamic Insights: Writings and Reviews*. Qum: Ansariyan, 2012).

Works Cited

Bukhari, Muhammad ibn Isma'il al-. *Sahih al-Bukhari*. al-Riyad: Bayt al-Afkar al- Dawliyyah li al-Nashr, 1998.

_____. *The Translation of the Meanings of Sahih al-Bukhari*. Trans. Muhammad Muhsin Khan. Lahore: Kazi Publications, 1983.

Ibn al-'Arabi. *The Bezels of Wisdom*. Trans. R.W.J. Austin. New York: Paulist Press, 1980.

_____. *Futuhat*. al-Qahirah: al-Hayah al-Misriyyah al-'Ammah li al-Kitab, 1972.

_____. *The Meccan Revelations*. Ed. Michel Chodkiewicz. Trans. William C. Chittick and James W. Morris. New York: Pir Press, 2002–2004.

Ikhwan al-Safa'. *Rasa'il*. al-Qahirah: al-Matba'ah al-'Arabiyyah, 1928.

Murata, Sachiko. *The Tao of Islam*. Albany: SUNY Press, 1992.

Muslim ibn al-Hajjaj al-Qushayri al-Nisaburi. *Jami' al-sahih*. al-Riyad: Bayt al-Afkar al-Dawliyyah li al-Nashr, 1998.

Mutahhari, Murtaza. "An Introduction to *'ilm al-kalam*." *al-Tawhid* 2: 2 (Jan.1985). Internet: www.al-Islam.org/al-tawhid/kalam.htm

Naqvi, 'Ali Muhammad. *A Manual of Islamic Beliefs and Practice*. London: Muhammadi Trust, 1990.

Creation

ANNA MARIA MARTELLI

He set upon the earth mountains towering high above it. He pronounced His blessing upon it and in four days provided it with sustenance for all alike. Then He made His way to the sky, which was but a cloud of vapor, and to it and to the earth He said: "Will you obey me willingly, or shall I compel you?" "Willingly," they answered. In two days He formed the sky into seven heavens with brilliant stars and guardian comets. Such is the design of the Mighty One, the All-knowing. (Qur'an 41:10–12)

Introduction

The conciseness of the Qur'an concerning the origin of physical existence poses a series of questions: first of all, was it a creation *ex nihilo* or not? Considering the evolution of the words and expressions employed in the Qur'an to render the concept of creation in its various forms, it is not easy to answer. In fact, the *kun fa-yakunu* (2:117): "When He decrees a thing, He need only say 'Be,' and it is," would support the thesis of a creation *ex nihilo*; however the Attributes in 49:24: "He is Allah, the Creator [*al-Khaliq*], the Originator [*al-Bari'*], the Modeler [*al-Musawwir*]," would presuppose an action carried out on a pre-existing matter. The pristine sense of *khalaqa* is "to refine, to model." It is employed for the creation of humankind starting from clay (6:2), from dust (22:5), and from a drop of fluid (16:4). "He moulds you in your mother's wombs by stages in three-fold darkness" (39:6)—this three-fold darkness is made up of the abdominal wall, the matrix and the placenta. *Khalaqa* is employed jointly with *sawwa* "to well proportion" (87:2) and is replaced by *sawwara* "to mould" (40:64).

Creation

"The creation of heaven and earth is greater than the creation of man" (40:57), yet it is not less certain that the terms expressing the creation of the physical universe all suppose a pre-existing matter: "He raised the heavens without visible pillars and set immovable mountains on the earth" (31:10); "We built the heaven with Our might, giving it a vast expanse, and stretched the earth beneath it. Gracious is He who spread it out" (51:47–48). Even more concrete is the following statement: "Are the disbelievers unaware that the heavens and the earth were one solid mass which We tore asunder?" (21:30). The concept of separation connected with the creating deed is strengthened in the Qur'an by two divine attributes: "He is the Separator of the heavens and earth" and "He is the Lord of the Separation."

16

In the Qur'an, the *kun fa-yakunu* expresses, at the same time, the command (*amr*) of Allah, His will (*irada*) and His decree (*qada*). Verse 16:40 presents the Word (*kalimah*) as the result of the divine will, while verse 36:82: "When He decrees a thing He need only say: 'Be,' and it is" identifies it with the command, the order. The creating Word expresses above all the divine Almightiness. Allah is He who creates: "Praise be to Allah, the Creator [*al-Fatir*] of heaven and earth. He multiples His creatures according to His will. Allah has power [*qadir*] over all things" (35:1). The main manifestation of the power of Allah is the ability to create: "Recite in the name of your Lord, who created" (96:1). One of the more important Attributes of Allah is that of Creator (*al-Khaliq* or *al-Fatir*) which, on the other hand, is the title of *Surah al-Fatir* (The Chapter of the Originator) (35).

The term *kun* has been an endless source of reflection for theologians and philosophers. For instance, it was the center of the theological debates about the uncreated character of the Qur'an. According to Sunnis, who relied on 7:54 "His is the creation, His is the command," here there is a distinction between the creation and the command of Allah: the Word expresses the command of Allah and therefore is not created. The expression *kun fa-yakunu* is at the origin of the thesis of a creation *ex nihilo*, supported by almost all theologians and commentators against philosophers, who, alone, maintained the thesis of the eternity of the world.

According to the Isma'ili philosopher Nasir-i-Khusraw, from Allah emerges His word "Be!," which brings into existence the Universal Intellect, perfect in potentiality and actuality. The Universal Intellect transcends time and space, containing all being within itself. The Universal Intellect enjoys a worshipful intimacy with Allah and derives perfection from this intimacy. From this worship emerges the Universal Soul, perfect in potentiality but not in actuality because it is separated from Allah by the Intellect. The Universal Soul recognizes its separation from Allah and moves closer to Allah in a desire for the perfection enjoyed by the Intellect. Through its search for perfection, the Universal Soul introduces the first movement into the entire structure, manifest in time and space.

The Sequence of Created Things

Then there is the question of the sequence of created things. Some things were created before the heavens and the earth and the *ahadith* (prophetic traditions) try to establish a primacy among them. Side by side with *ahadith*, *tafasir* (Qur'anic commentaries) enrich the image of creation. The Preserved Tablet (*al-Lawh al-Mahfuz*) comes first, followed by the Pen (*al-Qalam*); then there is water, which is the origin of life, and wind, which has to contain water. Yet, according to al-Bukhari (Book 4, vol. 54, *h.* 414), the Prophet said: "First of all, there was nothing but Allah, and (then He created His throne). His throne was over the water, and He wrote everything in the Book (in the heaven) and created the heavens and the earth."

The Qur'an does not show itself only as a Divine Revelation transmitted by an angel to the Prophet; it also states to be the result of the "descent" of a Book, the heavenly archetype of which is preserved beside Allah: "Surely this is a glorious Qur'an, inscribed on a Preserved Tablet" (85:21–22). When commenting upon verse 97:1: "We revealed the Qur'an on the Night of *Qadr*," the *ahadith* explain that the Tablet descended from above the seventh heaven, where it was located, down to the heaven of this world which is the lowest.

"Every age has its scripture; Allah confirms or abrogates what He pleases. His is the Eternal Book" (*Umm al-Kitab*, 13:39), which is often identified with the Preserved Tablet. "And with Him is the source of the Book," i.e. the Preserved Table, is reported in the *Tafsir Ibn 'Abbas*. The expression *Umm al-Kitab* in 13:39 seems to have a different meaning in 3:7 where it is acknowledged that some Qur'anic verses are clear and solid while others might be termed allegorical; the latter, in fact, being nonetheless sacred, may be interpreted in a personal way while their real meaning is known to Allah only. Some commentators thought they had to distinguish between two different tablets: one containing the primogenital text of the Qur'an, and another the repository of all past, present and future Divine decisions. The Pen is the title of *Surah* 68. The Pen is at the same time a Divine Instrument and a symbol of knowledge: "Recite! Your Lord is the Most Bountiful One, who by the Pen taught man what he did not know" (96:3–5) and: "By the Pen, and what they write."

"We made every living thing from water [*ma'*]" (21:30). This statement appears a total of four times in the Qur'an with some variations, including: "Allah created every beast from water" (24:45); "It was He who created man from water" (25:54); "He is created from an ejected fluid" (86: 5–7). Water is an essential element in paradise, the place of everlasting life, and for plants, animals and human beings of the earthly world. In the Qur'an, water is the element that gives life. Also the gardens of paradise are full of *ma' maskub*, namely, "gushing waters" (56:31).

On the water floats the Throne. In the Qur'an, two words are employed to describe it: *'arsh* recurs more often but in verse 2:255 the word *kursi* is used. *Kursi* also designates the throne of Solomon: "We placed a counterfeit upon his throne" (38:24), on the contrary *'arsh* is employed for the throne of the Queen of Sheba, transported on the air and altered beyond recognition by *jinn*: "And to his nobles he said: 'Which of you will bring to me her throne?'" (27:38). The image in 11:7: "Throned above the waters," is taken again by Ibn 'Abbas who reports that, before the creation of the heavens and earth, the Throne was upon the waters. The Throne is immense or sublime, *al-'azim* (23:86). Eelsewhere, it is called noble or *al-karim* (23:116). It is also said to be "as vast as the heavens and the earth" (2:255).

Air (*jaw*) refers to the space between earth and the sky where birds fly about. Their ability to hover is seen as a mark of the Divine Almightiness: "Do they not see birds that wing their flight in heaven's vault?" (16:79). However, in the Qur'an, air appears chiefly in the shape of a vital breath and of wind, air for antonomasia, in its quality of cosmological element. Wind was subdued to Solomon: "To him We subdued the raging wind" (21:81); "To Solomon We subdued the wind, travelling a month's journey morning and evening" (34:12); "We subdued the wind to him. So that it blew softly at his bidding wherever he directed it" (38:36).

As for the creation of the heavens and earth, most of the sources start with the creation of the latter stating that the heavens had already been shaped. However, the heavens and earth were a compact mass before the separation (21:30); only after that the seven heavens were molded. Several verses describe the creation as the work of an architect: the hills of Safa and Marwa are "beacons of Allah" (2:158), the 'Arafat mountain is qualified as a "sacred monument" (2:198). In the architecture of creation, Allah is "He who tore asunder the heavens and earth," the earth is compared to a bed (*firash*) and the sky to a dome (*al sama' bina'*): "Your Lord who has made the earth a bed for you and the sky a dome" (2:22); "It is Allah who has given you the earth for a dwelling-place and the sky for a ceiling" (40:64). The earth and all that covers it are assembled as if they were the components of a construction: "It was He who spread out the earth and placed upon it rivers and immovable mountains"

(13:3); "And in the land there are adjoining plots: vineyards and cornfields and groves of palm, the single and the clustered" (13:4). The beauty of the creation, its completeness and therefore its perfection are described as the work of the Supreme Artist. The sky is compared to a ceiling strongly held (*saqf mahfuz*). However this extraordinary creation is also a prodigy, because it is "without visible pillars" (13:2). It would seem that the only bearings for heavens were mountains: "He raised the heavens without visible pillars [*'amad*] and set immovable mountains on the earth" (31:10).

The universe is formed by the heaven (*sama'*) or the heavens (*samawat*), by the earth (*ard*), by the space between them (*ma bayna-huma*) and by that placed under the earth (*ma tahta al-thara*). In the Qur'an it is said that originally there was only a compact mass (*ratq*) which united the heaven and the earth. Allah separated them, creating the universe in six days. "Then He made His way to the sky, which was but a cloud of vapor [*dukhan*]" (41:10); "In two days He formed the sky into seven heavens, and to each heaven He assigned a task" (41:12).

"It is Allah who keeps the heavens and the earth from falling" (35:41); "He holds the sky from falling down" (22:65). Then, after completing the creation of the universe, Allah sat on His throne which, at the beginning of the creation, was floating upon the water. This passage, like others describing Allah anthropomorphically (*tashbih*), was one of the subjects of the long and virulent disputes among theologians. Hanbalis, for instance, interpreted literally such descriptions, while Mu'tazilites held that each analogy between Allah and His creatures had to be rejected and similar expressions required an allegorical explanation. According to al-Ghazali, the method of the *ta'wil* (symbolical exegesis) could be employed although a mystical intuition would be required to understand the inner meanings of the sacred text.

Between the seventh heaven and the Throne of God there are infinite spaces inhabited by enormous angels. Two points of this heavenly topography are interesting: *sidrah al-muntahah* and paradise (*al-jannah*): "He beheld him once again at the Sidrah-tree, beyond which no one may pass (Near it is the garden of Repose). When that tree was covered with what covered it, his eyes did not wander, nor did they turn aside: for he saw some of his Lord greatest signs" (53:13–18). The *Sidrat al-Muntaha* is also associated to the "light of Muhammad" (*nur Muhammadi*). According to the *Tafsir* of the Sufi al-Tustari:

"He beheld him once again" would mean: "In the beginning when God, Glorified and Exalted is He, created him as a light within a column of light [*nuran fi 'amud al-nur*], a million years before creation, with the disposition of faith [*taba'i al-iman*], in an unveiling of the Unseen within the Unseen [*mushahadat al-ghayb bi al-ghayb*], He stood before Him in servanthood [*'ubudiyyah*], by the Lote-tree of the Ultimate Boundary, this being a tree at which the knowledge of every person reaches its limit."

The Shi'ite *qadi* Sa'id Qummi, commenting the *Kitab al-tawhid* by Shaykh al-Saduq, identifies the Lote-tree with the *walaya* ("love," "alliance") of the (metaphysical) Imam that branches out in the hearts of believers. It is turned upside down because the Imam, archetype of the "light" of the *wilayah*, enclosed in himself all the shares of light assigned to the initiated.

"The lower heaven is decked with constellations" (37:6) which act as citadels (*buruj*). In addition, there are stars (*kawakib*) and lamps (*masabih*) "missiles for pelting devils" (67:5). Moreover, the heaven is guarded "from all accursed devils" (15:17) and filled with guards (*haras*) and flames (*shuhub*), that is: "mighty wardens and fiery comets" (72:8), for this reason elsewhere it is called *saqf mahfuz*: "provided with strong support" (21:32). Finally, a star identifiable with the sun (*siraj*) and a shining moon "set in it a lamp and a shining moon" (25:61), complete the ornaments of the firmament.

The heavenly realms are carefully guarded by means of gates. The gates of the sky can be opened to send down "water with which He caused all kinds of goodly plants to grow" (31:10) or "pouring rain that caused the earth to burst with gushing springs" (54:11). They also will be opened to reward believers: "Enter paradise and dwell in it forever" (39:73). The gates of heaven are the same of paradise. Angels watch over the gates of heaven: "From every gate the angels will come to them" (13:23). Heaven, place of the blessed souls, is provided with seven spheres (*tara'iq*): "We have created seven heavens above you" (23:17), in some manner surmounted by the Throne: "You shall see the angels circling round the Throne" (39:75). In reality, it is not a vertical architecture but a spherical one for the throne of Allah is everywhere: "Who is the Lord of the Glorious Throne?" (23:86).

The sun appears in the stories of the Cave (*ahl al-kahf*), of Solomon and the Queen of Sheba, and finally in that of Dhu al-Qarnayn. "You might have seen the rising sun decline to the right of their cavern and, as it set, go past them on the left, while they stayed within" (18:17). As regards Solomon, he was informed by the hoopoe that the Queen of Sheba: "and her subjects worship the sun instead of Allah. Satan has seduced them and barred them from the right path" (27: 23–24). Lastly, Dhu al-Qarnayn: "journeyed along another road until he reached the East and saw the sun rising upon a people whom We had utterly exposed to its flaming rays" (18:90); "He journeyed on a certain road until he reached the West and saw the sun setting in a pool of black mud" (18:86).

Like stars, mountains, trees, animals, and many human beings, the sun and the moon bow down before Allah. Allah, who presides over the alternation of day and night, and to the flying of time, decreed that: "The sun is not allowed to overtake the moon, nor does the night outpace the day" (36:40); "each running for an appointed term" (31:29; 35:13; 39:5); "each moves swiftly in an orbit of its own" (36:40); "which steadfastly pursue their course" (14:33). Allah made the sun and the moon a measurement of time since: "they pursue their ordered course" (55:5). Finally, "He has subdued to you the night and the day" (14:33).

Beyond the seventh land there is fire (hell) and this can be connected with two created entities: *al-Sirat*: "But We shall say: 'Call the sinners, their wives, and the idols they worshipped besides Allah, and lead them to the path of hell. Keep them there for questioning'" (37:23–24); and *al-Mizan*: "We have sent Our apostles with veritable signs and brought down with them scriptures and the scales of justice" (57:25). Therefore, on the Day of Judgment: "their deeds shall be weighed with justice. Those whose scales are heavy shall triumph, but those whose scales are light shall lose their souls, because they have denied Our revelations" (7: 8–9).

After creating the visible and invisible cosmos, Allah populated them. Then He created *jinn* "from smokeless fire" (55:15) and finally humankind (22:5; 6:2). The creation of Adam was announced by Allah to the angels: "I am placing on the earth one that shall rule as My deputy [*khalifah*], they replied: 'Will You put there one who will do evil and shed blood, when we have for so long sung Your praises and sanctified Your name?' He said: 'I know what you do not know'" (2:30).

Commentators generally agreed that the term *khalifah* should be extended to the sons of Adam, that is, to humankind, whose generations follow one another. Other commentators, on the contrary, emphasize such a substitution as a synonym for delegation of authority: so they see in Adam the *khalifah* of Allah, charged to establish on the earth a realm of truth and justice with reference to 38:26: "David, We have made you master [*khalifah*] in the land. Rule with justice among men."

Some Shi'ite authors recognize in Adam the first *khalifah* (he was succeeded by six others, namely: Noah, Abraham, Musa (Moses), 'Isa (Jesus), Muhammad and 'Ali or, according to some traditions, seven since they include David). The charge to do evil and shed blood fell either on *jinn*, or on the sons of Adam who did not comply with the law of Allah; commentators unanimously declare that in this formula there is no reference to Adam, owing to his rank as a prophet.

Allah created the first human being from clay. Commentators say that the name Adam derives from *adim al-ard* or from *adamat al-ard*, since it was created from the "surface of the earth." In the Qur'an, the words used to indicate the substance with which the first human being was created are dust (3:59), clay (7:12; 38:71), and molded loam (15:28). Allah fashions this matter and breathes His spirit into him to give him life (15:29; 38:72); besides, Allah created him by His own hands (38:75).

Clay and the lexical variants of the same are not prerogatives of the first human being as they also refer to the creation of humankind in general (6:2; 30:20–21; 37:11, 55:14). On the other hand, in the Qur'an there are other anthropogonies which cannot be brought back before the creation of the first human being: from an injected fluid, from a clot of blood (23:13), simply from water. This variegated whole was summarized by commentators in a single anthropogonic scheme. The creation of the human being occurred starting from clay or the Divine Breath, and that of his offspring from a drop (of seed) that, through a series of creative deeds, was transformed into a clot of blood and therefore into a human being. Only 'Isa (Jesus), like Adam, was created from dust and by breathing the Divine Spirit into him (3:59; 21:91; 66:12).

The lexical variations in connection with clay were widely and unanimously interpreted as the subsequent stages of a single substance in the manufacturing process of pottery. According to the best known version, Allah wet the dust (*turab*) to turn it into soft clay (*tin lazib*) that was left to ferment until it became black molded loam (*hama' masnun*); from this Allah fashioned the first human being and let it dry till it was transformed into dry clay, resounding like baked clay (*salsal ka al-fakhkhar*) (cfr. *Tafsir* Ibn Kathir). Authors insist on the fact that the clay dried or hardened without getting in touch with fire, according to the Qur'an which opposes two kinds of creatures: humankind, created of clay, and *jinn*, created of fire (15:26–27; 55:14–15).

The insistence that the Qur'an reserves to the physical and animal side of humankind does not mean that the intellectual and sensitive part of the human being is disregarded. A statement, often repeated, marks this side of the work of the Creator: "It was He who gave you ears, eyes and hearts" (23:78; 32:9; 57:23). "Have We not given him two eyes, a tongue and two lips?" (90: 8–9). Imam 'Ali's teachings, collected by Sharif al-Radi in the *Nahj al-Balaghah* (*The Peak of Eloquence*), state, with regard to the creation (Sermon 1), that Adam, once Allah had breathed His spirit into him, took the form of a human being provided with all physical faculties and intelligence. According Kulayni, the Shi'ite traditionist Kulayni,

When Allah created Intelligence He made it speak and then He said to it: "Come forward." It came forward. He then said: "Go back." It went back. Then Allah said: "I swear by My honor and glory that I have not created any creature more beloved to Me than you. I will not perfect you in anyone except whom I love. I, however, will command you only to do things and prohibit only you from doing certain things. I will grant blessings (rewards) to you only and will subject only you to punishments" [*al-Kafi*, H1, Ch1, h1].

According to a tradition of the Imam Ja'far al-Sadiq:

> The human Form is the supreme testimony with which God testifies His creation. It is the *Book* that He wrote with His own hand. It is the Temple that He has built with His wisdom. It is the reunion of the Forms of all the universes. It is the compendium of the knowledge originated from the *Guarded Tablet*. It is the visible witness that answers for all the invisible [*ghayb*]. It is the warrant, the proof against all deniers, it is the straight Path thrown between paradise and hell.

According to Corbin:

> That human Form in its pre-eternal glory is called the real Adam [*Adam haqiqi*], *Homo maximus* [*Insan kabir*]. This heavenly *Anthropos* is invested with and holder of the eternal prophecy [*nubuwwah baqiyyah*], of the essential primeval prophecy [*nubuwwah asliyyah haqiqiyyah*], opened pre-temporally in the heavenly Pleroma. He is also the reality of Muhammad [*haqiqat Muhammadiyya*]. The Prophet hinted at him when he said "God created Adam [the *Anthropos*] to the image of His form." And since the Prophet is the earthly epiphany [*mazhar*] of this *Anthropos*, he says: "The first thing that God created was my Light" (or Intelligence, or Spirit). This is what he meant saying: "I was already a prophet, when Adam (the earthly Adam) was still between water and clay (that is he was not yet created)."

"Surely worthier is He who has made His creatures and who will hereafter bring them back to life. Another god besides Allah?" (27:64); "Has He who created the heavens and the earth no power to create their like? That He surely has. He is the all-knowing Creator" (36: 81). The concept of a "new creation" or of a "continuous creation" (*khalq jadid*) was taken back by Sufis and, in particular, by Ibn al-'Arabi.

The Inner and Outer Meanings of Creation

The hermeneutics of Ibn al-'Arabi follow different ways, chiefly the *i'tibar* or the *isharah*, allusion to an inner state; it is characterized by a great care paid to the letter of the text from which the spiritual sense flows. For him, "there is no word in the universe that cannot be interpreted," because all the plans of existence are connected one with another. His metaphysical and initiatory doctrine brings him to formulate clearly a relationship of quasi-identity between the Qur'an, Word of Allah, and the Perfect or Universal Human Being, mediator and veil at the same time between Allah and the manifestation.

Some Qur'anic verses evoke the exterior signs of the creation and incite humankind to meditate on them in itself, thus establishing a principle of correspondence between the universe and the human being. "Your God is one God. There is not God but Him. He is the Compassionate, the Merciful" (2:163). The following verse recites:

> In the creation of the heavens and the earth; in the alternation of night and day; in the ships that sail the ocean with cargoes beneficial to man; in the water which Allah sends down from the sky and with which He revives the dead earth, dispersing over it all manner of beasts; in the movements of the winds, and in the clouds that are driven between earth and sky: surely in these there are signs for rational men [2:164].

The former verse clearly indicates how the latter must be read; it is a precise hermeneutic movement that allows the passage from macrocosmic signs to their microcosmic and spiritual meaning. Perhaps the expression of such a correspondence should be searched in the Qur'anic conception of the Book, the descent of which is often connected to the creation of the world, in particular at the beginning of the chapters starting with "isolated letters" (*al-huruf al-muqatta'ah*) (see 10, 11, 13, 14, 16, 20, 32, 41, 43, 45 and 46).

It is also through the mediation of the all-embracing book that the analogy between human and animal communities is expressed: "All the beasts that roam the earth and the birds that wing their flight are communities like your own. We have left out nothing in Our Book. They shall be gathered before their Lord" (6:38). Therefore, a triple relationship joins together humans and beasts and birds: the organization in a community, the Book that gathers them together in a same vision of the world and the final gathering of all beings.

The clearest statement of a necessary correspondence between the world and humans is in Qur'an 41:53–54: "We will show them Our signs in all the regions of the earth and in their own souls, until they clearly see that this is the truth. Does it not suffice that Allah is watching over all things? Yes, they still doubt that they will ever meet their Lord. Surely, Allah encompasses all things." Sufis have interpreted such verses in the sense of a correspondence between cosmic signs and souls. In fact, the Qur'an speaks of a vision conferred by Allah that brings back from the outside to the inside, in order to go beyond this distinction in the contemplation of the Truth which is Allah Himself, witness of Himself in everything.

Again, in 50:21–23: "On earth, and in yourselves, there are signs for firm believers. Can you not see? heaven holds your sustenance and all that you are promised. I swear by the Lord of heaven and earth that this is true, as true as you are speaking now!" Humankind is called here to perceive in itself the signs of earth and heaven, as mediator of their correspondence. Allah swears that this is true, because He is the Truth. The likeness between this truth and the words that the human being speaks, and the truth of which he cannot deny, confirms his *rôle* of mediator, through the inner vision of the world from high and from bottom, and supports his certainty that all that he finds in the lower part comes from the high. Here, as well, it is not question of a static vision of the relationship between macrocosm and microcosm but of an inner and analogical vision where the Revelation, which the human being articulates with his own tongue, is lived as nourishment and certainty. Even Qurtubi approached these verses to 2:163, quoted above, and drew the conclusion that: "there is nothing in the body of the human being, who is the microcosm [al-'alam al-saghir], that has not its correspondence in the macrocosm [al-'alam al-kabir]."

Conclusion

The theme of creation, one of the greatest of the Qur'an, can also be considered a fundamental one since it contains, concisely, the quintessence of the Qur'anic teaching: the absolute uniqueness of Allah, His creating power, His goodness, His mercifulness, His infallible justice. Like in a circle, creation finds its alpha and omega the divine will which created and regulates the whole of the creation to guide humans on the right path. So, creation, as a manifestation of the Divine Essence, is a series of "signs" allowing humankind to recognize their Lord and turn to Him. In fact, the great certainty of existence is the return to Allah. These signs have been interpreted according to different levels: literally and/or esoterically, on the ground of the beliefs of their commentators, whether Sunnis, Shi'ites or Sufis.

Works Cited

Amir-Moezzi, Muhammad 'Ali. *Le guide divin dans le Shi'isme original: Aux sources de l'ésotérisme en Islam.* Lagrasse: Verdier, 2007.
Bukhari, Muhammad ibn-Isma'il al-. *Kitab al-Sahih.* Internet: www.quranexplorer.com

Corbin, Henry. *Histoire de la philosophie islamique*. Paris: Gallimard, 1964.

Dawood, N.J., trans. *The Koran*. Harmondsworth: Penguin Books, 1956.

Ibn 'Abbas. *Tafsir Ibn 'Abbas*. 'Amman: Aal al-Bayt Institute for Islamic Thought, 2005. Internet: www.al-tafsir.com

Ibn al-'Arabi, Muhyi al-Din. *Les Illuminations de la Mecque*. Ed. M. Chodkiewicz. Paris: Albin Michel, 1988.

Ibn Kathir, Isma'il ibn 'Umar. *Tafsir Ibn Kathir*. 'Amman: Aal al-Bayt Institute for Islamic Thought, 2005. Internet: www.al-tafsir.com

Kulayni, Abu Ja'far Muhammad ibn Ya'qub Ibn Ishaq. *al-'Usul min al-kafi*. Ed. 'Ali Akbar al-Ghaffari. Tehran: Dar al-Kutub al-Islamiyyah, 1968.

Qummi, Muhammad ibn 'Ali ibn al-Husayn ibn Babuya al-. known as Shaykh Saduq, *Ma'ani al-akhbar*. Ahlul Bayt Digital Islamic Library Project, 2000. Internet: www.al-Islam.org.

Qummi, Qadi Sa'id. *Tafsir al-Qur'an*. 'Amman: Aal al-Bayt Institute for Islamic Thought, 2005. Internet: www.al-tafsir.com

Qurtubi, Abu 'Abdullah al-. *al-Jami' li ahkam al-Qur'an*. Ahlul Bayt Digital Islamic Library Project, 2000. Internet: www.al-Islam.org.

Radi, Sharif al-, ed. *Nahj al-Balaghah*. Collected sermons by Imam 'Ali ibn Abi Talib. Ahlul Bayt Digital Islamic Library Project, 2000. Internet: www.al-Islam.org.

Sadiq, Ja'far al-. *Ahadith*. Ahlul Bayt Digital Islamic Library Project, 2000. Internet: www.al-Islam.org.

Tustari, Sahl al-. *Tafsir al-Tustari*. 'Amman: Aal al-Bayt Institute for Islamic Thought, 2005. Internet: www.al-tafsir.com

Wrath

Amar Sellam

"They drew on themselves wrath upon wrath." (Qur'an 2:90)

Introduction

This chapter analyzes the symbol of wrath as a polysemic concept that is open to many levels of analysis. The method of analysis to be adopted will be mainly based on a content analysis method, supported by a linguistic (mainly semantic) and theological analysis.

The word "wrath" or "anger" (in Arabic *ghadab*) is mentioned many times in the Qur'an. But it has many synonyms such as *sakhat* or *ghayz* and near synonyms such as *la'nah* (curse), *maqt* (extreme hatred), and *khizy* (shame and ignominy). There are even expressions that denote meanings similar to the concept of wrath, such as *tabba* as in the following verse *tabbat yada Abi Lahab* (111:1), or *waylun* as in the following verse: "But woe betide those whose hearts are hardened against the remembrance of God" (39: 22). Through adjacency and context, meanings similar to wrath are expressed when, for example, the people incurring wrath are described as criminals, *mujrimun*, or when the intended meaning (or illocutionary intent according to Austin, 2005 and Searle 1969), despite the apparent remoteness of the expressions used, boils down to "wrath" and "anger," as is the case in the following example: "Give warning to the hypocrites that woeful punishment awaits them" (4:138).[1]

From an Islamic point of view, the idea of wrath, when related to God, should not be taken in the usual sense of human anger. God's anger is rather conceived of as a will to punish whoever has done wrong in His eyes. It is not an arbitrary desire to do ill, however, or some act of abusing status and power, so to speak, but rather an act of retribution against a category of people who, of their own accord, have chosen to defy the will and order of God. Islam is a faith based essentially on the total submission of humankind to the Divine will. God expects all humans to worship Him; that is, to show their inferiority and weakness, their need for the assistance of the Almighty, and to show through prayer, their allegiance to the Creator, and express their thanks to Him for His boons and munifencies and, above all, for having chosen humankind to be His representative on this earth. Indeed, God's purpose in creating humans (and also the jinn) is for them to worship Him. This meaning is clearly expressed in the following verse: "I created the jinn and humankind only that they might worship Me. I demand no livelihood of them, nor do I ask that they should feed Me" (51:56). It should be stressed that "to worship," here, has the sense of "to know." It was God's wish to be known that was the cause of creation.

Although the concept of wrath/anger is mentioned in various contexts pertaining to a variety of actors — considering both the entity that is "wrathful" or "angry" on the one hand,

and the entities incurring such wrath, on the other — our analysis will focus on the cases of God's wrath and on the parties that were the object of His wrath. We may note (in passing), the anger of the Prophet Musa (Moses) when he returned from his appointment with God, to be faced with the bad surprise of his people having reverted to the worship of the golden calf at which time he could not control himself with anger and took his brother Aaron by the beard and started scolding him for what had happened (20:94; 7:154). However, such a case of wrath will not be dealt with. What really matters for our present purpose is what these linguistic exponents express in the final analysis, namely the idea of retribution, or *al-Jaza'*, to be understood as either God's reward or God's punishment.

A Content Analysis Approach

In what follows, we shall use the content analysis method of analysis, to work out a set of lists in which a hand-count of clear cases in which the idea of wrath is used. As mentioned already, we shall focus on the cases in which the word wrath itself is mentioned, in addition to the cases of synonyms and near synonyms.

Strictly speaking, the word "wrath" (or *ghadab* in Arabic) is mentioned twenty-two times in the various chapters of the Qur'anic text (see Sawar 242). Most of the cases of wrath are attributed to God, with a couple of cases relating in one case to believers who distinguish themselves with the laudable act of willing to forgive when angered (42:37), and in another case to the spouses who have to swear, in the absence of witnesses to testify for them, that God's wrath (and curse) should afflict them if they have wrongly accused their husband or wife of adultery (24:9).

The cases of "wrath" or *ghadab* mentioned in the Qur'anic text are distributed as follows in the various chapters of the Holy Book:

The Exordium (*al-Fatihah*) (1:7)	Ta' ha' (20: 81, 86)
The Heifer (*al-Baqarah*) (2: 61; 90)	The Prophets (*al-Anbiya'*) (21:87)
The Imrans (*Aal Imran*) (3:112)	Light (*al-Nur*) (24:9)
Women (*al-Nisa'*) (4:93)[2]	Counsel (*al-Shura*) (42:16, 37)
The Table (*al-Ma'idah*) (5:60)	Victory (*al-Fath*) (48:6)
The Heights (*al-A'raf*) (7:71; 150, 152, 154)	She who Pleaded (or *al-Mujadilah*) (58:14)
The Spoils (*al-Anfal*) (8:16)	She who is Tested (or *al-Mumtahanah*) (60:13)
The Bee (*al-Nahl*) (16:106)	

Figure 1: The *wrath of God* as punishment and verses in which it is mentioned

In this list, the parties that incurred God's wrath or anger, so to speak,[3] are listed in the following figure (Figure 2):

People of the Book or Jews (1:7; 58:14; 60:13; 7:152; 42:16; 2:61; 2:91; 20:81)
Murderers (of believers in the passage) (4:93)
Those who turn their backs to the enemy in a fight (8:16)
Apostates[4] or those who have (willingly) recanted their faith (16:106)
Unbelievers (16:106)
Those who wrongly accuse their spouses of adultery (24:9)
Hypocrites (48:6)
Pagans (associators,[5] idolaters or *mushrikun*) (48:6; 7:71)

Figure 2: The groups who incurred *God's wrath*

Out of a total of 22 verses in which the word "wrath" is mentioned, 16 are relevant to our present purpose, as they are directly linked to the idea of God's wrath, so to speak (see Fig. 2 above). There are cases of repetitions (sometimes within the same chapter) where the word wrath is repeated twice. We should note that the serious sin that most incurs God's wrath, and which we have in the above data, is that of associating partners, as it were, with God, namely idolatry, commonly known in Arabic under the term of *shirk*. At the time of the Qur'anic revelation, most of the Arabs were known for worshipping idols, which they considered mediating channels between them and God. This means that the idols were not worshipped for their own sake. The Qur'an is quite clear in this connection when it states the following, quoting the idol worshippers: "We serve them only that they may bring us nearer to God" (39: 3).

Incidentally, the notion of God (under the name of Allah) was not unknown to the Arabs of the pre-Islamic period. What the new Islamic faith condemned in the Arabs' behavior was rather their acts of worship consisting of making sacrifices for the sake of their idols, and performing their annual rite of pilgrimage by circumambulating naked around the Ka'bah, to which were attached the idols that belonged to each Arab tribe; in addition to claiming that the angels were "God's daughters."

The *Sunnah* (i.e. the Prophet's compiled sayings) also condemns *shirk* for being the most serious sin. The Prophet in an authenticated saying or *hadith* is quoted by al-Bukhari and Muslim in their respective *Sahihs* as saying: "Avoid the seven deadly sins [*mubiqat*]." "What are they, Messenger of God?" his companions asked. He said: "Associating partners with God, [or *al-shirk bi-Allah*], sorcery, unjustified murder [in the eyes of Islamic law], practicing usury, misusing orphans' property, running away when engaged in *jihad*, and wrongly accusing chaste women [of adultery]." *Shirk* is considered the deadliest sin, and its perpetrator is condemned to eternal hell. All sins are so to speak "negotiable," except the act of *shirk*. The Qur'an is quite clear about the issue: "God will not forgive those who serve other gods besides Him; but He will forgive whom He will for other sins. He that serves other gods besides Him is guilty of a heinous sin" (4: 48, 116).

Synonyms of wrath such as "curse" (*la'nah*), "shame" or "ignominy" (*khizy*), and "execration" [*maqt*], are also related, as indicated above, to the concept of God's punishment and displeasure with the categories of people that deserve such a sorrowful destiny, as the Qur'an states. The following figure, used for the purpose of concision and space, will summarize how the linguistic expressions variably (or similarly as the case may be) deal with the idea of "God's wrath." It will also show the distribution, and therefore the relative significance of the allegorical sense of the central concept in question, and how important that will prove to be across the Qur'anic text.

Figure 3 shows the following facts: There are 31 cases of the use of the term "curse" related to God in the Qur'anic text, against 22 cases of the uses of the term "wrath" (see Fig. 2 above). The categories of people affected by God's curse are almost the same as those affected by His anger; we find almost the same types of people who incur God's wrath or curse. At the top of the list we find the unbelievers, the associators, the hypocrites, and the Jews. What is clearly visible is that both lists target specifically the enemies of the new faith under the first five groups in the two lists. This is understandable as what is crucial for Islam at its initial stages is its survival, the safeguard of its existence, and its protection from its enemies. These enemies are either physical (the warriors of Quraysh and the al-Ahzab,[6] who later engaged in various battles with the Prophet Muhammad; or theological in the case of the Jews, whose threat to Islam proved to be very serious (as they refused either to recognize the new religion, or to acknowledge the existence of passages in the Torah presumably heralding the arrival of the new Prophet (see verse 2: 89, *inter alia*).

Objects of curse and verses	Cause of curse	Nature of punishment
Unbelievers: (2:16; 11:19; 33:64)	failure to believe	eternal hell-fire
Hypocrites: (9:68; 3:61)	alliance with unbelievers	death sentence and hell-fire
"Associators" (48:6)	evil thinking about God	eternal hell-fire
Apostates: (47:23; 3:87)	recanting Islam	eternal damnation
Jews: (5:60; 4:46; 4:47; 4:52; 2:159; 5:13; 5:78; 5:64; 2:89)	failure to confirm Islam	eternal hell-fire
Accusers of chaste women: (9:68; 24:23)	accusing innocent women	grievous punishment
Hud's people: (11:60)	denying God's revelations	curse in life and in after-life
Those who lied about God: (7:44; 43:61; 3:61)	turning people from Islam	hell-fire
The Pharaoh and his warriors: (28:42)	arrogance and denial of God's existence	drowning and eternal hell-fire
Satan: (4:18; 15:35; 38:78)	leading people astray	eternal damnation
Corrupt people & covenant breakers (13:25; 40:25)	breaking God's covenant; corruption and discord sowing	hell-fire
Heart-tainted and scandalmongers: (33:61)	alliance with unbelievers	death sentence and hell-fire
Premeditated assassins (4:93)	premeditated murder	eternal damnation and hell-fire

Figure 3: The concept of *God's curse* as punishment in the *Qur'an* and the groups that incur it.

Murderers and spouse-defamers are also the object of both God's wrath and curse, respectively. We might therefore suggest that the concepts of curse and anger are synonymous in use and are frequently encountered and utilized interchangeably in the Qur'anic text. In fact, in some verses the two expressions are used side by side as is the case in the following verse, in which the object of curse (and also of wrath) is the murderer: "He that kills a believer by design shall burn in hell for ever. He shall incur the *wrath* of God, who will lay His *curse* on him and prepare for him a mighty scourge" (4: 93).

Let us now consider another term related to the idea of wrath in the Qur'anic text; the term is "shame" or "ignominy" as an equivalent of the Arabic word *sakhat* (see Figure 4 below). At the outset, it is important to note that not all the cases of the word "shame" used in the Qur'an will be taken into account; as only the items relevant to our present analysis will be focused on. Out of a total of 25 items, only 19 will be selected, as they are directly linked to the concept of God's punishment; in effect, it is God who will cast disgrace and utter humiliation on the wrongdoers.

Figure 4 above contains 19 cases of people or individuals that deserved, as it were, God's humiliation, the majority of which tend to fall within similar categories to the ones seen under the label of "wrath" and "curse." In other words, the groups that are targeted again by God's shame and humiliation are, once again the unbelievers or/and associators, the hypocrites, and the Jews. They incur God's wrath; they incur His curse, and they incur His disgrace and shame. The four groups are condemned to eternal punishment in hell for being the sworn enemies of God and His Messenger. They showed acts of defiance. They should therefore expect such a deserved punishment. In Islamic discourse, God only punishes those who deserve punishment, and this happens only after warning the people in question what they might encounter as a result of their wrongdoing. "Nor do we punish until we have sent forth a messenger" (17:15). Another verse is also relevant here: "He that does good does it for his own soul; and he that commits evil does so at his own peril. Your Lord is never unjust to His servants" (41:46). A third verse is also significant and points to the fact that God cannot possibly punish people who seek his pardon, even if they had been wrong-doers at some point in the past: "But God would not punish them while you were in their midst. Nor would He punish them if they sought forgiveness" (8:33). Here, the entire responsibility lies with the wrongdoers in terms of the likely punishment they might receive as a result of their own action.

Object of shame & verse	Cause of shame	Nature of punishment
Unbelievers (in general) (2:85; 2:114; 5:41; 5:33; 9:2; 39:26)	fighting the new faith	shame and disgrace
Unbelievers as arrogant associators (16:27)	worshipping idols	hell-fire
Hypocrites (5:41)	fighting the Prophet	eternal hell-fire
Associators (as thieves and highwaymen) (5:33; 9:14)	waging war against the God and His apostle	humiliation in this life and the next
Jews (5:41; 59:5)	retaliatory action in response to attempt to assassinate the Prophet	humiliation in life
Noah's people (11:39)	for mocking him for making the Ark	taken by an "everlasting scourge"
Shu'ayb's people (11:93)	refusing to follow the right faith of their prophet	struck dead overnight
The People of 'Ad (41:16; 41:6)	injustice and arrogance	punished in this life and the next
Muhammad's People (unbelievers and associators) (39:40)	refusing the faith of Islam	humiliated at the Battle of Badr await everlasting punishment
Those who defy God and His messenger (unbelievers and hypocrictes) (9:63)	defying God and ridiculing the Prophet	everlasting punishment
Those who dispute God's word without knowledge (22:9)	meddling in matters of faith	humiliation in life and hell-fire in the afterlife

Figure 4: "Shame" and "ignominy" as punishment in the Qur'anic text and the groups that incurred it.

By way of working out a general recapitulative summary of the above data, we might look at the Figures 4 and 5 from various angles and come to some tentative conclusions. For such a purpose, we shall posit the hypothesis that the idea of wrath with its various linguistic exponents, whether that is expressed as wrath (*ghadab*) proper, as a curse (*la'nah*) or as shame/disgrace (*khizy*), the common factor that binds together the various manifestations of "wrath" is that these tend to address the same groups with very few variations. At the top of those categories, we can clearly see the various groups: namely the unbelievers, the associators, the hypocrites, and the Jews. Naturally, people or individuals who commit heinous crimes such as murder, or those who wrongly accuse their spouses of adultery, are also targeted. But we should still ask the relevant question why it is that the Qur'an, through God and His messenger Muhammad, specifically points to those groups as sworn enemies with whom no negotiation, as it were, is possible. Why are they summarily condemned to eternal perdition and to everlasting hell?

This encompassing picture will be analyzed in terms of the order or sequence[7] of revelation, which is conducive to helping us better understand some phenomena and issues when seen from a historical perspective. In fact, the Qur'an — or rather its chapters or *suras*, or even some verses, or *ayat*— is classified into two major categories, Meccan or Medinan.

That is, each chapter or verse of the Qur'an, as the case may be, is either called Meccan or Medinan, according to whether it was revealed in Mecca or in Medina.

A cursory look at the data in question should spell out a number of useful indicators and, therefore, is liable to enable us to draw a number of conclusions. What should be focused upon here is how the various verses, and therefore chapters of the Qur'an, are distributed along the parameter of place of revelation (and therefore of the relevant period with which we are dealing in the life of the Prophet Muhammad). We should bear in mind that the period in which the Prophet moved from Mecca to Medina (what is known as *al-Hijra*, or Emigration/Flight) represents a landmark in his life, and in the life of the community of Muslims and of their faith in general. A recapitulative table might be useful for the present purpose; see Figure 5 below:

	Meccan suras or chapters[8]	Medinan suras or chapters	Total
"Wrath"	1; 7; 16; 20; 21 [Tot = 05]	2; 3; 4; 5; 8; 24; 48; 58; 60 [Tot=09]	14
"Curse"	7; 11; 15; 28; 38; 40; 43 [Tot= 07]	2; 3; 4; 5; 9; 13; 24; 33; 47; 48 [Tot= 10]	17
"Shame"	11; 16; 39; 41 [Tot = 04]	2; 5; 9; 22; 59 [Tot= 05]	09
General total	16 Meccan chapters	24 Medinan chapters	40

Figure 5: Distribution of the chapters analyzed in terms of place (and time) of revelation

Before dealing with the parameter of place of revelation, it might be useful to indicate the important total number of *suras* that deal with the symbol of wrath and its neighboring concepts which is 40. It is a relatively high number, representing 35 percent of the total number (114) of the chapters or *suras* of the whole Qur'an. This apparent emphasis and frequency of use of the categories in question seem to be quite significant.

With respect to the factor of place of revelation now, the data above show that a sizeable number of the *suras* dealing with the concept of wrath or its near synonyms were revealed in Medina (24 chapters, against 16 that were revealed in Mecca). In other words, the number of the Medinan *suras* dealing with wrath and its synonyms outnumber those that were revealed in Mecca. Although the figures do not show a clear-cut and tangible difference along the criterion we have set for the present analysis, they might, however, serve as a useful indicator, if only in a loose way, that points in favor of the posited hypothesis, which is that the Qur'anic discourse in the Medinan period tends to be more vehement in dealing with what are considered the enemies of Islam. Actually, from a historical perspective, we might consider the eventful life of the Prophet with its major upheavals as a proof of the change that occurred in that discourse, from an attitude of relatively peaceful tolerance, of putting up with the transgressors and their evil actions, to that of zero (or little) tolerance, so to speak.

We might here refer to this initial spirit of tolerance and coexistence (or shall we say an attitude of resilience and fortitude) on the part of the Prophet and his companions, who had to undergo all sorts of excruciating torments, alternated with luring and cajoling attempts at the hands of Quraysh. Such a spirit is clearly expressed in *Surah al-Kafirun* (The Chapter of the Disbelievers), which is a Meccan chapter: "Say: 'Unbelievers, I do not worship what you worship, nor do you worship what I worship. [...] You have your own religion and I have mine'" (109: 1, 6). During the Meccan period, despite the animosity and harassment of his foes, the Prophet adopted an attitude of "passive resistance," as it were, and never resorted to the use of force to defend himself and his followers, who were subjected to harrowing torture at the hands of the Meccan unbelievers (Morrow 330).

In Medina, however, the Prophet had indeed to wage many counterattacks, and even pre-emptive attacks in some cases against his foes, as the latter became increasingly aggressive and more and more belligerent. This is the time when God authorized him to defend himself against his enemies: "Permission to take up arms is hereby given to those who are attacked, because they have been wronged. God has power to grant them victory: those who have been unjustly driven from their homes, only because they said: 'Our Lord is God'" (22: 39). This is indeed the period when *jihad*, as a strictly codified[9] Islamic self-defense institution with humane[10] characteristics, was prescribed on Muslims. It was established with the creation of the Islamic state in Medina as a means for the Muslims to defend themselves, to defend their faith and to ensure its spread to the world at large inside and beyond the Arabian Peninsula (Morrow 330–332). The ultimate aim was the propagation of the principles of peace, love, brotherhood, equality and good conduct among peoples and individuals, to be summarized under the principle of "enjoining justice and forbidding evil."[11] Thus, the early Muslims had to fend off all sorts of aggressive assaults of the unbelievers from the Quraysh and their allies among the Bedouin and Jewish tribes, in such well-known Battles as those of Uhud, al-Khandaq, Mu'tah and Tabuk.

To be sure, the Prophet Muhammad's life is divided into two major periods, the dividing line between them being the migration from Mecca to Medina. During the first stage, although the Prophet had to face all sorts of problems, ranging from ridiculing his faith to attempts on his life, as is testified in such works as *Sirah Ibn Ishaq*[12] and *Tarikh al-Tabari*[13] and others, his attitude remained that of peacefully advocating and trying to spread his new faith. He had to endure all kinds of ordeals posed to him, and all sorts of obstacles laid down in his way by the lords of Mecca, who belonged for the most part to the tribe of Quraysh. Those lords saw in the new religion a direct threat to their economic as well as to their religious interests. In fact, the Quraysh lords had so far served as the custodians of the Ka'bah, to which all the Arabs turned for pilgrimage from time immemorial. And that was an important source of income. Besides, those lords felt that their prestige would be seriously undermined by Muhammad, a poor upstart, an orphan who had to seek the protection of his grandfather, then that of his uncle Abu Talib to survive. Remember that he started his life as guarding the sheep of the family. Social class had its saying here, to be sure. In any case, the Prophet bore with steadfast fortitude with the various testing tribulations (Qur'an 93).[14]

However, once in Medina, where he began to construct the new "State of Islam," the Prophet was in a position to counter his opponents at various levels of their defiance, including the military defense of his followers and of his nascent state. This is why we notice that the Medinan *suras* or chapters deal more defiantly with the foes of Islam, including what the Qur'an terms the *kuffar* (unbelievers), the *mushrikun* (associators or idol worshippers), the *munafiqun* (hypocrites), and their later allies, the Jews of Yathrib (namely Banu Qaynuqa', Banu Qurayzah and Banu al-Nadir). The latter Jewish tribe had chosen to antagonize the new religion of Islam and its Messenger. Such an enmity is reflected in the following verse: "You will find that the most implacable men in their enmity to the faithful are the Jews and the pagans, and the nearest in affection to them are those who say 'we are Christians'" (5: 82).

If Christians are described as being closer to the Muslims than the Jews, it may also be because they accepted 'Isa (Jesus) as the Messiah, while the Jews rejected him. It is equally possible that the verse in question alludes to the fact that, during the period of Revelation, it was the polytheists and the Jews who waged war on the Muslims, as opposed to the Christians. Historically speaking, however, there is no question that the greatest enemies of Islam have almost always been Christians. Whether they were Romans, crusaders, European colonizers, or modern-day Western imperialists, the atrocities against Muslims over the past 1,400 years have been overwhelmingly committed by Christians as opposed to polytheists and Jews.

To do some between-the-lines reading, we might suggest that the Jews of Yathrib disappointed the Prophet, who was expecting a different attitude on their part, namely an attitude of support for a faith which he had brought as a confirmation and a continuation of the other two previously revealed religions, i.e., Judaism and Christianity. In fact, Islam had preached from the start that it has come to confirm, revive, and purify the previously revealed religions of the Book. The Prophet indefatigably used this argument with the Jews of Medina, expecting them to support him against the sworn enemies of the new revealed religion, a religion that had come to reform and complete the ancient Abrahamic faith. The Prophet expected Jewish support against the declared unbelievers of Quraysh and some hypocrites among the dwellers of Yathrib, in addition to a group of Arab Bedouin tribes, such as Ghatafan and Banu Sulaym, etc (see al-Jabri 2009: 381). Instead, the Jews did just the opposite and rallied the enemies of the Prophet, thereby posing a serious threat to the new faith on the theological level. The unbelievers, who were in alliance with the Yathrib Jews, had occasion to resort to them for consultation on religious issues to provide arguments which they needed to use in an attempt to demolish the tenets of the new faith of Islam. A good example here is the challenging question posed by the unbelievers (apparently at the instigation of the Jews) to the Prophet defying him to spell out for them the nature of "the soul." The Qur'an answers for the Prophet in this connection by telling him to inform his foes of the following: "They put questions to you about the Spirit. Say: 'The Spirit is at my Lord's command. Little indeed is the knowledge vouchsafed to you'" (17: 85).

Theological Analysis

The Prophet's change of attitude mentioned above, and which is reflected in the Qur'anic discourse, may be further shown through some verses. For illustration, it suffices for us to mention a few verses that show the clear upheaval in the process of the Prophet Muhammad's calling people to espouse the new faith. While showing a lenient attitude of tolerance and coexistence with all the known religions at the time, including the faiths of the idol worshippers, Sabaeans, Jews, Christians and Magians, there came a time when such coexistence seemed to be no longer in order, at least if we just consider the literal interpretation of the verses in question. The challenges to the Prophet came from all places and all types of people. Compare the following two verses: (see 22:17) "As for the true believers, the Jews, the Sabaeans, the Christians, the Magians, and the Pagans, God will judge them on the Day of Resurrection. God is the witness of all things" (22: 17). A similar verse focuses on the people of revealed faiths, namely the Jews, Christians and Sabaeans, excluding the Magians and the Pagans: "Believers, Jews, Christians, and Sabaeans — whoever believes in God and the Last Day and does what is right — shall be rewarded by their Lord; they have nothing to fear or to regret" (2: 62). Compare this verse with the following one, in which no other religion should be accepted except Islam: "He that chooses a religion other than Islam, it will not be accepted from him and in the world to come he will surely be among the losers" (3:85).

On the surface there is an apparent contradiction or, at least, a paradox in the attitude of the Qur'anic discourse. While visibly tolerating not only the People of the Book (Christians and Jews), but also the non-Book people, including Magians and even Pagans (so far known as unbelievers), we may be struck by the apparent condemnation of all other faiths except Islam. According to al-Jabri (2009: 145), however, Qur'an scholars and commentators have diverged over the interpretation of the verses above. Some of them tended to adopt a literalist interpretation of the verses. This interpretation suggests at one time tolerating the other religions and, at another time condemning them, thereby giving birth to what might be considered a clear contradiction. Other commentators, however, such as al-Zamakhshari, according to al-Jabri (145), had a more insightful view, according to which, what is meant by *Islam* in 3:85 is not strictly speaking the new faith of Islam, but rather the monotheistic religion based on the Oneness of God (*al-tawhid*) and complete submission to God. In other words, both Abrahamic religions of Judaism and Christianity are to be tolerated. The proof of such an assertion, al-Jabri suggests, resides in the fact that "this is what the context and reality prove; Islam has recognized Judaism and Christianity and imposed *al-jizyah*[15] on their followers, as opposed to *zakat* [imposed on Muslims]" (see al-Jabri, 145). In this case, what is to be condemned is not any religion, but those faiths that specifically preach polytheism, paganism, and such like creeds.

Theologically still, and with respect to the idea of wrath in the Qur'an and in the Islamic tradition in general, we may suggest another facet of the issue that might be relevant to the present discussion. We stated earlier that "wrath" as a feeling or emotion is reprehensible when attributed to humans, but not so when it is ascribed to God's Will and Power. In other words, it is a prerogative of the Almighty, who permits Himself to behave in such a manner, in the same way as being the Only One, for example, that has the right to punish with burning fire. He alone can punish wrongdoers and therefore cast His anger (or rather it is the wrongdoers who incur His anger) on the evil doers. The issue is open as to how we should view the nature of this wrath or anger.

Such a discussion may lead us to the debate over God's attributes and most beautiful names. In Islamic discourse, there was once a controversy whether we should consider God's attributes literally or rather understand them in a metaphorical sense. The debate here had actually opposed the Sunnis with the more rationalist scholars known under the label of Mu'tazilites. The latter group based their theory on the premise that God clearly states in the Qur'an that there is nothing like him, that nothing should be attributed to him that belongs to human understanding; otherwise, one may sin by committing an act of anthropomorphism. The Qur'an indeed says: "Nothing can be compared with Him. He alone hears all and sees all" (42:11). Therefore, when we deal with the idea of wrath, we should, to be on the safe side, take it metaphorically, and avoid likening it to the common human feeling or emotion, since God transcends anything of the kind. Indeed, the Mu'tazilites deny the existence of attributes distinct from Divine essence.

A different view might be attributed to Imam al-Ghazali, the famous theologian and Sufi (12th Century CE), who had influential contributions to make on the issue of God's sublime names. In his book, *Attributes of Might and Power* (in Arabic titled *al-Maqsid al-asna fi asma'i Allah al-husna*)[16] he lists the ninety-nine divine names and defines them from his specific point of view. What is relevant for us in that list is a number of names that may be directly related to the idea of wrath, which is the focus of the present contribution. The names are the following:

1. *The Dominating One* (38)
2. *The One Who abases the unbeliever and exalts the believer* (48)
3. *The One Who raises to honor and abases* (49)
4. *The Avenger* (114)
5. *He Who is responsible for both good and evil* (120).

A brief look at the above *Names* might indicate that al-Ghazali seems rather bold in interpreting them in the way he does, at least by the standards of the Mu'tazilites, namely. In fact, to take the example of items (4) and (5), Robert C. Stade, states in footnote 144 that "This name is not found in the Qur'an" (120). Yet the essence of such Names may be considered to be consistent with the idea of wrath we have been trying to expose and explicate. If we take item (4) above, the *Avenger*, al-Ghazzali expounds it in the following terms:

> The Avenger is the One who breaks the back of the arrogant, the One who severely punishes the perpetrators, and presses punishment on the tyrants. He does that after excusing them (i.e. after forgiving earlier sins, after giving them many warnings [op cit 114].

So, as was stated earlier, despite "behaving" in a violent way, casting wrath, curse, and shame on the evil doers, God does not do so arbitrarily; God first gives a chance to people to seek repentance and ask for forgiveness. He warns them before inflicting His punishment.

Conclusion

By way of conclusion, we can say that the symbol of wrath in Islam, namely in the Qur'anic text, might be viewed and interpreted from various angles of vision. The content analysis and linguistic approach attempted in this study, together with some relevant theological discussion, have hopefully helped clarify the concept. The analysis of wrath (or anger) has been found to confirm the hypothesis that linking the text of the Qur'an with its historical context is likely to provide a clearer picture and a better understanding of the various meanings and messages that are relevant to our focal theme. The work of the late al-Jabri (2008 and 2009) has been of great assistance in this regard. Besides, using the Qur'an, as the primary source for analysis, has — it is hoped — contributed to focusing and tightening the discussion, away from undue ramification and hardly useful details. Furthermore, the theological element based on a Mu'tazili interpretation, besides a Sunni and Sufi one, has helped enhance the discussion and analysis of the topical concept. If anything, the concept of wrath, in association with things Divine, has been discussed here in close connection with the Qur'anic text. All temptations of partiality and subjectivity have been resisted to the maximum; the potential reader targeted, and to be borne in mind, is the academic, tolerant and rational type. Given its potential richness and possibility of openness on various other readings and interpretations, one may suggest, *inter alia,* an interesting comparative study, of the concept of wrath across the various monotheistic religions.

Chapter Notes

1. The translation of the Qur'an used throughout this chapter is by N. J. Dawood, Penguin edition, 2003.
2. The number here refers to the traditional sequence of the Qur'anic chapters.
3. God's anger can only be interpreted allegorically, as strictly speaking, from an Islamic point of view,

God should be disassociated from such known human feelings as anger or joy, or else we might be accused of committing an act of anthropomorphism. Yet this gave birth to a debate between a rational Mu'tazili point of view and a more literalist interpretation of *God's attributes* and *elevated names*.

4. Apostates and unbelievers are mentioned in the same verse.

5. The term "associator" is borrowed from Muhammad Mahmud Ghali's translation of the Qur'an, [4th ed.], *Towards Understanding the Ever-Glorious Qur'an*, (Egypt: Dar al-Nashr Lil-Jami'a, 2009).

6. Also called the "Confederate Tribes," they were mostly Bedouin tribes who contracted many military alliances with Quraysh, and secretly with the Jews, in their fight against Muhammad and his religion.

7. Order or sequence of revelation of the Qur'an is still, to date, a matter of debate. Some scholars (namely the late al-Jabri 2008 and 2009 in his 3 volumes) would prefer the sequence of the actual revelation of the various verses and chapters of the Qur'an to the rather traditional order of the Holy Book, compiled by the third Caliph 'Uthman. The ancient method adopted the length of chapters rather than the order of revelation. The majority of the copies of the Qur'an known today are based on what is called "the *Mushaf* of 'Uthman."

8. The sequence adopted here is that of the traditional *Mushaf.*

9. See a detailed discussion of this point in John Andrew Morrow's "*Jihad* in Islam" which is found in *Islamic Insights: Writings and Reviews* (329–336). The author shows how the Prophet insists on the obligation for the Muslim fighters to observe strict engagement rules such as the rule to spare non-combatants, women, children, old people, monks, the rule to refrain from cutting trees or destroying houses with people inside, the rule to spare people's means of sustenance, the strict observance of peace treaties, etc.

10. See also the list of rules of Islamic fighting engagement expounded by Morrow in "*Jihad* in Islam" (334).

11. See the Qur'an: "You are the noblest community ever raised: you enjoin justice and forbid evil." (3: 110).

12. See Ibn Hisham.

13. See Muhammad ibn Jarir al-Tabari, etc.

14. "Did he not find you an orphan and give you shelter?" (93:6).

15. *Al-Jizyah* is a former tax paid by *Dhimmis* (Jews and Christians living in an Islamic country against their protection) towards their contribution to the "state budget" or *Bayt mal al-Muslimin*, while *al-Zakat* is the contribution of Muslims to that budget.

16. Translated under the title of *Ninety-Nine Names of God in Islam*, by Robert Charles Stade (Ibadan: Daystar Press, 1970).

Works Cited

al-Qur'an. al-Qahirah: Dar al-Sahar li Tiba'ah, 2002.

Austin, John L. *How to Do Things with Words.* Harvard: Harvard University Press, 2005.

Dawood, N.J. trans. *The Koran.* London: Penguin, 2003.

Ghali, Muhammad Mahmud al-, trans. *Qur'an.* Egypt: Dar al-Nashr li al-Jami'at, 2009.

Ibn Hisham, Abu Muhammad 'Abd al-Malik. *Sirah al-Nabi.* Tanta: Dar al-Sahaba li al-Turath, 1995.

Jabri, Muhammad 'Abed al-. *Fahm al-Qur'an al-Hakim.* Dar al-Bayda': Dar al-Nashr al-Maghribiyyah, 2008 and 2009.

Mahalli, Jalal al-Din. *Tafsir al-Jalalayn.* 'Amman: Aal al-Bayt Institute for Islamic Thought, 2005. Internet: www. altafsir.org.

Morrow, John Andrew. "*Jihad* in Islam" *Islamic Insights: Writings and Reviews.* Qum: Ansariyan, 2012. 329–336.

Sawar, Marwan, ed. *Mukhtasar Tafsir al-Tabari.* Dimashq: Dar al-Fajr al-Islami, 1991.

Searle, John. *Speech Acts.* Cambridge: Cambridge University Press, 1969.

Stade, Robert Charles. *Ninety-Nine Names of God in Islam.* Ibadan: Daystar Press, 1970.

Tabari, Muhammad ibn Jarir al-. *Tarikh al-umam wa al-muluk.* N.p.: n.p., n.d.

Justice

Hisham M. Ramadan

"Judge with justice" (Qur'an 4:58)

Introduction

Allah, the Creator of the Universe, the Absolute Power, who is liable to no one for His actions, vested in Himself the adjective *al-Muqsit* (Just / Equitable) (3:18). He forbade injustice for Himself and made it forbidden to humankind (16:90). As Allah emphasizes in the Holy Qur'an: "O My servants, I have forbidden injustice for Myself and have made it forbidden amongst you, so do not be unjust to each other" (Muslim). This simple rule represents the very core of Islam. Justice is applicable to all creatures and to all actions notwithstanding race, gender, heritage or any other factor so long as the performed act is intentional and the actor is responsible and aware of his actions (6:131). In this context, all right conduct is just no matter how seemingly trivial and all wrong conduct is unjust. The following analysis shall briefly discuss a number of aspects of justice. It should be noted that the concept of justice is discussed from the perspective of Islamic sources, an approach which varies dramatically from the Orientalists' methodologies and points of view.

The Islamic Approach to Justice

Islam places the burden of enjoining justice on all Muslims. It is both an individual and a collective duty. It is absolute and is measured to the smallest degree (4:40). No one, regardless of race, religious affiliation (being Muslim or otherwise), gender, social status or any other factor, shall receive any advantageous treatment. All are equal before and under the law. Countless incidents confirm the rule of law doctrine. The Prophet Muhammad said:

> Help your brother, whether he is an oppressor or he is an oppressed one. People asked, "O Allah's apostle! It is all right to help him if he is oppressed, but how should we help him if he is an oppressor?" The Prophet said, "By preventing him from oppressing others" [Bukhari].

In another incident, the Prophet Muhammad asserted that no race is superior to any other. He emphasized that an Arab is not better than a non–Arab; a non–Arab is not better than an Arab; a red person, namely, a fair-skinned white person, is not better than a black person; and a black person is no better than a red person (Ahmad). Moreover, it has been reported by Muslim that a noble woman committed theft during the early days of Islam. After she was apprehended, her family sent a close companion to the Prophet Muhammad in an attempt to dissuade him from punishing her. The Prophet Muhammad refused to grant the request, noting that previous nations have been destroyed because they inflicted the punishment only on the weak while sparing nobles for the same misdeeds. According to Islam, however, justice must always be impartial and applicable to all.

The Prophet Muhammad's practice of enjoining justice and upholding the rule of law is a natural reflection of Allah's laws of justice. Allah is just even towards those who reject His very existence. Whosoever, believer or non-believer, does a good or evil deed, even if it is as small as the weight of an atom, shall see the consequences of his or her actions, reward or punishment, by virtue of Qur'an (99:7–8). However, because justice is measured to the least degree, believers and non-believers shall not be rewarded equally in the hereafter as belief in Islam is heavily weighed in favor of the believer. In his commentary of the Qur'an, known as *Ruh al-ma'ani*, al-Alusi, the renowned scholar explained that these verses 7–8 from Surah 99 imply that Allah is just to believers and non-believers in the sense that believers shall be rewarded for their deeds in this life and the hereafter, while the disbelievers will be rewarded for their good deeds only in this life.

A critical question then arises: what is *just* action? The depth and the importance of this question is apparent given that humankind is in a constant struggle to find the path to righteousness. Human desires, and self-constituted right and wrong standards, created and justified all sorts of injustices, including fascism, racism and Nazism. Islam's answer to this question is straightforward. Allah, in a *hadith qudsi* or sacred saying, declared: "O My servants, all of you are astray except for those I have guided, so seek guidance of Me and I shall guide you" (Muslim). Accordingly, the criterion for right and wrong, just and unjust, is compliance with Allah's guidance expressed within the indispensible basic sources of Islamic law: the Holy Qur'an and the *Sunnah* of the Prophet (16:89). If an issue was not expressly adjudicated in either Qur'an or *Sunnah*, Muslim jurists may engage in *ijtihad*, namely, exherting oneself to apply Islamic principles to changing times and circumstances. The alternative, as the Qur'an affirms (30:29), would be to follow one's desires and lusts, the end result of which is injustice. In Islam, morality is not what the majority believes is acceptable and appropriate. For Muslims, there are eternal ethical principles which are immutable. Murder is wrong and will always be wrong. Fornication and adultery are wrong and will always be wrong. While there are secondary matters, specific to time and culture, which are subject to adaptation, there can be no changes in the fundamental foundations of Islamic belief and practice.

Justice, as portrayed in the Qur'an, should not be accidental or incidental to Muslims. On the contrary, justice is part and parcel of faith. It should form part of a Muslim's creedal core. To be just in one's beliefs, one must believe in the Creator and Sustainer of the universe. The Qur'an (4:48) repeatedly confirms that the highest degree of injustice is disbelieving in Allah and/or associating others with Allah. It is considered the highest degree of injustice because it denies Allah His due, namely, to be believed in, worshiped, and obeyed. Because this injustice is so great, the consequences are severe, including hell-fire in the hereafter.

Not only should justice form a part of one's inner beliefs, it should form part of one's lifestyle. In other words, the belief in justice should be manifested in the actions of Muslims. They should believe in justice and act upon it. The Qur'an, on numerous occasions, gives examples of justice as a lifestyle. A justice-centered life is characterized by documenting debts to avoid future problems (2:282), protection the property of minor orphans (6:152), advocating reconciliation as a primary step to settle disputes and, if reconciliation fails, advocating repelling the aggressor until he desists (49:9). The Qur'an also gives examples of unjust lifestyles, including refraining from bearing truthful testimony (2:140) and forbidding others from doing the right conduct (2:114).

Justice as a lifestyle, as practiced by scores of Muslims, and the inconspicuous belief in Allah that is deeply rooted in Muslims' hearts, is fused to form the loop of justice. Belief in Allah motivates Muslims to practice justice as a lifestyle while the occurrence of justice evinces the existence of a Superior Being, Allah, who is inherently just. All this is condensed to formulate the norm of Islamic thought: justice is not a wish; it is a destiny. The Qur'an frequently confirms this fact in various forms. Chief among them is the notion of injustice to oneself. In the Qur'an, 2:231, it is asserted that unjust acts to others are not really what they seem. Because Allah is just, those who been subject to injustice in this life shall be relieved, to their satisfaction, and justice shall be restored, either in this life or in the hereafter. Yet, those who commit injustice intentionally, and do not repent, shall suffer the severe consequences in this life and/or in the hereafter, possibly for eternity.

Forms of Injustice

Injustice generally falls under two categories: (1) injustice to oneself by violating God's right to be worshiped exclusively and obeyed, namely, by associating other gods with God (2:51) or by violating God's prohibitory norms; (2) injustice to oneself by being unjust to others. Both forms of injustice are subject to correction by repentance. However, the method of repentance varies depending on the harm accrued. If the harm is limited to violating God's right, for example, consuming alcohol, then having sincere regrets for doing such an act and genuine desire not to commit this unjust act ever again, suffices for repentance (4:110). However, if such major sins are repeated habitually, punishment cannot be averted. Even God has limits. For certain major sins, there is exists a three strikes and you are out policy. As for sins and crimes which receive an earthly punishment according to Islamic law, they serve as expiation in this life and the hereafter for the repentant sinner.

For minor sins, repentance remains sound even if the actor commits the unjust act, repents, but repeats the action again in the future. The door for repentance for the new, albeit repeated, unjust act remains open and will never close as long as the individual is alive. On the other hand, if the harm caused by an unjust act encroaches upon others' rights, for example, committing theft, it is not sufficient to have sincere regret and a genuine desire not to re-offend. The actor must restore justice by returning the stolen property to its rightful owner (5:39). In such cases, God will only forgive the repentant sinner if he or she has been forgiven by his or her victim. In other words, in order to make things right in the next world, one must first make things rights in this world to the best of one's abilities. True and sincere repentance not only precludes punishment in the hereafter but also prevents triggering divine punishment in this life. Notably, if injustice becomes rampant in society, with no repentance in sight, it may bring total and absolute destruction to that population even though some righteous individuals may live among such wrong-doers (21:11).

Deterrence, Infusing Fear and Hope to Promote Justice

Muslim jurists represent belief in Islam as a flying bird. Its two wings are hope and fear. In the absence of either, the bird cannot fly. Hence, belief is incomplete. This account is inspired by the Qur'an's use of fear and hope to enforce divine obligations such as justice. Numerous verses in the Qur'an affirm that those who refuse to obey the divine command of justice shall be punished severely and those who comply with it shall be rewarded generously. As the Holy Qur'an implores,

> O you who believe! Be *Quwamin* (Stand out repeatedly and firmly) for Allah as just witnesses; and let not the enmity and hatred of others make you avoid justice. Be just: that is nearer to piety; and fear Allah. Verily, Allah is well-acquainted with what you do [5:8].

Initially, the verse starts with "O you who believe," which intended to capture the attention of listeners to the rest of the verse wherein lies the important matter. Addressing only the believers is unusual because the Qur'an generally addresses humankind at large. Singling out the "believers," however, infuses hope and desire in all Muslims who yearn to be included in this category for, as the Qur'an makes clear, only believers shall abide by the command contained in the verse. The command, which follows, urges Muslims to stand firmly for justice. *Quwamin*, as stated in the original Qur'anic Arabic text, references believers' steadfast efforts to uphold justice, as Allah mandates it, regardless of whether the upholder of justice is acting in an official or unofficial capacity, and whether a person is a witness or a party in a particular conflict. Remarkably, the command is to stand firmly for God, "Allah," All-seeing, All-knowing, and Master of the Day of Judgment. If the command were formulated by using alternative terminology, for example, "stand firmly for justice," it would have less impact on the listeners since justice is a relative concept and humans typically justify their erroneous acts and label them as just.

By making Allah the focus of the action, the Qur'an stresses that the commendable justice is the ultimate truth. As the verse reveals, Allah is not only Just; He is Justice. As the All-knowing and All-seeing — Who knows and sees what people think — He command justice and scrutinizes its enforcement. Subsequently, the verse commands: "and let not the enmity and hatred of others make you avoid justice." This portion attempts to tip the balance of human actions towards absolute justice if the balance is tilted towards injustice by strong emotions of enmity or hatred. Immediately after setting the balance right, the Qur'an repeats the order in very clear and strong language: "Be just." The incentive for being just is that it brings Muslims closer to the desirable status of piety. Finally, after the verse encourages Muslims to enjoin justice for its rewards, achieving two very desirable statuses in Islam, being pious and a true believer, the verse ends with a clear warning to deter injustice: "fear Allah." This final remark represents an implied threat of the punishment if Muslims avoid justice or even fail to stand firmly for it. The threat of the punishment is coupled with a reminder that Allah, the Master of the Day of Judgment, is "well-Acquainted with what you do." In other words, no human shall escape punishment for malevolent intentional conduct even if he or she attempts to conceal it because Allah knows what people think and do.

The basic sources of Islam, which consist primarily of the Qur'an and *Sunnah*, draw numerous examples that create mental pictures of justice in order to encourage general obedience to this primary principle. Typically, language of an emphatic nature is employed to create a terrifying or inspirational portrayal. According to the Qur'an, the *muttaqun*, namely, the pious God-fearing individuals who observe and command justice, "will be in the midst of gardens and rivers (paradise). In a seat of truth (i.e. paradise), near the Omnipotent King (Allah)" (54:54–5). A *hadith* confirms that, on the Day of Judgment, those who are just and enjoin justice will be contentedly seated on the pulpits of light beside God (Muslim).

In contrast, the Qur'an draws a dismal picture of the punishment that awaits the unjust. They will, it is warned, be thrown into hell-fire, the walls of which will surround them on all sides (18:29). If they ask for relief, they will be granted water like boiling oil that will scald their faces (18:29). Moreover, injustice is described as darkness on the Day of Judgment (Muslim). The Qur'an highlights the contrast between those who command justice and those who do not (16: 76). The unjust are analogous to a dumb, powerless slave who is a burden on his master while just individuals are on the straight path.

It is highly significant that the case of justice is presented in such a superior linguistic style. It generates inner belief that God, who is All-Seeing, All-Knowing, is watching and therefore the ultimate deterrent effect is in play. Also, it aims to neutralize human biases, motivated by ill feelings, to shift human judgment of what is just and right from a purely subjective standard to the sphere of ultimate objectivity as God mandates it. It re-prioritizes human intentions according to its importance on the Day of Judgment, and not in accordance with what an individual can achieve in his life by unjustifiable means. Ultimately, the employment of fear and hope creates a new normative attitude that shifts the individual's state of mind from what he can do to what he should do.

Islam, however, recognizes human frailty and the fact that individuals eventually may fail to conform to justice. Here, the door for repentance is wide open to cleanse oneself and avoid punishment. Repentance, in this context, comprises instant abstinence from injustice, deep sincere regret, a desire to never commit the act again, followed by restoration of justice, namely, helping the victim recover from the physical or material injury by every means possible. Yet, again, fear and hope are perfectly employed to encourage repentance and the restoration of justice as well as to deter the guilty party from further wrong-doing. The Qur'an, on the one hand, affirms that those who repent, and do righteous deeds, will have their odious deeds turned into good deeds by Allah (25:70–71; 27:11). The Prophet Muhammad, on the other hand, warned that although Allah gives respite to the unjust, He never releases them after they have been seized (Bukhari). Following the warning, the Prophet recited the following verse from the Qur'an: "Such is the seizure of your Lord when He seizes (population of) towns in the midst of their wrong: Painful indeed and severe is His seizure" (11:102).

Rights for Victims of Injustice

Islam affords a comprehensive theory of victims' rights. First and foremost, the restoration of justice is guaranteed. If it is not possible in this life, due to lack of evidence or otherwise, justice shall be restored on the Day of Judgment, even if the injustice seems trivial. The Qur'an speaks of Allah's promise to uphold justice even if justice was equivalent to the weight of an atom (4:40). In this context, Islam explains the phases upon which the victim shall take to restore justice. Initially, while the Qur'an forbids uttering evil, odious speech (4:148), it permits, as an exception, the individual who has been subject to injustice to complain and reveal the injustice. Justice restoration methodology varies depending on the circumstances and kind of injustice that has occurred. Generally, the accuser shall bear the burden of proof and the denier of the allegation must make an oath denying the truth of the allegation asserted (Bayhaqi). More specific rules were created to deal with various issues. For instance, the offense of *zina* (fornication/adultery) requires at least four credible witnesses to testify that they saw the repeated act of penetration or alternatively, the offender's uncoerced confession. The offense of murder requires two credible witnesses or the offender's uncoerced confession. Evidently, other forms of evidence, such as forensics, are equally important.

Once the injustice has been proven, a remedy, as prescribed by Islamic law, shall be instated. However, if injustice is not proven, due to lack of evidence or otherwise, the Islamic faith-based justice system shall stand as a psychological barrier that prevents the victim from taking law into his or her own hands and do what he or she believes to be right and reasonable to reinstate justice. When a victim is aware that justice will be restored, one way or another, in this life or the hereafter, such an assurance provides a great deal of mental relief. Such a state of awareness or certainty stems from the knowledge that Allah is Just and All-Knowing (4:40) and that there is no screen between the oppressed's invocation for justice and Allah (Bukhari). Moreover, fear of falling into error and becoming the transgressor prevents believers from taking the law into their own hands. As such, faith in divine justice can be a driving force that prevents retaliation (2:190). Nevertheless, the concept of *ihsan*, namely, the placing of faith into practice, plays a decisive role in implementing peace in society by encouraging forgiveness and preventing revenge. Although there is no synonymous word to *ihsan* in English, it can be translated as perfection in acting with the highest standard of ethics and skillfulness. In this context, while justice is equity in dealing with others, *ihsan* is the bountiful philanthropic act that falls beyond justice. The role of *ihsan* in peace building and its relationship to justice is best understood from the Qur'an, in general, and the following verse, in particular:

> Verily, Allah enjoins justice and *al-ihsan*, and giving (help) to kith and kin, and forbids *al-fahsha'* (i.e all evil deeds), and *al-munkar* (i.e all that is prohibited by Islamic law), and *al-baghi* (i.e. all kinds of oppression). He admonishes you, that you may take heed [16:90].

Remarkably, the word *ihsan* is immediately preceded by the command for justice. The sequence of commands suggests that justice is best followed by *ihsan*. Another verse affirms the same conclusion and describes best practices as follows: "Those (believers) ... who repress anger, and who pardon men; verily, Allah loves *al-muhsinun* [the good-doers who act in accordance of *ihsan*]" (3:134).

The sequence of commands in this verse illustrates the manners which are recommended after being a victim of injustice. Initially, victims shall restrain their anger, pardon those who harmed them unjustifiably, and then perform *ihsan* by showing grace and generosity to the offender. An incident occurred in the early years of Islam that illustrates the practical application of this verse. Imam 'Ali Zayn al-'Abidin, the son of Imam Husayn, and the grandson of Imam 'Ali, was accidentally injured by his slave-girl. When the slave realized her master's anger, she started reciting "those who repress anger," and the master responded: "I have restrained my anger." Then, the slave recited "those who pardon the people," and the master responded: "God has pardoned you." Finally, the slave recited "Allah loves those who perform *ihsan* [good deeds]" (3:134) The master responded: "Go, you are a free woman" (Zayn al-'Abidin 13 note 11).

Conclusion

Ultimately, as several Islamic law scholars have pointed out, the highest degree of *ihsan* is presented to the one who has harmed you. In this context, the renowned Islamic scholar al-Alusi in his commentary of the Qur'an, *Ruh al-ma'ani*, concluded that *'Isa* (Jesus) said that *ihsan* occurs when you present it to the one who harms you, not to the one who is good to you. Nevertheless, for individuals who are incapable of performing the recommended *ihsan*, simply because they could not reach such a stage of spiritual superiority, justice is always guaranteed. Again, the Qur'an (16:90) mentions justice before *ihsan* to explain that justice is the norm. This Islamic formula strikes a fine balance between creating a graceful tolerant environment, where individuals pardon one another, and upholding the interests of justice when it should be held firmly.

Works Cited

'Ali, 'Abdullah Yusuf, trans. *The Holy Qur'an.* Brentwood: Amana Corporation, 1983.

Alusi, Mahmud ibn 'Abdullah al-Husayni al-. *Ruh al-ma'ani.* Bayrut: Dar Ihya' al-Turath al-'Arabi, n.d.

Bayhaqi, Ahmad ibn al-Husayn al-. *Kitab al-zuhd al-kabir.* Bayrut: Dar al-Jinan: Mu'assasat al-Kutub al-Thaqafiyyah, 1987.

Bukhari, Muhammad ibn Isma'il. *Sahih al-Bukhari.* al-Riyad: Bayt al-Afkar al-Dawliyyah li al-Nashr, 1998.

Ibn Hanbal, Ahmad ibn Muhammad. *Musnad al-Imam Ahmad ibn Hanbal.* Bayrut: al-Maktabah al-Islamiyyah, 1969.

Muslim ibn al-Hajjaj al-Qushayri al-Nisaburi. *Jami' al-sahih.* al-Riyad: Bayt al-Afkar al-Dawliyyah li al-Nashr, 1998.

Zayn al-'Abidin, Imam 'Ali ibn al-Husayn. *The Treatise on Rights: Risalat al-huquq.* Trans. William C. Chittick. Qum: Foundation of Islamic Cultural Propagation in the World, 1990.

THE SPIRITUAL

The Path

John Andrew Morrow

"I have never seen a man lost who was on the straight path." (Sa'di of Shiraz)

Introduction

While the religion of Islam has many symbols, the image of the path (*al-sirat*; *al-tariq*; *al-sabil, al-nahj*) is among the most important symbolic expressions in Arabic-Islamic literature, language and culture. The image of the path, in its multiple manifestations as road, route, way, highway, pass and bridge, appears in the Arabic language in the form of various idiomatic expressions invoking guidance including: *Tariq al-salamah*, "May your road be peaceful"; *Tariq al-khayr*; "May your road be good"; *Fi sabil Allah*; "In the way of Allah"; *Allah yahdik*, "May Allah guide you"; personal names including *Sabil*, or "Way"; *Rashid* or "One who is guided"; *Irshad* or "Guidance," each related, literally or figuratively, to divine direction or *hidayah*, a concept intrinsically linked to the image of the straight path as agreed upon by Qur'anic commentators.

The image of the road, the "straight and middle path," is a primary principle in traditional Islamic thought, governing all domains: be it politics, economics, law or jurisprudence. Muslims are enjoined to moderation for as Almighty Allah says: "We have appointed you a middle nation" (2:143). In the field of politics and economics, Muslims are reminded to be neither conservatives nor liberals, neither socialists nor capitalists as embodied in Imam Khomeini's famous slogan "Neither East nor West." In the area of Islamic law, or *shari'ah*, Islam calls for moderation: "do not transgress limits" (2:190). In Islamic jurisprudence or *fiqh*, jurists follow the principle of moderation which states that, when two legitimate solutions exist, opt for the easier one. Even in the area of Islamic mysticism, we find many later orders who taught that the middle way, between excessive hunger and excessive eating, was the safest for the disciple's progress (Schimmel 117).

In Arabic-Islamic literature, language and culture, the image of the path, in its multiple manifestations as road, route, way, highway, pass and bridge, comes from the religion of Islam, its sacred text, the Holy Qur'an, and the Prophetic Traditions, the *ahadith*, namely the sayings of the Prophet Muhammad and, for Twelver Shi'ites, the apothegms of the Immaculate Imams — appearing in both exoteric and esoteric exegesis — literally, linguistically, allegorically, symbolically, religiously, theologically and philosophically.

The Image of the Road in the Qur'an

In the Holy Qur'an, the foremost symbol of the path comes from verse 6 of *Surah al-Fatihah*, the Opening Chapter, the Mother of the Book, the Core of the Qur'an, which reads "Guide us on the straight path" or *ihdina al-sirat al-mustaqim*. According to Tabarsi's *Tafsir majma' al-bayan fi tafsir al-Qur'an* and 'Allamah Tabataba'i's *Mizan al-Qur'an*, *al-sirat* means "the straight path" and is derived from *sarattu sartan*, "I swallowed it up completely," because this clear path swallows its walkers, without letting them go. According to al-Tabari, "The Arabs use the term *sirat* in reference to every deed and statement whether righteous or wicked. Hence, the Arabs would describe the honest person as being straight and the wicked person as being crooked" (Ibn Kathir). The word *al-sirat* (path) appears 46 times in the Holy Qur'an; the word *sabil* (way) ocurs 166 times; the word *subul* (ways) 10 times and the word *tariq* (road), 4 times, not to mention their multiple implicit appearances. The word *sirat*, written with both *sin* and *sad* in ancient times, is one of the few words in Arabic which is both masculine and feminine, making the path to God gender inclusive.

According to Sunnis, Shi'ites and Sufis, the "straight path" mentioned in the Qur'an refers to Islam in contrast to "the path of those who go astray" and "the path of those who incur your wrath" which, according to some Islamic sources, refers to Christianity and Judaism (Vernet 4). According to the Prophet,

> Allah has set an example: a *sirat* (straight path) that is surrounded by two walls on both sides, with several open doors within the walls covered with curtains. There is a caller on the gate of the *sirat* who heralds, "O people! Stay on the path and do not deviate from it." Meanwhile, a caller from above the path is also warning any person who wants to open any of these doors, "Woe unto you! Do not open it, for if you open it you will pass through." The straight path is Islam, the two walls are Allah's set limits, while the doors resemble what Allah has prohibited. The caller on the gate of the *sirat* is the Book of Allah, while the caller above the *sirat* is Allah's admonishment in the heart of every Muslim [Ahmad].

The Sunni and Salafi View of the Straight Path

In Sunni thought in general, and Salafi ideology in particular, the *sirat al-mustaqim*, the straight path, is typically viewed as one, consistent with a literalist, essentialist and reductionist interpretation of Islam. As Tabari explains in his *Tafsir jami' al-bayan fi tafsir al-Qur'an*, "The *ummah* [Muslim Nation] agreed that *sirat al-mustaqim* is the path without crookedness [*la 'iwaja fih*], according to the language of the Arabs." For the Salafis, however, these words are not sufficiently clear and exclusionary; as a result, they mistranslate them as "the straight path without branches," which is not only incorrect but a manifestation of their belief in a single path, to the exclusion of all others, and that it consists of their Salafi school (see www.tafsir.com). This conception is repeatedly reinforced in their writings.

According to Tabari, the "straight path" is interpreted as Islam or the Qur'an. According to Tabarsi, there are various opinions: for 'Ali, it is the Book of Allah; for Jabir and Ibn 'Abbas, it is Islam; for Muhammad ibn al-Hanafiyyah, it is the religion of Allah and for others, it is the Prophet Muhammad and the Imams who followed him. While Sunni scholars interpret the "straight path" as being Allah, Islam, the Qur'an and the Prophet, they hold that they are one and the same. In *Tafsir bahr al-'ulum*, Samarqandi quotes a *hadith* to support this contention. He relates a tradition on the authority of Ibn Mas'ud which says that the Prophet drew a straight line with various crooked lines beside it. The Prophet explained that: "This one is the straight path and the others are paths. At the head of each path is a devil encouraging people to follow it." Then he recited: "Verily, this is My way, leading straight: follow it: follow not [other] paths: they will scatter you about from His [great] path: thus doth He command you that ye may be righteous" (6:153). Despite the fact that some Sunni scholars believe in the sole nature of the straight path, their schools of jurisprudence are nonetheless divided in ways, *madhahib* and paths, *manhaj*, much as the Sufis denominate their religious orders as *turuq* (sing. *tariqah*) or ways, each following a particular *silsilah* or spiritual chain of initiation.

The Shi'ite View of the Straight Path

Among Shi'ites, however, a multiplicity of paths is acknowledged, consistent with the Prophetic Tradition which states that "The numbers of paths to God is equal to the number of human souls" (Chittick, 1989: 52, Note 1). 'Allamah Muhammad Husayn Tabataba'i, the Shi'ite commentator of the Qur'an, explains that "the straight path itself may be divided in various 'traffic lanes,' ways or branches." He observes that "Allah repeatedly mentions *al-sirat* [path] and *al-sabil* [way] in the Qur'an; but He has never attributed to Himself except one straight path; although He attributes several ways to Himself (29:69)." Tabataba'i stresses the fact that "the ways" is in plural and "the straight path" is in singular explaining that "[e]ither 'the straight path' is the same thing as 'the ways,' or 'the ways' on going further join together and then merge into the straight path." He further explains that:

> the ways of Allah are one with the straight path; but sometimes a way — the way of the believers, of the followers of the Prophet of those who turn towards Allah or any other way — suffers from some kind of deterioration, although the straight path is immune from all defects and imperfections... In short, the ways are of various grades near or distant; safe or unsafe; clean or unclean — but all are in the straight path, or, let us say, are one with the straight path. From the above analysis it may be seen that the straight path is a sort of controller of all the ways leading to Allah. We may say that a way leading to Allah leads a man to Him as long as it remains one with the straight path; but the straight path leads to Allah unconditionally, without any if or but.

According to Tabataba'i, there are many ways leading to Allah, guidance for one differs from those of others with each way having its own special guidance of its own, as is hinted to in the verses: "And [as for] those who strive hard for Us, We will most certainly guide them unto Our ways; and Allah is most surely with the doers of good" (29:69).

Unlike Tabataba'i, Taleghani maintained a distinction between way and path. In his exegesis, "*Sirat* means an open public highway because such a road draws wayfarers on into it, much like the alimentary canal. A *sabil* is a private road, which may lead to good or to evil" (161). If a road is traveled without guidance, and does not join the straight path, it will lead the wayfarer to nothing but aimlessness and distress (161). However, if the road is founded on faith and righteousness, it will lead to the straight path, the way of Truth (161). As Taleghani explains, "the straight way is itself a goal... As a person perseveres and his wayfaring becomes totally aligned with the road — as the *sabil* reaches the *sirat*, and the *sirat* grows straight and becomes the *sirat mustaqim* — rays will surround and envelop the wayfarer and fill his heart with fervor" (162).

In Shi'ite tradition, the "straight path" has a rich repertoire of meanings. According to Imam 'Ali, "The straight path, in this world, is that which stops short of excesses and rises above shortcomings, and remains straight; and, in the next world, it is the path of the believers [leading them] to the garden" (*Ma'ani al-Akhbar*). Imam al-Sadiq explains that the straight path is the path that leads to God's love, to His garden, and that protects people from following their own vain desires (*Ma'ani al-Akhbar*). In another *ahadith*, the sixth Imam says that the straight path "is the knowledge of Allah" (*Ma'ani al-Akhbar*).

In Shi'ite tradition, the "straight path" is often personified as being the *ahl al-bayt*, the Prophet Muhammad and his Household, namely 'Ali, his son-in-law, Fatimah his daughter, and their 11 direct descendants. As Imam 'Ali advised in *Nahj al-balaghah*:

> Regard the people of the household of your Prophet, adhere to the direction they take, and follow in their footsteps, since they will never separate you from guidance or lead you astray. If they stay, stay; if they rise, rise. Do not race ahead of them lest you become lost, and do not lag behind them lest you perish [qtd. Taleghani 171].

Ibn 'Abbas is reported to have said that "the straight path" refers to the love of Muhammad and his Family (Tabataba'i). According to Imam Ja'far al-Sadiq, "The straight path is *Amir al-Mu'minin* [the Leader of the Believers]" (Qummi, 1970; Qummi, 1960; al-'Ayyashi). In yet another tradition, the sixth Imam says that: "'Ali is the *sirat* whom God entrusted with the knowledge of everything in heaven and earth. He is God's *wali* [vicegerent] over the people and the Trustee of His truth" (Bursi 140). Imam Zayn al-'Abidin, speaking on behalf of the Household of the Prophet, proclaimed that: "We are the gates of Allah, and we are the straight path, and we are the [treasure] chest of His knowledge, and we are the interpreters of His revelation, and we are the pillars of His Oneness, and we are the place of His secret" (*Ma'ani al-Akhbar*).

According to 'Allamah Qummi, also known as Shaykh Saduq, one of the founding fathers of Shi'ite scholarship: "*Al-sirat* means the names of the Proofs of Allah," namely, the twelve immaculate Imams (1942: 71). As the sixth Imam explained, there are two paths: one in this world and one in the other. As for the path in this world, it is the Imam whose obedience is obligatory; he who knows him in this world and follows his guidance, he shall proceed on the path which is over hell in the next world; and whosoever does not know him in this world, his foot shall slip [over the bridge] in the next world, and he shall fall down into the fire of hell (*Ma'ani al-Akhbar*; Taleghani 171).

In Shi'ite tradition, the "straight path" referred to in *Surah al-Fatihah* also refers to *al-Sirat*, the bridge over hell, which every human being must cross as explained in the Qur'an: "Not one of you but will pass over it: this is, with thy Lord, a Decree which must be accomplished" (19:71). According to both Shi'ite and Sunni sources, it will be made wide for believers yet thinner than a hair, sharper as a sword and hotter than fire for unbelievers; true believers will cross it quickly and with ease like a flash of lightning; some will pass it with difficulty and yet be saved, and others will fall from it into the depths of hell (Merrick 406 Note 74; Qummi, 1942: 71–72). According to Qummi, he who acknowledges and obeys the Imams in this world, Allah will grant him permission to traverse *al-Sirat*, the bridge over hell, on the Day of Resurrection for, as the Prophet said to 'Ali: "On the Day of Resurrection, I will sit near the Bridge with you and Gabriel, and no one will cross the Bridge unless he can produce a writ [of absolution] by reason of devotion [*wilayah*] to you" (72).

According to Qummi, *al-Sirat*, the bridge which spans hell, passes through various mountain passes, each with a specific name: some are called *fard* or religious obligation, others *amr* or command; and yet others *nahy* or prohibition. If a human being has neglected any of his duties, he will be stopped and Allah will demand His dues. Finally, if he escapes from all the stages, he will arrive at *Dar al-Baqa'*, the Abode of Permanence (1942: 72). As Qummi explains, the name of one of the passes is *al-wilayah*, the love of Imams, before which all humankind will be stopped and questioned regarding their love for 'Ali, the Leader of the Believers, and for the Imams who followed him, for as the Qur'an says, "stop them for they must be questioned" (37:24) (1942: 72). Those who answer correctly will be saved, those who are unable to respond will be hurled into hell, a belief consistent with Imam 'Ali's saying: "I am Allah's division between heaven and hell" (Kulayni 1: 196–98).

While the meaning of the straight path is clear—it is a public road leading to good and well-being to a natural and universal goal—the imploration for guidance along the straight path is not always understood. According to the Commander of the Faithful, Imam 'Ali, the words *ihdina al-sirat al-mustaqim* or "Guide us on the straight path" mean "Sustain the grace that has held us to obedience to You, so that we may remain obedient through the rest of our lives" (qtd. Taleghani 169). When asked about the meaning of the verse in question, Imam Ja'far al-Sadiq said: "It means 'Grant us guidance to follow a road that leads to love and paradise, and restrain us from fancies and opinions that will bring us torment and destruction'" (169–170). As Taleghani explains, "These two traditions suggest that to seek guidance means to obey constantly and to eschew those fancies and opinions that assume a religious guise, leading us to deviate from the straithg way, for religious deviations—with the arrogance they incite—are more dangerous than irreligion" (170). Hence, while the path is straight, without perpetual effort and continued guidance, its travelers run the risk of going astray. As Taleghani expounds, "the prayer 'Guide us on the straight way' is not concerned with pre-existing involuntary guidance. If 'us' is a reference to the inner human reality, and the discriminating faculty, which is none other than the innate and potential intelligence, this is a prayer for guidance that is sustained and perfected" (169).

According to Taleghani, seeking the straight path is an innate and instinctual force (163): it is the spiritual yearning that draws one towards the Divine. For this Qur'anic commentor, "*al-sirat* (with the definite article) is a subjective or an objective promise; that road which is the promised goal of every seeker; the course of the evolution of living beings, or that of humanity advancing to perfection" (163). As he explains, "[a] road is spoken of as *mustaqim* either in suggesting a hypothetical straight line, or with respect ot a traveler who proceeds on it with steadfastness, where the road prevents him from deviating" (163–164). Together, then, "[t]he *sirat mustaqim* is the innate objective of humanity. It is the source-principle of evolution" (164). However, as the Ayatullah stresses,

> The *sirat* does not run to a limited, fixed goal, for perfections are limitless and God is above them all. Nor is the human being limited in capacity; each limit reached is the starting point for further movement toward the Limitless. If the *sirat* were just the means to a further goal, it would have been said, *Ihdina ilayka (ila jannatika) bi's-sirat (mina's sirat)*: "Guide us to You / to Your garden by the way" or something of that sort. Using logic, this means that either movement is identical with perfection and life or else it accompanies them inseparably and they are its manifestations and aspects. Lack of motion, then, is deficiency, death, annihilation [163].

For Taleghani, the straight path is a perpetual path, the road of spiritual evolution which brings one increasingly closer to the Source of Perfection: "It emerges in various forms and expressions pertaining to the 'worlds' and the stages of human perception; its final expression is that bridge over hell, which intelligent, responsible beings are bound to traverse" (171).

The Sufis, like the Shi'ites, believe that the "straight path" is a balance between extremes; equilibrium between the letter of the law and the spirit of the law, between the law, *al-*

shari'ah and mysticism, *tasawwuf*, *'irfan* and *ma'rifah*; it is the avoidance of extremes, following the milestones of moderation. According to Ibn Ajiba's *Tafsir al-bahr al-madid fi tafsir al-Qur'an al-majid*:

> The straight path is following the *shari'ah* outwardly and being humble inwardly. It is following the *shari'ah* outwardly and the *haqiqah* inwardly. Your appearance is submission, but your interior is freedom. The straight path which Allah has commanded us to seek is the balance between the *shari'ah* and the truth.

In *The Kernel of Kernels*, 'Allamah Tehrani's short treatise on spiritual wayfaring which is based on the lectures on practical *'irfan* delivered by 'Allamah Sayyid Muhammad Husayn Tabataba'i between 1949 and 1950, the esteemed Ayatullah comes to the same conclusion, namely, that the straight path is the one which combines the exoteric and the esoteric. As Tehrani explains,

> "the middle position" *(al-namaf al-awsat)* and "the median community" *(ummat wasat)* are represented by those who combine within themselves the outward and the inward and who have summoned all the levels and planes of their being to the worship of the Beloved and submission to Him, having equipped themselves adequately for the journey of the spirit [Introduction].

The Sufi View of the Straight Path

The Sufis, like the Shi'ites, acknowledge a wide array of ways. For them, the mystical path is a parallel path, a ladder of love towards spiritual perfection, a staircase that leads to heaven, on which the traveler slowly and patiently climbs towards higher levels of experience (Schimmel 105). According to Sufi thought, all human beings are on a road *(shari')* designated by God. Each individual is a "wayfarer" or *salik*. The word used in the Qur'an to refer to "wayfarers" is *ibn sabil*, namely, "the son of the path" (2:177; 2:215; 4:36; 8:41; 8:41; 9:60; 17:26; 30:38; 59:7). Interpreted by Sunni commentators of the Qur'an as merely "traveler," in Sufism, the *salik* and the *ibn sabil* are symbolically charged; they are adepts on a spiritual journey *(sayr wa suluk)*; they are travelers to *tawhid*, the existential affirmation of Divine Unity (al-Qushayri); they are wayfarers on the path of Allah as embodied in the example of al-Khidr, the patron saint of travelers, the immortal who drank from the water of life and whose encounter with Musa (Moses) appears in the Holy Qur'an (18:60–82).

According to the Sufis, the first stage of the path is abiding by the *shari'ah*, the Divine Law, which means literally means "road" or "path" (Qur'an 45:18; Nasr, 2002: 115; Larus 681). One of the 99 Names of Allah is "the Legislator" or *al-Shari'* which literally means "the one who guides on the path." The second stage of the path is the *tariqah*, the Order or the Fraternity, which literally means "path." Finally, the third stage of the path is the *haqiqah* or Divine Truth which can only be reached by following the spiritual paths of the *shari'ah*, the *via purgativa*, and the *tariqah*, the *via illuminativa*, in order to reach the *haqiqah*, the Divine Truth, the mystical quest for *unio mystica*. As Annemarie Schimmel explains:

> The *tariqah*, the "path" on which the mystics walk, has been defined as "the path which comes out of the *shari'ah*, for the main road is called *shar'*, the path, *tariq*." This derivation shows that the Sufis considered the path of mystical education a branch of that highway that consists of the God-given law, on which every Muslim is supposed to walk. No path can exist without a main road from which it branches out; no mystical experience can be realized if the binding injunctions of the *shari'ah* are not followed faithfully first. The path, *tariqah*, however, is narrower and more

difficult to walk and leads the adept — called *salik*, "wayfarer" — in his *suluk*, "wandering," through different stations [*maqam*] until he perhaps reaches, more or less slowly, his goal, the perfect *tawhid*, the existential confession that God is One [98–99].

This tripartite path to God can be traced back to a tradition in which the Prophet states that: "The *shari'ah* are my words [*aqwali*], the *tariqah* are my actions ['*amali*], and the *haqiqah* is my interior states [*ahwali*]," demonstrating that the *shari'ah*, the Path of Divine Law, the *tariqah*, the Sufi Path, and the *haqiqah*, Divine Truth, are mutually interdependent (Schimmel 105).

While the majority of mainstream Muslims circle the Mountain of Light, scaling it slowly and safely, sometimes barely moving from its base, the Sufis attempt a direct ascent to its vertiginous cloud-covered peak. Although the potential for a speedy ascent is alluring to the anxious, the path is fraught with peril. For surely, one wrong move, and one false step, can prove fatal. Although a select few have seen the summit in its entire splendor, most mountaineers have plummeted to their death. Slow as it may seem to some, the wide, well-trodden path, offers the surest road to success for those who are patient and persevere. The following interview summary provides a glance of Grand Ayatullah Bashir Najafi's (b. 1942) view on '*irfan* or mysticism:

> On the subject of studying mysticism, he stated that it is a necessity for the student to have mastered the other Islamic sciences, especially *fiqh* [jurisprudence] before entering into such areas. He explained that there were several avenues in achieving the recognition (*ma rifah*) of Allah; one is through the mastery of '*ilm al-kalam* (*aqa'id*) [religious beliefs]. The other is through being an expert in *fiqh*. Ayatullah Bashir concluded that it is only when one masters all Islamic sciences that he can dwell into understanding the science of mysticism. He specifically highlighted the example of Imam Khomeini: he was a *faqih* [jurist] and a scholar in all Islamic sciences and only then delved into the subject of mysticism. He warned that students who study mysticism at early stages of their *hawzah* [seminary] studies are likely to be lost and to deviate. He was, hence, against the teaching of mysticism in the mainstream *hawzah* curriculum, particularly for students whose basics were not strong enough [World Federation].

Similar views are also shared by the likes of the Grand Ayatullah Sayyid 'Ali al-Husayni al-Sistani (b. 1930), and Grand Ayatullah Ishaq al-Fayyaz (b. 1930), Shi'ite authorities who, while accepting Gnosis, wish to ensure that it remains within the realm of Islamic orthodoxy. In short, since mysticism is a steep mountain, foolish is he who enters its uncharted passes without a guide and proper preparation. In the words of Seyyed Hossein Nasr, one of the leading Sufi sages,

> The practice of religion, which is meant for everyone, is like walking on level ground or this "horizontal straight path." The Sufi path, however, is like mountain climbing or the "vertical straight path." Anyone who is able to walk can do so on this "horizontal path" by himself or herself, and of course with Divine confirmation, for even on the horizontal plane one can become lost. Mountain climbing is, however, something else. Especially in high mountains one cannot do it without an experienced guide as well as, of course, Divine aid. Now, the cosmic mountain is vastly higher than the peaks of the Himalayas, and one needs a guide to reach its peak and to ascend ever further to the Infinite Reality beyond the cosmos. Yes, some have achieved the climb successfully without a human guide, through the agencies of what Sufism calls "absent" or invisible guides (*rijal al-ghayb*), such as Khidr, or the Hidden Imam. But they represent the exception and not the rule [112].

As we have seen, both Sunni and Shi'ite scholars have traditionally viewed the path as a line, single or multiple, moving horizontally from point A to point B. While some Sufi scholars share this conception, others have viewed the straight path as a vertical ladder of spiritual perfection and yet others, have embraced the image of sphere, an interpretation more consistent with Islamic circular symbolism.

The Mystical Meanings of the Straight Path

At the heart of the Islamic universe is the Ka'bah, both earthly and ethereal, towards which all Muslims turn in prayer and around which they perform *tawaf* or circumambulation during the greater and lesser pilgrimage, counter clock-wise, a motion in universal harmony with cosmic cycles. This circular symbolism is found in Islamic art, architecture and social structure. When Muslims gather, for personal or religious reasons, they sit in a circle, a *halaqah*, which is equally used to describe a religious study circle. When the Sufis gather, they form a circle, a *halaqah*, around a pivot, or *qutb*. When Muslims invoke the Divine Name (*dhikr*), the royal path to spiritual realization, they use a circular rosary to perform *tasbih*, from the root *sabbaha*, which not only means "to declare His glory" but also "to rotate" and "to orbit" (Qur'an 17:44; Larus 603).

In Islamic mysticism, the *wasat* or center is the axis around which the world rotates and is referred to as the *qutb* or pole, generally represented by a wheel, referring to the absolute dominion over the worldly order. The title of *wasat*, center, *qutb*, pole, and *rukn*, pillar, is applied to Imam al-Mahdi, the twelfth Imam, the Spiritual Pole of the Age, *Qutb al-Aqtab*, the Pole of the Poles, around which the world revolves.

Islamic circular symbolism is particularly prevalent among later Islamic sages, especially the Sufis who spoke of the hierarchy of the *shari'ah*, the Divine Law, the *tariqah*, the Spiritual Path and the *haqiqah*, the Divine Truth, which is the origin of both. As Sayyed Hosein Nasr explains:

> Islam is then envisaged as a circle whose center is the *haqiqah*. The *radi* of the circle are the *turuq* (plural of *tariqah*), later identified with the Sufi orders, and the circumference is the *shari'ah*. Each Muslim is like a point on the circumference, whose totality composes the Islamic community, or *ummah*. To reach the *haqiqah*, one must first stand on the circumference, that is, practice the *shari'ah*, and then follow the *tariqah*, or Path to God, whose end is the Center, God Himself, or the *haqiqah* [2002: 60].

In Sufi philosophy, the soul is the cosmos and the cosmos is the soul, so much so that the primary function of Sufi cosmology and sciences is to provide a prototype of the cosmos for the traveler upon the path (Nasr, 1973: 46). As Shaykh al-'Arabi al-Darqawi explains: "The soul is an immense thing; it is the whole cosmos, since it is a copy of it. Everything which is in the cosmos is to be found in the soul; equally everything in the soul is in the cosmos" (4). In other words, the cosmos reflects aspects of the spiritual world in the mirror of the material and temporal (Nasr, 1973: 28). As such, Sufis view the straight path as a mystical quest, the journey of the soul from the outward to the inward, from the periphery to the Center, from the form to the meaning; it is at once a penetration to the center of the soul and a migration to the abode beyond the cosmos which are in reality but a single locus where the Divine Essence resides, the Presence which is at once completely our-Self and totally other than ourselves" (1973: 29).

In order to explain the cosmological concept of the celestial soul and its journey to its Center, Frithjof Schuon evokes the symbolism of the spider's web with its cosmic compartments and their contents:

[J]ust as the relationship of the center to space cannot be conceived except in this form of the spi-der's web with its two modes of projection — one continuous and the other discontinuous — so the relationship of Principle to manifestation — which makes up the universe — is only conceivable as a combination between worlds arranged according to gradation around the Divine Center and beings who pass through them. To speak of "Existence" is to proclaim the relationship between the receptacle and content, or between the static and the dynamic; the journey of souls through life, death and resurrection is nothing other than the very life of the macro-cosmos; even in our experience in this world we pass through days and nights, summers and winters; essentially we are beings who pass through states; and Existence is not to be conceived of otherwise. Our whole reality converges towards that unique "moment" which alone matters: our meeting with the Center [82–83].

According to Schuon, even the Qur'an is a picture of the cosmos: the chapters (*suwar*) are the worlds and the verses (*ayat*) are the beings (82).

In line with such circular symbolism, and for the sole purpose of scholastic philosophy (*kalam*) and intellectual exposition (*bayan*), we can conceive of the straight path as rays of light and Divine Truth as an imploded or inverted sun, a black hole, an event horizon, the sublime singularity, the absolute axis, an irresistible and inescapable force which draws all light. Although individual in origin, the rays or ways to Allah transcend multiplicity and attain singularity, the refracted rays becoming a totality, the many becoming One in universal unity. While each ray is a way, the countless rays combine, and unite in the Divine, leaving the lost to stray, without a way, damned in darkness, devoid of light and Divine Love, an interpretation consistent with the Qur'anic definition of the straight path as *sirati Allahi*, the path of Allah (42: 53), the Swallower of Souls, like space flowing into a black hole, "and to Him is our return" (2:1 56); "Everything will perish except His own face ... and to Him will ye be brought back" (28: 88).

Conclusion

As we have seen, the image of the path appears in the Arabic language in the form of idiomatic expressions; in the names of people, journals, magazines, books and businesses, and throughout Arabic-Islamic literature where it is derived from the Holy Qur'an and the Prophetic Traditions and is endowed with a multitude of literal and metaphorical interpre-tations. As we observed, Sunni and Salafi scholars, in their literalist line, believe in a single and unique path, devoid of branches. The Shi'ites and the Sufis, however, accept various paths to God and multiple interpretations of Islam, making them the farthest removed from the essentialist fundamentalist fallacy. Given the evidence presented here, it is evident that the path is one of the fundamental symbols found in Arabic-Islamic literature, language and culture, with far reaching philosophical implications in the realm of religious plural-ism.

Works Cited

'Ali, 'Abdullah Yusuf, trans. *The Holy Qur'an.* Brentwood: Amana Corporation, 1983.
Ayyashi, Muhammad ibn Ma'sud al-Salmi al-Samarqandi al-. *Kitab al-tafsir.* Tehran: Suq al-Shirazi, [1960].
Bursi, al-Hafiz al-Din Rajab ibn Muhammad al-. *Mashariq anwar al-yaqin fi asrar Amir al-Mu'minin.* 10th ed. Bayrut: Muassasat al-Alami, [1965].
Chittick, William C., trans. *A Shi'ite Anthology.* 2d. ed. Muhammad Husayn Tabataba'i. Qum: Ansariyan Press, 1989.

Darqawi, Shaykh al-'Arabi al-. *Letters of a Sufi Master*. Trans. T. Burckhardt. London: Perennial Books, 1969.

Ibn Ajiba, Ahmad ibn Muhammad. *Tafsir al-bahr al-madid fi tafsir al-Qur'an al-Majid*. 'Amman: Aal al-Bayt Institute for Islamic Thought, 2005. Internet: www.al-tafsir.com.

Ibn al-Naqib, Ahmad ibn Lu'lu'. *'Umdat al-salik wa 'uddat al-nasik / Reliance of the Traveller: The Classic Manual of Islamic Sacred Law* 'Umdat al-salik. Trans. Nuh Ha' Mim Keller. Evanston, IL: Sunnah Books, 1994.

Ibn Hanbal, Ahmad. *Musnad*. al-Riyad: Bayt al-Afkar al-Dawliyah, 1998.

Ibn Kathir, Isma'il ibn 'Umar. *Tafsir Ibn Kathir*. 'Amman: Aal al-Bayt Institute for Islamic Thought, 2005. Internet: www.al-tafsir.com.

_____. *Tafsir Ibn Kathir*. Internet: www.tafsir.com.

Kulayni, Abu Ja'far Muhammad ibn Ya'qub ibn Ishaq. *al-Kafi*. 2 vols. 3rd ed. 'Ali Akbar al-Ghaffari. Tehran: Dar al-Kutub al-Islamiyyah, 1968.

Larus. *al-Mu'jam al-'arabi al-asasi*. Bayrut: Alecso, 1989.

Majlisi, 'Allamah Muhammad Baqir. *Hayat al-qulub / The Life and Religion of Muhammad*. Trans. Rev. James L. Merrick. San Antonio: Zahra Trust, 1982.

Nasr, Sayyed Hossein. *The Heart of Islam: Enduring Values for Humanity*. San Francisco: HarperSanFrancisco, c2002.

_____ *Sufi Essays*. Albany: SUNY Press, [1973, c1972].

Qummi, 'Ali ibn Ibrahim. *Tafsir tafsir al-Qur'an*. 'Amman: Aal al-Bayt Institute for Islamic Thought, 2005. Internet: www.al-tafsir.com.

Qummi, Muhammad ibn 'Ali ibn al-Husayn ibn Babawayh al-. *Ma'ani al-akhbar*. Ed. 'Ali Akbar al-Ghaffari. Qumm: Intisharat-i Islami, 1361 [1982 or 1983].

_____. *Man la yahduruhu al-faqih*. Tehran: Dar al-Kutub al-Islamiyyah, [1970].

_____. *A Shi'ite Creed: A Translation of* Risalatu al-i'tiqadat *of Muhammad ibn 'Ali Ibn Babawayhi al-Qummi, known as Shaykh Saduq*. Trans. Asaf A.A. Fyzee. London; New York: H. Milford, Oxford University Press, 1942.

Qushayri, 'Abd al-Karim ibn Hawazin. *Tafsir lata'if al-isharat*. 'Amman: Aal al-Bayt Institute for Islamic Thought, 2005. Internet: www.al-tafsir.com

Samarqandi, Abi al-Layth Nasr ibn Muhammad ibn Ahmad ibn Ibrahim al-. *Tafsir al-Qur'an al-Karim: bahr al-'ulum*. 'Amman: Aal al-Bayt Institute for Islamic Thought, 2005. Internet: www.al-tafsir.com.

Schimmel, Annemarie. *Mystical Dimensions of Islam*. Chapel Hill: University of North Carolina Press, 1975.

Schuon, Frithjof. *Understanding Islam*. Trans. D.M. Matheson. London: G. Allen & Unwin, 1976, c1963.

Tabari, Abu Ja'far al-. *Tafsir jami al-bayan 'an ta'wil al-Qur'an*. 'Amman: Aal al-Bayt Institute for Islamic Thought, 2005. Internet: www.al-tafsir.com.

Tabataba'i, 'Allamah Muhammad Husayn. *al-Mizan*. Internet: almizan.org/Tafseer/fateha2.asp.

Tabarsi, al-Fadl ibn al-Hasan. *Tafsir majma' al-bayan fi tafsir al-Qur'an*. 'Amman: Aal al-Bayt Institute for Islamic Thought, 2005. Internet: www.al-tafsir.com.

Tehrani, M. Husayn Husayni. *Lubb al-Lubab (The Kernal of Kernels): A Short Treatise on Wayfaring*. Trans. 'Ali Quli Qara'i. Qum: al-Tawhid, n.d. Internet: www.al-islam.org/al-tawhid/lubb_al_lubab/

Vernet, Juan, trans. *El Coran*. Madrid: Planeta, 1991.

Servitude

Mustapha Naoui Kheir

"Allah is never unjust to His servants." (Qur'an 8:51)

Introduction

The life of a Muslim is composed basically of different realizations of conceptual images that undoubtedly have their roots in Islam, as a theological framework, and perhaps the most important one of those is that of the *'abd*. In English, the latter word is translated as "slave" or "servant." However, one would hardly talk about any full correspondence between these words since they are not equivalent theologically, culturally, and semantically. This is simply because the relevant concepts of *'ibadah* (worship) and *'ubudiyyah* (slavery) in Islam differ greatly and quite radically from all their counterparts in all other religions and languages. What is, then, peculiar to the concept of *'abd*, or *'ubudiyyah* in Islam and how can it be seen to constitute a sort of cornerstone in the Islamic worldview?

Islam and Not Muhammadanism

First of all, the particular image of the servant in Islam might not be easily visualized without a clear preliminary idea about its background image, namely, that of the Muslim and Islam. Unlike "Christianity," "Judaism," or "Buddhism," *Islam*, as an Arabic word, to start with, is not simply a word which designates a particular religion in order to distinguish it from others as is apparently thought by most people, including many Muslims. Whereas most religions, if not all of them, were named after founders like Buddha and Confucius, or after a prophet, as in the case of Jesus Christ, *Islam* is the name given by God Himself to His religion: *inna al-din 'inda Allahi al-Islam* "the only true faith in God's sight is Islam" (3:19). The noun *Islam*, it must be recalled, is derived from the verb *aslama* (to submit, to surrender), which is ditransitive in Arabic, namely, it calls for two objects: a direct one — say one's life and will — and an indirect one — obviously God. It is not insignificant, for example, that Pickthall (1930) should choose to render it in this verse as "The Surrender": "Lo! Religion with Allah (is) The Surrender (to His will and guidance)." As a result, many Muslims consider Islam to be God's final revealed religion in this life and in the hereafter. In the words of the Qur'an: "He that chooses a religion other than Islam, it will not be accepted from him and in the world to come he will be one of the lost" (3:85). "Muhammadanism," which is used by some Orientalists, and which is certainly a misnomer for the

Religion of God and all His prophets, should be rejected firmly as it makes Islam appear like a man-made religion when, in reality, the essence of the Islamic message of Muhammad was the same as the one sent to all of the prophets that preceded him. Many verses in the Holy Qur'an clearly testify to this point:

> Say, we believe in Allah and that which was revealed to Abraham and Ismail and Isaac and Jacob and the tribes and that which was given to Moses and Jesus and to other Prophets from their Lord. We make no distinction between any of them, and to Him we submit [3:3]

Life-Transaction and Not Religion

In addition, it ought to be stressed that the word "religion" itself does not necessarily mean the same thing as the word *din* in Arabic. While one can easily notice the narrow-scope meaning of the former in Germanic and Indo-European languages, the latter is rather multidimensional and comprehensive of everything pertaining to the life of humankind in every plausible sense. It incorporates, indeed, each and every single aspect of human life however insignificant it may otherwise appear, so it can only logically mean something like "a complete way of life" including people's beliefs, moral principles, and behaviors (both linguistic and actional). God Himself specified the scope of Islam fairly explicitly when He ordered believers to say: "My prayers and my devotions, my life and my death, are all for God, Lord of the Universe: He has no peer. Thus am I commanded, being the first of the Muslims" (6:163). In fact, when we consider the following verses, we cannot help realize that such a meaning of *din* is much wider in scope indeed: "Are they seeking a religion other than God's, when every soul in heaven and earth has submitted to Him, willingly or by compulsion? To Him they shall all return" (3:83).

Unfortunately, for many people, the bad behavior of Muslims is the criteria they use when judging the religion of Islam. Most Muslims, however, have not fully embraced Islam as a complete and total way of life which addresses all aspects of human existence. Hence, what is often portrayed as "Islam" is, in reality, a veneer of Islam placed upon a particular culture. With the onset of modernity, many, if not most Muslims, have developed two sets of values. They have religious values and wordly values. They live two different lives. They suffer from some sort of split personality, as it were, as reflected in expressions such as *din wa dunya* (religion and worldly life), and "a bit for my Lord and a bit for His servant." These expressions, in their content, are clearly reminiscent of the Western saying "render unto God what is God's and unto Caesar what Caesar's." Islam, however, is by nature and definition all-inclusive as far as the entire life of human beings on earth is concerned.

The Significance of the Slave

Interestingly, the concept of *'abd* in Arabic-Islamic culture is also by definition closely and thoroughly linked to that of *din* or religion. In its first sense, the word *'abd* refers to the ordinary meaning of "slave," namely, that of acknowledging the authority of another over oneself, of abdicating one's freedom and independence in favor of one's master, and of surrendering totally to his lordship without disobedience or resistance.

The following short narrative provides an idea of the two extreme meanings of *'ubudiyyah* (spiritual slavery) as experienced in Arabic-Islamic culture with, at one end, the ephemeral state of being a slave, in the sense of physical bondage, and the fully realized spiritual station of being God's slave, or *maqam al-'ubudiyyah* in Sufi terminology, at the other end:

> Ibrahim ibn Adham, one of the great mystics, once bought a slave. When he asked him what he would like to eat, the slave responded, "Whatever you wish to feed me." When the master asked the slave for his name, he said, "Whatever you wish to call me." When the master asked the slave what clothes he wanted to wear, he replied, "Whatever you wish to give me." And when the master asked him about the trade he practiced, he replied, "Whatever you want me to do." The master then asked him, "Do you not have a preference, a will of your own?" "A slave does not possess any will but his master's," answered the slave. Thereupon, Ibrahim ibn Adham thought about himself and his own situation and, crying, he said to himself "I am such a wretch! In all of my life, I have never, for even a single hour, held the same status towards Allah as this slave has towards me!" [al-Kharkushi 171].

In the Arabic language, the two meanings of *'ubudiyyah* are distinguished as follows: the plural of *'abd*, in the first meaning, is *'abid* and, in the second one, it is *'ibad*. Moreover, the second meaning is especially obtained when *'abd*, or *'ibad*, is attributed to one of God's sublime names like in *'ibadu al-Rahman*, or in proper names that start with *'abd* like *'Abd Allah*. This is, most probably why, according to a prophetic tradition, the best of names are those which start with *'abd* or those which are derived from the root *hamd*, like Ahmad and Muhammad: *khayru al-asma'i ma 'ubbidah aw hummidah*. The station of *'ubudiyyah* is, in principle, realized in these two types of names at least linguistically and optimistically, since the time it was incarnated in the person of the Holy Prophet *Muhammad* (Praiseworthy), who was also called *'Abd Allah* (Servant of Allah) in the Holy Qur'an: "when God's servant (*'abd Allah*) rose to pray to Him, they pressed around him in multitudes" (72:19)

Furthermore, the second meaning of *'ubudiyyah* (i.e. servitude or servanthood) is subcategorized by Muslim scholars into two kinds, which are traditionally referred to as *'ubudiyyah 'ammah* (general servanthood) and *'ubudiyyah khassah* (specific servanthood). The first type is called "general" because it is involuntary and common to all God's creation: "Not one of the beings in the heavens and the earth but must come to (Allah) Most Gracious as a servant" (19:93). In this sense, all creatures, including disbelieving ones, are consciously or unconsciously, willingly or involuntarily, God's servants since they act in accordance with the so-called natural laws that God placed within them as basic constituents of their beings. Therefore, we might, as well, go so far as to say that all human states can be referred to as states of *'ibadah* or *'ubudiyyah* regardless to how conscious one is of one's state at a given time or circumstance, which could shed more light on one of the much discussed verses: "And I did not create the jinn and humankind except to worship Me" (51:56)

Specific servanthood, on the other hand, is the result of deliberately submitting one's will to obeying God's Commands. Even the corresponding noun, in this case, is not the general *'abd* but *'abid* (worshipper) and this submission is called *'ibadah*. *'Abid* is commonly taken to mean someone who regularly performs devotional acts like prayer, fasting, pilgrimage, and other Islamic rituals; however, *'ibadah*, or the concept of worship in Islam, is much more than that though its plural is used in Islamic jurisprudence to differentiate technically between prescribed duties *'ibadat* and the other, apparently "free" transactional activities or *mu'amalat*.

Defined by al-Jurjani in his *Kitab al-ta'rifat* as "The action of an adult in glorification of his Lord and not necessarily in accordance with his own desires" (136), servanthood is understood in the Islamic tradition as a state in which every act, utterance, and intention is pleasing to God. In other words, in addition to the ritualistic acts prescribed by God and exemplified by His prophet, worship in Islam includes everything a Muslim does, or says, or even thinks of doing or saying, for the only purpose of pleasing God. It also includes the practice of refraining from saying or doing evil things and of not carrying out evil thoughts for the sake of God. In short, it is the whole of one's existence that God expects one to submit to Him if one wants to lead a life of a true Muslim, as is clearly specified in verse 6:163 above.

Islam: A Complete Way of Life

It is not only figuratively that Islam, as a whole edifice — a complete way of life — is said to be "built on five pillars" that constitute its primary duties, but what is implied is the rest of the "building" also should expectedly be constructed with material similar to that which the pillars are made of. All of this is perfectly realizable provided everything one says or does is preceded or accompanied by the pure intention of pleasing God exclusively.

For instance, earning a living can easily be turned into a worshipful action that is worthy of God's reward just like prayer and fasting. One day, the Prophet and some of his companions noticed a man performing hard work at his field. The companions wished the man had been doing it for the sake of God, but the Prophet replied that if the man was working to feed his children or his parents or even to keep himself occupied lest he might get indulged in a sinful activity, then it was indeed for the sake of God. This means that God-seeking intention is all that you need to transform a habitual action (*'adah*) into a devotional one (*'ibadah*). Therefore, practically all activities — like eating, drinking, and sleeping with one's wife, if done with the sincere intention of pleasing God, or preparing oneself to obey Him — are definitely counted as forms of worship in Islam. As the Prophet said in a famous *hadith*, "Actions are weighed through intentions and one gets only what one intends" as is stated in the famous *hadith* (Nawawi).

To encourage people to opt for the best of lives, the Prophet indicated that there are activities which are much more pleasing to God than others. "The pursuit of knowledge for one hour," for example, "is better than praying seventy years." Thus, the entire life of a Muslim can be converted into a continuous act of worship. All that needs to be done is to ensure that one's immediate and far-reaching aims are merged into that of seeking God's satisfaction and pleasure. In order to do so, one must opt for good deeds and utterances while avoiding evil ones.

Let us emphasize, in conclusion, that such an all-inclusiveness of the concept of *'ibadah* is explanatorily in keeping with, if not synonymous to, the religion of Islam itself as a complete way of life. After all, has not God said in *Surah al-Bayyinah* (The Chapter of the Proof), talking about the people of the Book, "Yet they were enjoined only to serve God and to worship none but Him" (98:5)? "To serve God," in this translation, stands for *li ya'bud Allah*, and "To worship none but him" for *mukhlisina lahu al-din*. In another verse, God has already commanded that we "worship Allah, making religion pure for Him" (39:12) and, in *Surah al-Kafirun* (The Chapter of the Disbelievers), He seems to present the notion of religion and that of worship as one and the same thing:

> Say, "O disbelievers, I do not worship what you worship. Nor are you worshippers of what I worship. Nor will I be a worshipper of what you worship. Nor will you be worshippers of what I worship. For you is your religion, and for me is my religion" [109:1–6].

What is more is that Islamic *'ibadah* is, in a sense, made much easier for Muslims as it is equated to just invocation or supplication (*du'a'*). There are texts, both in the Holy Qur'an and in the prophetic sayings, which clearly testify to this equation of worship and invocation in Islam. First, God says in 40:60 "Your Lord has said: 'Call on me [*ud'uni*] and I will answer you. Those that disdain my service [*'ibadati*] shall enter hell with all humility'" (40:60), which means that worshipping God consists essentially in supplicating Him, turning to Him for everything. It is said that God told Musa (Moses) not to hesitate in seeking His help even when it was something to tie his shoes with that he needed. That is to say whatever a Muslim is about to do he should have the appropriate invocation up his sleeve to start with, for it (*du'a*) is meant to be considered by the Muslims as "The weapon of the believer" (Hakim). Furthermore, God's Messenger is reported to have said that *du'a* was the marrow or essence of worship (*mukh al-'ibadah*), and, in another version, that it was worship itself (*al-du'a' huwa al-'ibadah*) (Nawawi).

The Stations of Spiritual Slavery

Finally, the most important dimension of the image of the servant concerns the quality of servant-hood, which is commensurate with the level or degree of *'ibadah* (worship). Since 'Ali ibn Abi Talib (cf. his *Nahj al-balaghah*), Muslim scholars have been unanimous that there are three main levels of worship. The first one is called *'ibadat al-'abid* (the slaves' worship) because it consists in worshipping God out of fear of His chastisement. The second level is referred to as *'ibadat al-tujjar* (the merchants' worship) which consists in worshiping God in the hopes of receiving a reward. The third, and top-most, rank of all worship is termed *'ibadatu al-'ahrar* (freemen's worship) because it is done out of pure gratitude and love to and for God, the Lord of the Universe. However, this rank of spiritual slavery is only reached by infinitely grateful servants, and these are very few indeed, as God Almighty informs us: "Yet few of My servants are truly thankful" (34:13). Such a rank is also known, particularly in Sufism, as excellence in worship. The term "excellence" or *ihsan* was defined in a well-known *hadith* as "worshipping Allah as though you were looking at Him, for if you don't see Him, He does see you" (Bukhari, Muslim). The Prophet, who is the perfect model of this rare class of devotees, used to get up during the night and stand so long for additional prayers that his feet got swollen up. His wife, 'A'ishah, once asked him the Messenger of Allah if he really needed to pray so much considering that God had forgiven his shortcomings. He responded, ""Can I not be a grateful servant then?" (*'afala akunu 'abdan shakuran?*) (Nawawi).

Most Sufi figures consider the last level of worship as the highest mystic station. Al-Nifari, for instance, went so far as to use a new noun derived from the root *'abd*, viz *'abdaniyyah* (slave-hood), specifically to designate it. According to him, such a station can only be attained by a servant if he or she succeeds in becoming a slave of God

> without any attribute, for if one were a slave with some attribute one's slave-hood would be attached to one's attribute, not to Him, and if it is attached to one's attribute not to Him, then one is a slave of one's attribute, not His slave [qtd. Dikri 2008: 179].

Rabi'ah al-'Adawiyyah (d. 801), an early female Muslim mystic from Basrah, Iraq, is reported to have addressed her Lord in the following words:

> If I were worshipping you so as to enter Your paradise, deny me such entry, and if I were doing it out of fear of Your hell, throw me in it, but if I am worshipping You for what You are, please do not prevent me from Yourself.

In fact, when one's unique aim in life is to abide by God's commands, and to do all that one can in order to serve Him out of love and gratitude, there expectedly results a feeling of liberation from all the worldly chains, and this is what opens a new gateway to the concept of freedom, whose inseparability from slavery and servitude is like that of the two sides of the same coin. In a *hadith qudsi* or sacred saying, God Himself is showing us the way to real freedom and happiness:

> My servant draws not near to Me with anything more loved by Me than the religious duties I have enjoined upon him, and My servant continues to draw near to Me with supererogatory works so that I shall love him. When I love him I am his hearing with which he hears, his seeing with which he sees, his hand with which he strikes and his foot with which he walks. Were he to ask [something] of Me, I would surely give it to him, and were he to ask Me for refuge, I would surely grant him it [Bukhari; Ibrahim and Johnson Davies].

Conclusion

It seems, therefore, that absolute servitude to God is the unique source of real and absolute freedom or, as al-Qushayri put it: "The truth of freedom lies in perfect servitude, for if you are truthful in your servitude to God, you will liberate His freedom from the slavery of dull things" (293). This amounts to saying that the true definition of freedom is nothing else than the true definition of slavery, slavery to God and freedom from any other potentially enslaving phenomenon, and that is precisely the meaning of *la ilaha illa Allah* (there is no deity but Allah): an everlasting process of affirmation after negation or, perhaps, affirmation by and through negation. Such a process, it must be recalled, involves the three fundamental components of the human servant, namely the heart, which is the abode of intention and inner belief, the tongue, which takes care of the linguistic confirmation, and the limbs which are responsible for the outer realization or concrete work.

Works Cited

'Adawiyyah, Rabi'ah al-. "Teachings." *Sufi Master*. Internet: http://sufimaster.org/teachings/adawiyya.htm.

'Attar, Farid al-Din. *Muslim Saints and Mystics*. Trans. A. J. Arberry. Ames, IA: Omphaloskepsis, 2000

Baghdadi, Mahmud 'Ali. *al-Islam wa al-hurriyyah*. Bayrut: al-Dar al-Jami'iyyah, 1985.

Bukhari, Muhammad ibn Isma'il. *Sahih Bukhari*. Internet: www.islamspirit.com.

Dawood, Nessim Joseph, trans. *The Koran*. Middlesex, UK: Penguin Books, 1956.

Dikri, Hifru Mohammad Ali. *Mu'jam Mustalahat al-Nifari*. Dimashq: al-Taqwin, 2008.

Hakim al-Nisaburi, Muhammad ibn 'Abd Allah. *Mustadrak 'ala al-sahihayn*. 'Amman: al-Dar al-'Uthmaniyyah, 2007.

Ibrahim, Ezzeddin and Denys Johnson Davies, trans. *Forty Hadith Qudsi*. Bayrut and Dimashq: Dar al-Koran al-Kareem, 1980. Internet: www.sunnipath.com/library/Hadith/H0005P0000.aspx.

Jurjani, 'Ali ibn Muhammad. *Kitab al-ta'riifat*. Bayrut: Dar al-Kutub al-'Ilmiyyah, 1983.

Kharkushi, 'Abd al-Malik ibn Muhammad. *Tahdib al-asrar fi usul al-tasawwuf*. Bayrut: Dar al-Kutub al-'Ilmiyyah, 2006

Muslim ibn al-Hajjaj al-Qushayri al-Naysaburi. *Sahih Muslim*. Riyadh: Dar al-Mughni, 1998.

Nawawi, Imam al- *The Complete Forty Hadith*. London: Taha Publishing, n.d. Internet: www.bogvaerker.dk/The_Complete_Forty_Hadith.html.

_____. *Gardens of the Righteous / Riyad al-salihin*. Trans. Muhammad Saghir Hasan Masumi. Islamabad: National Hijra Council, 1992.

Pickthall, Muhammad Marmaduke, trans. *The Meanings of the Glorious Koran*. Delhi: World Islamic Publications, 1930.

Qushayri, Abu al-Qasim. *al-Risalah al-Qushayriyyah*. Bayrut: Dar Ihya' al-Turath al- 'Arabi, 1998.

Perfection[1]

John Andrew Morrow

"Assume the character traits of Allah." (Prophet Muhammad)

Introduction

According to Muslim tradition, the most beautiful names of Allah (*asma' Allah al-husna*) are ninety-nine in number, all of which are found, in one form or another, in the Holy Qur'an (7:180; 17:110; 20:8; 59:24). As the essence of Allah, Islam, and the Qur'an, the divine names have played an important role in the interpretation of Islamic scripture. Invoked in prayer and in common speech, the divine names are also employed during *dhikr* or remembrance of Allah. Among the Sufis, be they Sunni or Shi'i, the ninety-nine names take on heightened significance as steps along the path of spiritual perfection, reaching its peak in the universal archetype of the Perfect Person who, by reaching the state of sublime submission, has become the microcosmic manifestation of all the divine names.

The Perfect Person in the Qur'an and Sunnah

According to a famous *hadith qudsi* or sacred saying, Almighty Allah says: "I was a Hidden Treasure [*kanz makhfi*], and I wished to be known. So, I created humankind, then I revealed myself to them, and they recognized me." In some Sufi versions of this saying, Allah not only reveals the reason for creation, but also the role of the created, saying:

> I was a Hidden Treasure that desired to be known. So I manifested all the creation to reveal the essence of the deep secret: knowledge of myself. He whom I created to reveal the treasure carries within himself this treasure but he must explode the mountain of his existence to discover the treasure which is hidden within it [Sufimaster.org].

As Almighty Allah says in the Holy Qur'an, "I created the *jinn* and humankind only that they might worship Me" (51:56). According to the Prophet's companion, Ibn 'Abbas, the verb "to worship" in this context is to be understood in the sense of "to know" (Murata 26; Ibn al-'Arabi, 131). The purpose of creation is inseparable from the concept of divine love. However, since human beings cannot know or love their Creator as an inconceivable transcendent Essence, Allah revealed His most beautiful names so that he could be invoked and remembered (Beneito v). In the words of Ibn al-'Arabi, "He brought the world into existence to make manifest the authority of the Names" (37). As Beneito explains,

Through His love and compassion, Allah —"hidden" with regards to His essence — epiphanates Himself in the cosmos, in human beings, and in the revealed Book, all places of His manifestation, through which he makes Himself "Manifest" to humankind. His names — which Ibn al-'Arabi considers as "relations" [*nisab*] — allow humankind to know Him through His similarity and to have knowledge of His incomparability, reconciling immanence and transcendence through a middle path which consists in the union of opposites.

The most beautiful names are the means through which Allah reveals the manifestations of His names throughout the cosmos (vi). They are the means of reaching Him, and the response to His command: "Call upon Me and I will answer you" (40:60). As a result, belief in God is not in itself enough. As 'Ali Muhammad Naqvi explains,

> A person must know the attributes of God, because it is the knowledge of the attributes of God which enables man to cultivate in himself the noblest of human qualities... The knowledge of God's attributes purifies man's mind and soul, his beliefs and actions, but mere intellectual knowledge of God's attributes is not sufficient. We must have an unflinching conviction, firmly rooted in our minds and hearts, so that we may remain immune from doubt and immoral action. If we have conviction that God is our Lord, that He oversees everything, then we may not commit a sin even at a place where there is no one to check us [Naqvi 3–4].

Knowledge of Allah is knowledge of the divine names. Knowledge of the divine names is knowledge of self, and the divine nature which lies latent in all human beings.

According to a well-known *hadith* (tradition) from the Prophet Muhammad, "Allah created Adam in His Own image" (*inna Allaha khalaqa Adama 'ala suratihi*). According to Islamic thought, this tradition indicates that the primordial nature (*fitrah*) of the human being is the epitome or universal synthesis of the Divine Essence in its earthly and spiritual manifestations. As Ghazali explains in *Mishkat al-anwar*,

> Allah, out of His grace and mercy gave to Adam a summary "image" or "form," embracing every genus and species in the whole world, inasmuch that it was as if Adam were all that was in the world, or was the summarized copy of the world. And Adam's form — this summarized "image" — was inscribed in the handwriting of Allah, so that Adam is the Divine Word [135].

Adam, as the Archetype of Man, embodies the Divine Presence and the divine names. As the Qur'an says, "He taught Adam the names, all of them" (2:31).

Assuming the Attributes of Allah

In Islam, in general, the goal of the believer is to conform to the character of the Prophet Muhammad, the greatest model of *al-tahalluq bi asma' Allah* or assuming the attributes of Allah, in which the qualities of the divine names manifest themselves in harmony (Beneito 310). As Ibn al-'Arabi says, "No one has realized this station [of servitude] to its perfection like the Messenger of Allah" (131). In Sufi thought, each step that the Prophet took during his ascension to heaven represented one of the divine names he had embodied. Besides the Messenger of Allah, the Imams, in Shi'ism, who are known as *hujjat Allah* or Proofs of Allah, and the *aqtab* or Poles in Sufism, are also sources of emulation (*maraj'i al-taqlid*). The goal of all believers is to literally become *muslimun*, those who surrender completely and absolutely to Allah, actualizing the divine names which exist within them as virtualities. This was clearly conveyed in the Prophet's words "Assume the character traits of Allah" (Ibn al-'Arabi 308, note 122) and the *hadith qudsi* in which Allah says, "My earth does not encompass Me, nor does My heaven, but the heart of My servant, the person of true faith, does encompass Me" (315, note 7; 323, note 37). In other words, all of Allah, all of His attributes, can fit in the heart and soul of a "Complete Human Being."

In Islam, a "Complete Human Being" is one who has reached the highest psychological, physical, and spiritual stage of being. This Perfect Person is like a sun around which the divine attributes revolve. Although the stages differ between different Sufi orders, they may include: the aspirant, the novice, the wanderer, the knower, the guide, the saint and, finally, the complete human being or perfect person. The "Complete Human Being" is the one who has effaced his ego, become selfless, abandoned his individual identity, erased his "I," and reached a state of union with the Supreme Identity. Ibn al-'Arabi uses the Arabic term *muwahhid* to designate the perfect spiritual union in which the believer loses himself in Divine Unity. It is the state in which the knower and the known are erased, which is known as *fana' al-fani* (annihilation of the annihilated). The person who reaches the state of *muwahhid* sees the Divine Unity in everything and does not associate or attribute anything inappropriate with it. Almighty Allah, in a famous *hadith qudsi*, describes the absolute surrender of a divine servant in the following terms: "When I love him, I am his hearing with which he hears, his seeing with which he sees, his hand with which he strikes and his foot with which he walks" (Bukhari).

According to Islamic thought, "Perfect People" are those who have fully submitted, who have become at one with the Divine, like the great spiritual guides, the Prophets in particular, the twelve Imams — among Shi'ite Gnostics — and the "Poles" (*aqtab*) — among Sunni Gnostics — namely, the *awliyya' Allah* (the Saints or Friends of Allah). For Shi'ite Muslims, the Fourteen Infallibles embody the divine attributes. It is for this reason that the Imams proclaimed: "We are the most beautiful names" (Kulayni). For Shi'ites, the Imam is the *khalifah* of Allah (the representative or vicar of the Divinity), the pillar of the divine names, namely, the manifestation of the divine attributes and qualities through which the Supreme Principle or the Universal Possibility make Himself known to His creatures. The Imam is the supreme mediator (*wasilah kubra*), synthesis of the divine attributes and qualities through which the Divinity is known by the creatures and through which the Divinity knows its creatures. The Imam is the one who has "become the Reality" (*al-mutahaqqiq bi al-Haqq*), namely, the one who, by perfecting himself, has fully manifested the totality of the divine attributes through the perfection of human attributes or moral virtues (*khuluq*), reaching the state of identification with His celestial model, the complete human being (*al-insan al-kamil*), the first creation, who has transformed into his own image of human form on earth. His limbs, acts and words are epiphanies (*mazahir*) of the Absolute. For Sufi Muslims, each Muhammadan pole has a *hijjir* or "constant invocation" specific to himself. The *hijjir* of the greatest Poles is the name Allah. This explains why the supreme Pole forever pertains to this name and is called 'Abd Allah. The constant invocations of the other Poles include well-known formulae that are used in prayer and invocation, including *la ilaha illa Allah* (There is no god but Allah), *Allahu Akbar* (Allah is the Greatest), *subhana Allah* (Glory be to Allah), *alhamdulillah* (Praise be to Allah), the most common phrases from the Allah Lexicon, as well as various Qur'anic verses.

On a more earthly as opposed to ethereal level, many Muslims have a favorite divine name and Allah expression, just like they have a preferred chapter or verse from the Qur'an. When Muslims give their children names of servitude like 'Abd Allah, they want their children to live up to them, to embody them, in the same way that divine names are actualized by the Friends of Allah. They do so in accordance with the words of the Prophet: "On the

Day of Judgment you will be called by your names and your father's names, so choose beautiful names [for your children]" (Abu Dawud). As Earl H. Waugh has observed, "This care about names has perhaps developed from the sensitivity to God's beautiful names in the Qur'an (17:110), and the great piety with which the ninety-nine names of God are recited" (224). When it comes to selecting names for one's offspring, the Messenger of Allah has said that "The names dearest to Allah are 'Abd Allah and 'Abd al-Rahman" (Abu Dawud). Parents who name their son 'Abd al-Halim, the Servant of the Gentle One, want him to be gentle; those who name their son 'Abd al-'Alim or 'Abd al-Hakim, want him to be wise; and those who name their sons 'Abd al-Rahman, want him to be compassionate. While each human being embodies the divine attributes, and often one in particular, many Muslims are actually named with the divine names.

According to Islamic thought, the Great or Complete Human Being (*al-insan al-kabir* or *al-insan al-kamil*), is the universal synthesis of the divine names and attributes. As Muslim Gnostics say, the universe is a Great Human Being, and the Human Being is a Small Universe (*al-kawnun insanun kabirun wa al-insanu kawnu saghir*) (Murata 23). In fact, the Complete Human Being (*al-insan al-kamil*) is the universal archetype in whose image was created the *humanized human* or *small man* (*al-insan al-saghir*), the "Son of Adam" (*ibn Adam*) in whom Allah placed all of the realities (*haqa'iq*) of the macrocosmos (*al-'alam al-kabir*), in such a way that the human being, despite the size of his/her body, represents the entire universe. The "Complete Human Being" is the universal synthesis of existence which embodies the virtual potentiality of all forms of being (*al-wujud*), through both divine and human attributes. As Ibn al-'Arabi explains, "[T]here is no name that God has applied to Himself that He has not also applied to us" (214). It is by means of these attributes that Allah brings Himself close to His creatures and gives them the opportunity to approach His essence (De la Torre 24). As Friedlander explains, "The names of Allah are connected with the life of man. All aspects of life can be seen in the names" (10). As such, there is a name of God for every human trait (De la Torre 25). This is why the Prophet Muhammad is quoted as saying: "He who knows himself, knows his Lord." In other words, the attributes of Allah are to be found in souls, the receptacles (*qawabil*) or place of manifestation of the Divine Presence. As Beneito explains,

> Human beings have the possibility, depending on their predisposition and receptivity, to adopt the qualities of the various names of the One and the Multiple, reintegrating them by means of his concentration, spiritual aspiration and breadth of his heart, in their essential Unity... It is essential to understand that the adoption of the qualities of the names does not imply appropriation. Human beings are the receptacle, the "place" in which the human attributes are manifested. Human beings participate in the attributes by which, through the grace of divine providence, they adorn themselves as faithful servants of God.

Human beings, by nature, possess all the possibilities of perfection. As a result, they have been placed in a central or axiomatic position in the universe. As Beneito explains,

> The servant ... is not a mere man or woman, a common person or individual believer ... but rather the human being *par excellence*, the Complete Human Being, created in the image of God, as a microcosmic synthesis and Pole or Axis of the Universe. Without a Complete Human Being, the cosmos would be annihilated.

To become a saint, from an Islamic point of view, is to fully realize all the possibilities of the human condition, uniting with the universal human prototype, "The Complete Human Being." From the perspective of *tasawwuf* (Sufism) and *'irfan Shi'i* (Shi'ite mysticism), spiritual realization (*tahaqquq ruhani*) consists in assuming each divine attribute step by step, eventually reaching union with the Divine (*Allah*) and the cosmos which is the representation of the "Complete Human Being," the mirror which reflects the highest grade of purity and simplicity of all the divine names. The entire process is one of unveiling. As the Prophet said, "Allah has seventy or seventy thousand veils of light and darkness" (Majlisi qtd. in Chittick, 1989: 264, note 49, and Ghazali, 1952: 76–77). The quest of each Muslim is to remove veils of darkness and veils of light. According to Nicholson, these light-veils correspond to various degrees of sainthood (78). As Ghazali explains, the first step along this path of spiritual purification is the understanding of the true meaning of the divine attributes (1952: 169). The adoption of divine names, Islam's ninety-nine point plan for human perfection, culminates in the creation of the "Complete Human Being," also known as 'Abd al-Samad, the Servant of the Eternal Universal Pillar, who serves as the place of manifestation of the divine names (Beneito 246).

According to Sufi thought, the Complete Human Being, who shares the original nature of Adam and the Muhammadan Reality (*al-haqiqah al-muhammadiyyah*), is the microcosmic synthesis of creation, the mirror in which the Divine Reality contemplates Himself, and the pupil through which He sees (Beneito v). As is often stated in Islamic mysticism, the Divine contemplates Himself and everything which He (*hu*) has achieved in the cosmos by means of the "Complete Human Being." As Beneito explains, "When a human being develops a divine character, adorning himself with the most noble qualities, he becomes the gaze of God from the cosmos ... the presence of the manifestation of the names of God" (243–44). It is for this reason that the "Complete Human Being" is known as the "Sole Prototype," the "Evident Prototype" which is spoken of in the Qur'an. In fact, it is the Universal Being which differentiates itself in successive polarizations, as active and passive, as species and individual, as male and female, as macrocosmos and microcosmos, as universe and human being. Each of these elements has their opposite in the plan of ontological perfection.

As the names of Allah are limitless, so are the ways to Allah. It is for this reason that it is reported that the Prophet said that "The numbers of paths to God is equal to the number of human souls" (Chittick, 1989: 52, Note 1) and it is why Yahya or John the Baptist told Ibn al-'Arabi in the fifth heaven that "Each person has a path, that no one else but he travels ... paths that come through the traveling itself" (223). Each person has a path, each path is a divine name, and each path starts with the most beautiful names, the source of the Allah Lexicon, and a ninety-nine step plan for human perfection.

Many people wonder how they can become pious Muslims. According to the spiritual tradition of Islam, the answer is to be found in the most beautiful names of Allah, the ninety-nine point plan for human perfection which is based on the *shari'ah*. The divine attributes, the most beautiful names, are also human attributes. If people pray, fast, pay the poor-due, perform the *hajj*, perform *jihad*, promote the good, forbid the wrong, love the Household of the Prophet, and keep away from their enemies, they are good Muslims. Complete and total submission to Allah, however, requires more than that. Performing the *wajibat* (religious obligations) and avoiding the *haram* (religiously forbidden) is merely the beginning of the journey towards Allah. And as Almighty Allah has promised: For every step one take towards Him, He will take two towards us. If one goes to him walking, He will come to us running (Bukhari, Muslim, Tirmidhi, Ibn Majah). So the first step is to cast off the veils of darkness and vice to pass through the veils of virtue and light.

The traveler on the path takes one attribute, any attribute, and attempts to embrace it and embody it. One Muslim may adopt the attribute of *al-Sabbur*, and work on his *nafs*, on his personality, his soul, his character, until he becomes perfectly patient. A Muslim woman, for example, may simultaneously embody the divine attributes of *al-Jamal*, the Beautiful, and *al-Batin*, the Veiled. Since beauty is a feminine attribute, a Muslim woman is a manifestation of divine beauty. When a Muslim sees the beautiful face of a woman, he is contemplating the beauty of the Divine. As the famous *hadith* says, "Allah is Beautiful and love beauty" (Bukhari). While Allah is Beautiful, He also hides His beauty behind the Veil (*hijab*) as divine beauty can only be contemplated by those who are pure of heart, the saints, the *awliyya'* or "Friends of Allah." Likewise, a Muslim woman's beauty can only be admired by her direct relatives (*mahram*). She is beautiful, but she is *batin* (hidden). The Muslim mystic, the *'irfani*, may adopt the attribute of *al-'Arif*, the One who Knows. The scholar may adopt the attribute of *al-Hakim*, the philosopher and the jurist the attribute of *al-'alim*, the *mujahid* the attribute of *al-Muntaqim*, the Avenger, the judge the attribute of *al-'Adil*, the Just, all assuming different attributes of Allah, and witnessing to the presence of the Divine. Of course, it is only the Friends of Allah who can adopt all the divine names, a state described by Ibn al-'Arabi as follows:

> [W]hen a servant ... knows that he is not [created] according to the form of the world, but only according to the form of God [*al-Haqq*], then God "makes him journey" through His names, "in order to cause him to see His signs" (17:1) within him. Thus [the servant] comes to know that He is what is designated by every divine Name — whether or not that Name is one of those described as "beautiful." It is through those Names that God appears in His servants, and it is through Them that the servant takes on the different "colorings" of his states: for They are Names of God, but "colorings" [of the soul] in us [213].

Adopting divine attributes, however, does not mean that one becomes Allah. As Ghazali warned:

> when one sloughs off the passions of his soul with its desires and concerns, no room remains in him for anything other than God, nor will he have any concern other than God... So if nothing exists in his heart but the majesty of God and His beauty, so that he becomes immersed in it, he does become as though he were He, but not so that he actually is God... But here lies a pitfall, for if one does not have a firm footing in things rational, he may fail to distinguish one of them from the other, and looking upon the perfection of his essence and how it may be adorned with the finery of truth which shines in it, he will think that he is He [God], and will say "I am the Truth" [1999: 153].

The fact that believers acquire one of the characteristics of the Divine Essence does not mean that they become Allah, since Allah is the synthesis of all the divine names, and the Muslim can only aspire to adopt one, some, or all of them, through their mention. In other words, everything in the human being manifests Allah's names and attributes, while the individual human being as a whole — at least in the case of those who are fully human and have become Allah's viceregents — manifests all Allah's names (Murata 37).

Conclusion

If the name *Allah*, which refers to the Essence, does not have a precise meaning, and cannot be comprehended, the most beautiful names, on the contrary, are divinely donned descriptions and the only means of understanding the Divinity. Ninety-nine in number, the most beautiful names are eloquent expressions of the multiplicity within the Divinity, and the conceptual core of the Qur'an. The most beautiful names are the foundational framework of Islamic speculative metaphysics, reaching its peak in the universal archetype of the Complete Human Being who, by reaching the state of sublime submission, has become the manifestation of Allah, the very reflection and image of the Divinity.

Chapter Note

1. This study was previously published in *Islamic Insights: Writings and Reviews* (Qum: Ansariyan, 2012) and *Sufi: A Journal of Sufism*. 71 (2006): 20–25. It also appeared in an expanded version in *Arabic, Islam, and the Allah Lexicon: How Language Shapes our Conception of God* (Lewiston: Edwin Mellen Press, 2006): 243–272.

Works Cited

Abu Dawud al-Sijistani, Sulayman ibn al-Ash'ath. *Sahih Sunan Abu Dawud*. Riyad: Maktabah al-Tarbiyyah al-'Arabi li Duwal al-Khalij, 1989.

Beneito, Pablo. *al-Kitab kashf al-ma'na 'an sirr asma' Allah al-husna / El secreto de los nombres de Dios*. Muhyi al-Din ibn al-'Arabi. Trans. Pablo Beneito. Murcia: Editorial Regional de Murcia, 1986.

Bukhari, Muhammad ibn Isma'il. *Sahih al-Bukhari*. al-Riyad: Bayt al-Afkar al-Dawliyyah li al-Nashr, 1998.

_____. *The Translation of the Meanings of Sahih al-Bukhari*. Trans. Muhammad Muhsin Khan. Lahore: Kazi Publications, 1983.

Burrel, David B. and Nazih Daher, Eds. *The Ninety-Nine Beautiful Names of God al-Maqsad al-asna fi sharh asma'Allah al-husna*. Abu Hamid al-Ghazali, Cambridge: The Islamic Texts Society, 1999.

Chittick William C., trans. *A Shi'ite Anthology*. 2nd ed. Muhammad Husayn Tabataba'i. Qum: Ansariyan Publications, 1989.

De la Torre, Purificación, et al., eds. *Sharh asma' Allah al-husna / Comentario sobre los nombres más bellos de Dios*. Madrid: Consejo Superior de Investigaciones Científicas, Agencia Española de Cooperación Internacional, 2000.

Friedlander, Shems, and al-Hajj Shaykh Muzaffereddin. *Ninety-Nine Names of Allah: The Beautiful Names*. New York: Harper Colophon, 1978.

Ghazali, Abu Hamid al-. *Mishkat al-anwar*. Trans. W.H.T. Gairdner. Lahore: Sh. Muhammad Ashraf, 1952.

_____. *The Ninety-Nine Beautiful Names of God: al-Maqsad al-asna fi sharh asma'Allah al-husna*. Ed. David B. Burrell, and Nazih Daher. Cambridge (UK): The Islamic Texts Society, 1999.

Ibn al-'Arabi. Muhyi al-Din. *The Meccan Revelations: Selected Texts of al-Futuhat al-Makkiyah*. Ed. Michel Chodkiewicz. New York: Pir Press, 2002.

Ibn Barrayan, 'Abd al-Salam ibn 'Abd al-Rahman ibn Muhammad ibn 'Abd al-Rahman al-Lajmi al-Ishbili, Abu-Hakam. *Sharh asma' Allah al-husna / Comentario sobre los nombres mas bellos de Dios*. Ed. Purificación de la Torre. Madrid: Consejo Superior de Investigaciones Científicas, Agencia Española de Cooperación Internacional, 2000.

Ibn Majah, Abi 'Abd Allah Muhammad ibn Yazid al-Qazwini. *Sunan*. N.p.: n.p., n.d.

Kulayni, Muhammad ibn Ya'qub al-. *al-Kafi*. Karachi: n.p., 1965.

_____. *al-Kafi*. Trans. Muhammad Rida al-Ja'fari. Tehran: WOFIS, 1981–82.

_____. *al-Usul min al-Kafi*. Tehran: Dar al-Kutub al-Islamiyyah, 1981.

_____. *al-Usul min al-Kafi*. Ed. A.A. al-Ghaffari. 8 vols. Tehran: Maktabat al-Saduq, 1957–61.

Majlisi, Muhammad Baqir ibn Muhammad Taqi. *Bihar al-anwar*. Tehran: Javad al-Alavi wa Muhammad Akhundi, 1956-.

Murata, Sachiko. *The Tao of Islam: A Sourcebook on Gender Relationships in Islamic Thought*. Albany: State University of New York Press, 1992.

Muslim ibn al-Hajjaj al-Qushayri al-Nisaburi. *Jami' al-sahih*. al-Riyad: Bayt al-Afkar al-Dawliyyah li al-Nashr, 1998.

Naqvi, 'Ali Muhammad. *A Manual of Islamic Beliefs and Practice*. London: Muhammadi Trust, 1990.

Nicholson, Reynold A., trans. *Rumi, Poet and Mystic*. London: Unwin Paperbacks, 1978.

Waugh, Earl H. "Names and Naming." *The Oxford Encyclopedia of the Modern Islamic World*. Vol. 3. Ed. John L. Esposito. New York: Oxford University Press, 1995. 224–26.

The Jinn

ANNA MARIA MARTELLI

"And the Jinn race, We had created before, from the fire of a scorching wind." (Qur'an 15:27)

Introduction

The term *jinn* indicates every kind of fantastic beings whose reality is stated in the Qur'an together with that of other creatures; consequently, to believe in their existence, as well as in that of angels, is part of the Muslim creed. Islam therefore reserves a place to these creatures who escape every perception, forming a sort of "hidden world" (*'alam al-ghayb*) that intervenes in the order of the "visible world" (*'alam al-shahadah*). In the following pages, the image of the jinn in the Qur'an and the *Sunnah* will be examined, exploring a dimension of Islamic cosmology of which little is known outside of the Muslim world.

The Jinn in the Qur'an and Hadith

In the Qur'an, interdimensional beings are described as *jinn, jinna* and *jann*, words which are all derived from the same root. The verb *janna* means first of all "to hide," "to cover," "to conceal," but also "to be abundant," "to be dark" and "to be or become mad." From this verb also derives *jannah* "garden," in particular the garden of paradise. *Jinna* together with *jinn* is the most frequently used word in the Qur'an to describe the inhabitants of the hidden world. If *jinn* means both "demon" and "genie," it also means "that which covers," "veil," or "the inside of something." As for the term *jinna*, it indicates not only demons and genii but also folly and fury. Finally, the term *jinn* is used both for demons and genii and for a type of snake, white and harmless, that lives in areas inhabited by humans. This word appears twice in the Qur'an in the meaning of snake, being the staff of Musa (Moses) that stirs like a *jann*: "And when he saw his staff writhing like a serpent" (27:10; 28:31).

In much of the Muslim world, madness is often associated with demonic possession, namely, possession by *jinn*. This popular belief is strengthened by the meaning of the root from which *junun*, "folly," took form. In this connection, the Qur'an relates that the Prophet himself was falsely accused of being possessed by *jinn*. The relationship between *jinn* and madness is specifically noted in the *Surah al-Jinn* (The Chapter of the Jinn), where they are accused of spreading falsehood against Allah, thus spreading folly among their misguided human subjects:

67

The Blaspheming One among us has uttered a wanton falsehood against Allah, although we had supposed no man or jinne could tell of Him what is untrue. Some men have sought the help of jinn, but they mislead them into further error. Like you they thought that Allah could never raise the dead [72: 5–7].

In his commentary of 2:275, Qurtubi, explains that: "This verse contains proof against those who deny the possession by way of *jinn*, claiming that it is a result of natural causes, as well as those who claim that *Shaytan* does not enter humans nor does he touch them." In reality, however, this verse does not support the belief in demonic possession; it simply states that the unbelievers among the *jinn* have the ability to communicate with human beings with whom they spread nothing but falsehood.

The Qur'an usually mentions *jinn* and human beings together, thus dividing the duty of worshipping God between two major classes of a different nature. A verse specifies that the *jinn*, like human beings, must worship God: "I created humankind and the jinn in order that they might worship Me" (51:56). Again, like humans, the *jinn* are thought of as being of both sexes. They were not, of course, created in the same manner of human beings but starting from fire: "And before him Satan from smokeless fire" (15:27), from a burning wind or from vapor. Yet this distinction is not always clear-cut for *jinn* are sometimes considered chthonic beings belonging to the same species of snakes, sometimes bodies composed of vapor and sometimes aquatic beings. This confusion, however, results from the fact that the *jinn* are shape-shifters. While invisible to human beings in their natural form, they may adopt various forms. They feign to be divinities, present themselves as fallen angels, claim to be spirits of the dead or assert to be extra-terrestrials; in short, whatever suits the taste of the humans they seek to deceive. Another point they have in common with humankind is that they can be devils: "Thus We have assigned for every prophet an enemy: the devils among men and jinn" (6:112). Like humans, the *jinn* have been granted freedom of choice: some opt to be righteous believers while others decide to be evil unbelievers. Although the *jinn* are demons, in the true sense of the Greek term, only the wicked among them can be categorized as devils.

The Qur'an is emphatic as to the obedience of the angels; however, the nature of the *jinn* and *shayatin* is distinct. This comes out in the case of Iblis: "And when We said to the angels: 'Prostrate yourselves before Adam,' they all prostrated themselves except Satan, who in his pride refused and became an unbeliever" (2:34), who, elsewhere, is said to be a *jinn*: "When We said to the angels: 'Prostrate yourselves before Adam,' all prostrated themselves except Satan, who was a jinnee disobedient to his Lord" (18:50). The question was debated by theologians and commentators who remarked that the angelic nature of Iblis was contradicted by the fallibility he showed and also by the fact that he had a progeny. Although raised by infallible Angels, Iblis was a fallible *jinn* who succumbed to the supreme sin of pride which resulted in his fall from grace and rejection from the realm of the Divine.

The *jinn* too had prophets; some of them are therefore destined to hell and others shall enter paradise. Theologians have discussed the identity of such prophets: it has been maintained that they were angels, but most of the authors, on the ground of the Qur'an itself, are convinced that they were human prophets:

Then He will say: "Jinn and men! Did there not come to you apostles of your own who proclaimed to you My revelations and warned you?" [6:130].
Nothing prevents men from having faith when guidance is revealed to them but the excuse: "Could Allah have sent a human being as an apostle?" Say: "Had the earth been a safe place for angels to dwell in, We would have sent forth to them an angel from heaven as an apostle" [17:94–95].

There are those, like Fakhr al-Din al-Razi, who believe that human prophets transmitted their revelations to certain *jinn* entrusted to bring them to their fellows. Some *jinn* are Muslims while others are Christians, Jews or unbelievers. The *Surah al-Jinn* (Chapter of the Jinn) contains a real profession of faith uttered by *jinn* and promises them a reward for obedience or disobedience. In addition, it states clearly that *jinn* are divided according to their faith:

> When we heard His guidance we believed in Him: he that believes in his Lord shall never be wronged or harmed. Some of us are Muslims and some are wrongdoers. Those that embrace Islam pursue the right path; but those that do wrong shall become the fuel of hell [72:13–15].

This peculiarity makes Muhammad "the messenger with two tasks" (*rasul al-thaqalayni*). In other words, he was a prophet and messenger to both the visible and invisible worlds.

In pre–Islamic Arabia, the *jinn* were viewed as the nymphs and satyrs of the desert, and represented the side of the life of nature still unsubdued and hostile to humans. However, in the time of Muhammad the *Jinn* were in the process of becoming vague, impersonal gods. The Arabs of Mecca asserted the existence of a kinship (*nasab*) between them and Allah (37:158), made them companions of Allah (6:100), offered sacrifices to them (6:128), and sought aid of them (72:6).

Jinn are thought of as intelligent beings, imperceptible to our senses, but capable of appearing under different forms and of carrying out heavy duties. According to popular tradition, they inhabit lonely places, reproduce, and have love stories with human beings. It ensues that their legal status was discussed and fixed and their possible relations with humans, especially in questions of marriage and property, were examined.

The different types of *jinn* form a sort of fantastic bestiary. There are at least sixteen types of *jinn* (*'ifrit, ghul, si'lat*, etc.). The word *'ifrit* appears only once in the Qur'an: "A demon from among the jinn" (27:39) to indicate a rebellious *jinn*. They were granted an important place in magic, thus acknowledging as a matter of fact a pre–Islamic influence. The employment of evil *jinn* by means of magic is strictly forbidden in Islam; in spite of that, it is good, in case of need, to defend oneself against them with magic activities and by means of amulets and talismans. In fact, devils (*shaytan*, pl. *shayatin*) are often regarded as impious *jinn*, enemies to human beings.

Jinn are much stronger than humans and, since they interact differently in the world of perception, they can carry out deeds that are impossible for humankind such as to shift at a very high speed. In the Qur'an it is said that Sulayman (Solomon) employed *jinn* to carry out a series of actions that were thought impossible. Yet, the Holy Book does not seem to distinguish between *jinn* and devils, as witnessed by the following two passages: "We subdued the wind to him, so that it blew softly at his bidding wherever he directed it; and the devils, too, among whom were builders and divers and others bound with chains" (38: 36–38); "Solomon marshaled his forces of *jinn* and men and birds, and set them in battle array" (21: 17).

The traditions of the Prophet offer a wider vision. Human beings are accompanied by a *jinn* who gives them suggestions. Prophets too can be assaulted by *jinn* and demons; it is said that the Prophet had to fight against a *jinn* who tried in all manners to prevent him from praying. According to another *hadith*, the Prophet recited the Qur'an to a group of *jinn* and, the following day, he showed his companions the trace that their igneous presence had left on the ground.

The connection of *jinn* with Iblis, the *Shaytan*, and to *shayatin* in general, is obscure.

In the *Tafsir al-Jalalayn* it is said: "and He created the *Jann*, the father of the *jinn*, namely, Iblis, of a smokeless flame of fire." In consequence there is much confusion, and many legends and hypotheses have grown up on this subject. In the Qur'an, Iblis is mentioned as a proper noun, and in relation to Adam. The Qur'an reports that he refused to obey: "I will not bow to a mortal created of dry clay, of black molded loam" (15:33), because: "I am nobler than he. You created me from fire, but him from clay" (38:76). Owing to his insubordination and his pride Allah cursed him: "'Begone' said Allah, 'you are accursed'" (38:77–78).

In the Qur'an, the term *shaytan* or Satan covers a much greater sense than Iblis. It indicates an evil being, whose nature and origin are not specified, an enemy to Allah and humankind, tempter and deceiver, who sows seeds of hatred and discord: "May your off-spring be enemies to each other" (2:36); "Must have been seduced by Satan" (3:155); "He that chose Satan for his friend, an evil friend has he" (4:38); "Satan would lead them far astray" (4:60); "Satan seeks to stir up enmity and hatred among them" (5:91). He transmits his message by whispering into the ears of his victims: "Say: 'I seek refuge in the Lord of men, the King of men, the God of men, from the mischief of the slinking promoter who whispers in the hearts of men; from jinn and men'" (114:1–6).

The Jinn in Muslim Theology, Sufism, Shi'ism, and Popular Beliefs

The figures of Satan, Iblis, and demons occupy an important place in Muslim theology, in Sufism and in popular beliefs; moreover, they determine, in a fundamental way, the religious conscience of Shi'ism. In fact, Shi'ism developed a vision of history in which the Qur'anic stories of the insubordination of Iblis and of the harmful deeds of Satan are reflected, repeating themselves endlessly. So, it was thought that every prophet and every Imam had his own adversary (*didd*) who, just like Iblis, refused to acknowledge his mission and incited human beings to rebel against him.

In the Islamic cycle, the "diabolic" adversaries of the early Imams would have been the first three Caliphs, along with the Umayyads, in particular Yazid, who was considered responsible for the death of al-Husayn at Karbala. Each of the later Imams also found his nemesis among the 'Abbasid Caliphs. The Shi'ite doctrine thus developed a dualistic vision of the world enlivened by the dialectics between Good and Evil: in front of the light of the Friends of God, stand the streams of his adversaries. The struggle between the Imams and their enemies was, in the Shi'ite view, a spiritual battle of cosmic proportions between the Party of Allah and the Party of Satan.

According to the Qur'an, Iblis is the first being who, by making use of his intellect, has singled out a scale of values among the created things; for this reason, later literature will assign to him the discovery of the analogy (*qiyyas*). The supporters of the *qiyas* in theology and in law had to examine the analogy used by Iblis and prove at least the incorrectness of his reasoning. Qurtubi, in his *Tafsir Jami' al-ahkam*, writes that Iblis "went wrong in the analogy because he relied too much on his judgment; in fact, he did not know that, even against all appearances, clay is superior to fire"; the author, in fact, remarks, among other things, that clay possesses the virtues of weight and immobility, calmness, slowness and temperance, life and patience, while fire is light and vacuous, mobile, inconstant and agitated. Not the least, remarks again Qurtubi, clay does not need at all fire while fire needs a place where to subsist and this place is nothing but the earth.

Moreover, Iblis is he who directed his attention on himself, and that is the same as saying that reason and pride proceed at the same rate: "Are you too proud, or do you think he is beneath you?" (38:75). Iblis' reasoning, in which he compared himself to the other creatures, would have therefore unveiled the evil of arrogance; namely, his presumed greater importance within the created cosmos. And arrogance involves the exclusion from the community: "Satan refused to prostrate himself" (15:30–31).

Detaching himself from his fellow peers among the angels, Iblis proves to be an exception. The only one to disobey, Iblis introduces individuality in creation, which is sacrilege, since it clashes with the individuality of the Creator and contradicts the Divine prerogative of Oneness (*al-tawhid*). This function as an antagonist to the Creator also finds expression in a sort of challenge that he issued to the Lord: "Do You see this being whom You have exalted above me? If You give me respite till the Day of Resurrection, I will exterminate all but a few of his descendants" (17:62).

Other passages suggest that the Iblis' desire to tempt humankind was a direct consequence of Allah's attempt to tempt him: "'Lord,' said Satan, 'since you have led me astray, I will seduce them all, except those that faithfully serve you" (15:39–40), and the Creator answered: "Learn the truth [*haqq*], then, and I speak nothing but the truth [*haqq*]: I shall fill hell with your offspring and the men who follow you" (38:84–85). Therefore, according to the Qur'an, Iblis misled humankind because, in his turn, he had fallen into error, and this is a truth that Allah acknowledges, equalizing the Word and, hence, the project of Iblis to His own word and project, both defined in the same way (*haqq*). In this way, the Qur'anic thought makes the devilish *rôle* a *rôle* of simple mediation and passage. The antagonism ends by serving the cause of the Oneness of Allah because it is inscribed in the design of creation since the beginning. While there are those who argue that Allah set up Iblis to fall, as part of some grand plan, this line of reasoning places the blame upon the Divinity and exonerates the disobedient one who acted according to his own free will. While it was the will of Allah that Iblis be expelled, it must always be remembered that the *will of Allah* represents the *knowledge of Allah*. While the Divinity knows everything that will come to pass, this does not imply that He is pleased with it.

In the mystic field, the refusal of Iblis to prostrate himself before Adam, a created being, would be motivated not so much by arrogance as by obedience to Allah's first commandment that is the declaration of his Oneness. The theologian and mystic Hallaj in his *Ta-Sin al-azal*, illustrates the tragedy of Iblis, who was ordered disobedience but who, at the cost of his punishment and the fire of hell, chose to prostrate himself only before the One. 'Ayn al-Qudat al-Hamadhani in the *Tamhidat* writes that Iblis is the guardian or the chamberlain of the Divine Presence because he divides those who deserve to approach it from those who are not worthy.

This view, which elevates Iblis to the realm of sainthood, is rejected by all major Muslim authorities among *ahl al-Sunnah*, *ahl al-bayt* and *ahl Allah*. Iblis is not the greatest of monotheists, as some mystics may claim: he is the avowed enemy of God and humanity. If he was cast out and cursed, it was not for professing the pristine purity of Divine Unity, it was out of pride. He did not refuse to bow down to Adam because he believed that only Allah was worthy of such worshipfulness. He refused to bow down because he believed that he was better than Adam. Iblis was proud and pride is a mortal sin. As Almighty Allah says in a *hadith qudsi* or sacred saying "Pride is My Cloak and greatness My Robe, and he who competes with Me in respect of either of them I shall cast into hell-fire" (Abu Dawud, Ibn Majah, Ahmad). As many Muslims mystics have themselves explained, Adam was created in the image of Allah. He was, as all prophets, messengers, and friends of Allah, the very manifestation of the divine attributes. As a perfect human being (*al-insan al-kamil*), he was the reflection of the divinity. In this sense, denying Adam was denying Allah.

According to the consensus of mainstream Muslim authorities, there is no belief without obedience. The profession of faith is not simply "There is no god but Allah"; rather it is "There is no god but Allah and Muhammad is the Messenger of Allah." Prior to the Prophet, the professions of faith included "There is no god but Allah and 'Isa [Jesus] is the Spirit of Allah" and "There is no god but Allah and Musa [Moses] is the Messenger of Allah" among others applicable to the prophets and messengers of the time. Hence, upon the creation of Adam, the testimony of faith was "There is no god but God and Adam is the Prophet of God." The *shahadah* is a two-fold clause which is interdependent. Professing belief in one God, while rejecting the message and messengers of that God, is undisputed disbelief. As the Qur'an clearly states, failure to obey Allah nullifies ones deeds (47:32). Direct disobedience is disbelief. A believer cannot openly defy the Divine.

In his role as *Shaytan*, the power and influence of Iblis has been greatly reduced. When he was once permitted in the presence of the Divine, he can no longer act as His interlocutor. He has been effectively exiled. As Almighty Allah addresses *Shaytan* in the Qur'an: "Go hence, and may your descendants be enemies to each other. The earth will for a while provide your sustenance and dwelling-place. There you shall live and there you shall die, and thence you shall be raised to life" (7:24–25). While he no longer has direct access to the Divine, he does have direct access to humanity. As the interlocutor of humans, however, he cannot speak, and has only been granted the power to whisper (114:4). Also, as regards action, his function is impoverished (2:35–36). As Qurtubi notes, *al-Shaytan* does not have enough strength to remove someone from the place where he resides, he can just push him and direct him; he does nothing but induce the human being to do evil (3:155). In this way, he pushes humankind to forget (6:68; 12:42; 18:63), to enmity and hatred (5:1; 17:53) and to fear (3:175).

Jinn often acted as "collaborators" of human beings. The charge that Muhammad was *majnun*—a mad poet or soothsayer—must be viewed in light of the belief that the *jinn* could inspire humans with messages of literary or divinatory purport. The charge against his predication and his Holy Book to be the product of a spirit of low level, and not of a Divine agent, evidently derives from these cultural data of seventh century Arabia. The answer of the Qur'an to the above is that *jinn* and demons would be incapable of producing such a revelation: "It was not the devils who brought down the Qur'an: it is neither in their interest nor in their power. Indeed, they are too far away to overhear it" (26: 210–212), and that it is Muhammad who teaches the religion, certainly not the contrary:

Tell how We sent to you a band of *jinn* who, when they came and listened to the Qur'an, said to each other: "Hush! Hush!" As soon as it was ended they betook themselves to their people and gave them warning. "Our people," they said, "we have just been listening to a scripture revealed since the time of Moses, confirming previous scriptures and directing to the truth and to a straight path" [49: 29–30; 71:1–14].

Jinn could also assault humans in different ways and specifically hit them or inhabit their bodies temporarily or permanently. Ancient Arabs explained in this way several diseases such as crisis of epilepsy, melancholy or depression, different types of madness, even fever or very common diseases. Traditional Islam has preserved the substance of these conceptions but added to the same an important change: by invoking Allah and the Holy Book, the believer gets an indisputable power over the *jinn*. Exorcisms are rites spread in

Islam and can be administered by qualified believers; a talismanic science based on the use of Qur'anic verses is employed to prevent the evil action of some *jinn*. There are, of course, many Muslims scholars who, while recognizing the existence of the *jinn*, reject the notion that they have any contact with humans. In their view, both worlds co-exist but do not intersect.

According to popular belief, *Jinn* are earthly and mortal beings who can accomplish many extraordinary deeds such as moving very swiftly in space or giving indications otherwise unapproachable. Most of them are neither better nor worse than human beings; they are simply greedy and selfish like them. Humans can have relations with them and get their help. The possibility of foretelling the future was connected to the existence of the *jinn*, yet it surpasses it. The person specialized in prediction was called *kahin*; he, through different procedures and, in particular, by resorting to *jinn*, tried to answer questions concerning the future. However, it is said in the Qur'an, these *jinn* did nothing but spy upon the heavenly council where Allah deliberated; yet, that is now precluded to them who are driven away by means of meteors: "They guard it against rebellious devils, so that they may not hear the words of those on high. Meteors are hurled at them from every side; then, driven away, they are consigned to an eternal scourge. Eavesdroppers are pursued by fiery comets" (37: 7–10; 15:17–18). As "real" as the *Jinn* may be for many Muslims, and as common as "contact" between them may be, most Muslim theologians prohibit "communicating" with these interdimensional beings.

A prophet strictly connected to *jinn* is Sulayman (Solomon): "To Solomon we subdued the raging wind: it sped at his bidding to the land which We had blessed. We have knowledge of all things. We assigned him devils who dived into the sea for him and performed other tasks besides; We kept a watchful eye over them" (21: 82–82). Here, the power of Solomon over nature and over invisible creatures, namely, the wind and devils subjected to his command, is celebrated. Another reference is in 34:12–14:

> To Solomon We subdued the wind, travelling a month's journey and evening. We gave him a spring flowing with molten brass, and jinn who served him by leave of his Lord. Those of them who did not do Our bidding We shall punish in the fire of hell. They made for him whatever he pleased; shrines and statues, basins as large as watering-troughs, and built-in cauldrons.

This passage ends the description of the hard labor imposed to *jinn* with an ironical note: Solomon watches over them leaning on a staff and:

> When We had decreed his death, they did not know that he was dead until they saw a worm eating away his staff. And when his corpse fell down, the jinn realized that had they had knowledge of what was hidden they would not have continued in their abject servitude [34:14].

So, *jinn* do not know the "hidden things" and foretellers who claim to receive their confidences are simply charlatans. However, since the *jinn* live very long lives, exceeding hundreds and even thousands of years, the evil-ones among them may falsely impersonate the dead, with whom communication is impossible, sharing detailed information about the past with those who supposedly communicate with spirits of the deceased. According to Islam, however, these spiritists are simply being deceived by agents of the Devil who spin a thread of truth in veils of falsehood and deceit.

Again, *jinn* are mentioned in the story of the Queen of Sheba. In the Qur'an her name does not appear, even if, according to commentators her name was Bilqis and her mother was thought of as belonging to the species of *jinn*. The conciseness of the Qur'an excited the interest of commentators with regard to the transfer of her throne:

And to his nobles he said: "Which of you will bring to me her throne, before they sue for peace?" A demon among *jinn* replied: "I will bring it to you before you rise from your seat. I am strong enough and faithful." But he who was deeply versed in the Scriptures, said: "I will bring it to you in a twinkling" [27: 38–40].

Theologians have proposed two sorts of interpretations about the nature of the *jinn*: some, such as al-Ghazali, thought they were made of an immaterial substance, like angels and demons; others, such as Ash'ari and Baqillani, affirmed that they were made of a material substance, but formed a simple body. In literature, since the pre–Islamic poetry where Ta'abbata Sharran boasted of his familiarity with the *ghilan*, through folk-tales, the image of the *jinn* has always been very popular. They also appear in miniature paintings and form part of the cultural beliefs of the Muslim world.

Conclusions

Changeable and elusive figures, the *jinn* represent an obscure force capable of doing evil deeds and driving humans to madness. Sometimes, they are diabolical; however, as the stories of Solomon witness, they are not always harmful. Before Allah, they seem to be in the same position of humans. The believers among the *jinn* are deeply different from Iblis since they do not rebel against Allah and are not an adversary to human beings, with whom they rather seem to compete. Consequently, the *jinn* are more similar to humans than to Iblis since some may err and some many not. They are, like humans, granted free-will and subject to choice. While the nature of the *jinn*, and their relationship with human beings, is subject to theological dispute and doctrinal divergence, these interdimensional creatures continue to play a prominent role in the lives and minds of many Muslims from Morocco to Indonesia and everywhere in between.

Works Cited

Abu Dawud al-Sijistani, Sulayman ibn al-Ash'ath. *Sahih Sunan Abu Dawud.* Riyad: Maktab al-Tarbiyyah al-'Arabi li Duwal al-Khalij, 1989.

Ash'ari, Abu al-Hasan al-. *Kitab al-Luma'.* Ed. and trans. R.C. McCarthy. Bayrut: Imprimerie catholique, 1953.

Baqillani, Abu Bakr Muhammad al-. *I'jaz al-Qur'an. EI Encyclopédie de l'Islam.* 2d. ed. Leiden: Brill, 1960.

Ghazali, Abu Hamid al-. *Mishkat al-Anwar.* Trans. Laura Veccia Vaglieri and Roberto Rubinacci. *Scritti scelti.* Torino: UTET, 1970.

Hallaj, al-Husayn ibn Mansur al-. *Ta-Sin al-azal. La passion de Husayn Ibn Mansur Hallaj, martyr mystique de l'Islam éxécuté à Baghdad le 26 mars 922.* Ed. Louis Massignon. Paris: Gallimard, 1975.

Hamadhani, 'Ayn al-Qudat al-. *Tamhidat. The Ocean of the Soul.* Ed. Helmut Ritter, John O'Kane, and Radke Bernd. Leiden: Brill, 2003.

Ibn Hanbal, Ahmad ibn Muhammad. *Musnad al-Imam Ahmad ibn Hanbal.* Bayrut: al-Maktabah al-Islamiyyah, 1969.

Ibn Majah, Abi 'Abd Allah Muhammad ibn Yazid al-Qazwini. *Sunan.* N.p.: n.p., n.d.

Mahalli, Jalal al-Din. *Tafsir al-Jalalayn.* 'Amman: Aal al-Bayt Institute for Islamic Thought, 2005. Internet: www. altafsir.org.

Qurtubi, Abu 'Abdullah al-. *al-Jami'li ahkam al-Qur'an.* Ahlul Bayt Digital Islamic Library Project, 2000. Internet: www.al-Islam.org.

Razi, Fakhr al-Din al-. *Tafsir al-Kabir.* Also known as *Mafatih al-ghayb. Routledge Encyclopedia of Philosophy.* John Cooper. London: Routledge, 1998.

Suyuti, Jalal al-Din. *Tafsir al-Jalalayn.* 'Amman: Aal al-Bayt Institute for Islamic Thought, 2005. Internet: www. altafsir.org.

Ta'abbata Sharran, in *EI* 2nd ed. *Encyclopédie de l'Islam.* Leiden: Brill, 1960.

Intoxication

Matthew Long

"They ask thee concerning wine and gambling. Say: 'In them is great sin, and some profit, for men; but the sin is greater than the profit." (Qur'an 2:219)

Introduction

Islam faces a number of challenges among Westerners today. Perhaps the greatest challenge is the lack of information the common person possesses on any aspect of Islam. Ask someone to identify any of the Islamic legal schools (*madhahib*), and one is likely to be met with silence. Ask that same individual to name any of the prophets in the Qur'an. Muhammad would most definitely be mentioned with perhaps a few others, such as Jesus, Moses, or even Abraham. A dearth compared to the line of prophets identified in the Qur'an. But when you probe the average person's knowledge of Islam on the matter of intoxication, specifically alcohol, odds are you will be met with an unequivocal, decisive response that Islam forbids alcohol. Despite most people's indubitableness on this matter, under the surface of this elementary, easily recognizable principle is an intriguing but convoluted image, the image of intoxication.

The image of intoxication is an image both controversial and complex. The complexities are borne out of the numerous, and often tantamount, linguistic expressions apropos intoxication as well as dissimilar positions formulated by the Islamic legal schools on substances deemed intoxicating. Those same divergent opinions formed by the Muslim legal traditions are the cause of some of the controversy on the nature of intoxicants in Islam. Controversy over intoxication is also prevalent in Sufism (*tasawwuf*), for the path of intoxication (*sukr*) is believed by some to be one of the means of achieving unity with the Divine while others prefer to follow the way of sobriety (*sahw*).

Intoxication in the Islamic tradition needs to be grasped from two viewpoints. First is the more pronounced and literal perception of intoxication. The Qur'an and *ahadith* provide our primary sources on intoxication followed by exoteric commentaries (*tafasir*) on the Qur'an and legal texts developed by Muslim jurists (*fuqaha'*) and scholars (*'ulama'*). Second are the metaphorical and allegorical interpretations of intoxication evoked by the poets and mystics of Islam, the Sufis. Mystical poetry, esoteric interpretations of the Qur'an, and Sufi manuals, detailing terminology and devotion, provide the substance of knowledge regarding the anagogic and metaphoric side of intoxication.

Alcohol, Drugs, and Earthly "Annihilation"

While intoxication is the focal point, it is not possible to portray the image of intox-ication fully without mentioning intoxicants (*al-muskirat*). Drugs and alcohol have been available to countless cultures for thousands of years; it is believed wine production dates back as early as 7000–6000 BCE and beer possibly even earlier. Evidence suggests that a wide range of cultures, Chinese, Indian, Egyptian, Mesopotamian, and Persian, for example, produced and consumed some type of alcoholic substances thousands of years before the arrival of Islam. When Islam did gain a foothold in Arabia and spread throughout the world, the majority of Muslims subscribed to a complete ban of intoxicants outlined in the Qur'an and by the Prophet Muhammad. However, drug and alcohol existence, production and consumption have remained in a number of Muslim countries and communities throughout the world to this day.

Prior to the advent of Islam, historical records and literature attests to the prevalence of alcohol, particularly wine, in the Arabian Peninsula. Wine was produced in neighboring regions, such as Yemen, and locally with Mecca and the city of Ta'if being known for the production of wine. Wine from Arabia was not held in high regard for either its quality or quantity given that the climate and terrain made for ill conditions to produce wine from grapes. More often merchants were the primary source of alcohol in Arabia importing wine from Iraq and Syria. Jews and Christians, according to the early Arabic poetry, were the prominent suppliers of wine. Further evidence for the prevalence of wine consumption is found in pre–Islamic poetry.

Before the advent of Islam, in the time of ignorance (*Jahiliyyah*), wine is mentioned often but not with the same frequency as will be seen in later poetry following the spread of Islam. In his translation and commentary of the *Hamasah*, a ninth century collection of poetry by Abu Tammam (Habib ibn Aws al-Ta'i) (d. 845–6), Lyall states, "Wine-drinking was a most prevalent habit among the præ-islamic [*sic*] Arab, and no old poem describing their daily life fails to make mention of it" (62). Poetry predating Islam is referred to as *al-shi'r al-jahiliyyah* (poetry of the time of ignorance). Arabic poetry was orally transmitted for centuries. It was not until the 8th century that poems were assembled into written anthologies. Therefore, knowledge of Arabic poetry in the time of *al-jahiliyyah* is limited to poets who lived during the 6th and early 7th centuries and whose poetry was recorded in these early collections.

The *Mu'allaqah* (or *Mu'qallat*), a compilation of pre–Islamic poetry purportedly col-lected by Hammad al-Rawiyah, makes reference to wine in nearly every single piece of poetry. Poets Tarafah ibn al-'Abd, Labid ibn Rabi'ah, 'Amr ibn Kulthum, 'Antarah ibn Shad-dad, and Imru' al-Qays all mentioned wine and drinking in some capacity in their individual contributions to the *Mu'allaqah*. Common topics were the color and odor of the wine, con-duct at and depictions of wine parties, and occasionally the effects of wine — with some authors never failing to point to the negative aspects of wine indulgence. "Drunkenness in the Jahiliya [*sic*] went hand in hand with ... profound forgetfulness, and the squandering away of wealth," says Kueny (104). A classical example of this behavior can be found in a passage from Tarafah stating, "I've ever quaffed the wine and took my joy, squandering my hoard and my legacy, till every one of my clan abandoned me and I was left alone" (qtd. in Kueny 96). Passages dedicated solely to wine in *Mu'allaqah* are minimal with some scholars reluctant to accept the authenticity of such lines claiming wine portions to be inserted, such as the case with the poems of 'Amr ibn Kulthum (Harb 220). According to Harb, al-'Asha

Maymun ibn Qays was the most prolific pre–Islamic wine-poet dedicating substantial sections of his works to wine (222). Al-'Asha describes drunkards as, "Some quite overcome with cheek in the dust, some (though no cripples) with no use of their legs" (qtd. Harb 221, ftn. 10). Collected in the latter half of the 8th century, the *Mufaddaliyyat*, a major anthology of poetry before and during the rise of Islam, also possess a number of poems discussing wine. 'Awf ibn 'Atiyya, 'Abda ibn al-Tabib, Masih ibn 'Asala, Rabi'ah ibn Maqrum al-Dabbi, 'Alqamah ibn 'Abadah, and Mutammin Nuwayra write of wine. Again though, many of these pieces demonstrate inserted statements on wine and not a thematic treatment of the subject. Poetry of 'Adi b. Zayd and 'Abda ibn al-Tabib begin to show signs of wine becoming more than an inserted statement; it is transforming into a theme upon which the entire poem would revolve.

Wine (*khamr*), produced from grapes, was known to Meccans and Medinans, but *ahadith*, records of the sayings and actions of the Prophet Muhammad, indentify the types of intoxicants which were more pervasive in the Hijaz. *Al-fadikh*, *al-ghubayra,'* *al-mizr*, *al-bit,'* and certain types of *nabidh*, *tila'*, *muthallath* were specific intoxicants reported in the *ahadith*; however, 357 names of intoxicating beverages are found in Firuzabadi's (d. 1415) *al-Jalis al-anis fi tahrim al-khandaris*. Wine produced with grapes (*al-a'nab*) was not as common as wine produced by "unripe dates (*al-busr*) and ripe dates (*al-tamr*)" in Medina (al-Bukhari *Kitab al-ashribah* no. 5258). Al-Bukhari (d. 870) further records, *hi min al-khamsahin al-'inabi wa al-tamri wa al-'isali wa al-hintahi wa al-sha'iri* (it [wine] can be produced from five things grapes, dates, honey, wheat, and barley) (*Kitab al-ashribah* no. 5259). Malik ibn Anas (d. 795) adds raisins (*al-zabib*) to the list crops which were fermented to create alcoholic drinks (*Kitab al-ashribah* no. 1593). Names of crops were occasionally applied euphemistically by Islamic writers to stand in for wine (*khamr*) and intoxicants (*muskir*).

Intoxicants and intoxication are mentioned several times in the Qur'an. One of the first verses pertaining to intoxication extols the users of intoxicating substances, for it reads, "And of the fruits of the palms and the vines, you take therefrom an intoxicant [*sakar*] and a provision fair. Surely in that is a sign for a people who understand" (16:67). This verse is unique for two reasons. First, this is the one occasion in the Qur'an when the term *sakar* signifies an intoxicating material, as opposed to *khamr* or *muskir*, and not the state of intoxication. According to the *Taj al-'arus*, *sakar* is synonymous with wine made from grapes (*al-a'nab*) or dates (*al-tamr*), *nabidh*, intoxicating fruit (*thamar*) and any substance which intoxicates (vol. 3, 274). Second, the consumption of intoxicants was a sign (*ayah*) given to the wise by God. That it is a sign for the wise is supported by the context of other verses in this section of *Surah al-Nahl* (The Chapter of the Bee). Proceeding and succeeding verses, 16:65–66 and 16:68–69, list other signs provided by God given to humanity, such as the honey of the bees, the milk of the cows, and the water from the skies. heavenly wine (*rahiq*), in Qur'an 83:25, is one of the many pleasures bestowed upon believers in paradise (*jannah*). Qur'an 37:45–47 and 56:18–19 describe a pure drink originating from flowing rivers and captured in a cup (*ka's*) which is reckoned to be some style of wine, referred to as *rahiq* but also *khamr* as in 47:15. However, partakers of the cup are not rendered "exhausted [*yunzifun*]." *Yunzifun*, from *nazafa*, is rendered as "intoxication" in Yusuf 'Ali's and Arberry's translations of the Qur'an and "drunk" by Asad. heavenly wine, therefore, does not have the same repercussions as earthly wine, namely intoxication (*yunzifun*).[1] Works from Jane D. McAuliffe and Suzanne Stetkevych along with Qur'anic commentaries afford invaluable investigation on the topic of heavenly wine.

The usefulness of wine remained overshadowed by the evils committed by those in states of inebriation. Drunken misconduct was rampant in society before the revelations condemning the use of wine and intoxicants. A rather sordid tale, found in Bukhari's and Muslim's (d. 875) *ahadith*, before the Qur'anic injunctions against intoxication and wine, involves 'Ali, Hamzah, and the Prophet. 'Ali one day found two of his camels had been slaughtered by Hamzah. When Muhammad called upon Hamzah, he supposedly found his uncle in a drunken (*thamilun*) stupor and became the recipient of drunken affronts from his uncle (al-Bukhari *Kitab al-Maghazi* no. 3781). *Thamil* does mean intoxication, according to the dictionary the *Taj al-'arus*, but is not used in the Qur'an and remains on the periphery of the vocabulary of intoxication (vol. 7, 247).[2] Hamzah's alleged drunken exploits may have been one of the first causes for the condemnation of intoxicants and intoxication in the Qur'an though it is not mentioned by Qur'anic commentators (*mufassirun*). It was not by any means the only occurrence, for commentators ascribe other drunken episodes to specific revelations. Shi'ite scholars, such as the modern scholar Muhammad al-Tijani, question the authority of such traditions. Such Shi'ites suggest that these incidents may have been fabricated by the Umayyads in order to dishonor the Household of the Prophet (382–383).

The Prophet Muhammad and the message of the Qur'an gradually shifted attitudes on the use of libations for the believers of Islam. Eventually, the Qur'anic text begins to criticize and question the use of wine. 2:219, 4:43, and 5:90–91 is the sequence of revelations the majority of Sunni and *Ithna 'ashariyyah* (Twelver) Shi'ite Qur'anic commentators accept with some including 16:67 as part of the arrangement (Tabari vol. 3, 681). Tabari (d. 923), Wahidi (d. 1076), and many other commentators state that the revelations came down in this order in response to 'Umar's demand for a ruling on wine usefulness (Tabari vol. 8, 657; Wahidi 48–49, 154–155). The first instance in which the status of wine undergoes a shift occurs in *Surah al-Baqarah* (The Chapter of the Heifer). It states,

> They will question thee concerning wine [*al-khamr*], and arrow-shuffling. Say: "In both is heinous sin; and uses for men, but the sin in them is more heinous than the usefulness." They will question thee concerning what they should expend. Say: "The abundance." So God makes clear His signs to you; haply you will reflect [2:219].

Notice how wine is not strictly proscribed, but rather it is condemned for the power it possesses to lead to sin. Despite this condemnation, the "usefulness" (*manafi'*) of wine is still acknowledged. The next revelation in *Surah al-Nisa'* (The Chapter of the Women) on wine prompted the believers not to attend the daily prayers while drunk,

> O believers, draw not near to prayer when you are drunken [*sukara*] until you know what you are saying, or defiled — unless you are traversing a way — until you have washed yourselves; but if you are sick, or on a journey, or if any of you comes from the privy, or you have touched women, and you can find no water, then have recourse to wholesome dust and wipe your faces and your hands; God is All-pardoning, All-forgiving [4:43].

At this stage, the prohibition against wine has not fully developed; rather, the Qur'an has set forth specific parameters on times when being intoxicated (*sukara*) is not allowed. Muslim, Zamakhshari (d. 1144), and Wahidi assert this revelation came down when a drunkard appeared at prayer reciting verses of the Qur'an incorrectly (Zamakhshari vol. 1, 146; Wahidi 112–113). This verse reveals many interesting nuances on the status of wine and intoxication in the Muslim community at this point. First, the Qur'an still has not forbidden wine; thus, it is possible to drink and come to prayers, as long as the drinking has not caused intoxication. In fact, Tabari asserts that a group of Muslims would habitually drink and then sober up before attending the daily prayers (vol. 3, 681). Second, intoxication is on par with other states of impurity, such as intercourse. Intercourse and other acts requiring ritual purification (*wudu*) are not evil or illicit by nature but do nullify the validity of prayer. This particular *ayah* equates intoxication with other non-illicit acts that prohibit the performance of specific duties. Such a position is at odds with the conclusion on the permissibility of intoxication eventually developed by the Islamic legal schools (*madhahib*).

When the final revelation came to the Prophet Muhammad concerning wine, it seems to have firmly established the prohibition against the substance. *Surah al-Ma'idah* (The Chapter of the Table Spread) relates,

> O believers, wine [*al-khamr*] and arrow-shuffling, idols and divining-arrows are an abomination, some of Satan's work; so avoid it; haply so you will prosper. Satan only desires to precipitate enmity and hatred between you in regard to wine [*al-khamr*] and arrow-shuffling, and to bar you from the remembrance of God, and from prayer. Will you then desist? [5:90–91].

Wahidi and Zamakhshari claim the final revelation on wine appeared after a violent encounter between the Helpers (*al-ansar*) and Emigrants (*al-muhajirun*). Sa'd ibn Abi Waqqas attended a gathering of Helpers and Emigrants at which meat and wine were served. After having drunk, to the point of intoxication, Waqqas asserted that the Emigrants were superior to the Helpers. Upon hearing this, one of the Helpers struck Waqqas in the nose (Zamakhshari vol. 1, 146; Wahidi 154). Following this event, the above and final verse on wine was revealed to the Prophet Muhammad and the community.

While this progression has many adherents, alternate accounts are found in Qur'anic commentaries. Fakhr al-Din al-Razi (d. 1209) indicates a sect of believers, among whom he counts himself, that affirmed that the prohibition of intoxicants actually arrived with the initial revelation in *Surah al-Baqarah* (The Chapter of the Heifer), but concurs with the order as established by Tabari (McAuliffe 165). Subsequent revelations merely reiterated and strengthened the original proscription. Respondents claim *Surah al-Baqarah* (The Chapter of the Heifer) is not definitive in the banning of intoxicants; furthermore, an outright ban would not have been successful. Lovers of the drink needed to be gradually weaned away from the use of intoxicants.

Shi'ite Muslims view the progression of prohibition differently and include additional revelations among the three enumerated by Sunni commentators. Tabataba'i (d. 1981), in the *Tafsir al-mizan*, believed the chain includes verse 33 of *Surah al-A'raf* (The Chapter of the Heights) and was revealed in the following order: 16:67; 7:33; 4:43; 2:19; 5:90–91. Qur'an 7:33 states, "Say: 'My Lord has only forbidden indecencies, the inward and the outward, and sin, and unjust insolence.'" Tabataba'i's, as well as al-Razi's, inclusion of this verses aims to temper the prohibition of *khamr*. He goes on to challenge the typical sequence of revelation as given by Sunni commentators and discuss at great length the pitfalls and dangers of alcohol. However, his critique focuses not on alcohol per se but rather the consequences of its consumption, intoxication. He claims,

> The social and moral disasters appearing in the wake of addiction to drink are too well-known to need any description. Depravity of character, debauchery, shamelessness, the leakage of secrets, scandals, slanders, destruction and damage to others, crimes, murder — name any immorality, alcohol will lead to it. In short, it nullifies all ethical laws and moral values upon which are based the felicity and bliss of this life and, more particularly, the values of chastity and probity.

Tabataba'i speaks of intoxicants, but patently alluding to intoxication as the root to all the ills of society. Disagreement over the traditional catenation of revelations between most

Sunni and Shi'ah halts with *Surah al-Ma'idah* (The Chapter of the Table Spread) firmly regarded as having established the final and unequivocal prohibition of wine.

The *ahadith* of the Prophet Muhammad fortify the stipulation against the consumption of intoxicants and the prohibition of intoxication. The *sahih ahadith* of both Muslim and Bukhari recorded the Prophet Muhammad's statements on wine and intoxication bolstering the Qur'anic precedence. Both contain *ahadith* related from 'A'ishah stating, *Kulla sharabi askara fa huwa haramun* (All beverages that intoxicate are forbidden) (Muslim *Kitab al-ashribah* no. 2001; al-Bukhari *Kitab al-wudu'* no. 239). The other major collections of *ahadith*, such as Malik ibn Anas' *al-Muwatta,'* contain variations of this same *hadith*. The *Sunan* of Abu Dawud (d. 889) and al-Tirmidhi (d. 892) add that the Prophet Muhammad said, *Ma askara kathiruhu faqaliluhu haramun* (what intoxicates in great amounts is forbidden in small amounts) (*Kitab al-ashribah* no. 3681; *Kitab al-ashribah* no. 1865). Additionally, these two collections add that the Prophet Muhammad said, *Kul al-muskirin khamrun wa kulla muskirin haramun* (Every intoxicant is wine and every intoxicant is forbidden) (Dawud *Kitab al-ashribah* no. 3679; al-Tirmidhi *Kitab al-ashribah* no. 1861). These *ahadith* provided the foundation for an all out prohibition against any intoxicant and becoming intoxicated.

Statements from the Prophet Muhammad appear to establish a prohibition against intoxicants; however, Islamic legal scholars would become divided on the matter of what counts as an intoxicant and whether certain circumstances override a proscription against such substances.[3] According to Deurash, jurists of the Hijaz concluded anything that could lead to intoxication should be banned in all circumstance (356). In a more transparent delineation of the legal positions on intoxicants, three of the Sunni—Shafi'i, Hanbali, and Maliki—*madhahib* and the Shi'ite *madhahib* deemed all intoxicating substances as forbidden.

Those subscribing to this ruling did so based on the aforementioned *ahadith* and Qur'anic interpretation (*tafsir*). The Arabic verb *yakhmur* meaning, "to cover or veil," is the verbal root of *khamr* which is the only form of intoxicating substance mentioned in the Qur'an. Applying analogy, the Muslim jurists, lexicographers, and commentators determined that *khamr* is anything that "covers" or "veils" the senses and the mind. According to the *Taj al-'arus*, *khamr* is to be regarded not just as the fermented juice of grapes, but the juice of any substance that intoxicates as well as an intoxicating substance covering the senses (vol. 3, 176). Al-Bukhari's *hadith*, *al-khamru ma khamara al-'aqla* (wine is what veils the mind), validates the claims of the jurists and lexicographers (*Kitab al-ashribah* no. 5259). Therefore, any other substance, such as *nabidh*, that does the same is to be considered *khamr* (Deurash 357). *Khamr* takes on a much wider definition beyond wine explaining why many English translators render *khamr* as a "strong drink" in Marmaduke Pickthall's *The Koran* or "intoxicant" in Muhammad Asad's *Message of the Qur'an*.

While the Shafi'i, Hanbali, and Maliki came to the same conclusion that intoxicating substances are forbidden (*haram*), each school had its own methods to reach this consensus. For instance, the bulk of Shafi'i scholars turned to the abundance of textual materials on *khamr* and *sukr* while the Maliki jurists focused upon the operative cause ('*illa*) (Haider 146,150).[4] Haider's study details the primary method sanctioning prohibition applied by each school along with central themes of the debated emphasized by each school, such as the Hanbali emphasis upon punishments (130–165). Fully developed expositions on topic of wine and intoxicants for each *madhahib* can be found in a number of sources: for the Shafi'i *madhhab* see al-Nawawi's *Minhaj al-talibin*, Ibn Qasim al-Ghazzi's *Fath al-qarib*, Abu Ishaq al-Shirazi's *al-Tanbih*, al-Mawardi's *al-Hawi al-kabir*, or *Reliance of the Traveller*;

for the Maliki *madhhab* see Zurqani's commentary on the *al-Muwatta,'* al-Qayrawani's *al-Risalah*, Ibn Abi Zayd's *Kitab al-nawadir wa al-ziyadat*, or Khalil ibn Ishaq al-Jundi's *Mukhtasar*; and for the Hanbali *madhhab* see Yunus Buhuti's *al-Rawd al-murbi'* or Ibn Qudamah's *al-Mughni* of al-Khiraqi's *Mukhtasar*.

Shi'ite jurists justified the prohibition of intoxicants along many of the same lines as the Sunni *madhahib* (schools). Many of the proofs for the prohibition of intoxicants come from the textual sources; the only difference from their Sunni counterparts is the use of traditions from the Imams. For example, Ja'far al-Sadiq (d. 765), the sixth Shi'ite Imam, states,

> Wine is the root of all evils and sins. A person who drinks wine loses his senses. At that time he forgets Allah, does not refrain from any sin, respects no one, and does not desist from committing evil openly. The spirit of faith and piety departs from him and only the impure and malicious spirit, which is far off from the blessings of Allah, remains in his body. Allah, His angels, His prophets and the true believers curse such a man and his prayers are not accepted for forty days. On the Day of Judgment, his face will be black and his tongue will come out of his mouth, the saliva will fall on his chest and he will desperately complain of thirst.

As a result of this tradition, and many similar sayings from the Prophet Muhammad and the Shi'ite Imams, Shi'ite jurists, like Abu al-Qasim al-Khu'i, have ruled that "Drinking wine is unlawful and in some traditions (*ahadith*), it has been declared to be a major sin" (#2642). Besides decreeing that all intoxicants were prohibited, most Shi'ite jurists have ruled that liquid intoxicants were *najis* or ritually impure. Although some contemporary Twelver Sources of Emulation do not consider alcohol to be impure literally, they all insist upon its spiritual impurity. Like their Sunni counterparts, since prohibition was agreed upon by all participants, divergence arose over specialized categories within the discourse of intoxicants and methods utilized to endorse the prohibition of intoxicants. Zaydi legal discourse, for instance, focused on the use of alcoholic substances in medicine (Haider 160). Imami positions can be found in Muhammad ibn al-Hasan al-Tusi's *al-Nihaya* and *Mabsut*; Zaydi opinions include al-Hadi's *Kitab al-ahkam* and *Kitab al-muntakhab* and Sharaf al-Din Husayn ibn Muhammad's *Shifa' al-uwam*; for the Zahiri opinion see Ibn Hazm's *al-Muhalla*; Isma'ili rulings can be found in Qadi Nu'man's *Da'im*. In direct opposition to proponents of the gross ban, a few questioned the meaning of *khamr* which led them to an atypical postulation. Jurists of Kufah and Basrah argue that only certain types of intoxicating beverages are prohibited while others are permitted even though those substances could intoxicate in substantial quantities (Deurash 356). Deurash identifies a few adherents to this position with the most recognizable being Abu Hanifah, an early Muslim jurist from whom the Hanafi *madhhab* takes its name. Thus, the Hanafi *madhhab* as well as a number of Mu'tazili theologians are regarded as the embodiments of this position even though a number of their fold rejected the use of any intoxicating substance, such as the great Hanafi scholar al-Shaybani (d. 804–5) (Rosenthal 112).

Proponents of this viewpoint applied numerous arguments to validate the permission of some alcoholic drinks. First, unlike the other *madhahib*, scores of the Hanafi literally understood the word as meaning, "dates and grapes that when fermented cause intoxication." That *khamr* was to be applied to all substances that have the ability to intoxicate was analogically inaccurate according to the Hanafi. This is what Reinhart refers to as "restrictive hermeneutics" and therefore substances, such as *nabidh*, are not to be counted as *khamr* (133). Furthermore, some do not assert that *khamr* is equated with the meaning "to cover or veil"; hence, to utilize the analogy that anything that veils or covers the intellect is *khamr* is not sound (Hattox 52). Second, those advocating the permission to consume intoxicants identified *ahadith* supporting their claim and regarded *ahadith* countermanding their position as either misinterpreted or abrogated (*mansukh*).

The *Sahih* of Muslim relates a number of *ahadith* alleging that the Prophet Muhammad was known to consume *nabidh* but with an important caveat (*Kitab al-ashribah* no. 2004–5). It is important to bear in mind that not all forms of *nabidh* led to intoxication. Determinants of whether or not a *nabidh* was intoxicating were the amount of time substances were left to steep and the container in which the substances and liquid comingled. *Nabidh* concocted in gourds (*dubba'*), such as a pumpkin, was forbidden while *nabidh* in a water skin was usually acceptable.[5] The *ahadith* which relate the Prophet Muhammad's supposed consumption of *nabidh* specifically state the *nabidh* was prepared in a water skin (*siqa'*) or earthen pot (*biram*) and not left for more than two days; therefore, the *nabidh* in these circumstances where non-alcoholic. As Tijani points out, however, it was this very tradition that served as a pretext for the Umayyad and the 'Abbasid rulers to justify the consumption of alcoholic substances (301). In another case, Malik relates that 'Umar permitted the consumption of *tila'* for residents of al-Sham (Syria) (*Kitab al-ashribah* no. 1600). Hanafi *fuqaha'* also reject the veracity of the *ahadith* employed by the other *madhahib* (Hattox 52–55). This collection of proofs capacitated Hanafi *fuqaha'* to contrive a less stringent posture on intoxicants. However, Abu Hanifah did not relinquish the standard view that intoxication is never permissible.

Appeals to communal consensus as well as sacred history were other tactics proponents of alcoholic beverages employed in support of intoxicants, particularly *nabidh*. According to Reinhart, drinkers routinely used the prophets of old to justify their consumption of *nabidh* (134–135). Nuh (Noah), Lut (Lot), and 'Isa (Jesus) in the Biblical traditions and Torah all imbibed in alcoholic beverages and furthermore became intoxicated. However, Muslim accounts of these prophets, in the Qur'an and Muslim historical literature, exclude episodes of drunkenness and the consumption of alcohol. Kuffan supporters of *nabidh* had to turn to sources outside of the traditional Islamic texts which probably lessened the impact of such an argument (Reinhart 134–135).[6] More influential was the utilization of communal consensus (*ijma'*). *Nabidh* enthusiasts pointed to its wide communal consumption, specifically in the region of Kufah, as proof of its licitness (Reinhart 133). A few scholars stated it was not the "substance" that was forbidden but rather the effects of the substance (Deuraseh 356, 358). Qur'anic commentaries relate the misdeeds of individuals who overindulged in wine. That overindulgence led to intoxication and with that came strife, misguided prayer, and neglect of Allah. Therefore, it was not the "substances" that led to these transgressions, just the intoxication. That explains why the Hanafi and Mu'tazili still concur that consuming any substance to induce a state of intoxication is prohibited and liable to punishment. For a full exposition on the Hanafi view of drinks (*ashribah*) see the *Fatawa 'alamgiri*, al-Quduri's *Matn al-Quduri fi al-fiqh*, Halabi's *Multaqa al-abhur*, al-Tahawi's *Mukhtasar* and *Sharh ma'ani al-athar*, al-Marghinani's *al-Hidayah*, or Sarakhsi's *Mabsut*. Reinhart's *Before Revelation* and Deuraseh present brief yet comprehensive summations of the strategies utilized by *nabidh* users and proponents of alcoholic beverages.

More captivating though are the degrees of intoxication articulated by the *madhahib*. Hattox states that, "the formulation of a definition of drunkenness is essential to the application of the beverage laws of any of the four schools" (56). *Madhahib* contested not only the substances engendering intoxication but what it meant to be intoxicated. Unsurprisingly, descriptions of a drunkard are markedly different in the Hanafi works of jurisprudence compared to the other *madhahib*. Ibn Qutaybah (d. 889) in the *Kitab al-ashribah* quotes various definitions of intoxication from legalists across the spectrum. Drunks were both ignorant (*jahl*) and engaged in silliness or foolishness (*safah*) according to Shafi'i, and Malik stated the drunkard was "forgetful [*yaghibu*] and mixed-up or confused [*yakhlitu*]" (Qutaybah 121, 124). 'Ali said that the drunk was the one who would madly rave (*hadha*) and fabricate (*iftara*) (Malik *Kitab al-ashribah* no. 1588). Hanafi characterizations of drunkenness are quite indulgent. Qutaybah quotes Abu Hanifah as having said a drunk is one whose, "intellect has left him so he does not understand a little or much (anything at all) [*yadhhabu 'aqluhu fa la ya'rifu qalil wa la kathir*]" (121). Even further to the extreme is a Hanafi scholar, Ibn Nujaym (d. 1563), who supplements Abu Hanifah's definition by adding that a drunkard "does not know (the difference) between a man and a woman or the earth from the sky [*la ya'rifu al-rajul min al-mar'a wa la al-ard min al-sama'*]" (qtd. in Hattox 152, n. 28). Hanafi jurists not only permitted adherents to indulge in alcoholic beverages but they could do so up to a near point of total "annihilation."

Punishment for transgressing the prohibition against intoxication is both corporal and perennial. The penalties for intoxication, and the consumption of intoxicants for that matter, are particularized in the *ahadith*. Corporal punishment (*hadd*) was carried out with lashings for contravening the laws against intoxication and consumption of wine. Forty lashes were administered to violators by the Prophet Muhammad, 'Ali, and Abu Bakr while 'Umar, 'Uthman, and Mu'awiyyah resolved that eighty lashes could be given (Muslim *Kitab Hudud* no. 1706–1707; Abu Dawud *Kitab Hudud* no. 4488). *Hadd* for drinking remains set at either forty or eighty lashes depending upon the legal school one opts to follow. Shi'ite jurists in contemporary Iran typically assign eighty lashes for public drunkenness; however forty is regarded as the appropriate punishment by some (Khu'i #2804). Besides the penalty of lashing, drinkers were to abstain from prayer for forty days (Abu Dawud *Kitab al-ashribah* no. 3680). In far more extreme cases, death could be imposed on those who habitually defied the mandates on alcoholic beverages. *Ahadith* of Dawud, Tirmidhi, Ahmad ibn Hanbal (d. 855), and Ibn Majah (d. 886–7) claim those found guilty of repeated drunkenness may be executed but only after the fourth offense though some Shi'ite scholars claim after the third offense death could be imposed (Khu'i #2804). The Shafi'i legal manual, *Reliance of the Traveller*, asserts capital punishment for drinking was superseded by *ahadith* found in collections such as Dawud and Tirmidhi (662; Abu Dawud *Kitab Hudud* no. 4485). In the one case in the *ahadith* in which a man was discovered to have broken the law for a fourth time, the Prophet Muhammad commuted the sentence of death. Lashings and beatings became the foremost punishment (*hadd*) means of disciplining drinkers.

Inebriation does not release individuals from certain acts committed while under the influence either. Particularly important for jurists are crimes (*jinayat*) and divorce (*talaq*) perpetrated while in a state of intoxication. Divergence of opinion on the efficaciousness of a divorce pronounced while intoxicated or crimes committed while drunk are more abundant than the permissibility of drinking itself. If a divorce pronouncement is made by one in a state of intoxication, that statement is considered legally valid according to *The Reliance of the Traveller*, a Shafi'i collection of legal rulings (Ibn Naqib 557). The same applies to those who committed a crime while in the state of intoxication; they are still considered liable to retribution (Ibn Naqib 584). Nawawi (d. 1277) a prominent Shafi'i scholar in his *Minhaj al-talibin* particularizes further crimes whose punishments cannot be absolved if perpetrated while intoxicated: apostasy (*al-riddah*), fornication (*al-zina*), and defamation (*namimah* or *ghibah*) (436, 439, 442). Contrarily, some jurists ruled that pronouncements of divorce are not binding upon those intoxicated. Abu Hanifah, for instance, denounced the legitimacy of a declaration of divorce while a person is intoxicated (Rosenthal 122). Unfortunately, this is an oversimplification of the matter.

An important element figuring into the determination of culpability in these cases relates to the grounds for intoxication. At some juncture in the debate, some of the *fuqaha'* felt an assessment of the motives for intoxication must impact the genuineness of a divorce or crime committed while in such a state. Intoxication is therefore subdivided into "excused" and "unexcused" intoxication (Zahraa 253; Anderson 826). Anderson illustrates this dichotomy in a survey of outcomes from a theoretical homicide case where the accused is intoxicated (826). If the homicide is committed by a drunkard who was in such a state due to ingestion of a medicine resulting in intoxication or the intoxication was not caused purposefully, i.e. "excused," the accused is not liable for retribution or talion (*al-qisas*) (Anderson 826). Nearly all jurists and scholars (*'ulama'*) concur on this point, for Ibn Naqib indicates that divorces pronounced and crimes committed under such circumstances are indeed null and void (557, 584). Blameworthiness for "unexcused" intoxication, meaning willful intoxication, found jurists partitioned. Ibn Hazm (d. 1064) of the Zahiri *madhhab*, Abu Thawr (d. 854) and Muzani (d. 877) claimed as Shafi'i jurists, and jurists among the Shi'ah ruled that intoxication — despite a person reaching such a state intentionally — renders certain actions as void, divorce an example (Zahraa 254, fn. 64; Nawawi *Majmu'* vol. 18, 204–207). Other Shafi'i, Maliki, and some among the Hanafi did not think inebriation, if reached purposefully, granted pardon for any offense (Zahraa 254, fn. 65; Nawawi *Majmu'* vol. 18, 204–207; Malik ibn Anas *al-Mudawwanah* vol. 3, 79). Jurists were divided not only about the culpability of crimes and divorce committed while intoxicated on alcohol, but on narcotics as well, a subject which shall be addressed subsequently. This added a new dimension to the discourse which further complicated the issue, creating more fissures on the opinion of crimes committed whilst inebriated or in a narcotic stupor.

Punishment for imbibing alcoholic beverages was not strictly confined to the terrestrial domain, for *ahadith* discuss penalties awaiting those who transgressed this statute in the hereafter (*al-akhirah*). Perhaps the most foul punishment awaiting is *tinah al-khabal*. Drinkers will be forced to consume this substance which is described by the Prophet Muhammad as pus (*sadid*) from wounds of the inhabitants of hell, according to Abu Dawud (*Kitab al-ashribah* no. 3680). *Tinah al-khabal* according to the Shi'ah is even worse. *Ahadith* from *al-Kafi* describes the substance as discharge from "pudendums of fornicators [*furuj al-zunah*]." Whether or not a transgressor of the law is forced to suffer the torments of hell (*al-nar*) without reprieve is ambiguous in the *ahadith* literature. Some *ahadith* count those found guilty of drinking more than three times or those who refused to repent among the inhabitants of hell (*al-nar*). *Ahadith* from Muslim and other collectors only state that those who drank wine or became intoxicated while on earth would be forbidden from partaking of the heavenly wine (*Kitab al-ashribah* no. 2003). This would suggest that admittance into paradise was possible but certain blessings and rewards could be withheld. A piece of later literature illustrating this belief is the *Risalat al-ghufran* of al-Ma'arri (d. 1058). The story goes that the pre–Islamic poet al-'Asha is discovered residing in paradise. While he had gained admittance into heaven, al-'Asha could not partake in the wine of paradise, a direct result of his quaffing of wine during his life. Even with corporal and eternal punishments established, the struggle to purge Muslims of alcohol had just begun.

Before proceeding, a note on the varying degrees of intoxication warrants further explanation. Recall that legal schools developed qualities and characteristics denoting a person who is intoxicated. Muslims loyal to the Hanafi *madhhab* most definitely required delimitation on intoxication given that some alcoholic concoctions were tolerable. But why would other jurists have felt the necessity to delineate the manifestations of intoxication if intoxicants, regardless of their substance, quality, or quantity, were banned? The answer is plain. Consuming intoxicants must have not entirely dissipated if the *madhahib* felt the compulsion to define intoxication. Such a thesis is supported with ample historical evidence that drinking remained a pastime in Islamicate society.

The Qur'anic narratives on drunkenness and spirits were suppressive measures, yet this scheme did not have the effect for which it was intended. Baladhuri's (d. 892) *Ansab al-ashraf* and the *Nahj al-balaghah* recount a tormenting situation originating from 'Uthman's appointment of his relative Walid ibn 'Uqbah as governor of Kufah. Walid, a known dipsomaniac, apparently led a congregation of followers in prayer while in an inebriated condition, though some doubt the validity of this account (Baladhuri vol. 6, 143–146). Goldizher identifies the 'Abbasid Caliphs al-Mutawakkil (d. 861) and al-Qahir (d. 950) as two excessive drinkers despite the former's strict application of wine and intoxication laws upon other Muslims (64). The Caliphs and other public officials are not the only people known to have refused to relinquish the pleasures of certain intoxicating drinks.

Throughout the centuries, both groups and individuals have circumvented or flouted the mainstream position forbidding the consumption of intoxicating drinks. The Isma'ili heresiographer Abu Tammam (Yusuf ibn Muhammad al-Nisaburi) identified at least seven groups in the *Bab al-shaytan* of his work known to consume wine: Bayhasiyyah, Dahhakiyyah, Mubayyidah, Mansuriyyah, Ya'furiyyah, and the Ashab al-Ra'y. Sufyan Thawri (d. 778), a second generation Muslim (*tabi'i*), a jurist, a memorizer (*hafiz*) and commentator of the Qur'an, was known to drink *nabidh*. While some forms of *nabidh* were not intoxicating, Ibn Qutaybah emphasizes that the drink would "redden his cheeks," indicating that perhaps some alcoholic content was present in Sufyan Thawri's *nabidh* (70). Opponents of wine and intoxicants even openly admitted that such a practice did not lessen the character or creditability of all those who consumed intoxicants. When asked who the most "outstanding [*khiyar*]" from among the Kufans was, al-Shafi'i pointed to the drinkers of *nabidh* (Qutaybah 71). A similar tale of the Shi'ite Imam Zayd ibn 'Ali, (d. 740) is found in the literature of Zaydi opponents. He is accused have having consumed *nadidh* though Imam Muhammad al-Baqir (d. 735) doubts the authenticity of such allegations, which sheds light on an important aspect of identifying sects and individuals as wine drinkers (Lalani 122). Caution must be exercised when reading many of these accounts of those said to have partaken in bacchian pleasures. Since the consumption of wine was seen as one of the most flagrant violations of the law for many Muslims, accusing individuals and groups of consuming intoxicants had the effect of discrediting and delegitimizing. Both Sunni and Shi'ite utilized this tactic when attacking views aberrant from their own.

The maturation of wine poetry (*khamriyyah*) during the Umayyad and 'Abbasid epochs further attests to the persistence of potables in Islamicate society. Wine poetry penned before and throughout the Umayyad dynasty remained akin to pre–Islamic poetry but possessed significant idiosyncrasies. Poets composing immediately following the enshrinement of Islamic principles found great difficulty adhering to the anti-wine injunctions. Expressions of these tribulations can be found in the poetry of Abu Mihjan al-Thaqafi, who was whipped at the command of 'Umar on numerous occasions for drinking (Ashtiany 223). Drunken revelry was common in the courts of Umayyads with days being specifically dedicated to imbibing in alcoholic pleasures (Ashtiany 224). Goldizher even asserts that it would not have been extraordinary to encounter a wine party in a mosque during Umayyad rule (64).

Al-Akhtal (d. 710), al-Uqayshir al-Asadi (d. 700), Abu al-Hindi, and al-Walid ibn Yazid (d. 744) are the most significant wine poets during the Umayyad period, but scores of others, including the school of poets from Kufah, contributed to the production of wine poetry. Wine poetry (*khamriyyah*) became a completely independent genre under the Umayyads. Al-Walid ibn Yazid, an Umayyad prince, is cited as one of the major influences on the wine poets and poetry. Much of the content in the wine poetry of the Umayyad period resembles that of pre–Islamic poetry. Sensory descriptions of wine are common as well as the effects of wine upon its partakers, but continued in the poetry of the Umayyads is a clear sense of bitterness and renunciation of the restrictions against wine and drunkenness. This conflict is typified in a piece by Ibn Harmah,

> The Prophet's descendant forbids me wine and gives me noble teaching; He says, "Abstain from it and leave it alone, for fear of God, not for fear of man." Yet how can I abstain from it, when my love for it is a love which has gained control over my frame? For me, the comfort of what is lawful is evil and my soul's comfort lies in the evil of what is forbidden [qtd. Harb 226].

Wine poetry reached a pinnacle under the 'Abbasids with the works of the *khamriyyah* champion Abu Nuwas (d. 815). Both his artistry and his passion for wine can be seen in his entire corpus of poetry with *Wa-Lahin Laha-ni* being a prime exemplar. Abu Nuwas sought out stupefaction on occasion saying, "Give me to drink till you see me think that a rooster is a donkey" (qtd. in Rosenthal 96). Though his ardor of wine is strong, some of his poems still exhibit contrition over his drunken behaviors as in the final lines of *Wa-Khaymati Naturin* when he states, "I woke in the morning to curse [my] drunkenness [*sukr*], though drunkenness [*sukr*] had been 'generous' to me — how often has 'generosity' been a burden to you" (qtd. in Kennedy 271, 278–9). While Abu Nuwas is credited as the dominant wine poet of the time, al-Jahiz (d. 868–9) and Muslim ibn Walid greatly contributed to the growth and prestige of the wine poetry in the 'Abbasid era. Characteristics of wine poetry developed in the writings Abu Nuwas lasted as wine poetry spread to Muslim Spain and other regions of Islamicate society. Poetry written during the rule of the Fatimid dynasty of North Africa demonstrates Nuwas' impact with Isma'ili Shi'ite poet Tamim ibn al-Muizz (d. 984–5) being a prime example of that influence. Images and symbols of wine poetry eventually were adopted by the Sufis. Images of intoxication and wine were transformed from literal to metaphorical, mystical expressions of love and union with the Divine which will be addressed later. However, some Sufis retained their physical desires for wine as a means of initiating states of transcendence.

Wine, alcohol, and intoxication carried with them a socio-religious stigma but ceased to ever really disappear from Islamicate society. Edicts aimed at ceasing wine production and sales, typically in an effort to restrain moral depravity associated with wine drinking and intoxication, crop up in various corners of Islamicate society nearly every century. The Fatimid ruler Hakim (d. 1021) of Egypt in the 11th century, a son of Saladin and ruler of Damascus in the 12th century, and Mamluk Sultan Baybars (d. 1277) in the 13th century all issued statutes against wine and intoxication despite Islamic precedents against such practices (Hamarneh 236). Many authors claim that Muslim physicians and alchemists, Ibn Sina (d. 1037), known as Avicenna; Jabir ibn Hayyan (d. 815?); Muhammad ibn Zakariya Razi (d. 925–935?), known as Rhazes; and al-Kindi (d. 866–874) to name a few, advanced the process of distillation and experimented with alcoholic substances.[7] Even the word itself, alcohol, originates from the Arabic *al-kuhl*. Ibn Battutah (d. 1369 or 1377) the great 14th traveler records a number of events in which he witnesses drinking and intoxication. The *A'in-e Akbari*, a Persian, administrative document written during the reign of the Moghul

Emperor Jalal al-Din Muhammad Akbar in the 16th century, mentions the process of distillation in order to produce highly alcoholic beverages.

While wine and alcohol certainly stand out as the trademarks of intoxication in the Islamic tradition, drug induced intoxication figures into the image of intoxication just as much as alcoholic intoxication. Poppy, opium, and heroin; hemp, hash, or cannabis; and *qat* are the dominant narcotics mentioned in Islamic literature. Qur'an and *ahadith* dispense little knowledge of these drugs, for many were foreign to the Prophet Muhammad and his early followers. Islamic medical texts, which were based on Greek medical treatises, provide the bulk of knowledge of narcotics in Islam. Legal texts and poetry paint vivid pictures of the use of narcotics, as well. Narcotics have been scrutinized — legally, socially, morally, and medically — nearly as microscopically as wine and alcohol. Therefore, the image of intoxication projected from drugs will be homogeneous to the image cast by wine and alcohol.

Muslim encounters with narcotics did not begin until a few centuries following the death of the Prophet Muhammad. This, of course, did not mean narcotics were unknown in the ancient world. Opium and poppy were known to many cultures including the Persians, Indians, and Mesopotamians. According to Hamarneh, the use of narcotics, specifically opium, is mentioned in the earliest of Greek literature, the *Iliad* and the *Odyssey* (227). Greek physicians wrote extensively on opium and poppy describing assorted species of poppy, medical applications of poppy, as well as the injurious side effects, such as intoxication. Initial encounters between Muslims and narcotics date back to the 9th century. 'Ali ibn Sahl Rabban al-Tabari (d. 855) wrote the *Firdaws al-hikmah*, the first major medical text by a Muslim author, which describes the applications and lethality of opium. It was not until the 10th century that interaction between Islam and narcotics occurred on a larger scale with a number of legal and medical works being dedicated to the subject from that time forward.

Narcotic terminology is equally as broad as the lexicon on wine and alcohol. *Banj*, *hashish/hashishah*, *afyun* (opium), and *qinnab/qunnab* (cannabis) are the names which appear recurrently throughout Islamic literature on drugs. Though some of these terms were technical, such as *qinnab*, *hashish* itself was a nickname and, what's more, authors often used terms indiscriminately with little precision (Rosenthal 19–21). *Banj*, for instance, referred to narcotics in general. It was often employed to speak of *hashish* in some instances but henbane in other texts. *Saykaran*, a second term referring to henbane, and *barsh*, a mixture of narcotics — sometimes opium and other times *hashish*— were terms employed with a great deal of frequency in the legal literature. While the list of narcotics is modest compared to drinks, metaphorical and euphemistic names of drugs are abundant. *Kif/kayf* (pleasure), *ghubayra'* (dust colored), *al-khadra'* (a reference to the color green) are a sample of the myriad of figurative names applied to various narcotics. Rosenthal provides a list of names for *hashish* and other narcotics from an unnamed source along with a well known list of appellations of narcotics from al-Badri's (d. 1489) *Rahat al-arwah fi al-hashish wa al-rah* (35–40). Different names for narcotics are enumerated by region and profession, but Rosenthal doubts the authenticity of all of the sobriquets listed.

The intoxicating effects after using anyone of the narcotics thus far discussed had long been recorded even before drug use began plaguing Muslims. Early medical texts describe the effects of narcotics in detail. Ibn Wahshiyyah's (d. 930–1) *Book of Poisons* (*Kitab al-sumum*) describes bodily reactions to various poisons introduced by means of ingestion, inhalation, or even by sight. Hellebore and coriander are both identified as producing "intoxication" and "drunkenness," respectively, in those who are poisoned or overdose with such products (Levey 93, 99). Traits of narcotic intoxication resemble many of those of alcoholic

intoxication, including the terminology. Badri adduced a few odes on narcotics and intoxication. Aybak al-Dimashqi (d. 1398) said, "They have broken it (*hashish*) into pieces,
enabling it to cause drunkenness [*sukra*] to settle in them," and in an assault on *hashish* Ibn
Ghanim (d. 1279–80) says, "The drug [*hashish*] has settled down in you and through its
intoxication [*sukr*] you have turned to walking as does someone born blind, feeling his way
around" (qtd. in Rosenthal 60, 168–9). *Sukr* and its derivations were applied to intoxication
from alcohol and wine but also to the state produced by narcotics.

Literature concerning drugs augmented the vocabulary of intoxication with additional
words to describe narcotic intoxication. *Nashwah*, from the verb *nashiya*, is a term Rosenthal
treated as analogous to alcoholic intoxication (*sukr*) and a descriptor of being "high" on a
narcotic. Evidence suggests that this term is near in meaning with *sukr*, for *nashwah* is commonly applied in conjunction with *al-khamr* although Ibn Taymiyyah (d. 1328) did use the
term when discussing narcotics. Based on this evidence, Rosenthal postulated that *nashwah*
must mean intoxication which is also the definition provided by Wehr (1135). The second
term of importance is *mastul*. *Mastul* (one intoxicated), rendered *masatil* in its plural form,
coming from the verbal form *satala* (intoxicated [by *hashish*]) was the chief term utilized in
the description of narcotic intoxication (Wehr 478). *Mastul* and its cognates were used by
a number of authors including al-Badri, Ibn Abi al-Surur al-Bakri (d. 1653), Aybak al-
Safadi (d. 1363) in *Wafi bi al-wafayat*, Ibn al-Wardi (d. 1349), and many others, according
to Rosenthal. While it is probable that some regarded the *sukr* and *mastul* as synonymous,
that phenomenon was not universal. The *Fawat al-fayat* of Ibn Kutubi (d. 1363) presents
a poem ascribed to the Islamic scholar Ibn Sayyid al-Nas (d. 1334). In said poem, al-Nas
enumerates many of the distasteful qualities of the *al-sufiya* which include dancing (*al-raqs*)
but more importantly for this discourse intoxication from alcohol (*al-sukr*) and narcotics
(*al-satl*) (Ibn Kutubi vol. 3, 291). In accordance with Rosenthal's assessment, it is clear that
some did not equate the state of alcoholic intoxication as tantamount with narcotic, or this
case specifically *hashish*, intoxication. Further proof of this appraisal is provided in legal
debate on narcotics.

Hashish and narcotic consumption escalated after Muslims first encountered such drugs
in the 9th and 10th centuries. Addiction became a problem in many cities, and it was not
long until Islamic scholars were forced to address the legal status of narcotics. On the one
hand, opponents of narcotics appealed to the earlier debates on wine and intoxication finding
those prior rulings to be the basis of adjudication on narcotics. Jurists permitting the use
of narcotics, contrarily, did so using argumentation and reasoning not exercised by the jurists
whose opinions on what was to be counted as an intoxicant was less stringent. Of further
interest were the jurists who opposed wine but permitted narcotics, creating a position
unprecedented in prior legal discourses on intoxicating substances.

Argumentation against the legitimacy of narcotics harkens back to the debate on
wine and alcohol. Islamic scholars and jurists, whether as opponents or proponents, agreed
on the intoxicating effects narcotics had upon users (Rosenthal 107). Given that narcotics
cause intoxication, anti-narcotic jurists appealed to the multiple *ahadith* of the Prophet
Muhammad with such pronouncements as "Every intoxicant is forbidden" (Dawud *Kitab
al-ashribah* no. 3679). Ibn Taymiyyah of the Hanbali *madhhab* and al-Dhahabi (d. 1348)
of the Shafi'i *madhhab*, a student of Ibn Taymiyyah, both came to the conclusion that any
product whose consumption results in intoxication of any form is an intoxicant (*muskir*)
and is outlawed (al-Dhahabi 91). These two are representative of the scholars whose analyses
led to the prohibition of narcotics. They are not representative, unlike the discussion on

wine, of their *madhahib*, for dissention of opinion within a legal school occurred with greater frequency on the issue of narcotics as compared to wine. Al-Qarafi (d. 1285), a Maliki jurist discussed below, ruled in favor of narcotics as does Nawawi, a Shafi'i. And though narcotic usage had many zealous opponents, most texts express a general laxity toward narcotic usage compared to wine and alcohol.

Those advocating the use of narcotics came from an array of the *madhahib*, and defended their opinions using two fundamental strategies. Nawawi, who vehemently prohibited wine, permitted the use of *hashish* in small amounts even though he acknowledged its ability to intoxicate (Zarkashi qtd. in Rosenthal 192).[8] Nawawi's justification was based on the premise that plants (*nabat*) are not impure (*najis*). Additionally, the *Reliance of the Traveller* asserts solid (*jamid*) intoxicants are pure (*tahir*) while liquid intoxicants are considered *najis* (Ibn Naqib 94).[9] Rosenthal indicates another Shafi'i, Ibn 'Imad al-Aqfahsi (d. 1405), concurred with Nawawi (105). Since narcotics, being plants whose substance is a solid material, are not impure, so they may be consumed in small amounts. Classifying narcotics as pure was one of the main grounds *fuqaha'* justifying the permissibility of narcotics. Narcotics, unlike wine, were never mentioned in the Qur'an and *ahadith*. Silence from the Prophet Muhammad and the Qur'an became the impetus for scholars to declare that what was not forbidden must be permissible. Ibn Kathir (d. 1373) records this principle in his *Bidayah wa nihayah*: "Forbidding what is not forbidden is forbidden [*haramun tahrimu ghayir wa al-harami*]" (vol. 17, 619). Many proponents of *hashish*, *banj*, and opium, along with *nabidh*, found this to be a compelling maxim. Even opponents, such as Ibn Taymiyyah, could not easily relinquish the sense of such a postulation (Rosenthal 101). These would be the strongest arguments for the permissibility of narcotics. Although Twelver Shi'ite scholars considered opium and hemp as *tahir* (ritually pure), they were nonetheless considered *haram* (prohibited) on the basis of *'aql* (reasoning).

An intriguing argument for the permissibility of narcotics was unearthed by Rosenthal in a short treatise on *hashish* by al-Zarkashi (d. 1392) and figures into this discussion. The main protagonist of this case was a Maliki jurist by the name of al-Qarafi. Al-Qarafi proposed that a narcotic (*murqid*) that is classified as intoxicating (*sukr*) must be only so labeled if it accomplishes the following two effects: interfere or befuddle the senses and create a sense of happiness or "confidence" (Zarkashi qtd. in Rosenthal 181–182). Wine certainly does both with ample evidence of the latter quality; however, al-Qarafi doubts the ability of a narcotic, such as *hashish* or *banj*, to instill a sense of confidence or joy. He concluded that since narcotics do not bring on a sense of joy or confidence, narcotics are to be deemed as merely corruptive (*mufsid*) (Zarkashi qtd. in Rosenthal 182). Certainly, al-Qarafi's ruling was on the periphery of judgments regarding narcotics, but its uniqueness illustrates the complexity narcotics and intoxication presented to Islamic scholars.

Just as the legalists quarreled over the legality of narcotics, so too did they squabble over the punishments for taking or becoming intoxicated with a narcotic. Forty or eighty lashes was the standard punishment (*hadd*) for consuming alcoholic intoxicants; thus, *fuqaha'* who equated the intoxication of narcotics to that of alcohol affirmed that the same punishment of lashes was applicable to those indicted of drug use. Ibn Taymiyyah, for instance, clung to this position. However, some jurists concluded that a different form of punishment referred to as *ta'zir* was recommended. *Ta'zir* means punishment, but unlike *hadd*, it was not strictly stipulated in Qur'an or *ahadith*. *Ta'zir* was typically less severe than *hadd* punishment and was decided upon by the particular judge (*qadi*) assessing the case. Shafi'i and Hanafi *fuqaha,'* such as Abu Hanifah, recommended the punishment of *ta'zir* for those becoming intoxicated on narcotics (Rosenthal 124–126). The culpability for divorce and crimes committed while intoxicated on narcotics is also reminiscent of debate that took place over culpability in cases involving a drunk. To name every figure to weigh in on the matter is far beyond the scope of this outline. Rosenthal and Camara have provided excellent studies on the actors involved in the disputations over narcotics and provided countless resources for more penetrating investigations.

An affinity between narcotics and wine is not only visible in the legal debates but extends to artistic grounds in the expression of poets. Narcotic poetry is minuscule compared to *khamriyyah* or even pre-*khamriyyah* poetry, and a great deal of this class of poetry focuses on one particular narcotic, *hashish*. Rosenthal railed such poetry as "repetitive," "perfunctory," "apologetic," lacking "exuberance," and not praised like much of the wine poetry which he sees as having an "honorable history" before Islam and remained "cherished by the highest social strata" following the spread of Islam (141–142). Despite Rosenthal's negative assessment, *hashish* and other narcotic poetry are reminiscent of wine poetry exposing the habits of users, the effects drugs have upon its user both favorable and harmful, and descriptions of narcotics and the intoxication brought on through usage. The lionization of *hashish* remains unparalleled to the poetry of Safi al-Din al-Hilli (d. 1339–1350?). Descriptions of *hashish*, its benefits, its advantages over the use of wine, and the intoxication which accompanies its use are all topics of exploration in his poetry. Appreciation for his loyalty to *hashish* can only be achieved by reading his poetry, but some of the following lines taken from his *Diwan* assist in portraying his feelings toward *hashish*:

> In the purse, not in the cup, I have a wine whose taste or smell makes me drunk [*askaru*]. The text of the Holy Writ has not forbidden it, neither has there been consensus in the law on its censure. Obviously useful, it possesses intoxication [*nashwah*] that saves the souls from their worries. The gratitude owed to it is greater than the drunkenness cause by it [*sukriha*], and its usefulness is greater than the sin of using it [629; qtd. in Rosenthal 172].
>
> It (*hashish*) has no hangover [*khumar*], except subtle thinking ... intoxication [*nashwah*] that the intoxication [*nashwah*] of wine [*al-rah*] is unable to offer [629; qtd. in Rosenthal 172].

Rosenthal provides a plethora of lines dedicated to the negative aspects of narcotics with figures such as Ibn al-'Afif al-Tilimsani (d. 1291) and Ibn Ghanim at the forefront of antagonists against narcotics. Al-Tilimsani stated that, "*Hashish* holds no advantage for its eater" (vol. 17, 621). Perhaps his harshest attack comes in the following lines which were probably taken from another source,

> This poor one whom you see
> Like a chick thrown to the ground featherless
> Has been killed by hashish intoxication,
> Killing being the custom of hashish [qtd. in Rosenthal 91].

No narcotic has garnered as much attention as *hashish* for the sole reason of a group of Nizari Isma'ili Shi'ites. The *Hashishin*, or Assassins as they are more commonly known, were a group of Muslims operating out of their fortress of Alamut between the 11th and 13th centuries. While there is no doubt that assassinations were carried out by its members, their notoriety arises from the accounts stating devotees were heavily intoxicated with *hashish* enticing them to carry out assassinations; hence their moniker *Hashishin*. Scholarship on this group has demonstrated the tales of drug use and intoxication were largely fabricated by Westerners, such as Marco Polo (Daftary 84). Contrary to the popular myth, the leader of this group, Hassan-i Sabbah (d. 1124), was stringent in the application of Islamic law. As proof, Daftary relates that Hassan had one of his own sons executed for consuming wine (145). A complete survey of the Hashishin can be found in the many works of Daftary but none more so than his work *The Assassin Legends*.

Drugs and alcohol remain the archetypal substances to usher in states of ecstasy and intoxication. A rather curious commodity that caught the attention of Muslim jurists for a time was coffee. Generally regarded to have been introduced into a number of centrally situated Islamic lands during the 15th century, coffee became both immediately popular and immediately controversial. Opponents of coffee despised its consumption for a variety of reasons. For example, coffee was touted as physically harmful and gatherings of coffee drinkers engaged in questionable or reprehensible behaviors, such as gambling and drug use (Hattox 43, 103–111). One strategy employed by some opponents of coffee was to label the substance as an "intoxicant" to ensure its prohibition. Coffee enthusiasts did not deny that it induced a mild form of euphoria (*marqahah*) according to al-Jaziri (d. 1568) (93). Likening coffee to wine persuaded few jurists and even fewer among the populous. Nearly everyone was acutely aware that the effects of coffee in no way resembled those of alcohol or drugs. Jurists found that classifying coffee as an intoxicant was quite outlandish. Furthermore, since nearly everyone drank coffee, legal scholars applied the principle of consensus (*ijma'*) as an auxiliary justification for coffee's permissibility. Tobacco underwent the same legal analysis as coffee with a few eccentric jurists labeling the product as intoxicating (Gerhan 1360). Overwhelmingly, tobacco too was identified as a product that induced a mild euphoria, not full blown intoxication, regardless of the amount smoked. Eventually, smoking was prohibited by most of the leading Sunni and Shi'ite scholars, not on the grounds that it intoxicated, but rather, on the basis of the Qur'anic principle that anything that causes harm to one's health is prohibited (2:195; 4:29).

Legal, religious, medical, and moral discussion on earthly or palpable intoxication has concerned Muslims, both pedestrians and scholars, from the time of the Prophet Muhammad to the present. A great deal of ink and words have been utilized to construct an image of intoxication in Islam that is expansive in scope yet intricate in detail. However, this remains only one dimension of the image of intoxication, the literal. In the succeeding section, attention will now be drawn to an image of intoxication not originating from mind-befogging substances.

Emotional and Mystical Intoxication

Worldly intoxication is a path anyone can travel who so desires it. Eating, drinking, or smoking an intoxicant can deliver most any individual into a state of inebriation. Even the name itself, intoxication, elicits notions of unruly behavior and less than reputable characters. Intoxication derived from wine and narcotics, however, only captures a fraction of the image of intoxication in any religious tradition, including Islam. Emotions and communion with the transcendental can lead individuals to an altogether different form of intoxication with psychological and spiritual intoxication override one's ability to control their actions and expressions. The distinction was best summarized in a short axiom, "There are two intoxications: intoxication of passion and intoxication of wine [*sukran-i sukru hawa wa sukru mudamah*]" (qtd. in Homerin 227). To this point the latter has been covered extensively. This section shall explore the former, intoxication of the mind and the soul simulated by emotion and experience.

Examples of emotional intoxication are found in the first source of knowledge for Muslims, the Qur'an. Many Qur'anic commentators and jurists preoccupied themselves with the intoxication resulting from wine and other substances, but this is not the only means by which an individual may come to be intoxicated according to the Qur'an. *Sakrah, sukarra,* and *sukara* are terms found in four other passages but they do not refer to alcoholic intoxication but emotional experiences leading to stupefaction. 50:19 speaks of the intoxication of death, "And death's agony [*sakrah*] comes in truth; that is what thou wast shunning!" 15:72 and 15:15 use *sakrah* and *sukirrat*, respectively, to mean confusion or "bedazzlement." Sahl al-Tustari (d. 896) in his *Tafsir* explains that this type of intoxication or confusion is brought upon by one's fascination with the world or the here and now while disregarding what waits beyond this world (105). He adds that obsession with the world is just as dangerous as an intoxicant (*muskir*) like wine (Tustari 105). *Surah al-Hijr* (The Chapter of the Rocky Tract) states, "Yet would they say, 'Our eyes have been dazzled [*sukirrat*]; nay, we are a people bewitched!'" Passages foretelling the Day of Judgment tell of the masses being plagued by intoxication. Qur'an 22:2 discusses the coming of the Hour (*al-sa'ah*) and how people will be intoxicated/drunk (*sukara*) but not by alcohol, rather with fear, confusion, and anger; hence "you will see people intoxicated [*sukara*] yet they are not intoxicated [*sukara*]." None of the states of intoxication were brought upon by the consumption of a drug or wine. Instead, the weight of events sparked an emotional response so profound as to cause individuals to act inebriated.

Emotional and spiritual intoxication were not the only ways in which one may find oneself inebriated. Tustari records a dialogue between himself and Sufi visitor, Abu Hamzah Muhammad ibn Ibrahim al-Bazzaz (d. 902), on matters of intoxication (Bowering 78). In the commentary following verse 67 of *Surah al-Nahl*, Hamzah mentions three forms of intoxication in addition to that of wine. They are the intoxication of youths (*shabab*), possessions (*mal*), and power (*saltanah*) (Tustari 109). To these four, Tustari appends two further forms of intoxication. The first is the intoxication of recognition or attention which befalls those in devotional practice, and the second is drunkenness of the learned individual who loves the world culminating into six forms of intoxication (109). Tustari's enumeration of so many varieties of inebriation may be based on his aversion of *sukr*. Commenting on verse 20:81, Tustari surmises that all types of intoxication are dangerous (126). However, most of the substances resulting in intoxication do not necessarily appear immediately dangerous in Tustari's scheme, wine excluded. Rather, it is the overindulgence, even in that which is beneficial, that can result in inebriation (126). For it is when one becomes supersaturated, by power, possession, the world, etc., that God is forgotten (126).

Muslim lexicographers did not neglect the emotional and spiritual aspects of intoxication when they defined the term *sukr*. The *Taj al-arus* quotes the same line of poetry describing the two types of intoxication in the definition of *sukr* and adds that intoxication can be brought on by either anger (*ghadab*) or passion/love (*'ishq*) (vol. 3, 273). Terms, such as *nashwah, thamil, mastul*, can be used to describe inebriation caused by the use of wine, drugs, and other substances.[10] Literature and poetry expressing spiritual intoxication repeatedly employ the term *sukr* or one of its cognates as opposed to the assortment of language for earthly intoxication. Within the Sufi mystical tradition, the term took on special meaning and a new set of terminology relating to intoxication developed. Proof of this can be found in three types of Islamic texts dedicated to the discussion of spiritual intoxication, Sufi poetry, biographies, and manuals.

Before setting out to explore the spiritual and mystical image of intoxication, understanding what the mystical tradition of Islam entails is paramount. Muslims believe that in the hereafter they will be reunited with God resulting in an unparalleled proximity to the Divine. In the Sufi tradition, through various techniques and methods, it is possible to gain proximity and even unity with the Divine while still alive. Methods include the performance of *dhikr*, a remembrance or invocation of God, done for the purpose of annihilating (*fana'*) the practitioner's self (*nafs*) to create uninhibited closeness or unity (*tawhid*) with God. For many Sufis, anything that blocks one from attaining this proximity is a veil to be removed. Experiences of this proximity and unity not easily conveyed by images or words, but words must be employed to convey the experience to others who seek this end.

Images of intoxication and wine were both absorbed from the literature and the poetry of the *Jahiliyyah* in the mystical tradition of Islam to depict their experiences of the Divine. Many poets of the *Jahiliyyah* spoke of longing for the beauty of a beloved and drinking wine to usher in ecstasy. The experience of unification a Sufi has with the Divine is usually described, in both poetry and manuals, as a feeling of ecstasy (*wajd*) or rapture (*ghalabah*) so great its descriptions and feelings match those of persons who are intoxicated. Wine was another theme adopted then morphed into a metaphoric device by the Sufi. Wine is the symbol of the love (*'ishq*) of God or rays emanating from the Divine's face (*wajh*) intoxicating the drinker.[11] Intoxication not only affects the mind of the drinker but especially the heart (*qalb*). It makes sense that the mystics of Islam would adopt language of such a "subversive" nature, according to Kueny (106). Earthly intoxication is a violation of the natural order; Sufi attempts to gain such proximity to God on earth are beyond the limits of typical human ability (Kueny 106). Opting to assume such dissident language had some degree of intentionality as well. Sufis applied these terms to chide the orthodoxy of the *fuqaha'* and their stringent understanding of the human relationship with God while on earth. This, in part, explains some of the long-standing tension that has existed between Muslims who demand strict adherence to the traditions, orthodoxy, and legal aspects of Islam and the Sufis.

Two classical works of *tabaqat*, Muhammad Sulami's (d. 1021) *Tabaqat al-sufiyah* and Abu Nu'aym Isfahani's (d. 1038) *Hilyat al-awliyya'*, identify individuals and their line of followers of various mystical paths (*tariqah*). These early biographers identify two of the most renowned mystics of early Islam, Abu al-Qasim al-Junayd (d. 910) and Abu Yazid al-Bistami (d. 874–5), who is sometimes referred to as Bayazid. Junayd and Bistami have traditionally been recognized as the propagators of two techniques or ways of achieving mystical union, sobriety (*sahw*) and intoxication, respectively.[12]

Mystics and mystical orders were often identified based on one of these two paths (*tariqah*) to achieve unity with the Divine. Mansur al-Hallaj (d. 922), for instance, is arguably the most controversial Muslim mystic of the intoxicated persuasion being executed for his rapturous utterances (*shathiyat*) viewed by the Muslim mainstream as heretical.[13] Abu al-Husayn (or al-Hasan) al-Nuri (d. 907–8), Abu Bakr al-Shibli (d. 944–6), Abu al-Hasan al-Kharaqani (d. 1033–4), Abu Sa'id ibn Abi al-Khayr (d. 1033), Abu Hamid ibn Abu Bakr Ibrahim (d. 1220), better known as Farid al-Din 'Attar, 'Umar ibn al-Farid (d. 1235), Ibn al-'Arabi (d. 1240), Jalal al-Din Muhammad Rumi (d. 1273), Yunus Emre (d. 1320–1) and Khwaja Muhammad Hafez-e Shirazi (or Hafiz) (d. 1389–92) are some who have been associated with Sufi concept of intoxication.[14] The classification system of sober and drunk mystics remained fixed throughout the centuries resulting in broad categorization of mystics and orders into these restrictive classes.

The dichotomy of sober and intoxicated is not indubitable; many individuals may have experiences which may be classified as "drunken" but recognize the validity of sober experiences and strive for such occasions. Burhan al-Din Gharib (d. 1337) of the Chishti Order once described the ideal Sufi master and included that, "His way is sometimes intoxicated and sometimes sober" (qtd. in Ernst 124). Ibn al-'Arabi, Shibli, 'Umar ibn al-Farid, and Farid al-Din 'Attar had occasions of drunkenness resulting from the joy of experiencing the Divine, but did not necessarily believe this to be the only state to achieve such ends or endorse this path. According to Kueny, only in a state (*hal*) of sobriety can the moments of intoxication be contrasted and appreciated (106). Furthermore, many Sufis see instances of mystical union as a gift from the Divine and not at the command of the practitioner. Thus, experiences of intoxication may simply come upon a practitioner. Evidence of this can be found in Sufi manuals which shall be examined shortly. For every Sufi is a unique *tariqah* which for some may include regular episodes of intoxication and for others regular occasions of sobriety with rare and intermittent bouts of mystical intoxication, a position corroborated by Nasr (179). In the end, the identification as being a "drunk" or "sober" Sufi may have been based on which path the practitioner gravitated toward with greater frequency. With the two forms or paths established, Sufi manuals and poetry become the well spring from which understanding what mystical intoxication entails.

Sufi manuals and poetry provide the greatest insight into the meaning and degrees of spiritual intoxication. Manuals and poetry also connect the concept of intoxication to other mystical expressions, states, and feelings creating an expansive set of vocabulary that is often contrasted with the vocabulary of sobriety. Sufi manuals echo similar perspectives on the state of intoxication. Additionally, many writers proffer their own biases and inclinations favoring one particular condition, resulting in value judgments of one particular path over another. One of the earliest manuals that does not evaluate the soundness of one path over another is the *Kitab al-Luma'* written by Abu Nasr al-Sarraj (d. 988). Intoxication is similar to the state of absence (*ghaybah*) except intoxication is stronger according to al-Sarraj (340). He also relates intoxication to unconsciousness (*ghashyah*) but unlike *ghashya* intoxication continues while *ghashya* is momentary (340–341). In a later discussion on *al-qabd* (contraction) and *al-bast* (expansion), Sarraj claims that intoxication, along with sobriety and a handful of other states (*ahwal*), is a state reserved for those whose hearts deeply exalt (*ta'zim*) God (344).

Al-Qushayri's (d. 1074) *Risalah* which built upon al-Sarraj's work provides further details on the concept of intoxication with particular emphasis placed on its relation to absence (*ghaybah*). Qushayri distinguishes between two forms of intoxication: genuine and "incomplete" (Qushayri 44). Proper inebriation goes beyond absence, for only those who reach this state through the witnessing of God's beauty will be granted "mystical ecstasy" (Mojaddedi 5). To convince his audience that intoxication is an acceptable path, he highlights Qur'an 4:173 describing Musa (Moses) falling unconscious upon witnessing God flattening a mountain (45). He claims that if a prophet can succumb to the power of God then other types of absence, namely intoxication, must be acceptable (45). Qushayri finds value in both sobriety and intoxication judging them as equally legitimate paths for the practitioner (Qushayri 44–45). He provides a short line of poetry (*bayt*) to illustrate his point. Qushayri and al-Sarraj remained neutral on the matter of whether sobriety or intoxication is the superior means of experiencing true mystical bliss.

Other Sufi manuals and treatises do not remain objective on the question of which means of coming to know the Divine is best. Mojaddedi cites 'Ali Hujwiri (d. 1071–1077) and Abu Bakr Kalabadhi (d. 990 or 994–5), who discuss mystical drunkenness but encourage the procurement of a sober state. Kalabadhi's definition, in the *Kitab al-ta'arruf*, of intoxication does not vary significantly from his contemporary, Qushayri, as he states that intoxication is near absence. However, Kalabadhi offers a caveat: intoxication is absence from the ability to discriminate (*tamyiz*) from what is painful and what provides pleasure but is not absent from the thing itself. According to Mojaddedi, this definition of intoxication is then contrasted with two forms of sobriety (3–4). Kalabadhi concludes that while both sobriety and intoxication lead to divine rapture only the sober can differentiate between the painful and pleasant and willingly accept what is painful (Kalabadhi 111). Despite his advocacy for sobriety, Kalabadhi cites a poem on sobriety and intoxication relating that both states are granted only by God and cannot be controlled by the Divine seeker (Kalabadhi 112).

Hujwiri also favored sobriety over intoxication but wrote extensively on intoxication. His work the *Kashf al-mahjub* was the first major Sufi manual in Persian. Hujwiri identifies the Tayfuriyyah, a Sufi order and followers of Bistami, as the proponents of mystical inebriation (184). "Drunkenness means a reduction of human attributes [*naqs-i sifat-i bashariyyat*]," reports Hujwiri arguing in the stead of the Tayfuriyyah which are a hindrance to attaining true unity (qtd. in Mojaddedi 7). Since only through intoxication can human attributes, one's will, and self-control (*tadbir*) be annihilated, intoxication is the superior path, according to the Tayfuriyyah.

Hujwiri, a student of Junayd and self-adherent to the path of sobriety, responds that due to the drunkard's inability to maintain control and stability, the state of soberness is better. Hujwiri then offers a teaching from his master found in many texts maligning intoxication, "Intoxication is the playground of children while sobriety is the place of annihilation of men" (Mojaddedi 8; Nicholson 186). Mojaddedi suggests that Hujwiri's proclivity for sobriety sprang from a sober practitioner's ability to discriminate, which is validated by the *ahadith* cited by Hujwiri (9). Being drunk would only exacerbate the practitioner's capacity to discriminate and prevent unity.

Hujwiri, like Kalabadhi, distinguishes between two forms of sobriety but also two forms of intoxication. He states that one type of sobriety arising from negligence (*ghaflat*) is actually a degree of intoxication for it too cloaks the practitioner (Nicholson 187–188). He continues describing the two forms of intoxication, one brought upon by the "wine of affection [*mawaddah*]" and the other by "the cup of love [*muhabbah*]" (Nicholson 187). The former type being "caused" continues to make the practitioner aware of oneself; however, the latter is not caused thereby obliterating the self which is not intoxication at all but rather sobriety (187).

Interestingly, Hujwiri, in the same vein as Kalabadhi and Qushayri, ends his discussion by noting that, "Both sobriety and intoxication appear to be intruders [*tufayli*] ... the end of one is the beginning of the other, and beginning and end are terms that imply separation... In union all separations are negated" (Nicholson 188). Hujwiri and Kalabadhi works greatly augment the meaning of and perspectives on intoxication. Futhermore, despite their partiality for sobriety, both authors regard them as equal with Hujwiri elaborating that notions of sobriety and intoxication continue to restrain the Sufi from reaching true union. Partiality for sobriety, but the recognized value of occasional intoxication, would become the mainstream doctrine of many Sufis and Sufi orders.

The *al-Futuhat al-Makkiyyah* and *Tarjuman al-ashwaq* of Ibn al-'Arabi delve deeper into the nature of intoxication providing further particulars without calling into question the validity of intoxication as some of its precursors had done. In *al-Makkiyyah* Ibn al-

'Arabi defines intoxication as absence from all things that encumber joy, glee, and the "disclosure of wishes" (qtd. in Chittick 198). Ibn al-'Arabi partitions intoxication into three echelons: natural (tabi'i) intoxication, rational ('aqli) intoxication, and divine (ilahi) intoxication. Natural intoxication is the joy and happiness when the wishes of the individual are manifested in the individual's imagination and are under the control of the individual (Chittick 198). For those who reach this station (maqam), God permits the forms created in the imagination to remain as the individual passes into sobriety. Rational intoxication is intoxication originating from one's reason built upon the necessity of proof and demonstration (Chittick 198–199). Ibn al-'Arabi constructs a useful analogy to explain this type of intoxication: a weaver and a piece of cloth. The cloth has no knowledge of the weaver just as the individual has no knowledge of God without God informing the individual. Those who choose not to accept this knowledge are the intoxicated. Through faith the drunkard can be sobered and no longer disqualify from God what is attributed to God (Chittick 198). He ends his discussion on "rational" intoxication by stating that "natural intoxication is the intoxication of the faithful, while rational intoxication is the intoxication of the gnostics" (qtd. in Chittick 199). Divine intoxication is the third form of intoxication mentioned, but Ibn al-'Arabi spends far less time detailing this level. He refers to this as the form of intoxication of "the perfect among Men" (qtd. in Chittick 199). Intoxication is also mentioned in the odes of the Tarjuman al-ashwaq. Ibn al-'Arabi writes of God's disclosure through phenomena, lightning (al-barq) specifically, in the poem in which he addresses intoxication (Ibn al-'Arabi 20). Individuals experience "manifestations" of God's essence in different degrees (Ibn al-'Arabi 75). The first of these degrees is tasting (dhawq), followed by drinking (shrub), and then "quenching" (ri) (Chittick 393 n. 36). He then extends the scale of experience to a fourth stage which he identifies as intoxication (Ibn al-'Arabi 75). Ibn al-'Arabi sought a balance (i'tidal) of both sobriety and intoxication, a position held by many Sufi masters, as indicated in the earlier words of Burhan al-Din Gharib.

Expressions of mystical intoxication in the form of poetry illustrate drunken experiences much more intimately and elegantly than the definitions provided thus far. An example of quintessential intoxicated poetry can be found in the work of Mahmud Shabistari (d. 1320) entitled Gulshan-i Raz (The Secret Rose Garden). His poem "The Wine of Rapture" captures many of the elements of al-khamriyyah, but now are a reference to the Divine.

> The wine, lit by the ray of his face,
> Reveals the bubbles of form,
> Such as the material world and the soul-world,
> Which appear as veils to the saints.
> Universal reason seeing this is astounded,
> Universal soul is reduced to servitude.
> Drink wine, for the bowl is the face of the Friend
> Drink wine, for the cup is his eye, drunken and flown with wine.
> Drink wine, and be free from heart-coldness,
> For a drunkard is better than one self-satisfied [qtd. Lederer 56].

Shabistari's poetry recounts many experiences Sufis feel when overcome with the intoxicating love of the Divine. Wine is the intoxicating substance which originates from the face or beauty of God. Having imbibed this wine, the practitioner becomes astutely aware of the veil that separates him from the Divine. Only through the consumption of the love of God can the mystic become free of the barriers of "self-satisfaction" and have the Divine enter the heart (qalb). 'Umar ibn al-Farid is best known for his two works "The Wine Ode [*al-Khamriyyah*]" and "Poem of the Sufi Way [*Nazm al-suluk*] (or The Great Poem rhyming in T [*al-Ta'iyyah al-kubra*])" each teeming mystical language expressing the intoxicating effect of the Divine. He opens his "Wine Ode" with the quatrain (*ruba'i*), "In memory of the beloved [*habib*] we drank a wine [*mudamah*]; we were drunk [*sakir*] with it before the creation of the vine" (Homerin 47; Farid 82).

In the commentary of Ibn al-Farid's Ode, al-Qaysari explains that the beloved (*habib*) is God, and the wine a drink called *Zanjabil*, originating from the springs of *Salsabil*, a reference to Qur'an 76:17–18 (Homerin 54–55). The wine leads to intoxication, but intoxication that comes not from the "vine," i.e. earthly wine. Instead, this drunkenness resulted from "God's beauty due to God's eternal majesty" (qtd. in Homerin 57). He repeats these metaphors in the "Poem of the Sufi Way" (Homerin 75; Farid 23).

Supposing that Ibn al-Farid preferred intoxication from this one poem is erroneous. He, like mainstream Sufis, found enlightenment in his intoxication but strove for sobriety as exemplified in a later portion of the "Sufi Way": "I imagined sobriety as my perigee [*hadidi*], and intoxication / my ascent to her, with effacement my lote tree's end in space" (Homerin 141; Farid 37). In other words, sobriety is the end while intoxication is the path to that end. Ibn al-Farid's position is similar to the great Persian mystical poet, Rumi.

While Rumi is widely held as one of the greatest intoxicated Sufi poets, he never endorsed the use of earthly intoxicants to arrive at the spiritual level about which he speaks. Rosenthal points to some Sufis and Sufi groups known to revel in products, particularly *hashish*, to abet the onset of a mystical state (53–54). Rumi disavows the legitimacy of such practices and the intoxication resulting therein in his poem "Many Wines" taken from the *Mathnawi Ma'nawi* or *Masnavi* (*Spiritual Couplets*):

> There are thousands of wines that can take over our minds.
> Don't think all ecstasies are the same!
> Jesus was lost in his love for God.
> His donkey was drunk with barley.
> Drink from the presence of saints, not from those other jars
> [Rumi *Mathnawi* vol. 4, 561–562, lines 2684–2720].

In this piece, Rumi acknowledges the two forms of intoxication: earthly and mystical. Both types share a common feature of overcoming the mind, but he cautions the imbibers of the former. He endorses the drunkenness arising from the love of God, a drunkenness in which even the prophets of God reveled. It is impossible to recount all the utterances of mystical intoxication. Thousands of lines have been dedicated to the experiences of those in Divine rapture plus most Sufis, whether labeled sober or intoxicated, have had instances of mystical ecstasy.

Conclusion

Every image in the Islamic tradition has many perspectives of understanding. Intoxication touches on the spiritual, psychological, emotional, and physical planes of our being forcing us to address intoxication from theological, legal, and metaphysical positions to come to an understanding of this image. Too often attention is directed toward more tangible, unadorned portions of the portrait of intoxication leading to oversimplified and austere statements about Islam, such as "Islam prohibits intoxication." The mysteries and beauties of the spiritual image of intoxication are often forgotten or passed over. Only through a comprehensive understanding of each Islamic image can one come to understand the complexities teeming within all the captions of Islam. With a better understanding of each image, a fuller appreciation for Islam will be born.

Chapter Notes

1. In *The Islamic Understanding of Death and Resurrection*, Smith and Haddad present a tradition on the authority of Abu Layth al-Samarqandi who speaks of inhabitants of paradise drinking heavenly wine to the point of intoxication.

2. *Thamala* refers to something (typically water) being left over. The designation of *thamil* as intoxication makes sense in light of another derivative of *thamala*: *thamlah*. *Thamlah* refers to dates or grains left in water, the typical process by which many fermented beverages were concocted.

3. Near the conclusion of this research, a new study on the prohibition of alcoholic substances was published. Chapter five of *The Origins of the Shi'a: Identity, Ritual, and Sacred Space in Eighth-Century Kufa* by Najam Haider examines a few of the specifics on the prohibition of alcoholic beverages according to the four Sunni legal schools and two of the Shi'ite schools. Its overview of the Shi'ite rulings; information, organized by charts, categorizing the traditions on alcohol based on school and permission; and tracing the lines of authority of these transmissions make this study an important contribution to the understanding of the legal understanding of intoxicants but little in the way of intoxication.

4. *'Illa* is an important feature of Islamic law particularly for those who rely upon analogy (*qiyas*) as proof permissibility or proscription.

5. See "*Nabidh*" and "*Khamr*" in the *Encyclopaedia of Islam* and Kueny's *Rhetoric of Sobriety* for details on receptacles for *nabidh*.

6. Kueny provides an excellent study of wine consumption by and intoxication of the prophets in the Torah and Biblical literature. She examines these traditions parallel to the Qur'anic and Islamic portrayal of the prophets drawing out distinctions and commonalities between Jewish and Christian images of the prophets, wine, and intoxication versus the Islamic depiction of prophets and intoxication.

7. Forbes, R J. *A Short History of the Art of Distillation: From the Beginnings Up to the Death of Cellier Blumenthal* (Leiden: E.J. Brill, 1970). Forbes argues that while "Arab" alchemist improved the art of distillation, they did not work with alcohol nor does any "Arab" text disclose information pertaining to the distillation of alcohol.

8. Al-Zarkashi's treatise *Zahr al-'arish fi ahkam (tahrim) al-hashish* is compiled from a number of manuscripts and presented as a single text in Appendix B of Rosenthal's *The Herb*; see pages 9–11 for details on the manuscripts and pages 175–197 for the Arabic text. This text is also found in *Tres tratados árabes sobre el cannabis índica* by Indalecio Lozano Camara; see pages 73–112 for the Arabic text and pages 113–146 for the Spanish translation.

9. Sadly, this discourse does not allow for a detailed exposition on the legal discussion of wine and narcotics on the subject of cleanliness which itself is a protracted and labyrinthine topic.

10. *Mast*, along with its cognates, is the Persian term for intoxication. It is frequently used by poets and saints to express mystical intoxication and has been adopted into other languages, such as Urdu, for the same purpose.

11. *'Ishq* is the primary term employed for "love" in Sufi literature. However, encountering other terms for love and beloved are not uncommon either.

12. Mojaddedi challenges this broad categorization and the authenticity of the assertion that either were the true propagators of sober or drunken mysticism in the article "Getting Drunk with Abu Yazid or Staying Sober with Junayd: The Creation of a Popular Typology of Sufism."

13. His expressions and teachings may have largely contributed to the marginalization of the intoxicated path from both mainstream Islam and Sufi circles. He was executed for such sayings as "I am the Truth [*ana al-Haqq*]" and "Nothing is in my cloak but God [*Ma fi jubbati illa Allah*]." Both of these statements were taken to mean that al-Hallaj, during his intoxicating trances, equated himself with God but were, in reality, his expression of the union he experienced.

14. This includes a number of Sufis as categorized by Ibn Taymiyyah, in his *Majmu'ah al-rasa'il wa al-masa'il*, as "intoxicated."

Works Cited

Abu Dawud al-Sijistani, Sulayman ibn al-Ash'ath. *Sunan Abi Dawud*. Online.

Abu Nu'aym al-Isbahani, Ahmad ibn 'Abd Allah. *Hilyat al-awliyya' wa tabaqat al-asfiya'*. Bayrut: Dar al-Kitab al-'Arabi, 1967–1968.

Anderson, J.N.D. "Homicide in Islamic Law." *Bulletin of the School of Oriental and African Studies, University of London* 13.4 (1951): 811–828.

Arberry, A.J. *The Koran Interpreted.* New York: Simon & Schuster, c. 1955.

Ayoub, Mahmoud. *The Qur'an and Its Interpreters: Volume 1.* Albany: State University of New York Press, 1984.

Baladhuri, Ahmad ibn Yahya ibn Jabir. *Jumal min kitab ansab al-ashraf.* Ed. Suhayl Zakkar and Riyad Zirikli. Bayrut: Dar al-Fikr, 1996.

Bowering, Gerhard. *The Mystical Vision of Existence in Classical Islam: The Qur'anic Hermeneutics of the Sufi Sahl At-Tustari (d. 283/896).* Berlin: de Gruyter, 1980.

Bukhari, Muhammad ibn Isma'il al-. *Sahih al-Bukhari.* Online.

Chittick, William C. *The Sufi Path of Knowledge: Ibn al-'Arabi's Metaphysics of Imagination.* Albany: State University of New York Press, 1989.

Crone, Patricia. *God's Rule: Government and Islam.* New York: Columbia University Press, 2004.

Daftary, Farhad. *The Assassin Legends: Myths of the Isma'ilis.* London: Tauris, 1994.

Deuraseh, Nurdeen. "Is Imbibing *al-Khamr* (Intoxicating Drink) for Medical Purposes Permissible by Islamic Law?" *Arab Law Quarterly* 18¾ (2003): 355–364.

Devasahayam, Theresa W. "Islam as Cultural Influence." *Alcohol and Temperance in Modern History.* Ed. Jack S. Blocker et al. Santa Barbara: ABC-CLIO, 2003. 324–326.

Dhahabi, Muhammad ibn Ahmad al-. *Kitab al-kaba'ir.* Dar al-Khulafa,' 1995.

Ernst, Carl W. *Eternal Garden: Mysticism, History, and Politics at a South Asian Sufi Center.* Albany: State University of New York Press, 1992.

Farid, 'Umar ibn al-. *Diwan Ibn al-Farid.* al-Qahirah: Maktabat al-Qahirah 1951.

_____. '*Umar Ibn al-Farid: Sufi Verse, Saintly Life.* Trans. E. Homerin. New York: Paulist Press, 2000.

Fulton, A S. "Firuzabadi's 'Wine-List.'" *Bulletin of the School of Oriental and African Studies* 12.4 (1948): 579–585.

Goldziher, Ignaz. *Muslim Studies (Muhammedanische Studien).* Vol. 2. Ed. C R. Barber and Samuel M. Stern. London: Allen and Unwin, 1971.

Haider, Najam I. *The Origins of the Shi'a: Identity, Ritual, and Sacred Space in Eighth-Century Kufa.* New York: Cambridge University Press, 2011.

Hattox, Ralph S. *Coffee and Coffeehouses: The Origins of a Social Beverage in the Medieval Near East.* Seattle: University of Washington Press, 1985.

Hamarneh, Sami. "Pharmacy in Medieval Islam and the History of Drug Addiction." *Medical History* 16.3 (1972): 226–237.

Harb, F. "Wine Poetry." *'Abbasid Belles-Lettres.* Ed. Julia Ashtiany et al. Cambridge: Cambridge University Press, 1990.

Hujwiri, 'Ali ibn 'Uthman. *The Kashf al-mahjub: The Oldest Persian Treatise on Sufism.* Trans. Reynold A. Nicholson. London: Printed for the trustees of the "E. J. W. Gibb Memorial" by Luzac, 1976.

Ibn al-'Arabi, Muhammad. *The Tarjuman al-ashwaq: A Collection of Mystical Odes.* Trans. into English by Reynold A. Nicholson. London: Royal Asiatic Society, 1911.

Ibn Hanbal, Ahmad ibn Muhammad. *Musnad al-Imam Ahmad ibn Hanbal.* Bayrut: al-Maktabah al-Islamiyyah, 1969.

Ibn Kathir, 'Imad al-Din 'Isma'il 'Umar. *Bidayah wa nihayah.* al-Qahirah: Hajar, 1997.

Ibn Majah, Abi 'Abd Allah Muhammad ibn Yazid al-Qazwini. *Sunan.* N.p.: n.p., n.d.

Ibn Qutaybah, Abi Muhammad 'Abd Allah ibn Muslim. *Kitab al-ashribah: wa-dhikr ikhtilaf al-nas fiha.* Ed. Yasin M. Sawwas. Bayrut: Dar al-Fikr al-Mu'asir, 1999.

"Intoxicants." *Encyclopaedia of the Qur'an.* Leiden: Brill, 2001–2006.

Jaziri, 'Abd al-Qadir ibn Muhammad. *'Umdat al-safwah fi hall al-qahwah.* Ed. 'Abd A. M. Hibshi. Abu Zaby: al-Majma' al-Thaqafi, 1996.

Kalabadhi, Abu Bakr Muhammad ibn Ibrahim al-. *al-Ta'arruf li-madhhab ahl al-tasawwuf.* al-Qahirah: Dar Ihya' al-Kutub al-'Arabiyyah, 1960.

Kalabadhi, Abu Bakr Muhammad ibn Ibrahim. *The Doctrine of the Sufis: Kitab al-ta'arruf li madhhab ahl al-tasawwuf.* Trans. A J. Arberry. Cambridge: Cambridge University Press, 1977.

Kennedy, Philip F. "Khamr and Hikma in Jahili Poetry." *Journal of Arabic Literature.* 20.2 (1989): 97–114.

_____. *The Wine Song in Classical Arabic Poetry: Abu Nuwas and the Literary Tradition.* Oxford: Clarendon Press, 1997.

"Khamr." *Encyclopaedia of Islam.* Leiden: E.J. Brill. 1960–2005.

"Khamriyyah." *Encyclopaedia of Islam.* Leiden: E.J. Brill. 1960–2005.

Khu'i, Abu al-Qasim al-. *Islamic Laws.* Trans. Muhammad Fazal Haq. N.p.: Islamic Seminary Publications, n.d. Internet: www.al-islam.org/laws/al-khui/

Kueny, Kathryn. "Islamic World." *Alcohol and Temperance in Modern History.* Jack S. Blocker et al. Santa Barbara: ABC-CLIO, 2003. 326–330.

_____. *The Rhetoric of Sobriety: Wine in Early Islam.* Albany: State University of New York Press, 2001.

Kutubi, Muhammad ibn Shakir. *Fawat al-wafayat.* Ed. Ihsan Abbas. Bayrut: Dar Sadir, 1974.

Lalani, Arzina R. *Early Shii Thought: The Teachings of Imam Muhammad al-Baqir.* London: I.B. Tauris in association with the Institute of Ismaili Studies, 2000.

Levey, Martin. "Medieval Arabic Toxicology: The *Book on Poisons* of ibn Wahshiya and Its Relation to Early Indian and Greek Texts." *Transactions of the American Philosophical Society*, 56.7 (1966): 1–130.

Madelung, Wilferd, and Paul E. Walker. *An Ismaili Heresiography: The* Bab al-Shaytan *from Abu Tammam's* Kitab al-Shajarah. Leiden: Brill, 1998.

Malik ibn Anas. *al-Mudawwanah al-kubra.* Bayrut: Dar al-Kutub al-'Ilmiyyah, 1994.

_____. *al-Muwatta'.* Online.

McAuliffe, Jane. "Wines of Earth and Paradise: Qur'anic Proscriptions and Promise." *Logos Islamikos: Studia Islamica in Honorem Georgii Michaelis Wickens.* Ed. Wickens et al. Toronto: Pontifical Institute of Mediaeval Studies, 1984. 159–174.

Metcalf, Barbara Daly, ed. *Moral Conduct and Authority: The Place of* Adab *in South Asian Islam.* Berkeley: University of California Press, 1984.

Mojaddedi, Jawid A. "Getting Drunk with Abu Yazid or Staying Sober with Junayd: The Creation of a Popular Typology of Sufism." *Bulletin of the School of Oriental and African Studies* 66.1 (2003): 1–13.

Murtada al-Zabidi, Muhammad. *Taj al-'arus sharh al-qamus.* al-Qahirah: Jamaliyat Misr al-Matba'ah al-Khayriyyah, 1888.

Muslim ibn al-Hajjaj, Abu Husayn. *Sahih muslim.* Online.

"Nabidh." *Encyclopaedia of Islam.* Leiden: E.J. Brill. 1960–2005.

Nawawi, Abu Zakariya Muhi al-Din Ibn Sharaf. *Kitab al-majmu' sharh al-muhadhdhab al-shirazi.* Jiddah: Maktabat al-Sawadi, 1995.

_____. *Minhaj Et Talibin: A Manual of Muhammadan Law: According to the School of Shafi.* Trans. E.C. Howard. Delhi: Adam Publishers & Distributors, 2001.

Nawbakhti, Abu Muhammad al-Hasan Musa. *Shi'a Sects: (Kitab Firaq al-Shi'ah).* Trans. A. K. Kadhim. London: ICAS Press, 2007.

Qushayri, 'Abd al-Karim ibn Hawazin al-. *al-Risalah al-qushayriyyah fi 'ilm al-tasawwuf.* Ed. Zakariyyah ibn Muhammad Ansari. al-Qahirah: Dar al-Tiba'ah al-'Amirah, 1870.

Reinhart, A K. *Before Revelation: The Boundaries of Muslim Moral Thought.* Albany: State University of New York Press, 1995.

Rosenthal, Franz. *The Herb; Hashish versus Medieval Muslim Society.* Leiden: Brill, 1971.

Rumi, Jalal al-Din. *Mathnawi.* al-Qahirah: Majlis al-A'la lil-Thaqafah, 2002.

"Saki." *Encyclopaedia of Islam.* Leiden: E.J. Brill. 1960–2005.

Sarraj, Abu Nasr 'Abd Allah ibn ali. *Kitab al-luma' fi al-tasawwuf.* Ed. Reynold Alleyne Nicholson. Leiden: E. J. Brill, 1914.

Shabistari, Mahmud. *The Secret Rose garden of Sa'd Ud Din Mahmud Shabistari.* Trans. Florence Lederer. London: J. Murray, 1920.

"Sufism." *The Oxford Encyclopedia of the Islamic World.* New York: Oxford University Press, 2009.

Sulami, Muhammad ibn al-Husayn. *Tabaqat al-sufiyyah.* Leiden: E. J. Brill, 1960.

Tabataba'i, 'Allamah Muhammad Husayn. *al-Mizan.* Online.

Tijani, Muhammad al-. *Ask Those Who Know.* Qum: Ansariyan Publications, n.d.

Tirmidhi, Abu 'Isa Muhammad ibn 'Isa ibn Sawrah al-. *Sunan al-Tirmidhi.* Online.

Tustari, Sahl al-. *Tafsir al-Tustari.* Trans. Annabel Keeler and Ali Keeler. Louisville, KY: Fons Vitae, 2011.

Wahidi Nishaburi, Abu al-Hasan 'Ali. *Asbab al-nuzul.* Misr: Matba'ah Hindiyyah, 1897–98.

Zahraa, Mahdi. "The Legal Capacity of Women in Islamic law." *Arab Law Quarterly* 11.3 (1996): 245–263.

Zamkhshari, Mahmud ibn 'Umar. *The Qoran: With the Commentary of the Imam Aboo al-Qasim Mahmood bin 'Omar al-Zamakhshari, Entitled the* Kashshaf 'an Haqaiq al-Tanzil. Ed. William N. Lees and Husain Hadim. Calcutta: Lees, 1856.

Fatimah

BRIDGET BLOMFIELD

"To thee have We granted the Fount (of Abundance)." (Qur'an 108:1)

Introduction

One of the defining tenets of Islam is the lack of images: Muslims do not worship idols or other images. Hence, there is no external image of the Prophet Muhammad's daughter Fatimah for the purpose of worship. The image of Fatimah must therefore be imagined within the landscape of the human heart. The mind's eye of each individual creates its unique image of her, making her deeply personal. It is through narrative that she is known best. Whether that is text or through storytelling and religious chants and poetry, Fatimah finds her place from piety to social activism. Imagery of Fatimah is found in all strains of Islam: Sunnism, Shi'ism, and Sufism. She is pure and spotless, an innocent young maiden, a loving wife, and the mother of a savior as well as the archetypal mother of the world. Fatimah inspires Muslim women to create change and justice in the modern world.

Fatimah is an archetype of the divine feminine revered by many Muslims, be they Sunni, Sufi or Shi'ah. She symbolizes the radiance of the divine and the blood and bones of humanity for she is the perfect balance of light and matter, the image of the divine feminine model, the prototype of woman. Allah fashioned the holy family one by one with Fatimah as the mistress of the universe where she is given earthly and mystical roles as a member of the *ahl al-bayt* (Holy Family of the Prophet Muhammad). Representing the sacred *bab* (gate), she is an open door to interior interpretation as well as an exhibitor of the external actions of social activism. As a bearer of religious authority, Fatimah mediates the human and divine and, for centuries, she has been an exemplary role model for women, as a political and social activist, fighting against oppression and injustice. Fatimah is the archetype of the suffering mother as well as the lady of celestial light. Relationship with Fatimah creates agency through identification with her sorrow as well as her piety. Today, particularly among Shi'ah Muslim women, the image of Fatimah is still such a role model.

Fatimah, the Object of Faith and Devotion

Fatimah bint Muhammad was the daughter of the Prophet Muhammad and is referred to as Fatimah *al-Zahra* which means the radiant, luminous, most shining one. As the wife of Muhammad's cousin 'Ali, and the mother of five children, one of whom is the highly revered Imam Husayn, she and her holy family play important roles in the development of Shi'i doctrine. Representing the soteriology of suffering and redemption, the Shi'i consider them to be the true leaders of the Muslim community who are responsible for the spiritual and lawful guidance of believers. According to the Shi'ah, Fatimah, after Muhammad and 'Ali, is the third leader of Islam.

Fatimah, as a heavenly intercessor, can sprinkle grace on all those who turn to her in search of intercession. She is the radiant mother who offers hope to the suffering and the possibility of redemption to those who emulate her. As the most holy of all the women in the Prophet's life, Fatimah is the absolute reflection of beauty and compassion, thus sharing the same high status as the Infallible Imams. On the Day of Judgment,

> Fatimah will pass over the bridge of separation on a she-camel of light with a crown adorned by jewels on her head. On her right and left, she will be surrounded by multitudes of angels and will advance until she is on the same level as the throne of God [qtd. Ayoub 213].

It is said that the fifth Imam, Muhammad al-Baqir, gave warning to those who were sinners, telling them that "on the day of Resurrection, Fatimah will stand at the gate of hell, and on the forehead of every human being will be written *mu'min* [believer] or *kafir* [unbeliever]" (214). But if you have loved Fatimah, "lover" will be stamped between your eyes and she will intercede on your behalf so that you are not sent to burn in hell. God gives her the grace to redeem those that have fallen and to lead them to paradise. These images of Fatimah increase faith and devotion to those who revere her.

Intercession is considered to be of the highest importance in Shi'i doctrine. Ibn Shahrashub believes Fatimah will be met by a divine voice that tells her "O my beloved and daughter of my beloved, ask me and thou shall be given, intercede with me, for thine intercession will be accepted" (107). Fatimah works as a redemptrix for all those who suffer and who come to her with tears for her family. She helps even those believers who have not gained quite enough merit to enter paradise. On the Day of Judgment, Fatimah will be compensated for her own suffering by being granted the power to save all those who asked her for intercession. She carries the *al-Jami'ah*, a scroll that is seventy yards long. Upon this scroll is written everything that humanity needs to know until the end of time (Mufid 414). Tears cried on her behalf, and on the behalf of her family, for the injustices done to humanity, will be recorded and taken into account, balancing transgressions that may be judged as sinful.

Images of Fatimah's Conception and Birth

"Then God created Fatimah from the Light and spirit without body." (Kulayni)

There are many hadiths that support the creation of Fatimah from light, maintaining that she was created "before there were heavens and earth, darkness and light, sun and moon, paradise and hell. Then God uttered a word from which he formed Light. With another word he created spirit." Then, "God expanded the Light of the Prophet's daughter, Fatimah, and from it He created the heavens and earth, and Fatimah became more excellent than both the heavens and earth" (Majlisi qtd. Moosa 58). These images of Fatimah portray her as the feminine form of the *Laylat al-Qadr* (Night of Power or Night of Destiny), the night that human beings are closest to God at the end of the fast of Ramadan. During the recitation of all night prayers and vigils, she appears as magnificent light and authority, the very essence of the Prophet.

Fatimah waited in heaven until God sent her through the loins of her father as the essence of the pomegranate fruit. According to Shi'ah tradition, the angel Jibril (Gabriel) descended upon the Prophet and told him to spend forty nights away from his beloved wife Khadijah. He was to spend this time in solitude, praying and fasting and was instructed to break his fast with heavenly fruits (fig, apple or pomegranate). After breaking the fast with this heavenly produce, the Prophet rose to pray. The angel Jibril descended once again and bid him not to pray, telling him: "*Salat* [ritual prayer] is forbidden to you at this time, until you go to Khadijah. Almighty Allah has indeed taken upon Himself to create for you in this night an excellent progeny. Thus he went to Khadijah's home" (qtd. Hosayni 25). The Prophet ate the fruit and the essence became sperm. When he returned he conceived Fatimah with his beloved wife Khadijah. Fatimah is the very essence of her father who said, "[We] were two, separated from one another, and yet of similar form" (Majlisi). According to a *hadith* narrated by 'A'ishah, the Prophet told her:

> Indeed, on the night during which I was taken to the sky, I entered heaven and I stood by its most beautiful tree, with the whitest leaves, and the most delicious fruit. So I took from its fruit and ate ... and when I descended to the earth, I approached Khadijah; and she became pregnant with Fatimah from that produce [qtd. Hosayni 27].

Fatimah was extracted from pure food, a pure action of *karamah*, a supernatural action performed by a godly person. Muhammad, the Messenger of Allah, was even told that the child would be female, and "that she is a pure and blessed child; and that the Almighty Allah will indeed create my lineage through her, and will choose from my lineage a number of *a'immah* [Imams] appointing them as His *khulafa'* [Caliphs] on His earth after the completion of His revelation" (qtd. Hosayni 28).

The Blessed Virgin Mary, Mother of 'Isa (Jesus), was believed to be a midwife to Khadijah at Fatimah's birth. Khadijah, (Maryam) Mary, Asiyah (the Pharoah's wife) and Fatimah are regarded as ritually and spiritually pure, whose conceptions, therefore, were "immaculate." Annemarie Schimmel retells the famous Shi'ah tradition that Fatimah's

> birth was surrounded by light; she was absolutely pure and had no menstruation. Thus she was honored with the title *batul*, "virgin," and later she assumed also the position of a true *Mater Dolorosa* after the death of her younger son Husayn [18].

Fatimah became part of the divine matriarchy of holy women who emanate and embody light, all three of them who are mothers of sorrow and radiance.

Fatimah is the representation of the Night of Destiny that "is better than a thousand months" for during this night there is a peace that lasts till dawn for it is the night that Fatimah is sovereign. During this night, any true believer that stays awake and prays until dawn is met by Fatimah's grace and is ushered into the symbolic moment that the divine gives birth to itself in each individual heart. What illumines this night is the light of Fatimah, for her attributes give birth to the perfect metaphorical child that takes humanity back to its celestial essence. Fatimah helps anyone who submits on this night the opportunity to give birth to his own divine essence (Corbin, *Cyclical Time* 101).

The Sacred Marriage

The Prophet Muhammad betroths Fatimah and 'Ali, a union that represents the mystical marriage as it takes place on simultaneous levels, the physical and the spiritual. This marriage is found in the arms of love, a partnership between two where a third aspect is present. It is in this relatedness to self and other that Fatimah creates this marriage. This marriage, as mystical union, transpires when one embodies the light of Fatimah in ordinary relationship. It is the inner perception, the *batin* that signifies an internal marriage with the divine and is lived out through *wilayah*. This pairing is found in the marriage of Fatimah and 'Ali because they represent receptivity to the will of God making their lives the holiest of the holy. Fatimah is the feminine form of creation and 'Ali is the authority by which creation can take place. Muhammad stated that the wedding between Fatimah and 'Ali had been initiated in heaven forty days before their earthly union. Her heavenly dowry was a portion of the earth where she reigns as the Queen of Women. The tuba tree in heaven dropped pearls and jewels and robes of light that were given to Fatimah by the maidens of heaven as a wedding gift.

Still told today, there is a story that Fatimah had a beautiful wedding dress and when a poor woman came to her saying she had nothing to wear to her own wedding (not knowing that Fatimah was soon to be married), Fatimah gave her the dress. As a result of her kindness, God dressed her and describes her as paradise itself: "He showed them a Being, adorned with a myriad of glittering lights of various colors, who sat on a throne, a crown on her head, rings in her ears, a sword drawn by her side" (Massignon 64–65). Fatimah was given the gift of "heavenly clothes" from the angel Jibril and on the day of her wedding she was accompanied by seventy thousand angels (Hosayni 41). Heavenly clothing can be interpreted as a mantle that concealed and enveloped her mystical powers. Her robes of light shield and protect anyone that turns toward her in need. Such imagery suggests that if one remains faithful there are heavenly rewards after death.

Fatimah's Death

When the Prophet Muhammad prayed in Fatimah's home after lunch one day, he foresaw the suffering of his daughter Fatimah and her family. The Prophet realized that his entire family would enter into the House of Sorrows. He warned those who would go against her in the future, saying: "Fatimah is a part of me; what hurts her hurts me, and what pleases her pleases me. Verily God gets angry when Fatimah is angry and is pleased when she is pleased" (Ibn Babawayh 303). Unfortunately, he could not change her destiny. Fatimah would experience a life of suffering and the majority of her family would be martyred.

Fatimah, as the body of Muhammad, is the carrier of the *nur Muhammad*, the light that illuminates suffering and gives it meaning. As the mistress of the House of Sorrows, she is also the bridge to heaven and the gate to the garden of the prophets. In the story of Fatimah's life, suffering is considered an unavoidable experience of what it means to be human. Because of their suffering, Fatimah and her family were surrounded by divine grace, for their suffering came at the hands of others. For the Shi'ah, this is extremely important for even today they continue to fight against religious oppression.

Fatimah died shortly after the death of her father. There are numerous accounts of her death but in the Shi'ah community the following is the most popular. Fatimah hides behind the door of her house because she is home alone and unveiled. Her husband's enemy, 'Umar, tells his forces to burn down the house. 'Umar then forces open the door and Fatimah is impaled by a large nail. She is then pulled from behind the door and beaten repeatedly until she miscarries. Fatimah dies hunched over in prayer after giving birth to a stillborn child. Because the last words that Fatimah uttered were prayers, and she was conceived in prayer, she is considered pure prayer, and because of her violent death at the hands of her oppressors, the image of Fatimah is that of martyr.

Fatimah was very close to her father. It was reported by 'A'ishah, the Prophet's youngest wife, that Fatimah's tears were the result of a broken heart caused by the loss of those that she loved most dearly. In the Sunni version, 'A'ishah relates that:

> The Prophet whispered something to his daughter Fatimah and she wept bitterly. He whispered to her again and she laughed. She had wept because he told her of his impending death, and when she wept, to console her, he asked "Does it not, however, please you that you will be the first of my family to join me and that you will be the first lady of heaven, and chief of the female believers?" [Shari'ati 162].

Fatimah's love for her father and family never wavered and thus at her death it was transferred to the family of humanity, as she became the redemptrix of all suffering that is transformed through love and faith.

Establishing Wilayah (Holiness)

Fatimah, through her actions, is a true mystic. The Sufi philosopher al-Hallaj describes the intention, commitment and qualities of a mystic as:

> He whose heart is of piety tested by God; who for his coat of arms has the Qur'an; for a cloak, faith; for a torch, meditation; for perfume, piety; for canonical ablution, contrition; for bodily hygiene, only the use of the lawful acts; and for ornament, continence; he lives only for the life to come; he cares for nothing but God; he keeps himself constantly in the presence of God; he fasts until death, breaking the fast in paradise; he espouses only good deeds; his only treasure is virtue; his silence is contemplation; his gaze is vision [qtd. Swartz 144].

Truly Fatimah fits into all of these categories. For this reason she is considered the embodiment of *wilayah*. *Wilayah* comes from the Arabic root word of *waliya*, which means to be near or close. The term *wali Allah* is a compounded word that means friend of God, which in English is interpreted as "saint." In the Qur'an, however, the term *wali* does not represent a friend but a guardian, intercessor or protector, giving *wali Allah* a social and metaphysical significance. The authority of the saint comes from one's ability to be *walayah* with people and constant *wilayah* with God. Fatimah is a spiritual intercessor and authority for "*walayah* and *wilayah* are best seen as semantic fraternal twins that coexist symbiotically, like yin and yang" (Cornell 273). These qualities are mutually dependent for meaning and authority. Fatimah's nature is that of sainthood based on an inner knowledge that manifests through actions and behavior that are witnessed by others.

The image of Fatimah as a saint depicts her as helping others communicate with God, acting on behalf of others, and as an inspiration through virtuous conduct. She is a master of the knowable and is a mediator between this world and the next. Her "gift" helps to regulate the social and spiritual standards of the community. Fatimah is the divine pole between this world and the next, where spirit meets flesh. Anointed as the Pure One, she is born pure and dies pure for "Fatimah's 'virginity' resides in her heavenly form, it is simultaneously sensual and pure, and finally converges with her role as mother" (Thurlkill 77) for "God has chosen you and purified you: He has chosen you among the women of the world" (Vaglieri 847). Carrying the offspring of Muhammad's ancestors, Fatimah is imagined as the archetypal Mother of Humanity.

Fatimah the Radiant as a Body of Light

The appearance of light and its transforming effects are critical to the formation of Islamic philosophy. Muslims write extensively about light as imagery of the divine. The *nur Muhammad* is the light that God transmitted to Muhammad and he passed to his family. Fatimah is a vessel of this holy light and she transmits it to all who weep in her name. Anyone in her presence felt that "the radiance streaming forth from her illumined the whole garden" (Thurlkill 64–65). In the Qur'an, it is written:

> God is the light of the heavens and of the earth. The parable of His light is as if there were a niche and within it a lamp: the lamp enclosed in glass: the glass as it were a brilliant star: lit from a blessed tree, an olive, neither of the east nor of the west, whose oil is well-nigh luminous, though fire scarce touched it: Light upon Light! [24:35]

Fatimah represents this lamp that not only shines in every *masjid* (mosque) but also illuminates the heart of every human being.

Fatimah, the Radiant, is also known as the great Mary, *Maryam al-Kubra*. She is considered a virgin like Mary the Mother of Christ. They differ in that Fatimah does not claim a virgin birth for any of her children. In this way, Fatimah is truly the bridge of heaven and earth. She is material and divine and gives birth to a body of illuminated matter — the human being that is full of the light of *barakah* (grace) transmitted from heaven though the Holy Mother. The substance of Fatimah is light; she is conceived of light and born into light. Midwifed by the Virgin Mary, mother of 'Isa (Jesus), Fatimah and her family occupy a position midway between human and divine beings for

> they are first conceived in God's mind as a principle of order, harmony and goodness in the world; then they were made substantial as luminous entities or conventicles of light transmitted in the loins of prophets and wombs of holy women until they reached actualization in the Prophet Muhammad [Ayoub 54].

Fatimah was first created as light and then shaped into a human being. Her children are considered shards of light, made from the compassion and love of God, who existed as essences of divine light before embodiment. Before assuming a body, Fatimah existed as a particle of God and was conceived by God through His divine will. God chose 'Ali as the Prophet's heavenly-appointed heir but it was Fatimah through whom that lineage is bestowed. God made the family of humanity (the family of the Prophet) in the "world of particles" (*'alam al-dharr*), an ethereal existence where the Holy Family is a reflection of God's light.

From the Islamic perspective a person born without a *nafs* (spirit; life-source; lower-self; animal nature) is a person who possesses the quality of '*ismah*, namely, freedom from sin and error. The *nafs* represents the part of a human being that is not yet illuminated; it still struggles with earthly dilemmas. In his description of Fatimah, Henry Corbin, scholar of Sufism and author of *Alone with the Alone*, interprets the lower-self or spirit (*nafs*) from a different perspective. He felt that the lower-soul was the humanness of our being, and should not be interpreted negatively. It is the anima, the feminine, the constitutive part of the human being. Fatimah is "the eternally feminine in man; that is why she is the archetype of the heavenly earth: she is both paradise and initiation into it" (Corbin, *Alone* 166).

The Womb of the World: Mother of Humanity

"Paradise lies beneath the feet of mothers." (Furuzanfar n. 480)

God fashioned the holy family from His light. This *nur Muhammad* was passed through his loins to the womb of his first wife Khadijah who birthed the Holy Mother Fatimah. The Prophet's joy that his offspring was a girl is described as such: (the angel Gabriel) "tells me that she is a female, and that she is blessed, pure progeny, and that Allah, Blessed and Exalted, will create my progeny from her" (Majlisi vol. 43: 2).

Not only does this image give value to women and femininity in the eyes of Islam, it indicates that they are the very resting place of the divine mystery, "their light is the divine light itself; their transparency allows it to shine through, retaining none of it as their own Ipsety" (Corbin, *Spiritual* 63). As ultimate Mother of the World and Universe, she generates and animates every living thing. She births, and rebirths, the light of Muhammad from which she was conceived. Through this imagery, it is suggested that she is the *nur Muhammad.*

Fatimah is also the mother of *al-rahmah,* mercy and compassion. She is derived from these two qualities and emits them to those that pray on her behalf. Her womb, *rahim,* is the growing place for every action that comes to life and initiates *rahmah* through the tradition of spiritual virtue. Fatimah-*Batul,* the Virgin Fatimah is the physical and spiritual mother of divinity for she is spirit embodied:

> Let him who wishes to breathe paradise in the manner of Muhammad breathing his daughter's perfume turn his mind upon her and upon what she reveals of the Secret hidden in her person; for she is the *Hujjat* of 'Ali, she establishes the esoteric sense of His knowledge and guidesthose who attain it. Through her, then, paradise is breathed, as the essential sense (*haqiqat*) of the *da'wat* [Corbin, *Spiritual* 108].

As *hujjah,* the proof of God, she represents the *batin* or esoteric aspect of the divine and also extends the exoteric manifestation of the divine through the birth of her holy offspring. As mother, the light of Fatimah is the source of life for all human beings. She is the mystical representation that gives birth to the Holy Family, and when still in the womb, "a light glows for him [her child] between heaven and earth" (Qummi 434). The light she embodies is a continuous determined creative force that existed before creation, through creation and continues to create itself, for it is the reflection of God. According to Shi'ah tradition,

> the same light (or alternately the hidden seed) which appears in some traditions as a pre-existential mystic essence, continues into creation, being passed on to a person in each generation and finally finding its eternal home in the descendants of 'Ali and Fatimah [Ayoub 139].

Their descendants carry this light into humanity whenever a child is born through this divine lineage. It is a seed that is dropped into the heart of each human being.

Conclusion

The multiple images of Fatimah continue to live today as she is continuously revered by Shi'ah practitioners. The religion of Islam is based on thought and love and in the Qur'an one cannot find the boundaries between love and faith for

Each religion, school of thought, movement or revolution is made up of two elements: wisdom and love. One is light and the other is motion. One gives common sense and understanding, the other, strength, enthusiasm and movement [Shari'ati 84].

Fatimah embodies the qualities of wisdom and love. She is the movement of love, receptive and active. Through the devotional love of Fatimah one learns to love divinely and naturally. Fatimah is daughter, wife, mother, and she encompasses all that is the divine feminine. Through her suffering humanity is redeemed. God sent Muhammad as a gift to the people of the world and in turn the Prophet gifted humanity with Fatimah:

As for my daughter, Fatimah, she is the mistress of the women of the worlds, those that were and those that are to come, and she is part of me. She is the human *houri* who when she enters her prayer chamber before God, exalted be He, her light shines to the angels of heaven as the stars shine to the inhabitants of the earth [Kulayni].

The Prophet continues to say after Fatimah suffers greatly,

She will come to me sorrowful and heavy with grief, persecuted and martyred. Then will I say, "O God, curse those who wrong her, punish those who persecuted her, humiliate those who humiliated her, and consign eternally into Thy Fire him who hit her side so that she lost the child" [qtd. Ayoub 239].

The *nur Muhammad* or light of Muhammad supports a lineage that is neither matriarchal nor patriarchal, but both. Fatimah is the vessel of light that is contained in the material world, the human body. From the Sufi perspective, Corbin described Fatimah as the "Virgin-Mother" who gives birth to the line of Holy Imams making her the matrix of creation. She is one of the endless reflections of the mystery and grace of Sophianic wisdom. The Prophet called her the "mother of her father" categorizing Fatimah in the same realm as Eve. She is "the feminine being who, in the image of divine compassion, is creatrix of the being by whom she herself was created — and that is why woman is the being *par excellence* in whom mystic love attaches to a theophanic image *par excellence*" (Corbin, *Alone* 162). The creative feminine births itself through numerous prophets and messiahs, embodying a spiritual potency that is the connecting point of the divine and the material. Without her, there would be no Imamate and, more importantly, no Imamic initiation. This holy lineage was the recipient of divine light and the guardian of the revelation.

Sorrowful yet courageous, Fatimah is a role model for women and serves as the divine feminine in the hearts of men as well. She resisted oppression and promises justice at the gates of paradise. She represents all beings on the Day of Judgment. When tears are wept for her, and supplications are made in her name, she is present to alleviate eternal suffering. For this reason, out of love and wisdom, the following salutation is offered to her:

Peace be with you, O you who were afflicted with trials by the One who created you. When he tested you, He found you to be patient under affliction...

Peace be with you, O mistress of the women of the worlds. Peace be with you, O mother of the vindicators of humankind in argument. Peace be with you, O you who were wronged, you who were deprived of that to which you were entitled by right...

God's blessings on the immaculate virgin, the truthful, the sinless, the pious, the unstained; the one who is pleasing to God and acceptable, the guiltless, the rightly guided, the one who was wronged; the one who was unjustly overpowered and disposed by force of that to which she was entitled; the one kept from her lawful inheritance, she whose ribs were broken; whose husband was wronged, whose son was slain; Fatimah, daughter of your Prophet, O God, flesh of his flesh, inner most heart of his heart... Mistress of women, proclaimer of God's friends, ally of pity and asceticism, apple of paradise and eternity... You, O God, drew forth from her the light of the Imams [Qummi 100–01, 539–40, 574].

The Prophet's cloak or mantle is the cocoon that embraces the holy family, "the closest relatives of the Prophet (Fatimah, 'Ali, Hasan and Husayn), who are wrapped in his cloak and form so to speak a sacred and blessed Unity" (Schimmel 37). Fatimah is Mistress of the night, a shining star, who gave birth to the sacred imamate of the Shi'ah. She wraps her cloak, the gift of her Father's mantle, around the world as she sprinkles *barakah* (grace) upon the earth, forever a role model for Shi'ah women.

Works Cited

'Ali, 'Abdullah Yusuf, trans. *Qur'an.* Brentwood: Amana Corporation, 1983.

Arberry, AJ, trans. *Koran.* New York: Macmillan, 1955.

Ayoub, Mahmoud. *Redemptive Suffering in Islam.* New York: Mouton, 1978.

Burton, John. *Introduction to the Hadith.* Edinburgh: Edinburgh University Press, 1994.

Corbin, Henry. *Alone With the Alone.* Princeton: Princeton University Press, 1969.

_____. *Cyclical Time and Ismaili Gnosis.* London: Kegan Paul International, 1983.

_____. *Spiritual Body and Celestial earth.* Princeton: Princeton University Press, 1977.

Cornell, Vincent J. *Realm of the Saint: Power and Authority in Moroccan Sufism.* Austin: University of Texas Press, 1998.

Furuzanfar, B. *Ahadith-i Mathnawi.* Tehran: Amir Kabir, 1968.

Hosayni, Mostafa. *Sayyedat Nesa al-Alamen: Chief of the Women of the World.* England: Islamic Propagation Center, 2003.

Ibn Babawayh, Abu Ja'far Muhammad ibn 'Ali al-Saduq. *Ma'ani al-akhbar.* Ed. 'Ali Akbar al-Ghaffari. Tehran: Maktabat al-Saduq and Mu'assasat Dar al-'Ilm, 1959.

Ibn Shahrashub, Muhammad ibn 'Ali al-Mazandarani. *Manaqib al-Abi Talib.* Najaf: al-Matba'ah al-Haydariyyah, 1956.

Kulayni, Muhammad ibn Ya'qub al-. *al-Usul min al-kafi.* Tehran: Maktabat al-Islamiyyah, n.d.

Majlisi, Muhammad Baqir al-. *Bihar al-Anwar.* Bayrut: Mu'assasat al-Wafa, 1983.

Massignon, Louis. "Die Ursprunge und die Bedeutung des Gnostizismus im Islam." *Eranos Jahrbuch* (1937).

Moosa, Matti. *Extremist Shi'ites.* Syracuse: Syracuse University Press, 1988.

Mufid, Shaykh al-. *Kitab al-irshad: The Book of Guidance.* Trans. I.K.A. Howard. Horsham: Balagha Books, 1981.

Qummi, Abu al-Hasan 'Ali ibn Ibrahim al-. *Tafsir al-Qummi.* Ed Tayyib al-Musawi al-Jaza'iri. Najaf: Maktabat al-Huda, 1966/1967.

Schimmel, Annemarie. *And Muhammad is His Messenger.* Chapel Hill: University of North Carolina Press, 1985.

_____. *Deciphering the Signs of God.* Albany: State University of New York Press, 1994.

Sells, Michael *Early Islamic Mysticism.* New York: Paulist Press, 1996.

Shari'ati, 'Ali. *Shari'ati on Shari'ati and the Muslim Women.* Trans. Laleh Bakhtiar. Chicago: KAZI Publications, Inc. 1996.

Swartz, Merlin L. *Studies on Islam.* New York: Oxford University Press, 1981.

Tabataba'i, 'Allamah Sayyid Muhammad Husayn. *Shi'ite Islam.* Trans. Seyyed Hossein Nasr. New York: State University of New York Press, 1977.

Thurlkill, Mary. *Chosen Among Women: Mary and Fatima in Early Medieval Christianity and Shi'ism.* Unpublished dissertation.

Vaglieri, Veccia. "Fatima." *Encyclopedia of Islam.* 2d. ed. Ed. Bernard Lewis, Charles Pellat, and Josepsh Schacht. Leiden: Brill, 1991.

THE PHYSICAL

Water

CYRUS ALI ZARGAR

"We made from water every living thing" (Qur'an 21:30)

Introduction

Water stands as one of the most symbolically significant images in most of the world's religious communities. Yet Islam's intellectual, contemplative, and popular traditions accord distinctive and variegated meaning to this image, uniquely influenced by pre–Islamic Arabic literary convention, the text of the Qur'an, Muslim rituals, Islamic literature, and the cultural context within which Islam blossomed. It is difficult to say that there is an image of water in Islam at all, but one can discern an accumulation of images and connotations that contribute to a concept of water as indefinite as it is rich. While, broadly speaking, that "image" relays life, knowledge, and purity, this work assumes that studying particular, illustrative instances of the meaning of water will yield a picture more indicative of Islam's unique symbolic heritage.

Water as Inherited Language

The Qur'an often mentions the centrality of water to a thriving and enjoyable life. It is not, however, the case that water was any *more* necessary there and then than it is here and now. Rather, the Qur'an's audience was cognizant of the scarcity and elusiveness of water, thus being very receptive to the Qur'an's descriptions of rain as a divine blessing, of the sudden drying of wells as a real possibility, and of water in general as the source of life. Moreover, the audience of the Qur'an had inherited a lexical and poetic tradition ample in the appreciation of water and rain.

While some of the many Arabic terms for rain are rare, others are common and occur in the Qur'an, specifically, *al-matar* (4:102, 7:84, 25:40, 26:173, 27:58, 46:24), *al-ghayth* (12:49, 31:34, 42:28, 57:20), *al-wadq* (24:43, 30:48), *al-wabil* (2:264–5), *al-ghadaq* (72:16), *al-tall* (2:265), and, arguably, *al-raj'* (86:11). The Qur'an's emphasis that the one true God grants all of these varieties of rain opposes the pre–Islamic practice among the Arabs of seeking rain from other gods. The exegete Mahmud al-Zamakhshari (d. 1144) raises the possibility, for example, that the name of the ancient Semitic deity al-Manat stems from the word *naw'* (an astronomical phenomenon used to chart rain times), possibly indicating that devotees sought rain in al-Manat's presence (al-Zamakhshari 4: 423; Varisco 253–3).

The Qur'an's audience inherited not only a vocabulary but also a poetic sensibility suited to value the sensory nuances of rain. The description of an impending rainstorm attributed to the famous pre–Islamic Arabic poet Imru' al-Qays (d. c. 550 CE) captures a sense of enchantment with rain echoed in the Qur'an:

> Help me gaze at this flash, at this glimmer
> that shines in piled cumulus mountains of white,
> its glow subsides at times, and at other times
> collapses like a tired, limping, brittle-boned beast.
> From it come bolts of lightning, as though they were
> the hands of a gambler stretched out for victory.
> I sit watching it, as the place of coming companionship shifts fast
> from a land of acacia-shaded water, to Yathlath's streams, to a valley.
> The rain strikes two smooth mountains in private lands, so their fine sand
> dissolves; it spreads to the valley of al-Badi, then turns to that fertile place,
> in a supple flatland in gardens with vegetation entwined,
> it then falls upon the garden's brooks as silvery liquid,
> territories vast and earth flourishing
> the outlet of the downpour in a wide expanse.
> At midmorning the water streams at every cloud-release
> forcing the lizards to gather in a barren, white plain.
> I ask my weak sister [the rain] for its water, although she is far away,
> and although visiting outside the realm of poetry is unlikely [Imru' al-Qays 88–90].[1]

The image of a mountain of clouds, lightning, and rain can also be found in the Qur'an. The power and capriciousness of the clouds found in the account of Imru' al-Qays here appear as humankind's weakness and dependence on one omnipotent entity:

> Do you not see that God drives the clouds, then brings them together, then renders them stacks, so that you see rain emerging from between them? And that He sends down from the sky mountains in which is hail, afflicting whom He wishes and turning it away from whom He wishes, the flash of its lightning almost taking away sights? [24:43].

While the sense of awe and beauty is shared by the two accounts, in the Qur'an natural phenomena function as signs of God, who is the creator and manager of the universe. Yet one finds in the Qur'an that water is much more than a symbol borrowed from a poetic tradition.

Water as Qur'anic Themes

Just as water is itself malleable, so too in the Qur'an does it assume numerous illustrative forms. It is a blessing. As is mentioned repeatedly, God sends rain down from the sky as a provision, reviving the earth, even if only those who apply reason recognize its source (45:5). It is also enjoyed in abundance in paradise (56:31). Yet, in hell-fire, water is also a punishment, for it is poured at boiling temperatures down the throats of its occupants (6:70), or over their heads (22:19). On the one hand, it becomes the paradigm for revelation and thus true knowledge. Out of 293 instances in which the root *n-z-l* is used to describe a divine down-sending, mostly referring to the down-sending of revelation, thirty-eight instances refer to water, drawing a connotative parallel between rain and revelation.[2] Just as rain is absorbed by the thirsty soil, revelation spiritually saturates the soul.

On the other hand, however, water can also be used to illustrate a *lack* of pious knowledge for those who reject the divine message; the sum of their actions is likened to a "mirage in a wide land, which the thirsty one thinks to be water," yet, when arriving at it, "finds to be nothing" (24:39). Their actions, and thus their lives, are like "levels of darkness in a fathomless sea, covered wave upon wave, upon which are clouds, layers of darkness on top of one another, such that when he brings out his hand, he almost cannot see it" (24:40).

Water is a source of life. The Qur'an asserts that every living thing, every animal comes from water (21:30, 24:45). Yet, having come from water, particularly from the "base water" that is semen, human beings should realize their lowliness, weakness, and need for spiritual purification in the form of belief and actions before they can enter paradise (77:20, 70:38–39).

Just as was the case with rain, springs number among the divine acts of grace, quenching the thirst of humans, watering gardens, and feeding cattle (26:133–4, 36:34; Johns 463). God can cause this blessing to dry up, rendering human beings impotent (67:30), sometimes on account of a people's ungratefulness or failure to heed their prophet (26:137–8). He can also cause a spring to appear as the sign of a prophet's veracity (17:90), as was the case famously with Musa (Moses), who struck a rock from which appeared twelve sources of water, one source for each branch of the Children of Israel (Johns 463). The association of Musa (Moses) with springs, particularly springs gushing out of rocks, as is described in the Qur'an 2:60 and 7:160, has caused locations in Syria and Jordan to be sites of reverence and even visitation (Sadan).

Rivers, wells, and seas also appear in the Qur'an, often relaying God's management of affairs, the neediness of humankind, or even a sense of mystery. Perhaps the most mysterious passage in the Qur'an is that which tells the story of a certain Musa, whom most exegetes agree to be the Prophet Moses, the "possessor of the Torah," along with Musa's unnamed companion, usually identified in the *ahadith* as Yusha' ibn Nun (18:60–82). They are in search of one more knowledgeable than Musa, a friend of God named al-Khidr, generally associated with eternal life, esoteric knowledge, and water (al-Bukhari 3:16 31, #74 and 65:18:3 1175, #4726).[3]

Indeed, Musa (Moses) knows he will find this teacher-figure at or near the "meeting of the two seas" (18:60), a place which the commentator Abu Ja'far Muhammad ibn Jarir al-Tabari (d. 923) identifies as the conjunction of the Sea of Persia and Sea of Rome (al-Tabari, *Jami' al-Bayan* 15:176; Wensinck 903–4). They find this location (or the rocky path to it) when a dead and salted fish, which he and his companion were planning to eat, or from which they had already taken a few morsels (al-Tabari, *Jami' al-Bayan* 15: 178), comes alive and swims away, possibly having been touched by the water of the meeting of the two seas, or by the waters of a spring of paradise, or by the water that the companion of Musa (Moses) uses for his ablutions (al-Razi 21: 480).

The commentator Abu 'Abd Allah Muhammad ibn 'Umar, known as Fakhr al-Din al-Razi (d. 1209), raises another possibility: "There are some who have said that the two seas are Musa [Moses] and al-Khidr [themselves], since they were two seas of knowledge" (al-Razi 21:479). This connection between water and knowledge appears often in Islamic texts, a connection here further emphasized by a comment al-Khidr makes when they see a sparrow sitting on a ship's edge, pecking at water: "My knowledge and your knowledge does not deplete God's knowledge even to the extent of what this sparrow takes from the sea" (al-Razi 21:478; al-Bukhari 65:18:3 1175, #4726).

A source of water associated with the *hajj* pilgrimage, as well as with Islam's sacred history, is that of Zamzam, in Mecca, a well associated with Hajar (Hagar) and her son

Ismaʻil (Ishmael). Hajar's bravery and reliance on God becomes apparent when Ibrahim (Abraham), who has been commanded to rebuild the center of monotheistic worship in Mecca, leaves Hagar and his son Ismaʻil in a place the Qur'an describes as a "barren valley" (14:37). Hajar's frantic search for water to give to her young son, causing her to rush between the hills of Safa and Marwah, has become memorialized as an action imitated by pilgrims during the Hajj (2:158; al-Tabari, *Ta'rikh* 1:252). Even to this day, pilgrims drink the waters of this well on their visit and take that water back home with them to treat the sick or more generally for blessings.

Water as Paradise

Water and other satisfying liquids feature prominently in the Qur'an's depiction of paradise. To those who believe and perform good deeds the Qur'an repeatedly promises "gardens beneath which rivers flow" (2:25, et al.). "Indeed, the Godwary are in gardens and in springs" (15:45), the Qur'an proclaims, a scene described by Qur'anic commentator Abu ʻAbd Allah Muhammad ibn Ahmad al-Qurtubi (d. 1272):

> When the people of paradise enter paradise, two springs are offered to them. They drink from the first one, and God erases all hatred and desire for vengeance from their hearts. Then, they enter into the second spring and wash themselves. Their faces become serene [El-Zein 467].

Thus, the Qur'an describes paradise as an ideal garden, in which believers are given various drinks from exclusive fountains, silver vessels, and exquisite cups. The springs, waters, and beverages have powerful names such as *Salsabil* and *Tasnim*, and even more powerful effects, such as the ability to purify the drinker (76:15–8; 83:25–8). Indeed, according to one *hadith*, one type of liquid given to paradise's inhabitants purifies its drinker from "anything other than God" (al-Tabrisi, Amin al-Din 10:623; al-Sulami 60). The paradisal body of water named *al-Kawthar*, the main theme of the Qur'an's shortest chapter (108:1–3), has been described in the traditions as a river of abundant good, whiter than milk, the pool of which serves as a meeting place for the Prophet's multitudinous nation (al-Tabrisi, Amin al-Din 10:835–9; Muslim 4:14 212, #400).

Water as Original Beauty

Water's loveliness need not only be enjoyed in paradise. The Prophet Muhammad, in a *hadith*, expresses ecstatic joy at fresh rainwater as a recent reminder of God:

> We were with God's Messenger when rain fell upon us... God's Messenger laid aside part of his attire, so that the rain would hit him [uncovered]. We asked, "Why did you do this?" He replied, "Because it is recent from its Lord, may He be Exalted" [Muslim 9:2 446, #898].

The Sufi and philosopher Abu al-Hasan ʻAli ibn Muhammad al-Daylami (fl. 974) uses this event to illustrate that ontological closeness to Universal Beauty functions as one factor causing the beauty of particular entities (Zargar 74; al-Daylami 23). In other words, the closer a given entity is to the source of beauty, the more beauty it emits. Sufism's famous thinker Muhyi al-Din ibn al-ʻArabi (d. 1240) also reads this *hadith* aesthetically, commenting that that which has more recently been with its Lord, here rain (but also other "fresh" entities, such as children), has the ability to subdue others, even those who hold the most exalted of spiritual ranks, namely, prophets (Ibn al-'Arabi 198). These two figures use this tradition to depict the Prophet as a lover of beauty, beauty of a very specific kind: a beauty of nature and its cycles, appreciated with a love that transcends the natural or the functional.

Water as Unity in Multiplicity

Esoterically inclined readers of the Qur'an, especially those within the Sufi tradition, appreciated the Qur'an's description of water as one entity with various manifestations. Ibn al-'Arabi uses verses describing two types of water, fresh and salt, or "sweet" and "brackish" (25:53, 35:12), to discuss the function of various faculties and senses: knowledge, like water, is one reality, but different organs acquire different sorts of knowledge, based on their created disposition, just as water varies in taste and quality depending on its location (Ibn al-'Arabi 107). Similarly Mawlana Jalal al-Din Rumi (d. 1273) comments that, as long as the water is sweet (that is, as long as one seeks knowledge from the proper spiritual guide), "from it would spring up one hundred plants" (Rumi 6:194, line 4321). Moreover, the repeated Sufi imperative to discover one unifying source for creation's multiple manifestations finds support in the Qur'an's description of manifold plants and fruits resulting from "one water" (13:4).

Water as Sufi Literary Tool

Rumi's lengthy narrative poem, *Mathnawi-i Ma'nawi*, manages — more than any other literary composition that comes to mind — to maintain the protean range of significance the Qur'an gives to the image of water. Water in Rumi's poetry, as in the Qur'an, never means one thing. For example, Rumi uses water to describe the relentlessly changing stream of events and time (Rumi 6: 152, line 3338), or to describe the power of an infinitesimal part to indicate the universal (Rumi 6:75, line 1502). Of course, this is partly due to Rumi's style, a style in which the fluctuating metaphor, reinterpreted in a secondary or tertiary way, is a central mode of discourse. Yet the range of significations for water also reflects the traditions that Rumi has inherited; not only the Arabic and Persian literary traditions, but also the exoteric and esoteric Islamic sciences.

An excellent example of Rumi's uses of water appears in the story of a poor Bedouin who, prompted by his starving wife's pleas, seeks out the caliph, famed for generosity. From the outset, the terms Rumi uses to describe this caliph employ the associations between generosity and water found in Arabic literature, such that, "in a world of dust," the caliph is "clouds and rain"; he is the "water of life and a sea of generosity" (Rumi 1:196, lines 2258 and 2262). When the Bedouin sets out, he brings his most prized possession as a gift to the caliph, namely, rainwater painstakingly collected and carefully transported in a prized new pitcher. Rumi uses this opportunity to introduce another facet of water's significance:

> What is that pitcher? Our body circumscribed,
> in which is the saline water of our senses.
> Dear God! This jug and pitcher of ours
> please receive, by the virtue of *God has bought* [*their souls*] (9:111),
> This pitcher, five-spouted for the five senses:
> keep its water clean from every impurity,
> so, in this pitcher, appears an opening to the sea,
> so that my pitcher absorbs the quality of the sea [Rumi 1:217, lines 2720–2723].

With this metaphor, Rumi entwines (1) the ethical, (2) the practical, and (3) the cosmological.

1. Ethically, the metaphor underlines the connection between *desirable* character traits and *divine* character traits; a human only needs to replace his own qualities (his own water) with divine qualities (pure, sea water).

2. Practically, the metaphor also intimates the means to acquiring divine qualities: controlling the spouts of the pitcher or, in other words, monitoring the senses. Here, Rumi probably alludes to a statement of Abu Hamid al-Ghazali that the heart or soul (since al-Ghazali intentionally conflates the two here) can be compared to a reservoir, and the five senses to five streams that flow into it from the outside. Drawing pure water from that reservoir involves stopping the streams' flow and clearing out the mud at its bottom; in other words, reaching the heart's inherent knowledge involves stopping the flow of sensory input and purifying the heart through remembrance of God (al- Ghazali, *Kimiya* 1:36–7). For both Rumi and al-Ghazali, monitoring and limiting the ebb and flow of the senses facilitates the wayfarer's acquisition of divine traits.

3. Cosmologically, Rumi's use of the image of water also indicates God's ultimate reality, since in the end, all water, whether in pitchers or in the sea, is the same: it is all water, subject to varying grades of purity. Such is also the case with meaning, which can be both spirit and existence. Meaning unifies all things and always suggests its source, namely, God. Yet form, the filter through which we encounter meaning, causes everything to seem distinct. The comparison of water (or wine) to meaning, and the pitcher (or goblet) to form, here the human form, is common to Sufi literature.

The message of the story might seem simple. There is only one true gift a person can bring the needless caliph, poverty, for poverty allows the ruler to implement his generosity. Similarly, God's servant should abandon hope of producing anything worthy from him or herself, and instead bring that emptiness and poverty to the needless source of creation. Yet the ontological implications of this metaphor constantly accompany Rumi's ethical discussion. Returning water to the caliph — who has command of the Tigris River — is the height of futility, just as approaching God with any sense of self corresponds to an ironic failure to acknowledge one's own nothingness.

Water as Primary Substance

"The body is composed of water, earth, heat, and moisture," al-Ghazali observes, and in doing so echoes an important mirroring in classical Islamic cosmology, one derived from Greek sources (al-Ghazali, *Kimiya* 1:18). The human body, as a microcosm, mirrors the macrocosm. Since the universe itself is composed of four elements, water, earth, fire, and air, the human body is composed of the four properties al-Ghazali mentions. This mirroring has esoteric implications. Revelation declared, for example, that God "created the heavens and the earth in six days, and His throne had been upon the water, in order to try you: which of you is most excellent in deeds" (11:7). As Sufi-inclined Shi'i thinker, al-Sayyid Haydar al-Amuli (d. after 1385), tells us, the divine throne was upon water because it, just as everything in creation, came to exist in a manner similar to the development of the human being:

> Its meaning is that He created the entire cosmos from water, and there was no barrier between the throne and water at that time, such that it [the throne] was "upon" it [water] — according to

the custom of Arabs. For when they see one thing upon another, without a barrier between them, they say, "It is upon it." The same can be said for the throne of the human heart, for it was upon water, namely, the water of the sperm-drop, until that point when they were separated and the form of the heart appeared [al-Amuli 5:111].

The author's argument eventually traces descending levels of creation after the divine throne, which all began from the primary element of all existence, water. This water derived from something that had existed before, a "gemstone" as it is called in various Shi'i *hadith* reports, one that melted when God gazed upon it with the "awe-inspiring eye" and became water (al-Amuli 5:112; al-Majlisi 54:220, #144). Thus, water, as the Qur'an declares, is the source of every entity that has life, that is, everything in creation (21:30). Yet "water" does not mean the compound of hydrogen and oxygen known in the material world. Water has two aspects, according to al-Amuli, form and meaning, both of which function in his understanding of the cosmos' genesis.

Water's "form" is of two types: first, it is the actualizing principle through which existents acquire bodies, and, second, it is also the water we all know. Water's "meaning" also has two categories: first, it is knowledge, and, second, it is the primary substance of all existent things. In other words, each of these primary, generative realities can be called "water," such that even angels trace their creation to water, because the basic element of their creation is knowledge (al-Amuli 4:46–7). Since, as a *hadith* states, "The heart of the believer is God's throne" (al-Amuli 5:121), the human heart also functions as the throne-like seat of knowledge and thus life for the entire human being. This is true of the physical heart as well as its more important spiritual counterpart, the real heart.

Water as Knowledge

The connection between knowledge and water is frequently found in Sufi and Sufi-influenced texts. According to al-Amuli, "From the perspective of dream interpretation, water invariably signifies knowledge. It has also been said, 'Were knowledge to congeal, it would be water'" (al-Amuli 5:117). In some ways, in declaring water to be knowledge, Sufi commentators reacted to a metaphor intimated in the Qur'an's connection between water, revelation, and individual capacity: "He sends water down from the heaven, and each waterway flows to its capacity" (13:17).

For Abu Hamid al-Ghazali, rainwater represented Qur'anic knowledge, and waterways of varying capacity represented the hearts variously prepared to receive that knowledge (al-Ghazali, *Ihya* 1:99). A later Sufi commentator, 'Abd al-Razzaq al-Qashani (d. 1329–35), uses this verse to describe the descent of knowledge from the Holy Spirit (*al-Ruh al-Qudus*) to hearts of varying preparedness, which washes away the base, earthlike attributes of the soul (al-Qashani 1:340).

Water as Ritual Purifier

As is intimated in the Qur'an (25:48), water is the key purifying substance in Islamic sacred law. In his Qur'anic commentary, *al-Durr al-Manthur*, the Shafi'i jurist, Shadhili Sufi, and prolific author 'Abd al-Rahman Jalal al-Din al-Suyuti (d. 1505) cites traditions supporting the stance that water "purifies, while nothing else purifies it" (al-Suyuti 5:73).

Not only does it purify substances that have been defiled, but water also functions as the main vehicle for purifying believers ritually. This is no minor function. Ritual purity can be considered the key to most Muslim acts of worship, most famously the prescribed daily prayer (Abu Dawud 1:45, #61 and 1:462, #618). Aside from *tayammum* (a process that does not involve water and is used only in exceptional cases), the two central purification rites in Islam, *wudu'* and *ghusl*, both involve washing with water. The first, *wudu'*, is a ritual ablution in which only certain parts of the body are washed, as described in the Qur'an (5:6).

The method for performing *wudu'*, along with some of its spiritual sense, appears in a series of prayers that the Prophet Muhammad's cousin and son-in-law, 'Ali ibn Abi Talib, is said to have made while performing *wudu'*:

> Then he inhaled the water and said, "God! Do not deprive me of paradise's breeze, but make me of those who smell the breeze, its fragrance, and its herbs." Then he rinsed his mouth and said, "God! Make my tongue mention Your Remembrance, and make me of those with whom You are pleased." Then he washed his face and said, "God! Brighten my face on the day when faces are made sombrous and do not make my face sombrous on the day when faces are brightened" [3:106]. Then he washed his right arm and said, "God! Give me my book in my right hand, and eternity in my left!" Then he washed his left and said, "God! Do not give me my book in my left, and do not render it fettered to my neck, and I seek refuge in You from the flames of hell's fires." Then he wiped his head and said, "God cover me in Your mercy, blessings, and pardon." Then he wiped his two feet and said, "God! Make firm my feet on the Path, on that day when feet slip, and have me strive to that which pleases You with me" [al-Kulayni 3:70–1].

The method of executing *wudu'*—and the corresponding interpretation of the verse describing this ritual (5:6)—varies. Thus, just to convey the precision and variety of opinions, Fakhr al-Din al-Razi offers no fewer than forty inquiries that have arisen surrounding the Qur'an's description of *wudu'* (al-Razi 11:296–307). These include whether intention is necessary before the act, whether observing order is necessary, whether the water must reach the skin beneath the beard, whether the elbows are included, whether the whole or part of the head is meant, and whether the feet are to be washed, wiped, or both.

One performs *wudu'* when ritual purity has been lost on account of minor occurrences, such as relieving oneself, expelling gas, losing consciousness either in sleep or by fainting, and, according to the Shafi'i legal school, skin-to-skin contact between a man and a woman who is not a near relative.[4] One performs *ghusl* or "washing" when ritual purity has been lost on account of major occurrences, which most commonly include penetration, ejaculation or menstruation. This washing mainly involves making the entire head and body wet. Needs surrounding *ghusl* begot a key architectural identifier of pre-modern Muslim-majority cities: the *hammam*, the public bath, in which participants enjoyed much more than relief from major ritual impurity, partaking in massages, exfoliation, depilation, steam baths, and social mingling (Sourdel-Thomine, 139–144). One's final purification ceremony, a *ghusl* after death and before burial, involves washing with water as well.

Lastly, the sacred law demands — or, when not demanding, strongly suggests — that a person wash with water after defecation or urination, for "God loves those who purify themselves" (9:108; al-Suyuti 3:278). One must bear in mind that in traditional Islamic scholarship the external, here the body and its faculties, and the internal, namely the soul and its faculties, are intertwined and interrelated. Possibly for that reason, the Sufi commentator Sahl al-Tustari (d. 896) reads verse 9:108, usually interpreted as referring to men praised for washing themselves externally, from an inner perspective: "Such purity refers to remembering God, the Exalted, secretly and openly, as well as obedience to Him" (al-Tustari 74).

Water as Treasured Resource

Islamic law concerns, of course, more than rituals. The Qur'an presents the human being as God's representative presiding over earth as part of a cosmological system in harmonic submission to its creator, clarifying, moreover, when it comes to human consumption, that "God loves not the extravagant" (Chamberlain 51; Qur'an 6:41 and 7:31). Thus, it should come as little surprise that the Prophet Muhammad was concerned with the conservation and fair distribution of water. The Prophet Muhammad reportedly discouraged his companions from wasting water even while performing ablutions and even if one draws such water from "a flowing river" (Ibn Hanbal 2:221). Moreover, despite facing opposition, he commanded landowners to be moderate in irrigation and to share water under their control with other landowners (al-Bukhari 42:6 568, #2359). In fact, one *hadith* describes "water, fire, and pasture" as public goods (al-Tabrisi, Husayn 17:114, #20914), although certain types of water qualify as a restricted public good and—in the case of reservoirs and other certain private locations—as a private good (Kadouri et al. 89–90). The notion that water is a precious and divinely-bestowed resource permeates Islamic writings, from the legal to the spiritual.

Water as Selfless Sympathy

The deprivation of water also has important resonances as an image among Muslims, especially, though not exclusively, those of the Shi'i school (Aghaie 112; Reid). Every year on the tenth day (*Ashura*) of the first Islamic month, many Muslims remember a grievous event that al-Tabari calls "the fiercest battle God created" (al-Tabari, *History* 140). The Prophet Muhammad's grandson, al-Husayn ibn 'Ali, suffered a gruesome death after the forces of the caliph Yazid ibn Mu'awiyyah slaughtered members of his family and a small group of supporters in the desert of Karbala, Iraq.

Water plays an important part in such remembrance, for the opposing army prevented al-Husayn and his followers from drawing water three days before their final stand, causing them to experience excruciating thirst (al-Tabari, *History* 107). Until the afternoon on the day of Ashura, pious Shi'i Muslims are encouraged to avoid drinking water and eating food and to remember al-Husayn's thirst—among his other trials—in a gathering known as *majlis 'aza'* in Arabic or *rawzah* in Persian (Qummi 502). Tears, also, reappear frequently as an important theme connected to al-Husayn's ordeal; Shi'i literature often emphasizes the pious value of weeping for the plight of al-Husayn (al-Tabrisi, Husayn 10:318, #12084).

Moreover, according to Shi'i Islam's most popular devotional manual, *Mafatih al-jinan*, "If a person is at the tomb of Imam Husayn on this day [of Ashura] and gives water to the people, it is as if that person has given water to that holy one's army and has been present with him at [the battle of] Karbala'" (Qummi 502). Giving water or carrying water echoes an act of heroism frequently remembered on this day, that of 'Abbas ibn 'Ali, al-Husayn's agnate brother, who was killed as he tried to gather water from the nearby Euphrates for al-Husayn's camp (al-Mufid 2:109–110).

The practice of water-carrying has, however, a broader memory in Muslim practice than the commemoration of al-Husayn. Water-carriers, in the past and in some places in Iran today, formed a fellowship under the guidance of an elder, a fellowship that celebrated the chivalric values classically associated with Islam's *futuwwah* movements (Zarvani and

Mashhadi 26–8). Indeed, the rite of water-carrying stands as a mark of the confluence of Iran's past Sufi heritage and its present Shi'i denominational affiliation. Distributing water, specifically to pilgrims coming to Mecca, was a prestigious endeavor in pre–Islamic practice as well, as mentioned in the Qur'an (9:19). The association of this practice with the martyrdom of al-Husayn ibn 'Ali has ensured its devotional longevity among Shi'i Muslims.

Conclusion

"Think of people [*khalq*] as water, clear and pure," says Rumi, "in which is the radiance of the attributes of the Possessor of Majesty" (Rumi 6:146, line 3182). Rumi advocates seeing God's beautiful names, the names so emphasized in the Qur'an, as the beauty in all created things. In doing so, he not only reminds us of the God-centeredness of his writings (and the monotheistic God-centeredness of Islamic literatures and practices more broadly), but also of water's function in such literary expressions. Water — pure, life-giving, essential, and multifarious — functions as a source of reverence but also as a perceived reflection of the self. It is, thus, a sign of water's universal conformability that so many have discerned in the image of water a sign of their own convictions.

Chapter Notes

1. Unless otherwise indicated, all translations are by the author.
2. This life-giving quality of both revelation and water sent down by God, along with much of the symbolic significance of water in the Qur'an, has been discussed in detail by Martin Lings.
3. Based on the love of prophets for knowledge, and their exalted ethical qualities, Fakhr al-Din al-Razi cites an argument rejecting a narration that alludes to Moses' supposing that he is the most knowledgeable of people or failing to recognize the limited nature of his knowledge (see al-Razi 21: 478). The spring of the Water of Life is often said to be the source of al-Khidr's immortality (see Poonawala).
4. The Hanbali and Maliki schools hold that such nullifies ritual purity only if done with sexual desire, and the Hanafi and Imami-Shi'i schools hold that such touching — excluding, of course, sexual intercourse — never cancels ablution (Katz 153–4; Chaumont 218–9).

Works Cited

Abu Dawud al-Sijistani, Sulayman ibn al-Ash'ath. *Sunan Abi Dawud*. Ed. Shu'ayb al-Arna'ut and Muhammad Qarah Balili. Dimashq: Dar al-Risalah al-'Alamiyyah, 2009.

Aghaie, Kamran Scot. "The Passion of 'Ashura' in Shi'ite Islam." *Voices of Islam* (vol. 2): *Voices of the Spirit*. Ed. Vincent Cornell. Westport, CT: Praeger, 2007: 111–124.

Amuli, al-Sayyid Haydar al-. *Tafsir al-muhit al-a'zam wa al-bahr al-khidamm*. Ed. al-Sayyid Muhsin al-Musawi al-Tabrizi. Qum: al-Ma'had al-Thiqafi Nur 'ala Nur, 1428 AH.

Bukhari, Muhammad ibn Isma'il al-. *Sahih al-Bukhari*. Dimashq/Bayrut: Dar Ibn Kathir, 2002.

Chamberlain, Gary L. *Troubled Waters: Religion, Ethics, and the Global Water Crisis*. Plymouth, UK: Rowman and Littlefield, 2008.

Chaumont, E. "Wudu' (a.)." *Encyclopaedia of Islam*. 2d. ed. Ed. P. Bearman, Th. Bianquis, C.E. Bosworth, E. van Donzel, and W.P. Heinrichs. Vol. 11. Leiden: Brill, 2002: 218–9.

Daylami, Abu al-Hasan 'Ali ibn Muhammad. *'Atf al-alif al-ma'luf 'ala al-lam al-ma'tuf*. Ed. Joseph Norment Bell and Hassan Mahmood Abdul Latif al-Shafie. Cairo: Dar al-Kitab al-Misri, 2007.

Firuzabadi, Majd al-Din al-. *al-Qamus al-muhit*. Ed. Muhammad Na'im al-'Arqasusi. Bayrut: al-Risalah, 2005.

Ghazali, Abu Hamid Muhammad al-. *Ihya' 'ulum al-din*. Bayrut: Dar al-Kutub al-'Ilmiyyah, 2004.

_____. *Kimiya-i sa'adat*. Ed. Husayn Khadiwjam. Tehran: Shirkat-i Intisharat-i 'Ilmi wa Farhangi, 1382 *hijri-shamsi*.

Ibn 'Abdallah, Muhammad ibn 'Abd al-'Aziz. *al-Ma' fi al-fikr al-islami wa al-adab al-'arabi*. Morocco: Wizarat al-Awqaf wa al-Shu'un al-Islamiyyah, 1996.

Ibn al-'Arabi, Muhyi al-Din. *Fusus al-hikam*. Ed. A. E. Affifi. Tehran: Intisharat al-Zahra, 1380 *hijri-shamsi*.

Ibn Hanbal, Ahmad. *Musnad Ahmad*. Bayrut: Dar Sadir, n.d.

Ibn Manzur, Jamal al-Din. *Lisan al-'arab*. Qum: Nashr Adab al-Hawzah, 1984.

Imru' al-Qays. *Diwan Imri' al-Qays*. Ed. Muhammad al-Iskandarani and Nahad Razuq. Bayrut: Dar al-Turath al-'Arabi, 2004.

Johns, Anthony H. "Water." *Encyclopaedia of the Qur'an*. Ed. Jane Dammen McAuliffe. Vol. 5. Leiden: Brill, 2001: 461–466.

Kadouri, M.T., Y. Djebbar, and M. Nehdi. "Water Rights and Water Trade: An Islamic Perspective." *Water Management in Islam*. Ed. Naser I. Faruqui, Asit K. Biswas, and Murad J. Bino. Tokyo: United Nations University Press, 2001: 85–93.

Katz, Marion Holmes. *Body of Text: The Emergence of the Sunni Law of Ritual Purity*. Albany: State University of New York Press, 2002.

Kulayni, Abu Ja'far Muhammad ibn Ya'qub ibn Ishaq al-. *al-Kafi*. Ed. 'Ali-Akbar al-Ghaffari. Tehran: Dar al-Kutub al-Islamiyyah, 1365 *hijri-shamsi*.

Lane, Edward William. *An Arabic-English Lexicon*. London: Williams and Norgate, 1863–93.

Lings, Martin. "The Qoranic Symbolism of Water." *Studies in Comparative Religion* 23 (1968): 153–160.

Majlisi, Muhammad Baqir al-. *Bihar al-anwar*. Bayrut: Dar al-Amirah, 2008.

Mufid, al-Shaykh Muhammad ibn Muhammad al-. *al-Irshad fi ma'rifat hujaj Allah 'ala al-'ibad*. Bayrut: Mu'assasat Al al-Bayt li-Ihya' al-Turath, 2008.

Muslim ibn al-Hajjaj al-Qushayri al-Naysaburi. *Sahih Muslim*. Riyadh: Dar al-Mughni, 1998.

Poonawala, I. K. "Ab ii. Water in Muslim Iranian Culture." *Encyclopaedia Iranica*. Vol. 1, Fasc. 1. Ed. Ehsan Yarshater. London: Routledge & Kegan Paul, 1985: 27–28.

Qashani, 'Abd al-Razzaq al-. *Tafsir Ibn al-'Arabi (Ta'wilat al-Qur'an)*. Ed. Samir Mustafa Rabab. Bayrut: Dar Ihya' al-Turath al-'Arabi, 2001.

Qummi, Shaykh 'Abbas. *Mafatih al-jinan*. Ed. Muhammad-Rida Ridwan-Talab. Qum: Ayin-i Danish, 2005.

Razi, Fakhr al-Din al-. *Mafatih al-ghayb*. Bayrut: Dar Ihya' al-Turath al-'Arabi, 1420 AH.

Reid, Megan H. "'Ashura' (Sunnism)." *Encyclopaedia of Islam, Third Edition*. Ed. Gudrun Krämer, Denis Matringe, John Nawas, and Everett Rowson. Leiden: Brill, 2011. Online Edition.

Reinhart, A. Kevin. "Impurity/No Danger." *History of Religions* 30:1, 1990: 1–24.

Rumi, Mawlana Jalal al-Din. *Mathnawi*. Ed. Muhammad Isti'lami. Tehran: Kitabfurushi-i Zawwar, 1990.

Sadan, Joseph. "'Ayn Musa." *Encyclopaedia of Islam*. 3d. ed. Ed. Gudrun Krämer, Denis Matringe, John Nawas, and Everett Rowson. Leiden: Brill, 2011. Online Edition.

Sourdel-Thomine, J. "Hammam." *Encyclopaedia of Islam, Second Edition*. Ed. B. Lewis, V. L. Ménage, Ch. Pellat, and J. Schacht. Vol. 3. Leiden: Brill, 1986: 139–144.

Sulami, Abu 'Abd al-Rahman Muhammad ibn al-Husayn al-. *Haqa'iq al-tafsir*. Tehran: Markaz-i Nashr-i Danishgahi, 1369 *hijri-shamsi*.

Suyuti, 'Abd al-Rahman Jalal al-Din al-. *Durr al-manthur fi tafsir bi al-ma'thur*. Qum: Kitabkhanah-i Ayatallah Mar'ashi-Najafi, 1404 AH.

Tabari, Abu Ja'far Muhammad ibn Jarir al-. *The History of al-Tabari (Ta'rikh al-rusul wa al-muluk)*. Ed. Ehsan Yar-Shater. Tr. I. K. A. Howard. Vol. 19. Albany: State University of New York Press, 1990.

_____. *Jami' al-bayan 'an ta'wil al-Qur'an*. Bayrut: Dar al-Ma'rifah, 1412 AH.

_____. *Ta'rikh al-umam wa-l-muluk*. 2d. ed. Ed. Muhammad Abu al-Fadl Ibrahim. Bayrut: Dar al-Turath al- 'Arabi, 1967.

Tabrisi, Amin al-Din Abu 'Ali al-Fadl ibn al-Hasan al-. *Majma' al-bayan fi tafsir al-Qur'an*. Tehran: Intisharat-i Nasir-i Khusraw, 1372 *hijri-shamsi*.

Tabrisi, Husayn ibn Muhammad Taqi Nuri al-. *Mustadrak al-Wasa'il wa mustanbat al-masa'il*. Bayrut: Mu'assasat Al al-Bayt li-Ihya' al-Turath, 1408 AH.

Tustari, Sahl al-. (d. 896). *Tafsir al-Tustari*. Bayrut: Manshurat Muhammad 'Ali Baydun, Dar al-Kutub al-'Ilmiyyah, 1423 AH.

Varisco, Daniel Martin. "The Rain Periods in Pre-Islamic Arabia." *Arabica* 34:2 (1987): 251–66.

Wensinck, A. J. "al-Khidr." *Encyclopaedia of Islam*. 2d. ed. Ed. C. E. Bosworth, E. Van Donzel, B. Lewis, and Ch. Pellat. Vol. 4. Leiden: Brill, 1997: 903–4.

Zamakhshari, Mahmud al-. *al-Kashshaf 'an Haqa'iq Ghawamid al-Tanzil*. Bayrut: Dar al-Kitab al-'Arabi, 1407 AH.

Zargar, Cyrus Ali. *Sufi Aesthetics: Beauty, Love, and the Human Form in the Writings of Ibn 'Arabi and 'Iraqi*. Columbia: University of South Carolina Press, 2011.

Zarvani, Mojtaba and Mohammad Mashhadi, "The Rite of the Water-Carrier: From the Circles of Sufis to the Rituals of Muharram." *Journal of Shi'a Islamic Studies* 4:1 (2011): 23–46.

Zein, Amira El-. "Water of Paradise." *Encyclopaedia of the Qur'an*. Ed. Jane Dammen McAuliffe. Vol. 5. Leiden: Brill, 2001: 466–7.

The Tree

SAID MENTAK

"And the herbs and the trees — both (alike) bow in adoration." (Qur'an 55:6)

Introduction

According to *The World Book Encyclopedia* (vol. 18:334), in addition to their being the biggest plants, trees "do not come and go with the seasons as flowers and farm crops do. Trees give shade, beauty, wood, and fruit to us all." Their uses range, then, from sheltering viewers to protecting and nourishing them. Although the *Encyclopedia* (345) classifies careless humans as the chief enemies of trees for the damage they cause them, it stresses the active role of conscientious and passionate people in growing and spreading trees. There are even those who have acquired the hobbies of cultivating interesting trees.

The Tree in the Arabic Language

In the Arabic dictionary (*al-Mu'jam al-wasit* 870), trees (*shajar*) refer either to erect plants with solid stalks or to plants that are not erect, as the use of the singular word (*shajarah*) in the Qur'an proves: "And we caused a plant [*shajarah*] of gourd to grow over him" (37:146). The Arabic dictionary also mentions the symbolic use of the word tree in the expression describing someone being from a good tree; that is to say, they are from decent origin. As in English, the phrase *shajarat al-a'ilah* (family tree) connotes the lineage of a certain family, the names of its members descending from a founding ancestor. It should be noted here that the Arabs are renowned for the preservation of their family trees; Sayyid Mahdi al-Raja'i informs us that the Arabs used to go to *'ukaz* market to mention their lineage, and Islam confirmed the importance of one's origin while repudiating fanaticism. Consequently, many books were written in Arabic to trace the genealogy of a family tree: Fakhr al-Razi's book, *The Blessed Tree in the Lineage of Talibiyyah*, is a case in point.

The Tree in the Qur'an

The tree is mentioned in the Qur'an in different situations, and at times with different meanings. The forbidden tree, or the tree that Allah warned Adam and Eve against approaching, was the cause of their fall from the garden of Eden, a world "of felicity, innocence,

124

trust, a spiritual existence, with the negation of enmity, want of faith, and all evil" (Yusuf 'Ali, fn 50):

> And We said: "O Adam! Dwell thou and thy wife in the garden; and eat of the bountiful things therein as (where and when) ye will; but approach not this tree, or ye run into harm and transgression" [2:35–36].

Regardless of the type of tree meant in this context, as commentators try to imagine, the forbidden tree was one among many other bountiful things offered to Adam and Eve. Mahmud ibn 'Umar al-Zamakhshari (70–71), for instance, draws our attention to the liberty and felicity Adam and Eve enjoyed. He also points out that the tree was not the only one in the Garden of Eden. Adam and Eve had ample choice and the decision to approach, not to eat, was theirs alone. It is important here to underline the meaning of the word "approach," which is used again in the Qur'an in the sense of "come nigh" with reference to adultery: "Nor come nigh to adultery: for it is an indecent (deed) and an evil way" (17:32), or with reference to indecent deeds, in general (6:151), or the orphan's property (6:152; 17:34). When Adam and Eve approached, or came near, the tree, they became easy preys to Satan; and, therefore, they were seduced to eat from the tree, thus disobeying Allah:

> Then began Satan to whisper suggestions to them, in order to reveal to them their shame that was hidden from them (before): he said: "Your Lord only forbade you this tree, lest ye should become angels or such beings as live forever" [7:20].

The tree, for Satan, a deceiving interpretation as it is, is a way to angelic life and eternity. Adam and Eve, being innocent, were convinced of his interpretation after he swore that he was their sincere adviser. Likewise, Satan managed to convince Adam and Eve to eat from the tree because, as Muhammad Rashid Rida (vol. 8: 249) has stated, it is in the nature of human beings "to love experience, explore the unknown, and desire the forbidden; thus, Satan's whispers have just inflamed their instinctive desires and pushed them to disobedience." From Adam and Eve's experience, Rashid Rida (vol. 1: 282–283) has drawn the conclusion, based on the Qur'anic verse (71:14): "Seeing that it is He that has created you in diverse stages?," that in the process of our life we go through stages: the first stage is that of childhood, where we are like innocent children in a garden full of trees with ripe fruit and running waters. At this stage, we are only inspired by knowledge of good and the prevention of the tree implies an inspiration of the knowledge of evil. The second stage involves the experience and distinction between good and evil. This is our fall from the garden of innocence (caused by our desires and Satan's whispers). The third and final stage is that of our maturity and return to Allah for forgiveness after our repentance. This reminds us of the Biblical connotations of the tree of knowledge in Western literature: the protagonists are innocent at first, taste from the tree of knowledge, are subjected to hardship, and finally acquired knowledge of self. However, from Adam and Eve's experience, the tree does not always have bad connotations. Although it is true that Rashid Rida (vol. 8: 353) believes the tree to be "a tree of instincts that fructifies sin and violation," on the basis that Allah has personified evil and good in the Qur'an by the accursed tree (17:60) and the blessed tree (24:35), trees were also useful to Adam and Eve as they enabled them to hide their shameful parts:

> So by deceit he [Satan] brought about their fall: when they tasted of the tree, their shameful parts became manifest to them, and they began to sew together the leaves of the garden over their bodies [7:22].

The cursed tree and the blessed tree are two types of trees in the Qur'an that have different connotations. The cursed tree is the tree that is referred to in *Surah al-Saffat* (The

Chapter of the Rangers) (37:62) and *Surah al-Dukhan* (The Chapter of the Smoke) (44:43) as the tree of *Zaqqum*. It is a tree that grows at the bottom of hell. When the Prophet's arch-enemy, Abu Jahl, has heard the verse about the cursed tree (17:60), he remarked in his mocking tone: "Your friend pretends that there is a tree that is not burnt by fire which burns stones" (qtd. Tahar ibn Ashur, vol. 15: 147). Abu Jahl ignores here, states Ibn Ashur (vol. 15: 147), the fact that Allah can create a tree that is not burnt by fire. In this sense, the cursed tree for Ibn Ashur is meant to be a trial for the wrong-doers. Additionally, it is also meant to frighten the unbelievers: "As also the Cursed Tree (mentioned) in the Qur'an: We put fear (and warning) into them, but it only increases their inordinate transgression!" (17:60). The cursed tree is described in the Qur'an as follows:

> For it is a tree that springs out of the bottom of hell-fire: the shoots of its fruit-stalks are like the heads of devils: truly they will eat thereof and fill their bellies therewith [37:64–66].

Surely, the fruits of the cursed tree are far from being attractive or agreeable, and the different types of delicious fruits that we taste almost daily stand in stark contrast, which makes the tree more frightening and thus disgusting. Wuhbah al-Zuhayli (vol. 15: 113) adds that the cursed tree is in the farthest place away from mercy.

On the other hand, the blessed tree represents all that is good, agreeable, and attractive. Above all, it is a tree that is used in Allah's description of His light:

> The parable of His light is as if there were a Niche and within it a Lamp: the Lamp enclosed in Glass: the glass as it were a brilliant star: lit from a blessed Tree, an Olive, neither of the East nor of the West [24:35].

Yusuf 'Ali (1016: fn 3000) remarks that "The olive tree is not a very impressive tree in its outward appearance. Its leaves have a dull greenish-brown color, and, in size, it is inconspicuous. But its oil is used in sacred ceremonies and forms a wholesome ingredient of food. The fruit has an especially fine flavor." John Andrew Morrow has rightly observed that the Muslim world "has always revered the olive as a source of food, oil, and medicine. The full appreciation of the olive was the direct result of both Qur'anic and prophetic guidance" (152). Then, Morrow cites many of its beneficial medicinal applications, among which we may mention that "The olive is considered nutritive, emollient, demulcent, and laxative. Internally, olive oil is used to treat constipation, flatulence, and colic, as well as peptic and gastro-intestinal ulcers" (152).

With the exception of the cursed tree, with its disagreeable sight and taste, trees in the Qur'an still retain their beauty, positive utility, and abundance of delicious fruits, thus reiterating in different ways the garden of Eden. It was from a tree in hallowed ground that the voice of Allah came to Musa (Moses) (28:30) after the latter had seen a fire in the direction of Mount Tur and had gone to get some kindling. Also, it was under a tree in the plain of Hudaybiyyah that the believers swore fealty to the Prophet Muhammad (48:18). Trees are used in the Qur'an, together with oceans to stress Allah's infinite signs and commandments:

> And if all the trees on earth were pens and the ocean (were ink), with seven oceans behind it to add to its (supply), yet would not the words of Allah be exhausted (in the writing): for Allah is exalted in power, full of wisdom [31:27].

Allah's "wonderful signs and commandments," explains Yusuf 'Ali (1219: fn 3616), "are infinite and cannot be expressed if all the trees were made into pens, and all the wide ocean, multiplied seven times, were made into ink." Trees, in this powerful image, are not used for their beauty, nor are they used for their nutritive purposes. Their wood is used for knowledge, which remains very limited in citing Allah's signs and commandments. Likewise, trees are used to demonstrate Allah's unlimited powers in creation and re-creation: "The same who produces for you fire out of the green tree, when behold! Ye kindle therewith your own fires!" (36:80).

Then, the positive utility of trees is for bees and humans alike. Allah inspired bees to build their cells in hills, trees, and human habitations:

And thy Lord taught the bee to build its cells in hills, on trees, and in (human) habitations; then to eat of all the produce (of the earth), and follow the ways of Thy Lord made smooth: there issues from within their bodies a drink of varying colors, wherein is healing for men [16:68–69].

The bee, as Tahar ibn Ashur (vol. 14: 204) has pertinently remarked, is a small, weak insect, and yet its healing power is amazing. The honey it produces has different colors and different healing effects. There is the common belief in Morocco that the honey from mountainous regions is better and more effective than that of the trees found in lowlying areas, and that the honey from lowlying areas is better than the honey obtained close to human habitations. The belief is drawn from the Qur'an's classification of the hills first, then the trees, and then men's habitations. Additionally, Allah created trees with abundant fruits for our enjoyment and nourishment:

With it [water] We grow for you gardens of date-palms and vines: in them have ye abundant fruits: and of them ye eat (and have enjoyment),—also a tree springing out of Mount Sinai, which produces oil, and relish for those who use it for food [23:19–20].

It is worth mentioning here that the word "gardens," which translates the word *jannat* in Arabic, does not reflect exactly its Arabic connotations of heaven. *Jannat* is the plural of *jannah*. This is to say that any time types of trees are assembled in the Qur'an in one scene they are described as being heavenly; it is in this sense that the Garden of Eden is reiterated.

A striking allusion to the Garden of Eden is similarly shown in *Surah al-Kahf* (The Chapter of the Cave), where two men are contrasted in their degree of faith in Allah.

Set forth to them the parable of two men: for one of them We provided two gardens of grapevines and surrounded them with date palms; in between the two we placed tillage. Each of those gardens brought forth its produce, and failed not in the least therein: in the midst of them We caused a river to flow [18:32–33].

The other man, however, lives in misery but has trust in Allah. The owner of the garden feels so proud that he forgets the power of Allah. Because of his lack of faith, the man is taught a lesson: the garden cannot stand for long without Allah's protection. Hence, the garden is suddenly turned into ruin, and the proud man finally recognizes his weakness before Allah's power. This kind of garden is what any individual would wish to have, and the Qur'an voices this wish somewhere else: "Does any of you wish that he should have a garden with date palms and vines and streams flowing underneath, and all kinds of fruits" (2:266). Still, with no faith in Allah's will and power, our life in the garden, in spite of its abundance and beauty, would be miserable.

The Tree in the Sunnah

In the *Sunnah*, trees are also copiously referred to, either as prophetic medicinal prescriptions (see Morrow 2011), or as economic blessings for Muslims. However, two striking images are worth mentioning in relation to trees. First, the palm tree, the Prophet Muhammad states, stands for the Muslim:

> "From among the trees, there is one tree whose leaves do not fall, and it is like the Muslim. Tell me what it is?" People thought of countryside trees. 'Abd Allah said, "I thought of the palm tree." Then, the people asked, "Tell us what it is Messenger of Allah." The prophet said: "It is the palm tree" [Bukhari 6216].

The benefits of palm trees are many, yet the fact that they are evergreen makes them more beautiful and more appealing to the beholder. The Muslim is supposed to be like a palm tree: more beneficial, helpful, and positive, thus making people comfortable. Second, the end of life, the Prophet Muhammad confirms, should on no account mean the end of hope in life: "If the Hour (of Judgment) comes, and one of you has a seedling in his hand and has time to plant it, he must plant it" (al-Albani 1424). Two interpretations are stressed in this *hadith*: by trying to plant the seedling in such circumstances the Muslim will be rewarded in the hereafter and, by so doing, he or she never despairs because there is no reason to do so. For a Muslim, life and death are Allah's creations potentially full of hope and good.

Trees are not neglected by the Prophet's companions, the Rightly-Guided Caliphs (*al-khulafa' al-rashidun*), who were vigilant enough to include everything in their discourses for the benefit of the Islamic *ummah* (community). When Abu Bakr decided to send a delegation to *Sham* or Greater Syria, he advised them: "Do not kill children; do not kill old men; do not kill women. Do not violate allegiance; do not truncate palm trees and do not burn them. Do not cut down fruitful trees" (qtd. Muhammad Bik al-Khudari 164). Islam has always been against useless destruction. If trees are needed to sustain human lives, they can be used moderately. Animals and all living beings have a share in trees, as well. 'Umar ibn al-Khattab, however, used the image of the tree to talk about Arabs in general. Talking to the messenger of Salamah ibn Qays, who visited him at home, 'Umar inquired about the price of meat in the town where he came from: "Tell me about *al-muhajirin* [the Emigrants]: how are they?" The envoyr replied, "They are well and victorious over their enemies." "Tell me about the price of meat among them," 'Umar asked, "for it is the tree of the Arabs and the Arabs are no good without their tree" (qtd. in al Khudari 211). The same way the Arabs feed on the fruit of trees, they cannot live without meat. 'Umar's remark reminds us of the Arabs' rural life and the abundance of sheep and camels among them. The image may also imply the analogy of the Arabs with the fruit of a tree: fruit without trees cannot ripen.

The Tree in Islamic Thought

The Tree of the Universe is the title of one of Ibn al-'Arabi's books. Ibn al-'Arabi, the famous Sufi Muslim mystic, thinks of the universe in terms of a tree. His mystic conception of the universe draws upon the following Qur'anic verse: "Seest thou not how Allah sets forth a parable?—A goodly word like a goodly tree, whose root is firmly fixed, and its branches (reach) to the heavens" (14:24). For Ibn al-'Arabi (41–2), and after he has looked at the universe (he says), he finds that the entire universe is a tree. From this tree appear two different boughs with the same root, the Will, whose branch is proportion and measure (42). "If you look at the different boughs of the tree of the universe," Ibn al-Arabi remarks,

You will know the root of that comes from the seed "Be!" "The first boughs grown from this tree were three (49): one bough took the direction of the right —'The companions of the Right Hand' (56:90) or the blessed; another took the direction of the left —'The companions of the Left Hand' (56:41), or the damned; and the third one is upright —'Those Nearest to Allah'" [56:11; 45].

The reason behind the difference in the boughs of this tree and the variety of its fruit is that Allah, Ibn al-'Arabi states (52–3), wants to show

> the secret of His forgiveness to the sinner... His mercy to the doer of good... His bounty to the obedient... His justice to the disobedient... His favor to the believer... and His indignation to the unbeliever. Because the tree of the universe never stops growing, there has sprung from it another bough, which he calls the Muhammadean bough which has spread mercy and blessing on all creations: "We sent thee not, but as a mercy for all creatures" (21:107). Therefore, blessed are those who follow the Prophet Muhammad's way and hold tight to the Islamic blessed bough.

Similarly, though modern in conception, 'Abbas Mahmud al-'Aqqad's book, *This Tree*, takes up the theme of Adam and Eve's forbidden tree to formulate his view of women. Al-Aqqad is a famous Egyptian writer renowned for his audacious views on literature and society. *This Tree* is a book about women, who, in al-'Aqqad's opinion, have inherited Eve's tempting nature. Undoubtedly, even if the book tends to be essentialist, its interpretation of the forbidden tree in the Qur'an is worthy of consideration. What happened to Adam and Eve is, al-'Aqqad (4) states, an eternal story that represents women's unchanging nature. They control men through temptation as men are naturally attracted to what is forbidden (5). The writer adds that the tree in the Qur'an delineates every trait encountered in the character of women:

> So this tree... This tree that the woman has eaten from because she is told not to, which she has fed on and told Adam to do the same... This tree is the symbol of submission that is in women, submission that leads to disobedience, of coquetry that leads to the pleasure of resistance, of mistrust... This is the story of "The Eternal Female," all of it in two words [9].

Whatever the case may be about this provocative description, which most would concede is sexist, as men are also sources of temptation for women, al-'Aqqad seems to have overlooked the fact that the Qur'an addresses both Adam and Eve at the same time; this is to say, they are both held responsible for their eating from the forbidden tree. Unlike the Biblical account, which blames Eve for expelling humankind from the Garden and allowing evil to enter the world in the same way that Pandora opened the prohibited box, the Qur'an states that both sinned, both repented, and both were forgiven (7:23; 20–121–122). Scholars who assert otherwise are grounded in religious and cultural traditions which operate outside of the framework of Islam.

Unlike al-'Aqqad, some other modern writers interested in Islamic jurisprudence have used the image of the tree to refer to the purposes behind the *shari'ah* (Islamic law). Ahmad al-Risuni (13), for instance, sums up the objective of the *shari'ah* in the following terms: "The purposes of *shari'ah* represent the intention of Allah and the purpose behind His charging His servants with laws; they are like fruits from a tree." After studying the goals of the *shari'ah*, Muhammad Jabrun draws on the image of the tree to explain what follows:

> The development of civilization is, generally, like the development of a cork tree which, as it grows, casts off its dead layers. This process continues so long as the tree exists... The analogy between contemporary reality and ancient reality in an Islamic framework can be compared to

the dead or dying layers of the tree of Islamic civilization and the living part that carries with it the possibility of development in contemporary Islamic civilization [173].

The image is a concrete representation of the heated debate permeating the Islamic intellectual scene. Scholars like Jabrun, and many others, favor renewal of the branches without damaging the Islamic trunk. In other words, they believe in the continual regeneration of Islam while remaining firmly attached to its religious roots.

Ironically, only in a story written by the Libyan Ahmad Ibrahim al-Faqih (1997: 11–17) does the tree lose the respect of five big beetles which have decided to eat it up after having put it to trial! The title of the short story is significantly funny: "Five Beetles are Judging the Tree." The olive tree planted near a mosque has protected and cured the town people for so long that it has acquired a historical dimension for the people who are very much concerned about its safety. For the beetles, nonetheless, the tree has just brought so many people to a previously deserted place to unintentionally trample on insects like beetles and kill them. Instead of blaming the people, the beetles find fault with the tree and decide to destroy it. Clearly, in this sense, it is not humans who destroy nature, though in Islamic culture insects, animals, and humans are all supposed to protect nature and benefit from it.

With the universal call for the protection of the environment, Yusuf al-Qaradawi relies on the Islamic heritage. However, instead of using the term "protection" he rather opts for "caring," which he thinks is more appropriate to describe human attention and concern about nature. In his book, *Caring for the Environment in Islamic law*, Qaradawi proves that Islam considers it the duty of every devout Muslim to care for nature since the entire environment in engaged in worshipping Allah (35) along with fellow human beings. The Qur'an itself urges readers and listeners to contemplate the wonders of creation and its submission to the Creator:

> Seest thou not that to Allah prostrate all things that are in the heavens and on earth, — The sun, the moon, the stars; the hills, the trees, the animals; and a great number among humankind? [22:18].

As to trees, Qaradawi cites many verses (58–59) from the Qur'an that encourage the plantation of trees without neglecting the beauty they spread on earth. Then, he moves to the *Sunnah* (60–63) to corroborate the Islamic caring for trees; for example, the Prophet Muhammad said, "Whoever plants a tree, preserves it, and cares for it till it bears fruit, he will receive, for each of its fruit, a reward from Allah" (qtd. Qaradawi 61).

Conclusion

In conclusion, "We urgently need," states Neil Sinden, "to find new ways of living with trees as cultural, spiritual, and emotional companions — as well as for ecological reasons" (qtd. Owain Jones and Paul Cloke 2002: 1). Owing to its reverence and respect for nature, Islam provides all of the necessary ingredients for a sound cultural, spiritual, and emotional relationship with trees as well as the environment as a whole. Regretably, the link between Islamic theory and Muslim practice has not always been evident, especially in modern times. Like people from all places and religious persuasions, the Islamic *ummah* has inflicted an enormous amount of damage upon the ecosystem. In order to protect the environment, a return to an Islamic attitude of admiration, veneration, and respect for nature is clearly in order.

Works Cited

Albani, Muhammad Nasir al-Din al-. *Sahih al-Jami' al-saghir.* Bayrut: al-Maktab al-Islami, 1408 AH.

'Ali, 'Abdullah Yusuf. *The Holy Qur'an: English Translation of the Meanings and Commentary.* Medina: King Fahd Holy Qur'an Printing Complex, n.d.

'Aqqad, 'Abbas Mahmud. *Hadhihi al-shajarah.* al-Qahirah: Dar Nahdat Misr, 1945.

Bukhari, Muhammad ibn Isma'il. *Sahih al-Bukhari* [The Book of Knowledge]. 2d. ed. Bayrut: al-Maktabah al-'Asriyah, 1997.

Faqih, Ahmad Ibrahim. "Five Beetles Are Judging the Tree." *Five Beetles Are Judging the Tree.* al-Qahirah: Dar al-Shuruq, 1997. 11–17.

Ibn al-'Arabi, Muhyi al-Din. *Shajaratu al-kawwn.* Ed. Riad al-'Abdullah. 2d. ed. Bayrut: Dar al-'Alam, 1985.

Ibn Ashur, Tahar. *Tafsir at-tahrir wa tanwir.* Tunis: al-Dar al-Tunisiyyah li al-Nashr, 1984.

Jabrun, Muhammad. *al-Maqasid fi al-fikr al-islahi al-islami.* Bayrut: Dar al-Kutub al-'Ilmiyyah, 2010.

Jones, Owain and Paul Cloke. *Tree Cultures: The Place of Trees and Trees in their Place.* Berg: Oxford and New York, 2002.

Khudari, Muhammad Bik. *al-Dawlah al-Ummawiyyah.* Bayrut: al-Maktabah al-'Asriyah, 2003.

Morrow, John Andrew. *Encyclopedia of Islamic Herbal Medicine.* Jefferson, NC: McFarland, 2011.

Razi, Fakhr al-. *al-Shajarah al-mubarakah fi ansabi al-talibiyyah.* Ed. Sayyid Mehdi al-Raja'i. Qom: Maktabat Ayatullah al-Uzma Mar'ashi Najafi, 1409 AH.

Rida, Muhammad Rashid. *Tafsir al-manar.* al-Qahirah: Dar al-Manar, 1947.

Risuni, Ahmad al-. *al-Fikr al-maqasidi.* al-Dar al-Bayda': Matba'ah al-Najah al-jadidah, 2008.

Qaradawi, Yusuf al-. *Ri'ayat al-bay'ah fi shari'at al-islam.* al-Qahirah: Matabi' al-Shuruq, 2001.

Zamakhshari, Mahmud Ibn 'Umar al-. *Tafsir al-kashaf.* Bayrut: Dar al-Ma'rifah, 2002.

Zuhayhli, Wahba. *al-Tafsir al-munir fi al-aqidah wa shari'ah wa al-manhaj.* Bayrut: Dar al-Fikr al-mu'asir, 1991.

The Sea

NAGLAA SAAD M. HASSAN

*"And if all the trees on earth were pens and the ocean (were ink), with seven oceans behind
it to add to its (supply), yet would not the words of Allah be exhausted (in the writing):
for Allah is Exalted in Power, full of Wisdom." (Qur'an 31:27)*

Introduction

In Islam, there is intensive use of natural imagery. Hence, images of the sun, the moon,
trees, stars, mountains, birds, rivers, winds, and seas abound in the Holy Qur'an and the
prophetic traditions. Mostly, these images are used as signs of God's existence and creation
defying the unbelievers' blasphemy and substantiating the believers' faith. In some cases,
however, images of nature carry deeper symbolic meanings. Predominant among these is
the image of sea.

The Sea in Arabic Language, Literature, and Culture

In the Arabic language, the sea is basically known as *bahr* or *yam* although the Arabic dictionary contains other synonyms such as *zafar, qamus, lujaj, tam, muhit* and *nawfal.* In terms
of vastness, the word *muhit* (ocean) comes first followed by *bahr* then *yem.* The word *bahr* also
denotes metric feet in Arabic poetry. In Arabic lexicography, *bahr* indicates vastness, broadness,
abundance, and generosity. According to Ibn Faris, in his dictionary *The Standards of Language,*
bahr comes from *istbihar* which means vastness. It is used to refer to both salty and fresh water.

The word *bahr* appears in the titles of many classical Arabic and Islamic books and it
usually denotes depth of knowledge and comprehensiveness. Examples include 'Abd Allah
Badr al-Din al-Zarkashi's *al-Bahr al-muhit (The Comprehensive Sea)*, Abu Bakr al-Bazaz's
al-Bahr al-Zakhir (The Plentiful Sea), Ahmad Farid's *al-Bahr al-ra'q fil al-zuhd al al-raqa'q*
(The Clear Sea in Asceticism and Heart–Softeners), and Ibn 'Ajiba's *al-Bahr al-madid fi tafsir*
al-qur'an al-majid (The Huge Sea in Interpreting the Holy Qur'an).

In Arab-Islamic culture, the sea is an important part of nature given the tropical climate
and the sprawling deserts characterizing most of the Arab countries. The Mediterranean,
the Red Sea, the Dead Sea, the Indian Ocean and the Arab Gulf are all major saline water
bodies. As well as being sources of food, jewelry, and oil, these water bodies are essential
means of transportation. They have also played a substantial role in developing and spreading
the Islamic civilization in its early days enhancing the exchange of goods and knowledge
with countries such as China, Spain, and India.

In Arabic literature, the image of sea is often used to imply abundance, opulence, growth, and generosity. Ever since the days of *jahiliyyah* (ignorance) Arab poets have often used sea images in their oeuvre. In addition to comparing their travelling convoys to ships, their beloveds to precious pearls deep in the sea, and their own poetic skillfulness to that of tricky whales ('Atwan 2), early Arab poets have used the image of sea — as well as rain — in their praise poems to commend the generosity and abundance of certain figures. The image of a raging tumultuous sea has often been used to describe mighty knights. During the Umayyad era, poets used to describe their sea voyages, the horrors of the sea, and the fright of those boarding their ships. In the second 'Abbasid era, al-Buhtri, the well known poet, initiated the description of marine battles between Muslim and Roman navies ('Atwan 6).

In prophetic traditions, the sea appears literally and symbolically. In one *hadith*, the Prophet refers to the purity of the sea affirming that its water is valid for *wudu'* (ritual ablution) and its meat is *halal* (permissible) for eating. Abu Hurayrah reported that a man asked the Prophet: "We travel in the sea and we carry with us little water. If we used it for *wudu'* then we would be suffering thirst. So should we still use this water for *wudu'*?" The Prophet replied: "Its [sea] water is pure and its dead is *halal* to eat" (Bukhari). In another tradition, the Prophet uses the sea as a symbol of profusion. He says, "Whoever says, *subhan Allah wa bi hamdihi* [Glory be to God and to Him be the praise] one hundred times a day, will be forgiven all his sins even if they were as much as the foam of the sea" (Bukhari).[1]

The Sea in the Qur'an

Mentioned thirty-two times in the Holy Qur'an, and sometimes substituted by *yam*, the name *bahr* is often used literally and symbolically. Significantly, and as some scientists put it, the ratio between the number of times the words *bahr* (sea) and *bar* (land) appear in the Holy Qur'an (32:13) equals the actual ratio between sea and land found on planet earth (71 percent / 29 percent). Except for a few times, *bahr* is almost always used in the singular indefinite form. When it comes in plural, it usually imparts the geographical entity of these water bodies. In addition to the verses in which Allah refers to the blazing and destruction of all seas on the Judgment Day, there is mention of *sab' bihar* (seven seas) — which indirectly hints at the geographical fact of the ancient world's seven seas.

When it comes in the dual form, the word refers to the parting of two water bodies, whether seas and oceans or seas and rivers. As we read in the Qur'an, "He has let loose the two seas, converging together, with a barrier between them they do not break through" (55:19–20). According to Harun Yahya, due to the difference in the density of the two seas' waters, the surface tension prevents them from mingling with one another, just as if a thin wall were between them[2] (49). In other verses, the parted *bahrin* refers to seas and rivers. Almighty Allah says: "And it is He Who has let free the two seas, this is palatable and sweet, and that is salty and bitter; and He has set a barrier and a complete partition between them" (25:54). The stress on the divider between fresh and salt water has been explained in terms of modern science too. According to Muhammad Wagdi, when the two bodies of waters meet,

> the salty water (the more dense) pushes the sweet water backwards starting with the deepest layer. The two opposing forces, the pushing force by the more dense salty water from one side and the current of the sweet water due to the slope in the river's bed from the other side limits the transition zone. The two opposing forces form a partition. Such partition prevents the salty water from going further into the sweet water region.[3]

The image of the two bodies of water, both salty and fresh, is particularly important in Sufi philosophy. For Sufis, the heart, the center of the body and the axis of its mysticism, is like the isthmus (*barzakh*) which separates the sweet fresh water being the domain of the spirit from the brackish salt sea which is the domain of and body (Linds 50). For them, the duty of the mystic is to reach this isthmus.

Like other aspects of the universe, the sea is also regarded by Sufis as a symbol of the Absolute, the *hijab,* the permanent and the immutable. As Seyyed Hossein Nasr explains,

> the sky, the sea, the mountains, the seasonal cycles, these realities manifest themselves now just as they did in the millennia before and they are the majestic testament of the Immutable in the process of becoming [91].

Because the cosmos in Sufi teachings is a reflection of the human psyche, the permanent elements in nature "evoke in the mind of man those permanent factors that are anchored in the immutable strata of his own being" (Nasr 92).

The sea also bears another symbolic significance for Sufis. In fact, in Sufi teachings, the image of the sea refers to true religion. For them, Allah's messages are like tides coming occasionally, but what remains always is the sea, namely, the truth. For Sufis, the image of the sea also denotes depth of knowledge required in their path towards Allah. As Sa'di of Shiraz explains, "deep in the sea there are riches beyond your imagination. But if you seek safety, that is at the shore."

In addition to the scientific and geographic information laid out in the previous verses, the Holy Qur'an represents other literal and symbolic images of the sea. Besides being included in the long chain of things created by God's hands, and hence destroyed by Him by the end of the world, the sea is mostly grouped with or metonymically represented by ships in order to testify to God's power over humankind and conversely humankind's ungratefulness and disobedience. It is also used as symbol of infinity, bounty and danger. In the stories of Musa (Moses), Nuh (Noah), and Yunus (Jonah), the sea is a two-fold weapon employed against both believers and disbelievers, saving the prophets and their partisans while causing their opponents to perish. Like other aspects of nature, the sea is referred to in the Holy Qur'an to testify to God's existence and to refer to his creation and bounty. Hence, in one verse, Allah refers to the sea along with its creatures, and how they are subjected to human use and benefit:

> And it is Who subjected the sea (to you), that you may eat from the fresh tender meat, and that you bring forth out of it ornaments to wear. And you see the ships plowing through it, that you may seek from His bounty and that you may perhaps be grateful [16:14].

In a number of verses, the sea materializes in the description of the horrors of the Resurrection Day. While in one verse, Allah swears by "the blazing [*masjur*] sea" (52:6), in another, He includes the enkindled sea in the list of natural landmarks that will be destroyed on the Judgment Day:

> When the sun (with its spacious light) is folded up;
> When the stars fall, losing their luster;
> When the mountains vanish (like a mirage);
> When the she-camels, ten-months with young, are left untended;
> When the wild beasts are herded together (in the human habitations);
> When the oceans boil over with a swell... [81:1–6].

In still one more verse, Allah speaks of the destruction of the seas:

> When the sky is cleft asunder;
> When the stars are scattered;
> When the oceans are suffered to burst forth... [82:1–3].

In other verses, the sea is tied to ships to represent divine omnipotence and human ingratitude. A considerable number of verses in the Holy Qur'an refer to the creation of seas and the subjection of ships to the service of humankind as signs of God's all-powerfulness. Hence, in *Surah al-Hajj* (The Chapter of the Pilgrimage), there is the verse:

> Seest thou not that Allah has made subject to you (men) all that is on the earth, and the ships that sail through the sea by His command? He withholds the sky (rain) from failing on the earth except by His leave: for Allah is Most Kind and Most Merciful to humankind [22:65].[4]

The sea is also used as a symbol of infinity. In one verse, Allah argues that the infinity of His words surpasses that of the sea:

> Say: "If the ocean were ink (wherewith to write out) the words of my Lord, sooner would the ocean be exhausted than would the words of my Lord, even if we added another ocean like it, for its aid." [18:109].

In *Surah Luqman* (The Chapter of Luqman), the image of multiple seas unequivocally pins down the matchless infinity and endlessness of God's Words. Allah says:

> And if all the trees on earth were pens and the ocean (were ink), with seven oceans behind it to add to its (supply), yet would not the words of Allah be exhausted (in the writing): for Allah is exalted in power, full of wisdom [31–27].

In another verse, this symbolic infinity is used to substantiate God's omniscience. Accordingly in *Surah al-Baqarah* (The Chapter of the Heifer), there is the clear statement,

> With Him [Allah] are the keys of the unseen, the treasures that none knoweth but He. He knoweth whatever there is on the earth and in the sea. Not a leaf doth fall but with His knowledge: there is not a grain in the darkness (or depths) of the earth, nor anything fresh or dry (green or withered), but is (inscribed) in a record clear (to those who can read).

In other verses, the sea is bound with the image of darkness to testify to God's creative powers on the one hand and to imbue a sense of expanse and danger. Hence, in one verse, the darkness of the sea is linked to the stars to show how the darkness of the infinite sea is offset by the light of the stars:

> It is He Who maketh the stars (as beacons) for you, that ye may guide yourselves, with their help, through the dark spaces of land and sea: We detail Our signs for people who know [6:97].

In another verse, the infinity of the sea is bound with its darkness to give an aggravated picture of its risks and to reflect the vulnerability and helplessness of people boarding ships:

> Who is it that delivereth you from the dark recesses of land and sea, when ye call upon Him in humility and silent terror: "If He only delivers us from these (dangers), (we vow) we shall truly show our gratitude?" Say "It is Allah that delivereth you from these and all (other) distresses: and yet ye worship false gods!" [6:63–64]

The reference to *shirk*, which suggests denying God's bounty and protection and attributing the end of the distress to someone else, is also suggestive of human ingratitude, an idea which is explicitly stated in another verse:

> When distress seizes you at sea, those that ye call upon — besides Himself— leave you in the lurch! But when He brings you back safe to land, ye turn away (from Him). Most ungrateful is humankind! [17:67]

In another place in the Holy Qur'an there is an image of a tumultuous sea whose deep dark depths are wedded to its roaring waves and both act as a vehicle in a metaphor describing the worldly deeds of the disbelievers:

> But the Unbelievers,—their deeds are like a mirage in sandy deserts, which the man parched with thirst mistakes for water; until when he comes up to it, he finds it to be nothing: But he finds Allah (ever) with him, and Allah will pay him his account: and Allah is swift in taking account.
> Or (the Unbelievers' state) is like the depths of darkness in a vast deep ocean, overwhelmed with billow topped by billow, topped by (dark) clouds: depths of darkness, one above another: if a man stretches out his hands, he can hardly see it! for any to whom Allah giveth not light, there is no light! [24:39–40]

Besides giving a sense of unfathomability and illusory abundance, the image has been further gauged from a scientific perspective. In fact, the verse refers to the immeasurable depths of darkness in deep seas and oceans, a fact which has recently been discovered by scientists. It also pinpoints the idea of internal waves lying beneath surface waves, "waves upon waves," a recent oceanographic discovery interpreted in terms of density differences. The internal waves, which cannot be seen by the human eye, but are rather detected by testing the salinity changes at a given location, occur on "density interfaces between layers of different densities."[5]

Where prophets are involved, the sea becomes a dual weapon, rescuing the prophets and the believers and swallowing their opponents. This is particularly clear in the story of Nuh (Noah), Musa (Moses), and Yunus (Jonah). Hence, in Noah's case, the sea carries the Ark on which Noah and the few believers are saved and transferred away from the Flood:

> But they rejected him, and We delivered him, and those with him, in the Ark: but We overwhelmed in the flood those who rejected Our signs. They were indeed a blind people! [7:64][6]

The idea of the sea as a double-edged weapon is particularly evident in the story of Musa (Moses) and the Pharaoh. Accordingly, whereas the Pharaoh and his soldiers are drowned while chasing the fleeing Musa (Moses) and the Jews, the latter are saved in the same sea which miraculously turn into a stretch of land letting them cross safely to the other shore. The details of this miracle are recounted in the Heights chapter:

> We sent an inspiration to Moses: "Travel by night with My servants, and strike a dry path for them through the sea, without fear of being overtaken (by Pharaoh) and without (any other) fear." Then Pharaoh pursued them with his forces, but the waters completely overwhelmed them and covered them up [20:77–78].[7]

The sea is, therefore, a punishment weapon for the disbelieving Pharaoh and his followers.

The use of the sea as a tool of punishment is continued in the narrative of the Jews. Hence, in other chapters, there is reference to the divine manipulation of sea and its creatures in testing the Jews—how they were prohibited to go fishing in the Red Sea on Saturdays, how Allah, to test their surrender and obedience, used to flood the sea surface with fish on Saturdays, and deny them this blessing on other days, how they broke God's command and hence deserved His curse:

> Ask them concerning the town standing close by the sea.[8] Behold! They transgressed in the matter of the Sabbath. For on the day of their Sabbath their fish did come to them, openly holding up their heads, but on the day they had no Sabbath, they came not: thus did We make a trial of them, for they were given to transgression [7:163].

The sea is also a main character in two other stories of Prophet Musa (Moses). Significantly, it is the sea which rescues Musa (Moses) from the Pharaoh when the former was newly born. Influenced by a prophecy that some newborn baby boy will dethrone him one day, the Pharaoh ordered that all infant boys be killed upon their birth. To rescue Musa (Moses), ironically the very person to which the prophecy refers, Allah inspires his mother to put the newly born Musa (Moses) in a wooden coffin and throw him in the sea (*yam*). He was then picked up by the Pharoah's wife who pleaded with the Pharoah not only to leave the baby alive but also to raise him in his own palace. The story unfolds in *Surah Ta-Ha* (The Chapter of Ta-Ha),

"Throw (the child) into the chest, and throw (the chest) into the river: the river will cast him up on the bank, and he will be taken up by one who is an enemy to Me and an enemy to him": But I cast (the garment of) love over thee from Me: and (this) in order that thou mayest be reared under Mine eye [20:39].

The second story in which Prophet Musa (Moses) is involved with the sea is when he goes out with al-Khidr. Described in the Holy Qur'an as "one from among Our servants whom We had granted mercy from Us and whom We had taught knowledge from Ourselves" (18:65), al-Khidr accompanies Musa (Moses) on a journey of divine learning. Musa (Moses) is first warned that he will not be patient enough to stand the actions done by al-Khidr but he promises that he will remain an uncomplaining disciple. In his first lesson and in an action that squarely fits the purposes of the image tackled here, al-Khidr makes a serious hole in the ship he and Musa (Moses) board. Oblivious of his previous oath, Musa (Moses) blurts out, "Have you made a hole in it to drown its inmates? Certainly you have done a grievous thing" (18:72). Khidr reminds Musa (Moses) of his warning, "Did I not say that you will not be able to have patience with me?" and Musa (Moses) pleads not to be rebuked. Later, al-Khidr will tell Musa (Moses) that he damaged the ship to prevent its poor owners from falling prey to the ruthless king who was seizing every ship by force. The sea here is a place of learning.

Continuing to play the same positive role with prophets, the sea emerges again in the story of Yunus (Jonah). Frustrated with his people who refuse to listen to his Message and continue to worship their inanimate idols, Yunus (Jonah) leaves his village and boards a sailing ship for an undetermined destination. The ship is then struck by a fierce storm. After several attempts at divination, Yunus (Jonah) is thrown in the sea to lessen its load. He is then swallowed by a huge fish which keeps him intact inside its belly, then throws him out ashore. Instead of swallowing the prophet and making him meet his end, the sea saves and protects him until, after admitting his sin and seeking forgiveness from Allah, he is tossed onto the land. The story is mentioned in detail in the following verse:

And verily, Yunus was one of the Messengers. When he ran to the laden ship: Then he (agreed to) cast lots, and he was among the losers. Then a (big) fish swallowed him as he had done an act worthy of blame. Had he not been of them who glorify Allah, he would have indeed remained inside its belly (the fish) till the Day of Resurrection. But We cast him forth on the naked shore while he was sick. And We caused a plant of gourd to grow over him. And We sent him to a hundred thousand (people) or even more. And they believed; so We gave them enjoyment for a while [37:139–148].

Conclusion

Essential to the image of the sea, therefore, is a continuum of paradoxes between life and death, provision and ungratefulness, destruction and re-construction. Hence, while the atheists are made to drown during the Flood and the Exodus, prophets and believers are rescued in the same water body. Although willingly plunging himself into it, Prophet Yunus (Jonah) remains unharmed and is even aided by a sea creature until God grants him forgiveness expel him — safe and sound — unto earth. As such, the sea is as much a symbol of destruction as it is of salvation. Considering the oceanic depth of sea imagery in Islamic sources, where it stands as a sign of Allah, this study, has simply explored it surface in the hopes of enticing others to take a symbolic plunge.

Chapter Notes

1. The image of sea foam is used in other *hadiths* as well. One more example is the *hadith* that says "whoever keeps the *zuhr* [noon] prayer, will be forgiven all his sins even if they are as much the froth from the sea" (Tirmidhi).

2. According to Harun Yahya, this is clear in the area where the Mediterranean Sea and the Atlantic Ocean meet. Although water from the Mediterranean Sea enters the Atlantic between Gibraltar and Morocco, its temperature, salinity, and density does not change because of the barrier that separates them.

3. This fact has been revealed by oceanographers only toward the end of the nineteenth century. They have shown that in estuaries, where fresh (sweet) and salt water meet, there is "pycnocline zone with a marked density discontinuity separating the two layers" (Davis 92–93).

4. This meaning is repeated in *Surah al-Isra*: "And when harm touches you upon the sea, those that you call upon vanish from you except Him. But when He brings you safe to land, you turn away. And man is ever ungrateful" (17:67). It is also touched upon in verse 33 of *Surah Ibrahim* (The Chapter of Abraham) and verse 164 of *Surah al-Baqarah* (The Heifer).

5. Internal waves cover the deep waters of seas and oceans because the deep waters have a higher density than the waters above them (Islam Guide).

6. "Because of their sins they were drowned (in the flood), and were made to enter the Fire (of Punishment): and they found — in lieu of Allah. None to help them" (71:25).

7. The gist of this story is repeated in other verses. "So We exacted retribution from them: We drowned them in the sea, because they rejected Our signs and failed to take warning from them. And We made a people, considered weak (and of no account), inheritors of lands in both east and west, — lands whereon We sent down Our blessings. The fair promise of thy Lord was fulfilled for the Children of Israel, because they had patience and constancy, and We levelled to the ground the great works and fine buildings which Pharaoh and his people erected (with such pride). We took the Children of Israel (with safety) across the sea" (7:136–138). The miraculous transformation of part of the sea into a land path is reiterated in *Surah Ta-Ha* (The Chapter of Ta-Ha): "We sent an inspiration to Moses: 'Travel by night with My servants, and strike a dry path for them through the sea, without fear of being overtaken (by Pharaoh) and without (any other) fear.' Then Pharaoh pursued them with his forces, but the waters completely overwhelmed them and covered them up" (20:77).

8. According to Muhammad ibn Ishaq, Dawud ibn al-Husayn, and others, the village mentioned here is Aylah on the Red Sea.

Works Cited

'Ali, 'Abdullah Yusuf, trans. *The Holy Qur'an*. Brentwood: Amana Corporation, 1983.
'Atwan, Husayn. *Wasf al-bahr wa al-nahr*. Bayrut:Dar al-Jil, 1982.
Davis, Richard A. *Principles of Oceanography*. Boston: Addison Wesley Longman, 1977.
Ibn Faris, Abu al-Husayn Ahmad. *Mu'jam maqayis al-lughah*. Bayrut: Dar al-Fikr, 1979.
Ibn Kathir, Isma'il ibn 'Umar. *Tafsir Ibn Kathir*. 'Amman: Aal al-Bayt Institute for Islamic Thought, 2005. Internet: www. al-tafsir.com
Khan, 'Inayat. *Sufi Teachings: Lectures from Lake O'Hara*. Victoria, BC: Ekstasis Editions, 1994.
Lings, Martin. *What is Sufism?* Berkeley: University of California Press, 1975.
Tabarsi, al-Fadl ibn al-hasan. *Tafsir majma' al-bayan fi tafsir al-Qur'an*. 'Amman: Aal al-Bayt Institute for Islamic Thought, 2005. Internet: www.al-tafsir.com
Tirmidhi, Muhammad ibn 'Isa. *Sunan al-Tirmidhi*, Homs: Maktabat Dar al-Da'wah, 1965.
Wagdi, Mohammad N. *Exploring the Scientific Miracles*. Internet: www.scienceinquran.com
Yahya, Harun. *Miracles of the Qur'an*. Toronto: al-Attique Publishers, 2001. Internet: harunyahya.com

The Ship

Said Mentak

"And among His signs are the ships, smooth-running through the ocean." (Qur'an 42:32)

Introduction

The word "ship" is used, according to *Merriam-Webster's Collegiate Dictionary*, to refer to "a large seagoing vessel." However, linguistically, it can, at times, denote a large boat or simply a boat "propelled by power or sail," and both ship and boat are subsumed under the word "ark." In translating the word "ship" into Arabic, the choice falls between *fulk*, *safinah* (ark and ship), or *zawraq* (a boat). It is interesting to note, in this context, that the word *safinah*, used many times in the Holy Qur'an, is translated once into English as "ark" with reference to Noah's Ark, and another time as boat in describing the journey of Musa (Moses) with Khidr, the knowledgeable servant of Allah, who was sent to teach Moses the hidden meanings of things in their connection with human perception and acts in ordinary life. This difference in the translation of the same word is deduced by the translator from the context only. Symbolically, in both English and Arabic cultures, the words "ship" and "ark" connote fortune, protection, and safety. Still, it is only in Arabic culture that the word "ship" is used in the expression "the ship of the desert" to refer to the camel, which patiently crosses the desert with an astounding resistance to thirst.

The Ship in the Qur'an

Building the ark took Nuh some time and incited acrimonious reactions on the part of the unbelievers. The unbelievers looked at the surface of things and ridiculed Noah who, for them, was working on an ark far away from the sea and there was no sign of water anywhere. Besides, the passers-by satirically inquired, did Noah change his mission, a prophet turning into a carpenter?

> Forthwith he (starts) constructing the Ark: every time that the chiefs of his people passed by him, they threw ridicule on him. He said: "if ye ridicule us now, we (in our turn) can look down on you with ridicule likewise!" [11:38].

The unbelievers were ignorant of the secret meaning of the ark and never asked what sort of future ridicule Noah was talking about (Asha'rawi 42).[1] Logically, an ark required water but since they rejected Noah's saving message they would consequently disbelieve in miracles:

At length, behold! There came Our command, and the fountains of the earth gushed forth! We said:

"Embark therein, of each kind two, male and female, and your family — except those against whom the Word Has already gone forth, — and the Believers." But only a few believed with him [11: 40].

Therefore, water sprang out of earth all of a sudden and the ark acquired its otherwise lost significance. In a flood, where waves were like mountains, an ark was the only means to save those who believed. Those who did not believe were doomed to drown even if they were very close members of Noah's family — his wife and his son — who wrongly thought that if he went to a mountain he would be saved. Nevertheless, the ship obviously proved more useful than the mountain in times of flooding waters. Finally, the ship physically saved the believers and took them away from the troubling unbelievers to a place more secure.

Symbolically, Noah's Ark could also be called the ship of faith in Allah's straight path, the path of salvation. Allah showed humans the straight path but humans chose their own crooked ways. Noah selected the believers to save them for the one purpose of guaranteeing the continuation of the straight path. Thus, the ship has gained larger dimensions than those of simply moving believers from a place to another, and it is thanks to the ship that the very few who believed in God remained alive. For Sayyid Qutb, what happened to Nuh (Noah) is an example, among many others in the Holy Qur'an that is meant to show people the outstanding landmarks for strongly built societies:

Landmarks have become clearer to this ummah (Muslim community), and this outstanding landmark (Nuh's dialog with his son) was built on the true nexus that should construct the Muslim society, and on nothing else. Allah has asked the ummah to go straight on the road with resolution and clarity represented by many situations and by the many instructions in the Holy Qur'an [1887].

Since Noah's son refused to join the believers onboard the ship, thus claiming his disbelief in his father's message, he was drowned like the others. His blood nexus with his father could not save him; the true nexus, therefore, was belief in Allah. The Flood event was of such paramount importance that the blood nexus could not have assured the fair continuation of a race of believers; Allah's mercy is shown through His justice: "And a Sign for them is that We bore their race (through the Flood) in the loaded Ark; and We have created for them similar (vessels) on which they ride" (36: 41–2).

Still, Muhyi al-Din Ibn al-'Arabi, the Sufi philosopher, has his mystic reading of Noah's Ark and the flood. In a strange manner, the downpour from the sky and the springing waters from the earth were meant to fuse light with soul and self. The waters of the earth pushed up "the light through the soul to the mind," and the waters of the sky sent down "the soul through the light to the self" and we can imagine a ship sailing in such a mystic flood (236). No doubt it is not a normal ship; is it real or spiritual?: "When the soul reached the self, they became Noah's; and when the light reached the mind, the light turned into pictures" (236). The mystic finds in Noah's Ark a symbol for a voyage into the soul to reach the unexplainable.

Allah's messenger Yunus (Jonah) wrongly thought his escape would be assured by means of the ship. However, being overladen with passengers, the ship might sink. Yunus despaired of ever convincing his people to profess Allah alone, so he planned to escape via the sea to another people who might listen to him. As soon as Yunus had left, storms and strong winds started and his people, as if reminded of Nuh's Ark and the storm, were frightened and ran back to belief. Regarding Yunus, the Holy Qur'an informs us,

When he ran away (like a slave from captivity) to the ship (fully) laden, He (agreed to) cast lots, and he was of the rebutted [37:140–1].

Many times did the passengers draw lots for the person to be thrown from the ship to the sea to make it lighter and it was Yunus who should be the one. The ship is not always a safe means after all. Allah's help is necessary. Besides, had the ship been in a favorable context (not over laden, that is) Yunus could have safely reached his destination. Both Nuh (Noah) and Yunus were Allah's messengers, yet, being the captain and having Allah's support, as it were, the ship moved smoothly to its secure shore. Yunus had to learn that there was no escape from Allah's destiny.

The ship, when small, can also have particular connotations for individuals. It becomes a means of sustenance for some and an attractive commercial target for despots. Khidr, the good man, sent by Allah to teach Musa (Moses) the hidden meanings of things, scuttled a ship belonging to poor people. Musa (Moses) did not like the good man's act in sympathy with the poor owners, but he was not aware of the hidden, bigger harm: an unjust king was going to deprive the poor of the ship. Therefore, once the ship is scuttled, the king will not think of ever taking it. The poor owners would surely dislike Khidr's act, but the Holy Qur'an teaches us through this example that we may dislike something while we are ignorant of the impending good that might come out of it.

The image of the ship can be generally understood in positive terms once the bounty of Allah is not ignored or denied. The ship is a means of economic prosperity as it is a means of communication. People used to discover other people and other cultures, used to trade with them and communicate thanks to the sailing ships: "It is Allah Who has subjected the sea to you, that ships may sail through it by His command, that ye may seek of His bounty" (45: 12). Hence, believers are supposed to thank Allah and show gratitude:

He it is who enableth you to traverse through land and sea; till when ye even board ships;— they sail with them with a favorable wind, and they rejoice thereat; then comes a stormy wind and the waves come to them from all sides, and they think they are being overwhelmed: they pray unto Allah, sincerely offering (their) duty unto Him, saying, "If Thou dost deliver us from this, we shall truly show our gratitude!" [10: 22]

The whole universe is Allah's creation and humans, with their ingenuity (Allah's bounty) have created ships. Nonetheless, ships cannot sail smoothly without favorable winds or favorable waves, over which humans have no control. And here is introduced the element of faith that connects humans to their Creator and stresses the importance of gratitude.

The Ship in the Sunnah

During the time of the Prophet Muhammad the ships helped some Muslims out of their predicament. After two years of the call to Islam, the Prophet found it difficult to protect his followers due to the suffocating pressure exercised by the unbelievers on Muslims. Hence, he advised some of them to go to Ethiopia, where there was a Christian king with a strong sense of justice. Muslims were to move to the coast where two ships were about to leave to the south. By the time a Qurayshi group reached the coast to kill the fleeing Muslims, the latter had already moved far away. Once in Ethiopia, the Christian king treated the Muslim escapees with justice and assured their protection. In this sense, we could venture to say that while the two ships literally took the Muslim escapees safely to the Christian kingdom, they symbolically built a bridge between Islam and Christianity. This is how Imad al-Din Khalil indirectly established this connection of the literal to the symbolical: the journey to Ethiopia was "made easy by the ships, and by the help of the monsoon to this sea journey in such circumstances in addition to the good doctrinal relationship between Islam and Christianity" (65).

Nonetheless, never has the image of the ship taken its wider symbolical dimension as in the *hadith* about the individual, social responsibility, and the limits of liberty. The Prophet Muhammad once said:

> The example of the persons abiding by Allah's restrictions and those who violate them is like the example of those folks who drew lots for their share in a ship. Some of them got the upper part of the ship, and the others the lower. When the latter needed water, they had to go up to bring water and pass by those above, so they said, "Let us make a hole in our share of the ship and get water instead of harming those above us." If the people in the upper part left the others to do what they wanted, all the people onboard the ship would perish, and if they prevented them, they would all survive [Bukhari 749–750].

The first striking feature of this vivid picture lies in the connection between the people of the ship to those outside. Obvious as the connection might be, there still remain certain basic intrinsic and extrinsic constituents to explain to make the image clearer for a discussion of its expanded implications for Islamic culture to date.

The first constituent is that only two types of people can be involved: those who abide by Allah's rules and those who do not. However, in another version of the same *hadith* there is a third type: those who flatter and ignore taking action against the sinners. The three types could exist but it is impossible, as al-Asqalani has perceptively put it, to have only the sinners and the flatterers, or the whole society would collapse (369–70). However, the existence of the two types, those who abide by the rules and those who do not, is possible because not all the people in a society choose destruction over survival.

The second constituent refers to the human choice to build or destroy the common good. The people of the ship have signed up for drawing lots on their share in the ship and it is obviously the case that both parties will rest content with the results. The social agreement between the two parties also stems from the conviction that sharing is necessarily imposed by life circumstances; otherwise, each party would wish to live in isolation. That is why the image of the ship here is very pertinent. There is only one ship and the only choice people have is to share. However, sharing does in no way indicate doing harm to partners, by making a hole in the one ship that is supposed to save them all.

The third constituent relates to social duties. Those who have taken the upper part of the ship are not as privileged as they might think they are. Their responsibility to protect the common good is greater than those below. They are required to be always vigilant. On the other hand, those who have taken the lower part of the ship do not, interestingly enough, complain of being below or in the lower class. They have ironically interpreted taking water from above as a harmful act and making a hole in the ship would save them embarrassment and not lead to their extinction.

The fourth, and final, but this time extrinsic constituent of the *hadith* has to do with its wider implications in Islamic culture, especially the modern Islamic culture in its connection with the West. Muslims in traditional times found in the image of the ship two major implications: one implication covers the importance of promoting virtue and preventing vice, and the other implication is connected with Islamic jurisprudence. Drawing lots (*al-qura'*) to decide on shares as the *hadith* proves is allowed by Islam. Thus, the image of the ship was not given its due as an image, yet with the advent of Western modern theories the image is read by Muslim scholars, in addition to what was stressed in tradition, in different ways.

For instance, the Muslim scholar, Muhammad 'Ali al-Sabuni bases his discussion of personal freedom on this image of the ship. For him, the image is a perfect example to those who blindly believe in individual freedom regardless of religious restrictions:

> The Prophet means by this image those who have lost their way, and gone astray, and have wrongly understood freedom; so they have lived their lives according to their whims and desires ... and the image is another example to those who have seen evil and closed their eyes as if they are not concerned and thought they are doing good [33–34].

Those who overlook evil and those who believe in individual freedom share in floundering the common good because, al-Sabuni explains, "our situation in this life, living on the planet earth, is like ship passengers. Among us are the righteous and the immoral, the good and the bad, so if we leave the evil ones free doing what they like, without even advising them, or preventing them, we will all perish" (34).

Similarly, Bakri Shaykh Amin and 'Abd al-Fatah Tabbarah think of the *hadith* as reflecting the right of the individual and the right of the community. Bakri Shaykh Amin remarks that some people invoke the right of the individual and others hesitate as to the right of the community when the right of the individual is invoked while, in fact, the right of the community is at stake when many individuals claim their right to do what they like. Hence the importance of the image of the ship:

> The two parties have owned this ship, which has two floors, and each passenger has his/her place and his/her own property in the ship. When a passenger comes and says: my place is my property I will do in it what I like, and it is my right to make a hole in my place to draw water and avoid harming others [146].

The individuals, like this passenger, Bakri Shaykh Amin further explains, by claiming their right proper to them alone, overlook the fact that they are going to cause not only the death of the other passengers but theirs as well. Bakri Shaykh Amin calls such individuals fools because they ironically think they are not harming the others by making a hole in their own property. Then, in this sense, using force can be justifiable for the protection of these individuals. Almost the same idea is advanced by 'Abd al-Fatah Tabbarah who specifies the people who are qualified to protect the community. It is the political leaders and the *'ulama'* (Muslim scholars) who must show continuous vigilance against the spoilers. The Prophet Muhammad, he adds, "wanted that Muslims spread in their society the spirit of the community and that the individual remain a member in it ... and that individual freedom is connected to the benefit of the society" (35).

On the other hand, according to Hasan Habannaka al-Maydani, the image of the ship is not confined only to Muslims but to all human societies. If the sea stands for life with its calm and sweet moments, hardship and darkness, the passengers onboard the ship will definitely risk a lot unless they agree to work for the common good and establish values of solidarity and mutual understanding (194). Therefore, the passengers of the ship inside a Muslim society are required "to apply Islamic jurisprudence and socially push the wrongdoers to respect Islamic social norms" but outside Muslim society they are supposed to give a good example to other cultures and spread the values of justice and democracy (198–99). In this context, it is not enough for all passengers of the ship to reform themselves alone and ignore others; individuality with social responsibility can always positively contribute to the welfare of all human societies. Above all, once at sea, egoism will not save the ship from sinking.

Finally, with his political and religious overtones, Muhammad Qutb gave the image of the ship a new perspective imposed by the context of Muslim Brotherhood in Egypt in his time. Qutb does not see in the ship merely that sea vessel, but even the earth for him could become a sea of troubles when religious control gets loose and carelessness prevails. In this sense, the ship for him is a ship of society: "Many people forget — in the midst of it all — this truth. They forget the ship of society or the ship of life. They forget. And they think they are on land, fixed without being disturbed or removed. That is why they become debauched or despots" (158). Hence, after giving concrete examples of different individuals onboard this ship of society, he warns against leniency and seeking excuses. The first time a misdeed is condoned, it spreads and becomes the rule. But Qutb has two remarks to make about the image of the ship: first, the two floors, one above and the other below, do in no way reflect hierarchy (the masters and the slaves); they rather reflect degrees of faith in Allah. Those below could be more faithful than those above. Second, both parties onboard the ship have very close interests — to keep the ship going safely (167–68). Corruption spreads like fire, and once the ship is scuttled for one reason or another, everybody's interest will certainly come to an end.

Conclusion

The image of the ship in the Holy Qur'an, the *Sunnah*, and Islamic culture takes different facets and can go beyond cultural boundaries. From the image as image to the image as idea, or from the image as concrete object to the image invoking symbolical notions, the image of the ship remains over time very effective. We might not agree in this sense with Thomas W. J. Mitchell, who believes that "it is a commonplace of modern cultural criticism that images have a power in our world undreamed of" by those before us (7–8).[2] Images have always had power over humans all over the world and, in Islam, the Holy Qur'an and the Prophet Muhammad have resorted to images to make messages clear and lively. Also, if ever asked about the degree of cross-language equivalence in the translation of the image of the ship, which some might think is culture specific and therefore topical, one might argue that in spite of its "fixed language-specific expressions" in Islam the image of the ship is universal since many cultures make use of the image in their different disciplines (Trim 66). Finally, in discussing Jean-Jacques Rousseau's political philosophy, Christopher D. Wraight states that "The essential and distinctive feature of Rousseau's model is that all these individuals are in the same boat: all make the laws applied to them equally" (46). It is not surprising, then, if he mentions later in his analysis that one of Rousseau's influences was the Prophet Muhammad (81). Did Rousseau read the *hadith* of the ship? At any rate, there is a striking analogy between the prophet's image of the ship and Rousseau's *The Social Contract*, where "as every individual gives himself absolutely, the conditions are the same for all, and precisely because they are the same for all, it is in no one's interest to make the conditions onerous for others" (Wraight 36). Clearly, the image of the ship in Islam can be a useful catalyst for new cross-cultural ideas in social, political or religious organization.

Chapter Notes

1. The translation of the text is mine throughout where the source title is not in English.
2. It is worth noting here that Mitchell thinks that the power of the image is undreamed of by the

ancient idolaters, but I have referred to those before in general because we think that no human civilization has used the image as we, the moderns, do.

Works Cited

'Ali, Abdullah Yusuf. *The Holy Qur'an: English Translation of the Meanings and Commentary.* al-Madinah al-Munawwarah: King Fahd Holy Qur'an Printing Complex, n.d.

Amin, Bakri Shaykh. *Adabu al-hadithi al-nabawi.* al-Qahirah: Dar Shuruq, 1979.

Asha'rawi, Muhammad Mitwali. *Qisas al-anbiya': Durusun wa Ibarun.* Bayrut: Dar al-Qalam, 2000.

Askalani, Ibn Hajar. *Fathu al-bari sharhu Sahih al-Bukhari.* Vol. 5. Bayrut: Dar al-Kutub al-'Ilmiyyah, 1989.

Bukhari, Muhammad ibn Isma'il. *Sahih al-Bukhari* (The Book of Partnership). Vol. 2. Bayrut: al-Maktabah al-'Asriyyah, 1997.

Ibn al-'Arabi, Muhyi al-Din. "Faslun fi Sharhi Mobtada' Attufan." *Rasa'il Ibn Arabi.* Abu Dabi: Cultural Foundation Publications, 1998. 227–241.

Khalil, Imad al-Din. *Dirasah fi al-sirah.* Bayrut: Dar al-Nafa'is, 1997.

Maydani, Hasan Habannakah. *Rawai' min aqwali Rasul.* 10th. Ed. Dimashq: Dar al-Qalam, 2005.

Mitchell, W. J. Thomas. *Iconology: Image, Text, Ideology.* Chicago: University of Chicago Press, 1986.

Qutb, Muhammad. *Qabasat mina Rasul.* al-Qahirah: Dar Shuruq, 2003.

Qutb, Sayyid. *Fi Zilali al-Qur'an.* Vol. 4. Bayrut: Dar Shuruq, 1982.

Sabuni, Muhammad 'Ali al-. *Min kunuzi al-sunnah: Dirasat adabiyyah wa lughawiyyah min al-hadith al-sharif.* Bayrut: 'Alam al-Kutub, 1985.

Tabbarah, 'Abd al-Fatah. *al-Hikmah al-nabawiyyah kama tatajala fi ahadith Rasuli Allah.* Bayrut: Dar al-'Ilm li al-Malayin, 1986.

Trim, Richard. *Metaphor Networks: The Comparative Evolution of Figurative Language.* New York: Palgrave McMillan, 2007.

Wraight, Christopher D. *Rousseau's The Social Contract: A Reader's Guide.* New York: Continuum, 2008.

Food

Naglaa Saad M. Hassan

"Eat of the things which Allah hath provided for you, lawful and good" (Qur'an 5:88)

Introduction

At the heart of Islamic religion and culture lies the image of food. In fact, food (*ta'am*) is intrinsically tied to Islamic faith and practices; hence, fasting (*al-sawm*), the fourth pillar of Islam, and the concept of *halal* (permitted) and *haram* (prohibited), are integral to Muslims' eating practices, through which food habits emerge as a testimony to faith and surrender to God's will. Eating practices and food choices are, therefore, intrinsic to Muslim identity be it Sunni, Shi'ite or Sufi. For observant Muslims, Islamic dietary laws represent a major identity marker, granting them a sense of spiritual solidarity, and differentiating them from others.

Food in the Qur'an and Sunnah

In the Holy Qur'an and the traditions of the Prophet Muhammad, food and eating appear with remarkable frequency. The Holy Qur'an mentions worldly and heavenly food. It stresses that food is a blessing and delight in this life and the hereafter. In fact, the significance of food in the Holy Qur'an is underlined by the fact that one chapter carries the name "Fig," another is entitled "Heifer" and still a third is named "The Table Spread with Food" (*al-Ma'idah*). In addition to these straightforward implications, the Holy Qur'an shows food laden with multi-layered symbolism. Apart from being a symbol of reward and punishment, as both a blessing and a curse, food is presented as a sign of God's miraculous power, a testimony to the nature of angels, and a proof of the idea of divinity and humanity.

In different places in the Holy Qur'an, food is referred to as *ta'am* from which comes the verb *yut'im* (feed). However, the noun *rizq* (provision) and the verb *yurziq* are sometimes used to give a generic meaning of feeding and food, whether heavenly or worldly. In universal terms, Allah draws attention to His provision — the diversity of fruits and plants and animals which are *ayat* (signs) inviting humankind to ponder over God's existence and inducing gratitude: "Then let man look at his food: We pour forth water in abundance. And We split the earth in clefts. And We cause therein *habb* [seeds] to grow. And grapes and nutritious plants [*qadb*]. And olives and date palms" (80:24–29). Some verses elaborate on how Allah creates different fruits "both similar and dissimilar although they spring from the same soil and water: There are signs in that for people who believe" (6:99). Even when the more universal word *rizq* is used, the message continues to be the same: "Who is it that can provide for you [*yarzuqum*] if He should withhold His [*rizq*] provision Nay, but they continue to be in pride, and flee" (67:22).

Notably, some kinds of food, particularly fruits, are mentioned repeatedly across the Holy Qur'an. Besides underscoring their being a sign of God's bounty, this Qur'anic phenomenon indirectly hints at their nutritional and medical values. Among these fruit plants recurrently appearing in the Holy Qur'an are date-palms, grapes, olives, and pomegranates. Date-palms, for instance, are mentioned twenty times, eight alone and twelve grouped with other fruits, particularly grapes, itself appearing eight times in the Holy Qur'an: "Then We brought forth for you therewith gardens of date-palms and grapes, wherein is much fruit for you, and whereof you eat" (40:19). Olive is mentioned six times and is grouped with fig in a divine oath initiating the *Surah al-Tin* (the Chapter of Figs): "I swear by fig and olive and this secure country" (95: 1–2).

These aforementioned implicit medical and nutritional benefits of these fruits are explicitly stated in Prophet Muhammad's traditions (*ahadith*). The medicinal properties of olives, for instance, are clearly stated in many traditions. Abu Hurayrah narrates that the Prophet stated: "Eat olive oil and apply it locally since there is cure for seventy diseases in it, one of which is leprosy" (Abu Nu'aym). Sayyid al-Ansari narrates that the Prophet said "Consume olive oil, and massage it over your bodies, since it is a holy tree" (Tirmidhi, Ibn Majah). 'Uqbah ibn Amir also narrates that the Prophet stated: "[yo]u have olive oil from this holy tree; treat yourself with this, since it cures the hemorrhoids [*basr*]." In addition, 'Alqamah ibn Amir narrates that Prophet said: "There is olive oil for you, consume it, and apply it on your bodies since it is effective for hemorrhoids" (Ibn al-Jawzi).

When the Holy Qur'an describes these fruit plants as an aspect of heavenly felicity, food ceases to be a sign of worldly provisions and rather becomes a symbol of blessing and reward. The dwellers of paradise are described as living "Amid thornless lote-trees, and banana-trees (with fruits), one above another. And extended shade, and water flowing constantly, and abundant fruit, neither intercepted nor forbidden" (56:28–33). Verses referring to how food is part of the felicities of paradise abound: "And We shall provide them with fruit and meat such as they desire" (49:23); "And with fruit that they may choose. And with the flesh of fowls that they desire" (56:32–33); "Eat and drink with happiness because of what you used to do" (49:19). On the other hand, sinners and wrongdoers are threatened to have "a food that chokes, and a painful torment" (73:13). In fact, the Holy Qur'an specifies three kinds of food for the hell people: *ghaslin* (pus), *al-dari* and *al-zaqqum*: "No food will be there for them but ghaslin [pus]" (69:36); "No food will there be for them but a bitter obnoxious thorny plant, which will neither nourish nor satisfy hunger" (88: 6–7); "Verily, the tree of *zaqqum* will be the food of the sinful, like molten brass, it will boil in their insides, like the boiling of scalding water" (44:43–46).

Accordingly, food can be a blessing and a curse, a means of both reward and punishment, an idea which is particularly evident in the stories of Adam, Musa (Moses), the Pharaohs, and the Jews. In the Holy Qur'an, the story of Adam shows how God had blessed him and his wife with heavenly food and has saved them the throes of hunger. For Adam and Eve, heavenly eating was a kind of blessing, a sort of delight: "You will never be hungry therein nor naked. And you (will) suffer not from thirst therein nor from the sun's heat" (21:119–120). "And we said: 'O Adam! Dwell you and your wife in paradise and eat both of you freely with pleasure and delight, but come not near this tree or you both will be of the *zalimun* [wrong-doers]'" (1:35). Because food is a worldly and earthly desire, Allah uses it to test Adam's will and obedience. It is the lust for food which drags Adam and Eve to commit the first sin that expels humanity from the Garden: "Then Shaytan whispered to him, saying: 'O Adam! Shall I lead you to the Tree of Eternity and to a kingdom that will never waste away'" (21:121). And in another verse, "Then the Shaytan [Satan] made them slip therefrom (paradise) and got them out from that in which they were" (1.36).

The story of Prophet Musa (Moses) and the Jews carries this symbolic use even further. Hence, the Egyptians were punished by lack of fruits in return for oppressing the Jews: "And indeed We punished the people of Fir'awn [Pharoah] with years of drought and lack of fruits (crops), that they might remember (take heed)" (7:130). Leaving Egypt and heading to Jerusalem, the Jews, who withstood the atrocities of the Pharoah, were given heavenly food as a sign of God's blessing: "and We shaded you with clouds and sent down on you *al-manna wa al-salwa*, saying: Eat of the good lawful things We have provided for you'" (1:57). As the stories of the Jews unfold, references to how food was divinely used as means of reward and a testimony to God's bounty and blessing continue: "And remember when We said: 'Enter this town (Jerusalem) and eat bountifully therein with pleasure and delight wherever you wish and enter the gate in prostration and say: 'Forgive us'" (1:58). Demonstrating their restlessness and their rejection of this divine blessing, the Jews invoke Musa (Moses) to ask God for other kinds of food:

> And remember when you said: "O Musa, We cannot endure one kind of food. So invoke your lord for us to bring forth for us of what the earth grows, its herbs, its cucumbers, its *fum* (wheat or garlic), its lentils and its onions." He said, "Would you exchange that which is better for that which is lower? Go you down to any town and you shall find what you want!" And they were covered with humiliation and misery and they drew on themselves the wrath of God [1:61].

At that point, the change of food is matched by a change in its symbolism. It shifts from being a sign of God's blessing to a symbol of His wrath; hence, becoming a curse and a means of punishment. This argument can be developed further when light is shed on the kinds of food divinely forbidden to the Jews in their dietary laws: "For those who followed the Jewish Law, We forbade every (animal) with undivided hoof, and We forbade them the fat of the ox and the sheep, except what adheres to their backs or their entrails, or is mixed up with a bone: this in recompense for their willful disobedience for We are True (in Our ordinances)" (6:146). Although the Torah and the Talmud do not explain the reason why certain foods, such as animal fat, shellfish, camels, and the hare, were prohibited to the Jews, the Qur'an makes it clear that this prohibition was tightly linked to their "disobedience" (6:146) and wrongdoing: "For the wrongdoing of the Jews, We made unlawful for them certain good foods which had been lawful for them and for their hindering many from Allah's way" (3:160). This idea is further underscored by a verse refuting the Jewish claim that this prohibition has its roots in Prophet Jacob's days. Allah states clearly that "all food was lawful to the Children of Israel, except what Isra'il [Israel] made unlawful for himself before the *Tawrah* [Torah] was revealed" (3:93).

In the Holy Qur'an, food is also used as a symbol of God's miraculous power. In *Surah al-Baqarah* (The Chapter of the Heifer), the second chapter in the Holy Qur'an, there is reference to the story of the pious man who "passed by a town which had tumbled over its roofs" (2:259) wondering "how will Allah ever bring it to life after its death?" According to *Tafsir Ibn Kathir*, the man is said to be either 'Uzayr, or one of the children of Israel, and the village was Jerusalem, after Nebuchadnezzar destroyed it and killed its people. The verse narrates how Allah causes the wondering man to die for a hundred years and then raises him up again. Looking around, the man thinks that he was dead for a day or a part of a day. Allah guides him to look at his food, which is said to have included figs, grapes, and juice: "look at your food and your drink, they show no change" (1:259). Allah also asks the man to look at the bones of his donkey to show him how He is able to resurrect the dead, fleshing out the animal's bones and bringing it back to life. Thus, while the donkey was made dead in order to demonstrate Allah's miracle of resurrection, of bringing the dead back to life, the food remained fresh, with no traces of rottenness, in order to show God's ability to stop natural decay and death. In so doing, Allah demonstrated the contested idea of eternity in the afterlife.

The idea of food and God's miracles is also demonstrated in the story of the *ma'idah* (the table spread with food) which was sent to 'Isa (Jesus) and his apostles from heaven. According to the Holy Qur'an, the disciples asked 'Isa (Jesus) to invoke God to grant them some miraculous table spread with delicious, heavenly food, one that can be left as a sign for all generations and will help accentuate their faith. Although 'Isa (Jesus) warned them: "Fear God, if you have faith" (5:112), the Disciples persisted in their request: "We want to eat from that heavenly table until our hearts are satisfied. Then we will know you have really told us the truth. We want to be witnesses of this miracle" (5:113). Thereafter 'Isa (Jesus) invoked God to send them this table: "O God, our Lord, send us this table from heaven set with choice foods that will be a festival for us and a Sign for thee. Provide our sustenance for you are the one who sustains us" (5:114). In response, Allah sent them the table warning them that if they persist in their doubts, they will receive His utmost punishment and torment. Thus, while in the story of al-'Aziz food is miraculously manipulated in order to underscore the concept of resurrection and eternity after death, in the story of the apostles, it is used to substantiate the existence of God and heavens.

Another strategic use of food in the Holy Qur'an is targeted at the controversial issue of humanity and divinity. Hence, while God provides for His creatures — itself a sign of His existence — He Himself is not fed: "Say: 'Shall I take as a guardian any other than Allah, the Creator of the heavens and the earth And it is He Who feeds but is not fed'" (6:14). Being fed means being subject to hunger; it suggests dependability and perishability which both contrast with the idea of perfection and wholeness associated with divinity. Allah says: "I seek not any provision from them nor do I ask that they should feed Me. Verily, Allah is the Provider, Owner of Power, the Most Strong" (51:58–59). Notably, the Holy Qur'an refutes the controversial question of the divinity of 'Isa or Jesus by showing how he and his mother were eating food:

> The Messiah 'Isa, (son of Maryam), was no more than a Messenger; many were the Messengers that passed away before him. His mother Maryam as a *siddiqah* (saintly woman). They both used to eat food. Look how We make the *Ayat* (signs) clear to them; yet look how they are deluded away (from the truth) [5:75].

The need for food is a sign that should drive people away from considering 'Isa (Jesus) their God. 'Isa (Jesus), Allah is careful to declare, is a human being in need for God's bounty in order to survive and can perish by hunger in case God stops His provision. Notable also is the fact that the Qur'an refers to how prophets, including Muhammad, were mocked and rejected by their own people on basis of their consuming earthly food, rather than heavenly one (23:33, 25:7).

The Qur'an also manipulates food images in order to demonstrate the nature of angels and how it differs from that of human beings. There is reference to the story of the angels who materialized to Prophet Ibrahim (Abraham) as mortal guests, "then he turned to his household, and brought out a roasted calf. And placed it before them (saying): 'Will you not eat.' Then he conceived fear of them (when they ate not). They said: 'Fear not.' And they gave him glad tidings of a son having knowledge" (51:25–29). Although the honored guests appear to be human beings, their abstinence from eating the succulent food refutes their apparent flesh-and-blood human figures.

Food is also tightly entangled with Muslim devotional practices (*'ibadat*). In fact, eating is a matter of faith in Islam. This is clearly demonstrated in four facets. The first is *halal* (lawful) and *haram* (unlawful) food by which all Muslims are to abide in their daily meals. The second is fasting the holy month of Ramadan, the fourth pillar of Islam, and arguably one of the greatest religious observances in Islam. The third is the slaughtering of sheep during *hajj* on *'id al-adha*. And the fourth is doing *kaffarah* or "expiation" by which Muslims expiate their oaths, and compensate for their unfasted days in Ramadan.

Islamic Dietary Laws

All practicing Muslim believers are expected to obey God by eating lawful foods (*halal*) and avoiding the forbidden ones (*haram*) which are mentioned in the Qur'an and in the Prophet's traditions. Goodness and dedication to none but Allah are two primary provisions for food to be lawful in Islam. These two provisions are referred to in many verses in the Holy Qur'an: "They ask you as to what is allowed to them. Say: the good things are allowed to you" (5:4). This comprehensive image of goodness as a key to lawfulness is elaborated in other verses wherein are listed all kinds of unlawful food. Allah says:

> He has only forbidden you dead meat, and blood, and the flesh of swine, and that (any food, meat or not) which has been dedicated to other than Allah. But if one is forced by necessity, without willful disobedience, or transgressing due limits; then he is guiltless. For Allah is Oft-forgiving Most Merciful [Qur'an 2:173].

Hence, *haram* food in Islam includes four main categories: blood, carrion, swine, and food dedicated to other than Allah. In other verses, these four categories branch into subcategories; the dead animals, for instance, are further categorized into "animals which have been strangled, and animals which have been killed by a blow, and animals which have fallen to their death, and animals which have been gored, and animals which wild beasts have eaten — except those you are able to slaughter properly" (5:3). Also the quality of blood forbidden is explained in another verse: "say: I do not find, in what has been revealed to me, any food that is forbidden to eat except for carrion, flowing blood or blood poured forth, and pork — for that is unclean — or some deviance consecrated to other than Allah. But if anyone is forced to eat it, without desiring to or going to excess in it, your Lord is Ever-Forgiving, Most Merciful" (6:145).

What is common in all the verses referring to lawful and unlawful food is the idea that there is no punishment for anyone who is forced to eat *haram* food. The idea of allowing the consumption of unlawful food under certain conditions is known as the law of necessity in Islamic jurisprudence or *fiqh*, "that which is necessary makes the forbidden permissible," which, in the case of dietary laws, allows one to eat normally prohibited products if one were starving. This law underlines the flexibility of the Islamic faith. It does not, however, permit Muslims to indulge in forbidden food for any other reason. For meat to be *halal*, it must belong to a category of animals whose consumption is permitted. The animal in question must also be slaughtered by a Muslim in the name of Allah in accordance with the method specified by the *shari'ah*.

In general, all Muslims, including Shi'ites, Sunnis and Sufis are to abide by the food regulations dictated in the Qur'an. Minor differences between Shi'ahs and Sunnis in food practices, can, however, be traced. Foods or parts of animals forbidden based on exclusively Shi'ite hadiths include hare and rabbit, fish without scales, sea creatures with shells, with the exception of shrimp, and certain body parts such as the gallbladder, spleen, bladder, eye balls, and sexual organs. Similar prohibitions are also found in the Hanafi school of Sunni jurisprudence on the basis of *ijtihad* (interpretation of Islamic law to new issues not directly addressed in the Qur'an and *Sunnah*).

Islamic Food Etiquette

Besides setting what is *halal* and *haram* (permitted and prohibited), the Qur'an and *Sunnah* put regulations to eating practices and etiquettes. Hence, mentioning Allah's name over all kinds of food is a must, and its negligence is a sin. Allah says: "So eat of that (any food, meat or not) on which Allah's name has been mentioned, if ye have faith in His signs" (6:118) and in one more verse, Allah says: "And do not eat from that which the name of Allah has not been mentioned, for it is a transgression and a sin" (6:121). Further regulations relating to eating etiquette are laid down in the Prophet's traditions. 'Umar bin Abi Salamah said: "When I was a young boy, I was in the care of the Messenger of Allah and my hand was wandering all over the plate [while eating]. So the Prophet said 'Young boy, mention the name of Allah [before you start to eat], eat with your right hand, and eat from what is in front of you'" (Bukhari and Muslim). 'Abdullah ibn 'Umar narrates that the Prophet Muhammad said: "When one eats then, one should eat with the right hand and, when one drinks, then one should drink with the right hand" (al-Bukhari and Muslim). Also 'Abd Allah ibn 'Abbas narrated that the Prophet said: "Do not blow from your mouth into food and water" (Tabarani).

Although Islam encourages people to eat from the various lawful provisions on land and sea, it warns against excessiveness: "and eat and drink but waste not by extravagance, certainly He (Allah) likes not those who waste by extravagance" (7:31). The Islamic faith requires moderation and reasonableness in handling food is sustained in *hadith* literature. The Prophet is reported to have said: "The son of Adam does not fill any vessel worse than his stomach. It is sufficient for the son of Adam to eat a few morsels to keep him alive. If he must fill it, then one-third for his food, one-third for his drink, and one-third for air" (Tirmidhi). And in another tradition, he says: "We (Muslims) are a people who do not eat until we are hungry. And if we eat, we do not eat to our fill" (Ibn Kathir).

Self-Sacrifice and Charity

The emphasis on moderation and economy in the politics of Muslim eating is much sustained by fasting. All Muslims — Sunnis, Shi'ites and Sufis — are required to fast Ramadan, the ninth month in the Muslim calendar, by abstaining from food, drink and sexual intercourse from dawn to sunset. Fasting is meant to control human desires and lusts; it also aims at creating a coherent society driving the rich to sympathize with the poor given that all Muslims, regardless of their class, experience the throes of hunger. In Arab and Islamic culture, fasting strengthens relationships among members of the community. The prophetic tradition which says "He who gives food for a fasting person to break his fast will receive the same reward without reducing the fasting person's reward" (Ahmad, Tirmidhi, Ibn Majah, Ibn Hibban) drives Muslims to invite each other during this holy month to gain reward, an attitude which spreads cordiality and sociality among Muslims. Fasting Ramadan is also considered a unique opportunity to revive one's bond with Allah. The Prophet said "Perhaps a person fasting will receive nothing from his fasting except hunger and thirst" (Ibn Majah, Darimi, Ahmad, Bayhaqi). Hence, during their fasting, all practicing Muslims, regardless of their schools of law, are usually keen on keeping their prayers, reciting Qur'an, abstaining from sins, giving alms and feeding the poor — this activity which bears great significance in Islam.

In fact, the relationship between feeding the poor and true faith is essential to Islamic beliefs, an idea which is evident in a considerable number of verses in the Holy Qur'an. Accordingly, the believers are asked to give food that they most desire and love to the needy. This is because, among the residents of paradise are those who "give food, in spite of their love for it, to the poor, the orphan and the captive (Saying): 'We feed you seeking Allah's Face only. We wish for no reward, nor thanks from you'" (76:8–9). Alternatively, among the inhabitants of hell are those who refused to feed the poor: "'What has caused you to enter hell' They will say: 'We were not of those who used to offer the salah, nor did we feed the poor'" (74:43–44). The Prophet's traditions further solidify this Islamic attitude. The Prophet is quoted as saying that "among the things that expiate sins and increase one's rank are offering food and praying at night while people are sleeping." In another hadith, Prophet Muhammad equates feeding the poor and saying a good word with one complete pilgrimage. Furthermore, when the Prophet was asked to define faith, he replied that is consisted of "offering food and giving the greeting of peace" (Muslim).

The Symbolism of Sacrifice

The third aspect of Islamic 'ibadat (devotional acts) associated with food is the slaughtering of sheep during 'Id al-adha (the Feast of the Sacrifice). Like Christians and Jews, Muslims acknowledge the holy sacrifice of the monotheist Prophet Ibrahim (Abraham) when he opted to sacrifice his own son, and symbolically the material word, in return for God's consent and the spiritual world. The 'id celebrates God's bounty in allowing Ibrahim (Abraham) to substitute a sacrificial ram. Each year, a billion Muslims worldwide celebrate 'Id al-adha which comes at the end of al-hajj, the pilgrimage to Mecca that constitutes the fifth pillar of Islam and is to be made once in a Muslim's lifetime. All Muslims — Sunnis, Shi'ites and Sufis — are entitled to perform al-hajj (the greater pilgrimage) provided that they can afford it. Part of the rituals includes slaughtering a sheep, a camel or a calf. Muslims who are not performing the hajj should slaughter a halal animal on the first day of the eid and share its meat with family members, friends, and the poor. As per Sunnah, one third should be donated to the poor, one third to the relatives, and the last third to one's immediate family. This ritual is shared by all Muslims — Sunnis, Shi'ites and Sufis. Symbolically, the slaughtering act points to one's willingness to sacrifice the physical flesh in return for God's consent and spiritual reward. As the Qur'an explains, "It is not their meat or their blood that reaches Allah; it is your piety that reaches Him" (22:37). It is piety and the search for God's acceptance that Allah means by animal sacrifice. At the social level, and as is the case with fasting Ramadan, the ritual also helps strengthen ties among families and friends and reach social harmony between the rich and the poor.

Food and Social Harmony

This keenness to encourage social harmony between the rich and the poor is also found in the concept of *kaffarah* (expiation), by which Muslims expiate pre-determined mistakes including intentional oaths, unfasted days in Ramadan, and the *zihar*.[1] Notably, expiation in Islam is done by either giving food to the poor or abstaining from food through fasting. In case of breaking one's oath, Allah dictates that one should "feed ten poor, on a scale of the average of that with which you feed your own families; or clothe them; or free a slave. But whosoever cannot afford, then he should fast for three days" (5:89). Since the act of freeing a slave is not applicable nowadays, Muslims are to opt between feeding the needy, clothing them, and fasting for three days. The *kaffarah* of *zihar* as well as unexcused leaving out a fast of Ramadan is one of three options: freeing a slave, fasting for two months or feeding sixty poor people to their fill.

The Symbolism of Food in Shi'ism and Sufism

Food and eating customs play a prominent role in some Shi'ite practices. During Ashura, the tenth day of the Islamic month of Muharram, Shi'ites commemorate the martyrdom of Husayn, son of Caliph 'Ali, and grandson of the Prophet Muhammad, in the battle of Karbala. Unlike most Sunnis, Shi'ites regard Ashura as a mourning occasion marked by large public parades in which loud lamentations are accompanied by chest-beating rituals. During the whole month of Muharram, however, the affluent Shi'is provide food and drink to the whole community wherein they live. Children distributing ladles of water to passersby and tables laden with food to the poor are common scenes in Shi'ah communities. Symbolically, this is meant to compensate for the bitter fact that Husayn was hungry and thirsty when he was killed. It also aims at easing the thirst and hunger of the socially oppressed.

Food also carries specific symbolism in Sufism. Given that Sufism rose up as a reaction against the growing worldliness of Muslims in the second half of the seventh century C.E, (Hoffman 469) it has long been associated with fighting one's passions and appetites. Differentiating between the earthly soul and the heavenly spirit, Sufis advocate methods through which the soul can resist its fleshly desires. According to Valerie Hoffman, "the earliest Sufis practiced almost incredible feats of self-denial, shunning all forms of luxury, eating the barest minimum necessary to keep alive, avoiding sleep ... and spending their nights in devotion and self-examination" (469).

Poverty and hunger were two main demands for early Sufis. When Abu Yazid al-Bistami, an early mystic Sufi, was asked how he reached the peak of mystic mystic knowledge, he said that he had done so "with a hungry stomach and a naked body" (qtd. in Hoffman 470). Abu Hamid al-Ghazali, a leading pioneer of early Sufism, has cited fasting as one of the tools necessary in the path of God. Al-Ghazali holds that hunger is the fiercest weapon against Satan. Citing how Satan used food lust in his trick to expel Adam and Eve from paradise, Sufis ascertain that Satan seeps into human veins the moment he starts to eat to his fill. Fasting, therefore, is highly regarded by Sufis. In addition to the obligatory fasting during the holy month of Ramadan, Sufism encourages its advocates to adopt fasting in order to quench physical desires whether for food or sex. Citing the Prophet's tradition which urges young men to fast if they cannot afford marriage, Sufis hold that fasting is a form of castration (qtd. Hoffman 471).

In Sufism, even eating manners are exercises in piety, modesty, and submission to God. For them, what comes first is the intention. Whether eating or fasting, all acts must be done for the sake of God (Hoffman 476). Following the examples of the Prophet, who is regarded as the highest example of spiritual mysticism, Sufis transform earthly eating into a religious ritual. In addition to mentioning God's name, meals are started and finished with prayers. Even though modern Sufis, particularly Egyptian ones, have deviated from the course of the early ones with their emphasis on hunger and poverty as two important conditions in the path to God, the significance of food in Sufi discourse has never ceased. In modern Egyptian Sufi circles, food is served in *mawlids*, celebrations of the birth of certain Sufi saints and shaykhs, an act which is meant to transfer the *barakah* (blessing) of the dead saint to the attendees. Even in narrower Sufi circles when a living shaykh is offering food to others, he is offering his spiritual *barakah* along with it. Food therefore, continues to bear the same symbolic spiritual dimensions.

Conclusion

Whether esoterically or exoterically, literally or symbolically, food is highly significant in Islamic teachings and culture. Apart from being one of the provisions of the Creator, food performs a social and cultural function in Islamic societies while, in the same breath, testifying to Muslims' commitment to their worshipping acts. As a symbol of life and death, blessing and curse, purity and impurity, food plays a rich part in Islamic imagery, thought, and ideas.

Chapter Note

1. In *tafsir* books, the word *zihar* refers to the pre–Islamic Arabian custom whereby a man divorces his wife by simply saying that she is to him like the back of his mother and, hence, unlawful. The word is derived from *zahr* which means "back" in Arabic. In the time of *jahiliyyah*, the pre–Islamic days of ignorance, this divorce was irrevocable and a woman divorced this way had no right to re-marry.

Works Cited

Abu Nu'aym al-Isbahani, Ahmad ibn 'Abd Allah. *Hilyat al-awliya' wa tabaqatal-asfiya'*. al- Qahirah: Maktabat al-Khanji, 1932–38.
'Ali, 'Abdullah Yusuf, trans. *The Holy Qur'an*. Brentwood: Amana Corporation, 1983.
Bayhaqi, Ahmad ibn al-Husayn. *al-Sunan al-kubra*. Bayrut: Dar Sadir, 1968.
Bukhari, Muhammad ibn Isma'il. *The Translation of the Meanings of Sahih al-Bukhari*. Trans. Muhammad Muhsin Khan. Lahore: Kazi Publications, 1983.
Darimi, 'Abd Allah ibn 'Abd al-Rahman al-. *Sunan al-Darimi*. Dimashq: Muhammad Ahmad Dahman, 1930/31.
Hoffman, Valerie J. "Eating and Fasting for God in Sufi Tradition." *Journal of the American Academy of Religion* 63.3 (Fall 1995): 465–484.

Ibn Hanbal, Ahmad ibn Muhammad. *Musnad al-Imam Ahmad ibn Hanbal.* Bayrut: al-Maktabah al-Islamiyyah, 1969.

Ibn Hibban, Muhammad. *Sahih Ibn Hibban.* Bayrut: Mu'assasat al-Risalah, 1984.

Ibn Kathir, Isma'il ibn 'Umar. *al-Bidayah wa al-nihayah.* Bayrut: Maktabat al-Ma'arif, 1966.

_____.*Tafsir Ibn Kathir.* 'Amman: Aal al-Bayt Institute for Islamic Thought, 2005. Internet: www.al-tafsir.com.

_____. *Tafsir Ibn Kathir.* Internet: www.tafsir.com.

Ibn Majah, Abi 'Abd Allah Muhammad ibn Yazid al-Qazwini. *Sunan.* Trans. Muhammad Tufayl Ansari. Lahore: Kazi Publications, 1994.

Islam Guide. Internet: www.islam-guide.com/frm-ch1-1-e.htm.

Muslim ibn al-Hajjaj al-Qushayri. c1963. *Sahih Muslim.* N.p.: n.p., n.d.

Tabarani, Sulayman ibn Ahmad. *al-Mu'jam al-kabir.* Baghdad: al-Jumhuriyyah al-'Iraqiyyah, 1984–1990.

Tirmidhi, Muhammad ibn 'Isa. *Sunan al-Tirmidhi,* Homs: Maktabat Dar al-Da'wah, 1965.

The Phallus

Mahdi Tourage

"Then Allah sent a raven, who scratched the ground, to show him how to hide the shame of his brother." (Qur'an 5:31)

"Image is a perfectly transparent and straightforward term," writes Margaret Miles, "until one begins to consider its complex past and present usages" (160). This cannot be truer in regard to Islamic imagery, as it is often treated as an abstract enterprise detached from the cultural context that gives rise to it. Its subject matter is routinely viewed as a de-contextualized universal that can be accessed in its unmediated and pure form. However, quite to the contrary, these abstract images are inevitably "filtered," as it were, through the intermediary of variable cultural formations such as language.[1] This is particularly true in regard to the imagery from the mystical cache of Islam. The subject matter of mystical imagery, like love, may be "ineffable" (James 414) or, like the heart, be "wholly transcendental and spiritual" (Underhill 81), as the Western classical texts on mysticism explain. But the Islamic images' abstract subject matter inevitably emerges within a symbolic matrix of muta-ble cultural terms. One such image, whose complexity of use in the past and present has been completely overlooked, is the image of the phallus. This is despite the often overt ref-erences to it in Islamic sources (Qur'an, circumcision as emphasized in the *Sunnah*, and attention paid to genitals for ritual purity) (Wheeler 89–119; Kueny 166–7). In the Qur'an, for example, immediately after eating from the forbidden tree, Adam and Eve's private parts become apparent to them and to the reader (Qur'an 20:121–122, repeated also in 7:20–22). The Qur'anic term variously translated as their "genitals," or their "shame" is *saw'a* (sing.), which standard Arabic dictionaries translate as "the external portion of the organs of gen-eration" (Lane 4.1458). It could also denote "an unseemly sight," as in the case of a corpse, or more precisely a corpse whose organs of generation are exposed. The Qur'an relates the story of Adam's sons, where the immediate concern after one brother kills the other becomes how to hide the "shame/corpse" of the victim. Allah sends a raven who scratches the ground to show the murderer how to hide the "shame/corpse" of his brother. "'Woe is me!' said [the murderer]; 'was I not even able to be as this raven, and to hide the shame of my brother?'" (5:31) In some other passages in the Qur'an, this term is used in its plural form where God informs the Children of Adam: "We have revealed to you garments to cover your shame parts [*saw'atahuma*]" (7:26); and God warns the Children of Adam against seduction by Satan who got their parents out of the garden, stripped them of their clothes and exposed their "shame" (7:27).

Assuming that a distinction can be made between the image, the Greek term *eikon* which could correspond to the Arabic term *surah*, and its meaning, *ma'ana*, we can ask: what is the significance of this image in the Qur'an and the meaning intended by it? Muslim scholars draw the legal principle of the prohibition of exposing one's genitals from these passages. They also read in them connotations of moral negativity associated with nudity and its consequent shame and evil intentions (Katz 548). For the purpose of examining the image of the phallus in Islamic sources, and to give some possible answers to these questions, focus will be placed on the symbolic use of the image of the phallus in the work of the great Persian mystic of the 13th century, Jalal al-Din Rumi. Focusing on Rumi's work is due to the fact that the cautiously implicit use of this image in non-legal sources has been limited to *hazl* (bawdy, facetiae), *hija'* (satire), and *hajw* (verbal aggression, rooted in pre–Islamic poetry), and, at best, as an appendix or to enhance more "serious" works (Rosenthal; van Gelder). Furthermore, Rumi uniquely stands out as the only mystic who exploits the significance of this image amidst his mystical poetry. The uniqueness of Rumi among all other mystics, saints, and scholars is particularly due the nature of his mystical enterprise which is to hint at the inner meaning of *everything*. Even the vulgar and the "obscene" are frequently noted and their inner meaning explained. From the verses of the Qur'an to the sounds of the bazaar and boiling of the chickpeas, esoteric concepts and worldly tales merge in poetry of otherworldly quality. His mystical epic, the *Mathnawi*, a poetical form peculiar to the Persian language, struck a chord which resonated deeply in the hearts of the Persianate world and beyond, and assured it a success denied to other mystical works. Not surprisingly, Rumi was the best selling poet of the 1990s in the United States, and the *Mathnawi* is often referred to as the "Qur'an in Persian language" (Lewis). Among the mundane cultural formation, through which deeper meanings are explained in the *Mathnawi*, is the image of the phallus. A few instances in Rumi's work where the phallus has been used as an esoteric symbol will be presented. This will provide a background to re-examine the use of this image in some of the Qur'anic passages quoted above.

The Image of the Phallus Literalized

There are a quite a few references to the phallus in the *Mathnawi* but, in at least two instances, this image is used specifically for mystical purposes, which include effecting transformation. The first story is in Book Five of the *Mathnawi*, where the short story of a prankster who donned a woman's veil and sat among women in a religious gathering is related (5:3325–3350).[2] A "learned" preacher was speaking about how pubic hair longer than a grain of barley was objectionable and had to be removed in order for the daily ritual prayer to be complete. The prankster turns to the woman next to him and says: "O sister, would you for God's sake bring your hand forward and check the length of my pubic hair?" (5:3333–3334). The woman unknowingly puts her hand in his trousers and her hand touches his penis. She screams loudly, causing the preacher to say: "My preaching touched her heart!" (5:3335). The prankster corrects him: "No, it did not touch her heart, it touched her hand / Woe to her if it had touched her heart, o wise one!" (5:3336). In the next line, Rumi goes on to give an example of the kind of transformation that could change the heart: "A bit [of it] touched the hearts of [Pharoah's] magicians / [when Moses'] staff and hand became as one before them" (5:3337). The transformation of the hearts of the magicians is a reference to the well-known Qur'anic tale (which would have been familiar to Rumi's readers) of the encounter of Moses with Pharoah's magicians. In this encounter, the magicians defeated by Moses acknowledge the greatness of his God. Pharoah becomes angry and orders their hands and feet to be cut off alternately and that they be crucified. They say:

"There is no harm, indeed to our Lord we return" (Qur'an 26:50). In the tale of the prankster, Rumi incorporates this utterance of the magicians into the text: "Their cry of 'There is no harm' reached the heavens / [they said to Pharaoh]: 'lo, cut [them off], for the soul is liberated by such pain.'" (5:3339)

Shaving of the pubic hair is a hygienic cultural practice which could also be connected to eroticization of genitals (Bouhdiba 203–5). By connecting this practice to the perfection of the ritual daily prayer, and his own discourse to something that has touched the woman's heart, the preacher is wrongly *sublimating* the external forms only to back his claim of superiority. Sublimation, which in psychoanalytical terms means a redirection of suppressed (sexual) desires to different and apparently "higher" aims, is an apt characterization of the preacher's action in this tale (Freud 69–70). Here, sublimation describes the preacher's discursive maneuvering that effects an alteration in the significance of his own identity structure. Hence, it is his own identity that is changed and mistakenly elevated, not anyone's heart, as he deceptively supposes. However, his goal of laudatory self-promotion is expressed through his linking of the shaving of pubic hair and the perfection of one's daily prayer. The preacher's sublimation, that is, the resurfacing of his true desire (which is self-promotion) in a socially acceptable form, has an illusory orientation. Hence, it must be understood as a deceptive, misplaced, and *imaginary* reading of a sublime and symbolic value into a culturally produced formation.[3] Whereas Rumi usually contests the literalization of symbols and ideals, in this reverse strategy he renounces the imaginary sublimation of external forms by literalizing them. One of his goals is evidently to effect transformation, not the imaginary/illusory kind of transformation that the preacher purports, but the kind that was effected in the hearts of the Pharaoh's magicians. The former is substantive, but the latter is literally skin deep, equated with the literal image of the phallus. As Rumi himself warns us, "true manliness" lies beyond the literalized object: "[True] manliness is ... not beard and penis, otherwise the donkey's penis would have been the king of men" (5:3711–12).

This strategic literalization is repeated in a few other passages in the *Mathnawi* where human bodies are presented as naturally and biologically functioning entities. For example, there are human bodies that emit gas (4:768–69) and semen (5:2202), eat and defecate (6:1256), urinate (4:3148–49), experience hunger, and have needs for sexual gratification. In one tale, the inner organs of the body, such as the liver (5:1387) and intestines (5:1337), blood (5:1389), and uterus (5:1337), as well as lips (5:1357), throat (5:1398), and neck (5:1410) are put on display. In all of these examples, parts of the body are related to eating and reproducing. In fact, throughout the *Mathnawi*, Rumi repeatedly connects "genitals" and "throat." For example 5:3938–9 he writes: "Because for him [the uninitiated] reality consists of genitals and throat / do not explain the mysteries of the Beloved to him." In one tale, the greedy eyes of a woman view the large organ of a donkey as honey and confection (5:1430). In this tale, the greed of the woman for this disproportionate "morsel" (the donkey's penis) causes her to choke to death when she engages in sexual relations with the donkey (5:1398). Also, the donkey's testicles, and its penis, with its attributes, large and erect (5:1385), injurious (5:1387), moving up and down (5:1356) are noted. In that tale the woman's vagina is described as coming to life: "Out of joy that woman's vagina became a nightingale / restless and inflamed in sexual urges for the donkey" (5:1363). In other passages, menstruation (5:3920 and 3230) and the foul smell of a vagina (4:3148–49) are noted. In an allusion to the Qur'anic idea that on the Day of Resurrection tongues will be sealed, and parts of the body (hands and feet specifically) will testify (Qur'an 36:65), we read: "[on the Resurrection Day] the vagina will say: 'I have fornicated'" (5:2214). These examples dispute the assumptions that the body is a coherent and self-subsisting entity while countering the tendencies of abstracting the body as unified and autonomous. In these examples, bodies are literalized and situated in their cultural context. They re-enact their elemental function as a way of remembering their (corpo)reality. If we take the body as a vital site of memory, as cultural anthropologists do, we can argue that in these bawdy examples significance is invested back into the human body (Connerton 72–104). This is not to say that the body contains any intrinsic significance. On the contrary, the parts of the body, and the functions associated with them, have no meaning of their own until they are placed in their cultural context and become endowed with the ideological assumptions of a given culture. As Eilberg-Schwartz, in regard to the views of the body in Judaism points out, "[w]hen people relate to discrete organs of their bodies, they are not just relating to themselves but to symbols of their culture" (12). Therefore, when we discuss the image of the phallus we are not simply discussing a discrete organ of the male body, but a symbol of the culture.

The Image of the Phallus Sublimated

Before answering the question, "what is the symbolic significance of the image of the phallus?" we must note that literalization is one side of Rumi's project. If the external forms are erroneously sublimated, Rumi highlights their corporeality by drawing attention to their margins, orifices, and elemental functions as noted above. But if symbols and images are erroneously objectified, Rumi brings them back into communication with their ideational matrices. A good example of this, related to the image of the phallus, can be found in the tale of "The Slave Girl who Satisfied her Sexual Urges with a Donkey" (5:1333–1429). The tale begins with a slave girl who had trained a donkey to engage in sexual intercourse with her in the manner of men. The slave girl would slide a gourd over the organ of the donkey to prevent it from fully penetrating and injuring her during intercourse. The donkey becomes thinner every day because his time of feeding and resting is spent in the sexual act with the slave girl. The mistress of the house, the owner of the donkey, becomes concerned about the state of the donkey and begins to investigate the reason for its thinness. She finds her slave girl satisfying her sexual urges with it. Having become sexually excited and jealous herself, she sends the slave girl away and begins to engage in the sexual act with the donkey. However, not having noticed the important protective function of the gourd used by the slave girl, she dies in the process. Rumi's voice is heard asking the reader: "A bad death with a hundred disgraces, o father / have you ever seen a martyr of the donkey's penis?" (5:1390).

Against this background, Rumi warns the reader against the harms of unrestrained sexual urges which, he argues, are the product of overeating. Therefore, one has to eat less or to get married. The tale then turns to the discussion that, on the spiritual path, the external forms are only "borrowed forms." Knowledge of the external forms is an incomplete knowledge that, like a snare, traps heedless birds. Complete knowledge is the knowledge of the secrets of the inner meanings that is possessed by a true master. As long as we see only the organ, the true meaning of the tale, exemplified by the function of the gourd, eludes us. The focus of the tale, thus, is not the literal aspect of the image of the phallus but the transformative possibilities fostered by its representational strategies.

One example of transformative possibility is instantiated in the tale where Rumi manipulates the contiguity of a sign and the thing signified by that sign resulting in the emergence of a transformation of the significance of a character. By the virtue of the signifiers defining the slave girl's sexuality at the beginning of the tale (satisfying her sexual urges with a donkey), she is an aberration from the perceived heterosexual norms. Yet with the choice of the words "master," "external form," and "secret" in line 1419, the slave girl's sexual encounter with the donkey turns out to signify the master's prerogative of engaging the secrets. The "stratagem" of the slave girl using a gourd in her sexual encounter (5:1335) now becomes the ingenious approach of the master to the secret by using the term "craft" (5:1423). More importantly, the words "external form" and "secret" in line 1419 are displaced by the terms "penis" and "gourd" in the next line (1420): "You saw the external form (not) the secret. You saw the penis (not) the gourd." In these examples one signifier displaces another, creating new sets of meanings and alternative significations. Thus the possibility of a closed literal interpretation that precludes other meanings is disrupted.

Of course, the transformation is not limited to the characters and signifiers in the text, the ultimate goal of a tale like this, or the entire corpus of Rumi's mystical work, is to effect transformation of subjectivity in the reader. In a sense, Rumi is "textually manipulating" the reader, distracting the non-initiates from the inner meaning of the text, that is, its symbolic significance (Quilligan 281). In other words, like many other rhetorical devices and linguistic manoeuvrings, Rumi's use of the image of the phallus could be about distracting "outsiders," or veiling the inner meaning of the text, from the uninitiated. The "insiders" potentially or actually already know the inner meaning, and the uninitiated are already outside, dismayed by the "frivolous and mendacious interpretations," as Kermode puts it (3). So Rumi could very well be setting up a trap for the uninitiated reader. Hence line 1420, which admonishes the mistress for seeing only the donkey's organ and not the gourd, must be viewed in conjunction with the last line of the tale that rebukes the reader for hearing the external form and not the inner meaning: "You saw the penis as honey and sweetmeat / why did you not see that gourd, you greedy one?" (5:1420); "Having heard the external form you became the translator, that is, commentator, like parrots, unaware of your own speech" (5:1429).

These examples show Rumi's dynamic approach to the strategic use of the image of the phallus. As the example of the tale of the Prankster and the Preacher shows, the preacher's self-promotion, by linking the shaving of pubic hair to the perfection of one's daily prayer, is a deceptive and delusional reading of a sublime and symbolic value into a culturally practice. Rumi draws attention to the cultural context that endows the shaving of pubic hair and the image of the phallus with its meaning in order to counter the hegemonizing discourses that erroneously sublimate the external forms. In other passages quoted above, he highlights the corporeality of the body and its functions by drawing attention to their margins, orifices, and elemental functions. In the tale of the Slave Girl and the Donkey, however, he hints at the symbolic significance of this image.

The Image of the Phallus and Subjective Transformation

Surely the significance of the image of the phallus exceeds its objectification and its literal meaning in these texts. One effect of the use of this image, or more broadly bawdy passages and their "vulgar" terms, is to produce an open system of interplay of the sublime and the vulgar, the mystical and the non-mystical, with the aim of effecting subjective transformation. In line 3340 of the prankster's tales, Rumi alludes to this transformative function by stating: "We understood that we are not this body." This transformation of subjectivity is effected through a communication that is established between the literal (even vulgar) and the sublimated (or sublime). In this tale, a non-mystical theme (the shaving of pubic hair) and vulgar words, like "penis," are mixed with esoteric themes (like Moses' miracles) and essential Sufi terminology, like the "heart" (3335–36) and "essence" (3341). It is evident that the vulgar and the sublime are not completely disassociated but are put in communication with each other. Thus, in their transformative itinerary, sublimation and objectification are not mutually exclusive possibilities.

The communicative aspect of the relationship between the literalized and the sublimated formations is at least partially aimed at effecting a transformation on the subjective level. The "subject" in this formulation may be understood as the human subject, or the subject of the text. As a reference to the human subject, transformation occasions recognition of the subject as a culturally constituted configuration. Evidently, this is the aim of a mystical discourse (like the *Mathnawi*); in line 3340 of the Prankster and the Preacher's tale we read: "We have come to know that we are not this body." As if anticipating the question "What are we, if not this body?" Rumi continues: "(It is) beyond the body that we touch God." That which is beyond the body is named in the following line "Fortunate is he who recognized his [true] essence." This is a reformulation of the famous saying "Whosoever knows his soul, knows his lord" (Altmann 196–232). It means all things other than one's essence are cultural formations, that are, to use Sufi terminology, so many *veils*. Thus, the transformation of subjectivity entails the recognition of the locatedness of the subject and our knowledge of it. As Sufis put it, this is the recognition of "veils as veils," that is to say, they lack intrinsic significance (Chittick 59–86). It is this recognition that Rumi alludes to in the tale of the prankster where he states: "We have come to know that we are not our body / it is beyond the body that we touch God" (5:3340).

More relevant to the goals of this study, subjective transformation in the tale of the Prankster and the Preacher may also be an allusion to change in the ways that the subject of this tale is perceived. That is to say, intervening in the process of meaning production can alter the perception of the bawdy content of this tale. Closed models of signification limit themselves within the constructed boundaries of epistemological conventions that can admit only certain terms and imagery as "mystical" into its signifying repertoire. An example is the interpretive approaches of commentators and scholars of Sufism who have dismissed or completely overlooked the mystical significance of these two tales and other bawdy passages of the *Mathnawi*. For example, they have been viewed as reflecting the failing imaginative faculties of an aging mystic, simply as a literary device to grab the attention of the reader or merely the symbolic opposites of the otherwise sublime *Mathnawi* (Nicholson 6.vii; Schimmel 51; Bürgel 46).

These are closed models of interpretation that dichotomize Islamic/Sufi imagery into mystical/non-mystical. They disassociate the crude, even vulgar, imagery of these tales from the bulk of the *Mathnawi*'s otherwise "mystical" passages. Such a dichotomizing reading is not supported in the text, nor is it evidently envisioned by Rumi himself. This is not to say that the text does not differentiate the vulgar and the sublime. Rather, the two are put in purposeful communication with each other. This communication between the literalized (the vulgar) and the sublime (the mystical) points to the transformative efficacy of their dynamic interplay. The communicative aspect of the relationship between the vulgar and the mystical that is effected in these tales upsets the totalized regimes of signification by demonstrating how the "vulgar" and "non-mystical" can operate in mystical ways. Therefore, the subjective transformation can be understood as a change in the culturally constructed distinction between the mystical and non-mystical.

The Image of the Phallus and Its Symbolic Significance

What is the symbolic significance of the image of the phallus in the *Mathnawi* (or in the Qur'an for that matter)? If we continue along the same lines of thinking, outside the dichotomizing and constraining epistemological boundaries, we can uncover further layers of meaning related to the symbolic significance of the image of the phallus in these two tales of the *Mathnawi*, and perhaps in the Qur'an. Rumi gives us some clues as to the symbolic significance of the image of the phallus in the tale of the Prankster and the Preacher. There is an abrupt shift in the tale (5:3337), turning the focus from the organ of the prankster to another phenomenon that remains unnamed in the text: "A bit [of 'it'] touched the hearts of [Pharaoh's] magicians / [when Moses'] staff and hand became as one for them." If touching the hidden organ by hand caused such a reaction in the woman, how much greater would the degree of transformation have been had "it" touched her heart. The Qur'anic narrative of the encounter between Moses and the Pharaoh's magicians is an example where something of "it" had actually touched someone's heart. Rumi does not need to tell the reader who the magicians were. In the story of Moses, as it is related in the Qur'an, God gives Moses his staff, which turns into a serpent, as a sign to prove his prophecy. (Qur'an 26:15) Upon seeing this miracle, the Pharaoh's sorcerers prostrate themselves before Moses and acknowledge the greatness of Moses' God. Pharaoh becomes angry and orders their hands and feet to be cut off alternately and that they be crucified. To this they respond: "There is no harm, indeed to our Lord we return" (Qur'an 26:50).

With some exceptions, for emphasis or clarity for example, expressed pronominal subjects are not necessary in Persian because they are implicit in the verb. This grammatical peculiarity is even more subtle in the third person singular past tense of the verb *zad* used in this line (3337). The enclitic personal ending, which is added to the past stem of the verbs, is not needed at all, leaving it to even more covertly allude to that which has been provisionally translated as "it" here. So we can ask: What is that "it" that cannot be revealed in the text even pronominally and the slightest of its touch can cause such a massive transformation?

We do know that whatever that "it" is, it is not the organ; rather, it is its symbolic opposite. Taking a cue from Rumi himself, in order to consider what this symbolic configuration may be, we must transform our phenomenological approach and think outside of the delimiting conventions and the usual epistemological confines. This strategy of reading mystical texts through the prism of selective conceptual tools from postmodern theories (such as semiotics) has been fruitfully attempted in studies of Kabbala, for example (Wolfson 113–154). The theoretical works of the French psychoanalyst Jacques Lacan have been shown to be particularly relevant to studies of Persian/Islamic text (Glünz 223–243; Sells and Webb 195–215; Tourage, *Rumi* 56–64). Relying on Lacanian theory of signification, it can be argued that the symbolic opposite of the organ in this text, the "it" that touched the magicians' hearts, can be understood as a reference to the phallus. The phallus is an unrepresentable symbolic configuration that is neither imaginary nor literal neither entirely abstracted nor completely exposed (Lacan 289). It is disclosed in its concealment, which is not possible unless it is concealed in its disclosure. Even though the phallus transcends the cultural construction of the organ, its symbolic function is not entirely dissociated from the biological operations of its corporeal correlate, the phallus. The phallus is not the organ, but it does symbolize the organ in a relationship that designates the organ as "the privileged referent to be negated" (Butler 84). This is characterized as a relationship of negation and identity.

In the story of the Prankster and the Preacher, the organ that touched the hand of the woman signifies nothing beyond the corporeality of the body or the external form of the text, which, combined with its negative cultural connotations, can rightly warrant the dismissal of its significance in the text as non-mystical and perhaps distasteful. However, when we consider the organ's relationship of negation and identity with a transcendental signifier, the phallus, that, according to Rumi, can only touch one's heart we can see that its significance exceeds its apparently non-mystical literalization and biological corporeality. The organ is dissociated from the phallus, but nevertheless provides the occasion for its signifying effects. That is to say, the significance of the phallus is irreducible to the function of the organ, the phallus. To repeat, the penis is not the phallus. The penis is a veil that covers and distracts. On its own, it signifies nothing beyond the lust for self-gratification in the *Mathnawi*. However, the crucial point here is that as Sufis well understood this, a veil does not only conceal, it also reveals. In this text, the veil conceals *as* it reveals — the penis simultaneously distracts and alludes to a profound hidden meaning signified by its hidden symbolic opposite, the phallus. This is the kind of hidden meaning that, as Rumi points out, touches that spiritual organ of perception that the Sufis designate as the "heart" (Rustom 3–13). Only "something of it," that is, only something of the phallus as the veiled signifier, touched the hearts of Pharaoh's magicians, causing a transformation of their heart. In this context, the phallus is the signifier of esoteric secrets.

To decipher precisely what the esoteric secrets are is a futile endeavour because of the limitations of language, on one hand, and the hidden nature of secrets, on the other. No language can contain the secrets. Or, as Sufis would say, "the veils will never be lifted" (Chittick 81). And a secret that is openly divulged is no secret at all. Only the existence of secrets may be intimated through allusions, symbolizations, and paradoxes that hint at the secrets without actually revealing them. The content of secrecy forever eludes decipherment. To quote Chittick: "'What' is a question applying only to the entities of things, which is to say it can be asked only of the veils; the whatness of that which the veils veil can never be known" (85). How can we be sure of the existence of secrets? The proof for their presence is found in their effects, that is, in the subjective transformation effected by secrets, for example, as happened to the Pharaoh's magicians' hearts.

The same dynamics of negation and identity that characterize the phallus-penis relationship are found in the tale of the Slave Girl and the Donkey. In that tale, the organ of the donkey actively determines the mistress' desire and conditions its intensity. When partially concealed by the gourd it also signifies the esoteric secret known only to the master, alluding to the phallus because of what it signifies, rather than for what it actually is. A novice, jealous of the master's ease of access to the secrets, and too proud to humble herself before her to learn, takes the organ for the phallus. The phallus and the organ itself are two different things; however, the organ that assumes the function of a signifier can take on the value of a "fetish" (Lacan 285, 290). Here, fetish is an "*imaginary* fixation on literalized ideal entities and related symbols and practices" (DiCenso 58, emphasis added). The donkey's organ, in this story, functions as a fetish in relation to the mistress' object of desire.

Can we not see the same relationship of negation and identity to be conditioning the Qur'anic story of the sons of Adam where the "shame" of the murdered brother becomes exposed after the killing? "Penis" may not be the first or only translation of the Arabic term *saw'a* in that passage. In fact, most classical and modern commentators, both Sunni and Shi'a, read *saw'a* as the "corpse" of the dead brother (Busse 270–272). For example, among the classical major commentators, Tabari is not concerned about the alternative meaning of this term as the genitals of the dead brother (5.196–198), nor is Ibn Kathir (5.176). Modern commentators are also mainly concerned with other aspects of this tale. For example, in following his own particular concerns, Qutb comments that this passage provides guidelines for standing up against crime and punishing criminals in order to set up an Islamic Society (4.68–73). In his monumental commentary on the Qur'an, the Shi'a scholar Tabataba'i only briefly notes that *saw'a* is that which is displeasing to humans (5.306). However, at least two of the major classical commentaries of the Qur'an specifically note sexual organ (*awra*) as a possible meaning of this term even though they do not elaborate beyond the legal requirement for covering it. Zamakhshari specifically notes genitals (*'awra*) as one meaning of this term and distinguishes it from corpse (*jasad*) (2.227). Razi also takes *saw'a* to mean genitals (*'awra*) of a corpse (*jasad*) or a dead body (*jayfah*) which is not allowed to be disclosed (11–12.209). If we take the penis as a possible translation of the term *saw'a* as supported by Zamakhshari and Razi, we can ask, Why is there so much emphasis placed on its textual exposure? It seems there is even more concern with this exposure and subsequent imperative to conceal it than with the killing. Even the regret of the murderer seems to be more for failing to conceal the sexual organ of the victim than for the killing itself:

> [After the murder] Allah sent a raven, who scratched the ground, to show him how to hide the shame of his brother. "Woe is me!" said he; "Was I not even able to be as this raven, and to hide the shame of my brother?" Then he became full of regrets [Qur'an 5:30–31].

Not only was it shameful for Cain to have killed Abel, it was even more shameful that he failed to cover his naked corpse. Rather than bury his brother, Jalal al-Din al-Mahalli and Jalal al-Din al-Suyuti report that he carried him on his back, not knowing what to do with his earthly remains (*Tafsir Jalalayn*). There is no doubt that the *saw'a* or shame refers to the dead body of the brother. However, since the word also has the sense of "shameful parts," it may also refer more broadly to the "dead, naked, body" of the brother. In fact, in their *tafsir*, the two Jalals interpret the *saw'a* as "the nakedness" and "the carcass" of the brother. In the *Miqbas*, a Sunni *tafsir* attributed to 'Abd Allah ibn 'Abbas, *saw'a* also has the sense of "naked corpse." The sin of Cain, therefore, was not simply premeditated murder; it was also disrespecting a cadaver. As Man is the manifestation of Allah and the mirror in which He sees Himself, to desecrate him is a defamation of the Divine.

It is plausible to argue that the "truth" of the story, which the text tells us at the outset will be "recited," could very well be related to the organ of the murdered brother: "Recite to them the truth of the story of the two sons of Adam" (Qur'an 5:27). Of course the truth of the story is irreducible to the exposed organ. In fact, any relation between that truth and the organ must be negated. But in its exposure and subsequent concern for its concealment, the organ in this text alludes to the function of the phallus, the esoteric symbol which, though unrepresentable, reorients the subject in relation to the truth of this story. As argued elsewhere, the phallus signifies the "truth" of the text beyond the reified literalized organ and the historicity of the story itself (Tourage, "Erotics of Sacrifice").

Concluding Remarks

For obvious reasons the image of the phallus has not been viewed favorably by scholars and commentators. This is especially true in studies of Sufism where more sublime imagery is elevated to the level of the universal, and narrow interpretive modality focusing only on abstract ideas has been privileged. Thus the study of Islamic imagery in general, and Sufism in particular, have limited the significance and range of symbolizing practices of a mystic like Rumi. Many bawdy passages in the *Mathnawi* are embodied reminders of the reality of the body as a culturally produced formation. The representation of parts of the body in the bawdy examples in the *Mathnawi* may be viewed as a re-incorporation of the private parts, orifices, and their basic functions back into the erroneously sublimated body of Persian mystical texts and its abstracted universalities. They aim to transform the canonization of a mystical language that instead of effecting transformation of the hearts may end up supporting the structure of literary and cultural totalization as the example in the tale of the Prankster and the Preacher demonstrates. In these tales, Rumi ventures outside the normative range of Persian mystical conventions to bring about a transformation of subjectivity through the communicative strategies of a mutual and dynamic interplay between the sublimated and the literalized systems of symbols. As the examples of the bawdy passages in the *Mathnawi* demonstrate, this dynamic interplay is a two-way process in which not only lofty mystical concepts, but apparently non-mystical images like sexual organ too can initiate subjective transformation. Rumi's goal is to disrupt, or "unveil" in the technical terminology of Sufism, the illusory position of subjectivity through which humans distort images and the sublime goals of the mystical path. The vulgar products of the culture, for example, coarse terms like *kir*— arguably one of the most vulgar terms in Persian language, which perhaps should be translated into an even more of a vulgar term than the penis — are Rumi's tools to effect this "unveiling."

Thus, we do not need to oppose, redeem or remedy these bawdy tales or the use of the image of the phallus in the *Mathnawi*. We do need, however, to appreciate what Rumi is trying to achieve, that is, re-establishing the link between abstract ideas and their cultural contexts when this link has been disconnected either by a fetishistic literalization of symbols and ideals (as in the case of the mistress in the tale of the Slave Girl and the Donkey), or by religious/mystical totalization based on the sublimation of culturally constructed norms (like shaving the pubic hair as in the tale of the Prankster and the Preacher). What all these mean is that the process of meaning production can never be reduced to a single interpretative modality or a particular norm. As has been argued in this study, far from being limiting, vulgar images like the penis are among the resources of the culture that can contribute to the open-endedness of the process of meaning production. There is nothing vulgar in the image of the penis itself; it is only in its cultural contexts that it takes on a sense of vulgarity. However, when this image is re/signified in the mystical context of the *Mathnawi*, we can be sure there are hidden layers of meaning intended by it.

One such hidden layer of meaning is found in at least two tales in the *Mathnawi*, where a vulgar term, the penis, is used to simultaneously distract and allude to the presence of hidden secrets in the text. This concealment and disclosure is effected through negation and identity that characterizes the relationship of the present organ and its symbolic unrepresentable opposite, the phallus. In this context, these two passages can be interpreted as phallocentric, that is, the phallus functioning as an esoteric symbol and the signifier of esoteric secrets. The same phallocentric orientation can be detected in the Qur'anic story of the two sons of Adam, one killing the other. In that tale, the exposure of the "shame" of the murdered brother and concern for its concealment, highlight the function of the phallus, which is not the organ, yet through its symbolizing function conditions the symbolic structure of concealment and disclosure. Even though the text announces that "the truth of the story of the two sons of Adam" will be told, we end up with the impossibility of guaranteed access to this truth. The "truth" of the story, it could be argued, is precisely this symbolic absence of the truth as signified by the phallus. In other words, the definite closure in the process of meaning production, or the full disclosure of the "truth" of the story is deferred indefinitely. Whereas, in a postmodern context, this deferral of closure of truth often leads to alienation of the subject, in the religious context of the Qur'an this indefinite deferral produces a sense of awe and wonder at the grandeur of the truth which cannot be captures in any language (Tourage, "Erotics of Sacrifice"). This parallels the two tales of the *Mathnawi* in which the precise nature of secrets is not disclosed because in addition to the veil of language safeguarding them, the signifier of secrets, i.e. the phallus, is concealed. Any claim of a definite disclosure of the truth (for example, the claim that there is only one "correct" interpretation of these texts) is an imaginary fixation on a literalized form substituted for inner meaning which could be formulated as fetishism.

It would be too reductive to view the image of the phallus as a negative category, denoting a deviation from a norm or convention, which then is contrasted with other more sublime imagery. No norm, convention, or context can utterly deplete the interpretive possibilities of Islamic imagery. The symbolic matrix of Islam remains an open-ended system of unfolding the latent meanings and significances that cannot be reduced to a single mode of interpretation or a particular convention. Therefore, decontextualized abstract (sublime) concepts cannot be universalized as the only convention of signification. Nor can literalized images, even vulgar terms like the penis, be decoupled from their ideational matrices. As the examination of the significance of the image of the phallus in these few passages shows, we need neither to dichotomize the literal and the abstract, or vulgar and the sublime, nor compound them. We can interrupt the logic of contraries between these purportedly polar opposites by establishing a transformative dialogue between the two in ways that acknowledges their differences as well as their interconnectedness through a relation of negation-identity.

Chapter Notes

1. It should be noted at the outset that this is not to reject any claim to "truth" outside of culture as some postmodernists do. In fact, as it will be argued below, it is precisely through cultural elements that the allusion and hints of "something" beyond them, that is, something that transcends, yet is bound by cultural contexts, could be intimated.

2. All references to the *Mathnawi* are to Nicholson's edition, indicated by book number, and followed by the line number. All translations are mine.

3. Here, "imaginary" is synonymous with illusory and should not be confused with imagination. Corbin offers the best articulation of this distinction in relation to the esoteric works of Muslim mystics. He explains that between the empirical world and the world of abstract understanding is the intermediate world of *mundus imaginalis*, an ontologically real world which requires its own faculty of perception. He writes: "This faculty is the imaginative power, the one we must avoid confusing with the imagination that modern man identifies with 'fantasy' and that, according to him, produces only the 'imaginary'" (Corbin 9).

Works Cited

Altmann, Alexander. "The Delphic Maxim in Medieval Islam and Judaism." *Biblical and Other Studies.* Ed. Alexander Altmann. Cambridge, MA: Harvard University Press, 1963.

Bouhdiba, Abdelwahab. *Sexuality in Islam.* Trans. Alan Sheridan. London: Saqi Books, 1998.

Bürgel, J. Christoph. "'Speech Is a Ship and Meaning the Sea:' Some Formal Aspects of the Ghazal Poetry of Rumi." *Poetry and Mysticism in Islam: The Heritage of Rumi.* Ed. Amin Banani, Richard Hovannisian and Georges Sabagh. Cambridge: Cambridge University Press, 1994.

Busse, Heribert. "Cain and Abel." *Encyclopaedia of the Qur'an*. Ed. Jane Dammen McAuliffe. Vol.1. Leiden: Brill, 2001–2006.

Butler, Judith. *Bodies That Matter: On the Discursive Limits of "Sex."* New York: Routledge, 1993.

Chittick, William C. "The Paradox of the Veil in Sufism." *Rending the Veil: Concealment and Secrecy in the History of Religions*. Ed. Elliot R. Wolfson. New York: Seven Bridges Press, 1999.

Connerton, Paul. *How Societies Remember*. Cambridge: Cambridge University Press, 1989.

Corbin, Henry. *Swedenborg and Esoteric Islam*. Trans. Leonard Fox. West Chester, PA: Swedenborg Foundation, 1995.

DiCenso, James J. *The Other Freud: Religion, Culture and Psychoanalysis*. London: Routledge, 1999.

Eilberg-Schwartz, Howard, ed. *People of the Body: Jews and Judaism from an Embodied Perspective*. Albany: State University of New York Press, 1992.

Freud, Sigmund. *On Sexuality: Three Essays on the Theory of Sexuality and Other Works*. Trans. and ed. James Strachey and Angela Richards. London: Penguin Books, 1977.

Gelder, Geert Jan van. *The Bad and the Ugly: Attitudes Towards Invective Poetry (Hija') in Classical Arabic Literature*. Leiden: Brill, 1989.

Glünz, Michael. "The Sword, the Pen and the Phallus: Metaphors and Metonymies of Male Power and Creativity in Medieval Persian Poetry." *Edebiyat* 6.2 (1995): 223–243.

Ibn 'Abbas, 'Abd Allah (attributed). *Tanwir al-miqbas fi Tafsir Ibn 'Abbas*. Trans. Mokrane Guezzou. *Aal al-Bayt Institute for Islamic Thought*, 2012. Internet: www.altafsir.com/.

Ibn Kathir, Emad al-Din Abu al-Fida Ismail. *Tafsir al-Qur'an al-'Azim*. Ed. Mustafa al-Sayyid Muhammad, et. al. 10 vols. Jizza: Qurtuba, 2000.

James, William. *The Varieties of Religious Experiences: A Study in Human Nature*. New York: The Modern Library, 1999.

Katz, Marion Holmes. "Nudity." *Encyclopaedia of the Qur'an*. Jane Dammen McAuliffe. Vol. 3. Leiden: Brill, 2001–2006.

Kermode, Frank. *The Genesis of Secrecy: On the Interpretation of Narrative*. Cambridge, MA: Harvard University Press, 1979.

Kueny, Kathryn. "Abraham's Test: Islamic Male Circumcision as Anti/Ante-Covenantal Practice." *Bible and Qur'an: Essays in Scriptural Intertextuality*. Ed. John C. Reeves. Atlanta: Society of Biblical Literature, 2003.

Lane, Edward William. *Arabic-English Lexicon*. 8 vols. New York: Ungar, 1955–6.

Lewis, Franklin. *Rumi, Past and Present, East and West: The Life, Teachings and Poetry of Jalal al-Din Rumi*. Oxford: One World, 2000.

Lacan, Jacques. *Écrits: A Selection*. Trans. Alan Sheridan. New York: Norton and Company, 1977.

Mahalli, Jalal al-Din al-, and Jalal al-Din al-Suyuti. *Tafsir Jalalayn*. Trans. Feras Hamza. Amman: Aal al-Bayt Institute for Islamic Thought, 2012. Internet: www.altafsir.com/Al-Jalalayn.asp.

Miles, Margaret R. "Image." *Critical Terms for Religious Studies*. Ed. Mark C. Taylor. Chicago: University of Chicago Press, 1998.

Quilligan, Maureen. *The Language of Allegory: Defending the Genre*. Ithaca, NY: Cornell University Press, 1979.

Qutb, Sayyid. *In the Shade of the Qur'an*. Trans. and ed. Adil Salahi and Ashur Shamis. Leicester: The Islamic Foundation, 2001.

Razi, Fakhr al-Din Muhammad ibn Umar al-. *al-Tafsir al-kabir*. 32 vols. Egypt: Matba'ah al-Bahiyyah, 1938.

Rosenthal, Franz. *Humor in Early Islam*. Leiden: Brill, 1956.

Rumi, Jalal al-Din. *The Mathnawi of Jalalu'ddin Rumi*. 8 vols. Ed. Reynold A. Nicholson. London: Luzac, 1925–1940.

Rustom, Mohammed. "The Metaphysics of the Heart in the Sufi Doctrine of Rumi." *Studies in Religion/Sciences Religieuses* 37.1 (2008): 3–13.

Schimmel, Annemarie. *The Triumphal Sun: A Study of the Works of Jalaloddin Rumi*. Albany: State University of New York Press, 1993.

Sells Michael A., and James Webb. "Lacan and Bion: Psychoanalysis and the Mystical Language of Unsaying." *Theory and Psychology* 5.2 (1995): 195–215.

Tabari, Abi Ja'far Muhammad al-. *Jami' al-bayan 'an ta'wil al-Qur'an*. Egypt: Mustafa al-Babi al-Halabi, 1954–68.

Tabataba'i, Muhammad Husain. *al-Mizan fi tafsir al-Qur'an*. 21 vols. Bayrut: Mu'assasah al-'Alami li al-Matbu'at, 1970–1985.

Tourage, Mahdi. *Rumi and the Hermeneutics of Eroticism*. Leiden: Brill, 2007.

_____. "The Erotics of Sacrifice in the Qur'anic Tale of Abel and Cain." *International Journal of Zizek Studies* 5.2 (2011): n. pag. Web. 12 May, 2012.

Underhill, Evelyn. *The Nature and Development of Spiritual Consciousness.* Oxford: Oneworld, 1999.

Wheeler, Brannon. *Touching the Penis in Islamic Law.* Chicago: University of Chicago Press, 2004.

Wolfson, Elliot R. "Occultation of the Feminine and the Body of Secrecy in Medieval Kabbalah." *Rending the Veil: Concealment and Secrecy in the History of Religions.* Ed. Elliot R. Wolfson. New York: Seven Bridges Press, 1999.

Zamakhshari, Abi al-Qasim Mahmud ibn 'Umar al-. *al-Kashshsaf 'an haqa'iq al-tanzil wa 'uyun al-aqawil fi wujuh al-ta'wil.* 6 vols. Riyad: Maktabah al-'Abikan, 1998.

Eyebrows

Aida Shahlar Gasimova

"And (there will be) companions with beautiful, big, and lustrous eyes." (Qur'an 56:22)

Introduction

Azeri-Turkish poetry was a fertile stream of Medieval Turkish literature. Supposedly, its flourishing owes to the thirteenth century Mongol invasions which brought to Azerbaijan new waves of Oghuz tribes who united there with the local Oghuz Turks who had long inhabited the region and who used Turkish as a spoken vernacular.[1] The union with these newly arrived Oghuz Turks, the triumphant fellow tribesmen, gave impetus to the revival of ethnic consciousness and stimulated the growth of outstanding poetry in Azeri-Turkish (Köpruluzade 11). Furthermore, the emergence of some sovereign Turcoman and Turcophone states, such as Qara-Qoyunlu (1375–1468), Agh-Qoyunlu (1378–1508) and the Safavids (1501–1722), stimulated the use of the Azeri vernacular, for "it enjoyed high prestige as the language of the ruling family and the Qizilbash tribes" (Perry 278).

The unique Azeri-Turkish literary tradition is noted for having carried elements of Islam and Muslim culture. It was also deeply impacted by Ibn al-'Arabi's teaching of *wahdat al-wujud* (unity of existence). Furthermore, the *hurufi* notions which emerged in Tabriz exercised a great influence on Azeri poetry. Hurufism, for those who are not familiar with the term, refers to a kabbalistic mystical Sufi movement which granted a sacred symbolism to Arabic letters. It is therefore not surprising that the images related to the Qur'an consti-tuted a great portion in this tradition, particularly in the depiction of facial features which, according to *hurufi* teachings, were a manifestation of divine letters.

The human face in *hurufi* teaching was considered to be the holy writing itself men-tioned in the Qur'an by the phrase *wa kitabin masturin fi raqqin manshurin* (By a book scribed, in a parchment unfolded) (52: 2–3). The Face was *lawh mahfuz*, because all the eternal and everlasting knowledge and divine orders have been written on the Human Face (Usluer 289–293). The detailed analysis of the image of eyebrows in the context of Medieval Azeri-Turkish poetry, especially in the poetry of great *hurufi* poet Imaduddin Nasimi[2] (1369–1417), Shah Isma'il Khata'i (1487–1524),[3] Muhammad Fuduli (1494–1556)[4] and others gives us ample grounds to suggest that the Qur'anic text was the source which inspired, not only Sufi symbolism in general, but the traditional symbolism of the eyebrows in par-ticular.

169

Eyebrows in Sufi Symbolism

Utilization of Qur'anic imagery in the depiction of facial features has been conditioned by the natural shape and functions of the feature itself: the more dynamic the feature, the more intense and meaningful are its images. From this point of view, the curl, lips and eyes, with dynamics of shape, motion and such derivative factors as tears, breath, aroma, sheen, and other elements, produced a great number of poetical images and esoteric meanings. Meanwhile, the image of eyebrows and its Sufi symbolism is more limited and traditional in scope due to its static nature. This can be explained by the fact that eyebrows do not play an important function in the face, besides preventing sweat from entering the eyes and diverting the sun from one's pupils. Although lacking in motion, and derivative factors, eyebrows beautify the face. In fact, according to many cultures, the eyebrows are the single most important feature on the face of a woman.

The description of eyebrows has sprung from both number and configuration. Arched, bow-shaped, eyebrows have produced various images related to Islamic and Qur'anic motifs, such as *mihrab, shaqq al-qamar, qaba qawsayn, nun,* and *qaf,* which carry the elements of a circle, thus expressing inner Sufi meanings. As Carl W. Ernst accentuates, circular elements were considered to have cosmic significance in the medieval Muslim world. The stress on circularity introduced into Arabic calligraphy by Ibn Muqla accentuated the metaphysical and spiritual properties attributed to the Arabic script. In his *Tuhfat al-muhibbin,* Siraj al-Shirazi spoke of circular symbolism in the following fashion:

> And since by the principles of wisdom it is demonstrated that God (glory be to the Most High) created the world in a circular form, even so the explanation of this meaning has occurred in the words of the sages. "The world is circle, the earth is a dot, the heavens are bows, accidents are arrows, and man is a target; so where is one to flee?" This is based on the judgment that, "the best of shapes is the shape of the circle" [Ernst 436].

Being semicircular in shape, eyebrows symbolized the proximity to God as a mean of ascension (*qaba qawsayn*). Furthermore "the eyebrows were likened to the niche [*mihrab*] of the Palace of Oneness [*Wahdat*] which directed the attention of Gnostics to the Divine Beauty [*Jamal*]" (Geyushov 359–360).

The lexicological repository of eyebrows in Azeri-Turkish poetry consists of a remarkable combination of synonyms in Turkish, Persian, and Arabic. They are the Persian *abru,* Arabic *hajib,* and Turkish *qash,* among others. There are several epithet-metaphors such as *mihrab, qiblah, taq, qaws, kaman,* and so forth, which are usually associated with eyebrows. The fact that eyebrows come in pairs has promoted the emergence of dual images such as two bows (*qaba qawsayn*), the split moon (*shaqq al-qamar*), as well as the two wings belonging to Qur'anic and post–Qur'anic birds (*hud-hud, 'anqa,* etc.).

Since eyebrows are similar in shape to bows, pens, and feathers, they inspired poets to produce a body of Qur'anic images which usually were accompanied by images of eyes, lips, single moles, and eyelashes, that entered into Sufi poetry as frequently used dichotomic constructions ('Alibayli 409). The positive image was usually accompanied by its diametric opposite. This was some kind of reflection on various contrapositions beginning from the contradictory character of spiritual worlds up to divaricating of psychological feelings of the Gnostic (*'arif / murid*) as *khawf / raja* (fear / hope), *bast / qabd* (expansion / contraction), *sahw / sukran* (sobriety / intoxication) and so on (Bertels, *Accounts,* 111).

In some cases, the eyebrows, along with the curl and eyelashes, represent seven congenial lines of hair in the human face that have a special symbolic meaning in *hurufi* teachings. Safarchioglu, while analyzing the hidden meanings of the eyebrows in the poetry of the prominent Ottoman poet Nevi, notices that their meaning is closely related to that of eyes, eyelashes, and cheeks. For example, if eyes and eyelashes are acts of homicide, eyebrows are murder weapons. In other words, they are the bows that shoot the arrows of coquetry and flirtatiousness. The association of seductive eyes with spiritual death and destruction seems to have been inspired by some sayings attributed to the Prophet Muhammad. In a tradition cited by Muslim, the Messenger of Allah is reported to have said that: "The [evil] gaze is a poisonous arrow from the arrows of Iblis. He that abstains from it out of my fear, I will grant him in return such faith, the sweetness of which he will experience within his heart." In yet another tradition, the Prophet warned that "Gazing at strange women is the adultery of the eyes" (Muslim).

If some Sufi poets compared eyebrows to weapons, others equated them with animate objects. For example, if the face is the ocean, eyebrows are fish (*nun*) within it (Safarçioglu 51). This motif echoed in Nasimi's poetry as follows:

> If someone looked at the beloved whose eyebrows are like Yasin,
> He would make his soul and breast (a target) for her arrows [*nawekler*].
> She has already drawn her eyebrows as bows and shed my blood,
> If you do not believe, look at her bloody arms [Nasimi 227].

Utilization of extensive antithetical constructions was a specific feature and stylistic device in ancient Turkish literature. Besides the above-mentioned Sufi contrapositions, "collection of the semantic contrapositions related to the dualistic myths has also become an important part of the poetical creation" in Turkish literature (Stebleva 182). The most commonly used figures in these antithetical constructions were metaphors, comparisons, constant epithets, allegories etc. Particularly metaphors — personifications (*tashkhis*) — were the most applied ones that gave a profound vivacity to the poetical self-expression of the poetry.[5] In the tradition under review, all these images were used to demonstrate the world of emanations that has been illustrated in the shape of a loop or link-gripping Sufi, who was longing for the union with the Supreme Essence, and who tried to release himself from the chains of the lower world (Bertels, *Accounts* 115). The following passage from Fuduli's *Sahhat and Marad* (*Health and Sickness*) is in tune with such speculations:

> Love and Spirit reached a very dreadful home. The home was called *Cheshm-i Shahla* (Brown eyes). Its inhabitants were artful. Its king was Coquetry, the Murderer [*Qatil Ghamza*]. Then, they reached a very glorious place where saw two fine rooms which served as a sanctuary and a prayer niche. In beauty, they looked like *qaba qawsayn*. They were an abode of gratefulness of hearts. Their name was *taq-i abru* [Fuduli, *Health* 76–77].

As has been mentioned above, eyebrows may be depicted as a separate part of Beauty's face, expressing proximity to Divinity. Eyebrows can also be described along with other features, particularly with curls and eyelashes, representing seven congenial lines in the human face. Such facial features have been ascribed a great of importance in *hurufi* teaching for their being the fourth part of the mysterious number 28.[6] Clearly, the Qur'anic text served as a rich repository for expressing the scope of Sufi eyebrow symbolism.

In accordance with *hurufi* notions, Classical Azeri-Turkish poetry likens eyebrows to the Arabic letters *nun*, *ra*,' and to the attached letters (*al-huruf al-muqatta'ah*) *ya*,' *sin*, *ta*'. From the *hurufi* point of view, Shah Isma'il Khata'i's poem is very important in that every feature is likened to an Arabic letter, among them the eyebrows' comparison with the letter *nun* is noteworthy (Khata'i 88). In *hurufi* poetry, the congenial lines are frequently employed as images associated with with *ayats* and *surahs* of the Qur'an, with such expressions as *Umm al-Kitab* (Mother of The Book), *al-ism al-'azam*—the greatest name of God. The cited below distiches from the poetry of Nasimi depict the facial features in compliance with *hurufi* notions:

> Your lock, eyebrows and eyelashes are verses of the Book [*ayat-ul-kitab*],
> These are the Tablet [*mushaf*], look at its *surahs* and *ayats* [Nasimi 28].
> Your eyebrows, eyelashes and black lock are *Umm al-kitab*
> The Qur'an is the Imam and *Murshid* of the People of Oneness [*ahl-i tawhid*] [Nasimi 59].
> Your eyelashes and eyebrows are the Greatest Name [*ism-i 'azam*]
> There would not be fear of the demon [*div*], if they were my resort [Nasimi 105].[7]

The *hawaris* or apostles from the story of 'Isa (Jesus) (3:52; 61:14) and *Sehr-i Samiri* (*Samiri's* sorcery), (20:85, 87, 95) are also common images related to the eyebrows, eyes, eyelashes, and cheeks. Alongside with such common images, the eyebrows, when taken separately, have some traditional Qur'anic images which may be classified as follows: *Qaba qawsayn* (accounts of the Ascension of the Prophet) (53:9); *Qalam wa nun* (Muslim cosmogony), (68:1); *Shaqq al-qamar* (Miracle ascribed to the Prophet Muhammad) (54:1); Wings of the bird of the mountain *Qaf* (post–Qur'anic story of the prophet *Sulayman*); and wings of *hud-hud* (hoopoe, the story of Sulayman) (27:28). As can be appreciated, it is scarcely possible to fully understand the semantic layers of the images related to eyebrows without a thorough knowledge of the Qur'anic or post–Qur'anic stories hidden behind the poetical word.

As has been mentioned above, the mythic-ritual implications of the semi-circular eyebrows have inner metaphysical meanings in Sufism. In Sufi cosmogony, the wholeness of the universe is imagined as a circle which consists of two semicircles (bow, arch), one of which symbolizes the descent (*nuzul*) through the degrees and stages of universe — namely, God's most beautiful nameswhich embody multiplicity (*kathrat*)—while the other one indicates ascent (*'uruj*). The descent begins from the highest stage — that is, the the stage of eternity which leads to total *tawhid*—and ends in humanity (Geyushov 60). The configuration of the eyebrows, which is represented as two semicircles, provides a full scope of expression to convey the Sufi perception of the universe while corresponding with the mythopoetical meaning of the archetype of the bow and arch. It is not by pure accident that the most applied Qur'anic image of the eyebrows that of two bow-lengths or *qaba qawsayn*.

Surah al-Najm (The Chapter of the Star) alludes that the Prophet Muhammad, during his Night Journey to the highest heavens, was at a distance of but two bow-lengths (*qaba qawsayn*) or nearer to the Divinity. For Muslim mystics, this symbolizes "the highest degree of proximity the heart can reach" (Schimmel, *Mystical* 221). In Lahiji's interpretation, *qaba qawsayn* represents a stage of Oneness and Holiness. In this stage, the Perfect Human Being has transformed into a manifestation of the Divine Substance and Names (259). It is a stage of Muhammad, the Messenger of Allah, who, passing the semicircles, descended (*nuzul*) and ascended (*su'ud*), ultimately reaching the station of unification of unification (*jam'i-jam'*). For al-Qushayri, such a stage consists of the "total self-dissolution [in God] and loss of perception of anything other than God" (112). In Nizami's *Iskandarname*, we see that, when the Prophet Muhammad was released from his corporeal being, he found himself surrounded inside of a spiritual circle (33).[8]

The idea of bows being a symbol of proximity seems to go back even further all the way to ancient mythology. This is because classical Azeri-Turkish literature had links to both ancient Turkish mythology and the Arabic and Islamic tradition. In ancient Arabian and Turkish mythology, the *yay* or bow was considered to be a symbol of the Divinity. Emerging from the cult of the sun, the bow, in Turkish mythology, has been a symbol of the heaven which manifested the Supreme Deity. For this reason, the ancient Turks usually wrote "belonging of God" inside of their bows (Seyidov 269). Furthermore, as the bow symbolized the sun god, the divine abode which has been lost for human beings, by the use of magical and semi-magical means, ancient humans thought about the return of their soul to this glorious land. Ancient people imagined that the ladder, made from fairy arrows shots to the heavens by the bow, could lead him to this glorious land (Spense 76).

Similar views existed among pre–Islamic Arabs, as well. Ancient Arabian soothsayers (*kahins*) utilized bows and arrows, which resembled the rays of the sun, in their mystical and magical practices (Ibn Hisham 222).[9] Sometimes, the bows were denotative of the contact between the ancient nomadic tribes.[10] Subsequently, they seem to have taken on a special symbolic meaning in their mystic practice as the union between God and human being. Therefore, if we consider some logical relation between the direct meaning of the bow and its symbolical meaning, it becomes clear how the symbols of *qaba qawsayn* were used to express several layers of perception. These layers represent the Qur'anic notions (*qaba qawsayn*, 53:9) about nearness to God, the widely spread motif of ascension (*'uruj*); the Sufi perception of the universe; as well as ancient mythological notions regarding the bow.

One can suggest that the utilization of the bow as an oracle by priests and shamans somehow found its way into sacred books and Sufi teachings. In the process, the bow came to symbolize the release from the corporeal world and union with God. Nevertheless, in the poetry under review, both mythological thought and Sufi perception are occulted in the hidden strata, while the Qur'anic images are dominant and obvious: "Mystery of your *qaba qawsayn* eyebrows cannot be understood, / He who sacrificed himself for those bows comprehended this mystery" (Nasimi 218).

Thus, Nasimi expresses the transcendent substance of God, which cannot be comprehended without the Sufi's self-denial. However, the first image that represents itself through the distich is that of *qaba qawsayn* was very familiar to medieval readers of the Qur'an: the Prophet's Nightly Journey or Ascent. From here, it is logical that Azeri poets depicted bow like eyebrows as a mean to convey the symbolic meaning of the *Mi'raj*: "Nobody would understand the symbols of *qaba qawsayn*, / without seing the brows of that full moon [*mah-i badr*]" (Nasimi 245).

The antithesis observed in this verse between the dark brows and bright cheeks (or face / full moon), which expresses the contradictory character of Sufi perception, has been even further developed in Nasimi's other poems:

> The night of your lock is like *qadr* [destiny], your red cheeks are like the moon
> The Ascension is your face, the lotus [*sidrah*] is your stature, and two bows are your
>   eyebrows [Nasimi 246].
> I joined the ascent with your eyebrows; they are *qaba qawsayn*
> In this night of union [*wuslat shabi*], I became irradiant from head to toe [Nasimi 153].

In Classical Azeri-Turkish poetry, as can be seen from the above, night and day, along with dark and light, form dichotomic constructions that are reflected in the Human Face. According to Muslim Tradition, the *Mi'raj* occurred at night (*Laylat al-Isra*) but ended with bright light. According to the *hadith* literature, the Messenger of Allah was asked whether or not he had seen God during his ascension, to which he responded: "I have seen a light" (*ra'aytu nuran*) (Ibn Kathir, 3/11). Such a symbolic image is seen in *Tarjuman al-ashwaq* by Muhyi al-Din Ibn al-'Arabi, one of the most influential figures in Azeri-Turkish Sufi poetry:

> The whiteness of her forehead is like the sun,
> The blackness of the hair on her brow is like the night
> Most wondrous of the forms is she: combining sun and night together!
> Through her, we are in daylight during the night, and in the night of her hair at noon.

While interpreting this passage, Ibn al-'Arabi states that "the blackness of the hair on her brow" represents the mysterious sciences of which she is bearer. "We are in daylight during the night" indicates that we are in the essence of God's invisibility" (*Tarjuman* 123–4). Emphasizing this motif, Shabustari says:

> When one is too close, he cannot see,
> Everything goes dark before his eyes, and his mind cannot comprehend.
> Be aware that this darkness is the light of the Essence
> Inside darkness resides the water of life [Lahiji 194–196].

The comprehensive explanation of this spiritual state has been given by Lahiji, who observes that a look from the nearest distance can cause a blackout. The inner eyes become blind when they reach the substantive manifestation after passing through the names and attributes. "Inside darkness resides the water of life," means that in the darkness of the world of Multiplicity (*kathrat*), the water of life is usually hidden (Lahiji 194–196; Schimmel, *Mystical Dimensions* 144). In other words, Absolute Unity is shrouded in Multiplicity, namely, the many lead to the One.

In Nasimi's following distich, one can see a hidden reminiscence to the ascension. The poet employs the symbolic meaning of eyes and brows of coquetry and flirtatiousness which lead to temptation, meanwhile the poetic vocabulary (*yay, falak, malak*) is deeply associated with account of the *Mi'raj*: "O God [*Ya Rabb*]! Whose tempting eyes and eyelashes are like arrows and bows / Heaven [*falak*] is a target of Your arrow, the angel the sacrifice for Your bow" (N.177). The image of bows inspired the poet to create one more original image of eyebrows — that of rainbows (*qaws quzah*) (N.163). Inspired by Nasimi's poetry, Haqiqi says that "the beloved's *qaba qawsayn* eyebrows are *fitnah* [temptation] for the crescent moon [*hilal*]," seemingly claiming that they lead astray from Islam, the symbol of which is the crescent moon (*Anthology* 258).[11]

In studying images related to the eyebrows, it would be worthwhile to consider the arch, a widely spread mythopoetical image which represented by a rotated semi-circle. As can be seen in the quatrains by Nasimi, the arched niches (*mihrab*) of mosques are similar to brows. As such, they indicate proximity to God:

> Your eyebrows were the highest arch [*a'la taq*],
> The spirit was longing to ascend to them.
> Your face was a locus of the Creator's manifestation [*mazhar-i khallaq*]
> It was the Ka'bah of the soul [*Kabey-i jan*] and the prayer niche [*qiblah*] of the lovers [Nasimi 312].

It is worth noting that the *mihrab* is one of the most commonly applied images applied to eyebrows, opening broad horizons for the poetic imagination. In *Surah Maryam* (The Chapter of Mary) in the Qur'an, the *mihrab* means a "prayer niche" (19:11). Semi-circular eyebrows, much like a *mihrab*, attract the attention of believers towards the *qiblah* (direction of prayer). In the poetry of Fuduli, the whole scene from a Muslim mosque is depicted in the human face. Eeyebrows resemble the *mihrab* or "prayer niche," eyes stands for the *imam* or "prayer leader," and eyelashes are believers lined up for congregational ritual prayers (233). Reminiscence is made to the *Surah al-Saffat* (The Chapter of the Rangers) by the use of expression *saf-saf* (lined). Another poem on this subject runs as follows: "I wonder whether the hermit [*zahid*] is madly in love with her eyebrows, / Causing him to talk to himself while staring at the *mihrab* all the time" (Fuduli 137). A unique scene of this kind has been imagined by Qadi Burhanuddin, which includes not only the process of praying, but also the act of ablution before performing *namaz* (ritual prayers), and all these using the parts of human body: "I never conduct a prayer [*namaz*] in front of the niche of your eyebrows, / without performing ablution [*ghusl*] in the blood of the heart" (Qadi 40).

The main poetic figure used here is *husn-i ta'lil*. By using the images of eyebrows, the poet explains the hermit's unceasing prayers before the mosque's niche. A similar image is found in Kishwari's poetry, in which the hermit abandons the world and secluded himself in corner of the mosque due to the "*mihrab*'s likeness to the eyebrows of the Beautiful" (Kishwari 101).[12] A mosque-like scene is also depicted in the face of beloved in the poetry of Habibi (1470–?), the court poet of Shah Isma'il Khata'i: "The sacred sanctuary [*Bayt al-haram*] is around of your cheeks / Your eyes are like the prayer leader [*imam*] of your eyebrows' niche [*mihrab*]" (*Anthology* 258). Even before these poets, Nasimi had likened eyebrows to the niche and eyes to the preacher (*khatib*) (Nasimi 33).

As can be expected, bows produced a whole arsenal of images related to the human face. In the poetry of Fuduli, an awesome martial scene is represented in the face of the Beautiful: "Your bow-like eyebrows colored by indigo [*wasmah*] / They are like swords rusted away through shedding blood" (140). The target of the arrows thrown by bows-eyebrows is the true lover who, according to Kishwari, never tries to avoid them (Kishwari 132). In another poem by Kishwari, the lover's bleeding heart is longing over the beloved's eyebrows which, like a hero (*dilaver*), entered combat with the two bows (Kishwari 81). In this military scene, the image of a Turkish warrior is very appropriate for Turkish marksmen were considered to be the most skilled in the art of fighting: "Your Turkish eyes put arrows in the bows of your brows, / the Heart made itself a target for this arrow" (Qadi 360).

Images related to the moon, particularly to the prophetic tradition of *Shaqq al-qamar*[13] or the splitting of the moon is one of the most interesting mythopoeical figures connected with the eyebrows. If the full moon (*badr*) is an image of the face, its dichotomic image is the eyebrows when compared with the half moon (*hilal*). The *beyts* (verses) of Nasimi, which are cited below, reflect recurring Qur'anic motifs: "On the Night of Ascent, your two bows divided the full moon / Who is not aware of this miracle cannot appreciate the crescent moon [*hilal*]" (Nasimi 120). The eyebrows, as symbols of the new moon, are developed in Fuduli's poetry with some specific anthropomorphic, cosmogonical nuances:

Every month, the universe [*dahr*] fancies your bows
That is why, in the beginning of every month, the new moon [*hilal*] appears.
The new moon [*mah-i nov*] became a wanderer [*sergeshte*], longing for your bows
From town to a town as a vagrant [*avara*] and through months and years [*mah-i sal*] [218].

This verse is full of poetic figures. These are the *tashkhis* (the universe and the new moon which "fell in love"), *tasghir* (the lover who became as slender as a new moon), and *husn-i ta'lil*, the explanation for the emergence of the new moon. The semantic shades of meaning of the *mah* (month, moon) give an opportunity to create a whole number of puns (*jinas* and *tasdir*). Lahiji, while explaining the similar motive in the poetry of Shabustari, stresses the importance of verse thirty-nine of *Surah Yasin* where the moon is compared to the slender and covered branch of the palm. According to him, the lover (universe) falls ill with eternal love which resembles the slender branch of the date palm (Lahiji 277–8).

Dichotomic images of the face (full moon) and eyebrows (bows) in the following passage by Fuduli apparently derived inspiration from the Qur'anic story of 'Isa (Jesus): "Oh Painter (*musawwir*)! You are painting this beauty with the face like the moon. / Although, it is hardly possible to paint someone with eyebrows like bows" (Fuduli 332). These verses are reminiscent of the Qur'anic story of '*Isa al-Masih* (Jesus, the Messiah), in which he is presented as a *musawwir* or "fashioner of figures." The Qur'anic account reads as follows:

> And (appoint him) an apostle to the Children of Israel, (with this message): "I have come to you, with a Sign from your Lord, in that I make for you out of clay, as it were, the figure of a bird, and breathe into it, and it becomes a bird by Allah's leave" [3:49].

Some metaphorical images of eyebrows also draw from the symbolic Pen of Majesty. Kishwari says: "Pen of Majesty [*kilk-i qudrat*] has drawn your eyebrows over your eyes / Building a niche of obedience [*mihrab-i ta'at*] above the land of disbelief" (Kishwari 90). Haqiqi expresses this motif which alludes to the Qur'anic story regarding the creation of the first man and the prostration of the angels before him (*al-Baqarah* 30–34): "The hand of omnipotence [*qudrat eli*] paints [*cheker*] with the pen [*qalam*] the half-moon of your brows, / Prostrate yourself before the soil of your creation if you are an initiate [*'arif*]" (*Anthology* 246).

These verses contain echoes of the cosmological function of the Qur'anic Pen. It must be mentioned that the Qur'anic verses related to the Pen provided inexhaustible topics, mythopoetical images and artistic expressiveness for the poetry. Besides the verse 44 of the *Surah Al 'Imran* (The Chapter of the Family of 'Imran), there are several Qur'anic verses connected with this instrument which represents a mean of creation and perception: they are: *al-Qalam*, 1; *al-'Alaq*, 4; and *Luqman*, 27. Almost all the exegetes, while interpreting the meaning of *qalam*, recount the following prophetic tradition with minor variations: "The first thing God created was the Pen, then *nun*. *Nun* is ink. God ordered the Pen to write. The Pen asked: 'What should I write?' God said: 'Write all human actions until the Day of Judgment, their livelihood, and life time.'"[14] After the Pen had written everything, God sealed it, for "the Pen will not speak until the Day of Judgment" (Ibn Kathir 4/427; al-Tabari 12/177; Sam'ani 6/16; al-Qurtubi 18/223).

In medieval Muslim society, the pen was an instrument of pre-eternal and divine character. It is not surprising that medieval scribes did not throw away the shavings produced by sharpening their pens but, rather, buried them in a pure place (Kaziyev 294). They were treated as shards of a sacred instrument. In his *Fihrist*, Ibn al-Nadim said that "The Pen is a messenger of the mind, its envoy and tongue. The intelligence of people is dripping from the tip of their pen... While the people are crying the pens are laughing" (21). The metaphorical meaning of the pen has been stressed in Sufism. As Schimmel has explained, one of the qualities required in a pen is that its tongue, or even its head, be cut off: the pen becomes the symbol of the mystic who must not divulge the secret, and who speaks without tongue (Schimmel, *Letter*, 415). It is noteworthy that the pen has been used in the poetic texts under review not only for "drawing" the eyebrows, but also as their metaphors: "*Nun wa qalam* has been revealed in honor of your eyebrows, / Who reads this letter, will imagine the full-moon [*badr*] as half-moon [*hilal*]" (Nasimi 54).

The poetic figure *laff-i nashr* is used in this distich with *nun* representing the full moon and *qalam* representing the half-moon. *Nun wa al-qalam* is the beginning verse of the *Surah al-Qalam* (The Chapter of the Pen). The verse *nun wa al-qalam* is an oath taken in the name of the Pen: "Nun. By the Pen [*qalam*] and all that they write [therewith]!" (68:1). In Azeri-Turkish poetry, writes Schimmel, "the *nun* represents the beautifully arched eyebrow, even though it is upside down, and the pupil or the mole could then represent the dot inside *nun*" (*Calligraphy* 139). There is no consensus when it comes to the symbolism of the letter *nun* which seems to have deep mythological roots.[15] Common knowledge considers it to be an attached letter. In Qur'anic commentaries, a great variety of definitions have been given to *nun* as an attached letter. It is frequently imagined as a fish (*hut*) carrying seven layers of the earth on its back. Another definition given to *nun* is that of an inkpot (*dawat*) (Ibn Kathir 4/427; al-Tabari 12/176; Sam'ani 6/16; al-Qurtubi 18/223). Sometimes *nun* is defined as a brilliant tablet (*lawh min nur*) on which everything is written. In this case, the pen's luminous origin is observed (Ibn Kathir 4/428; al-Tabari 12/176; al-Qurtubi 18/223). Some commentators say that the oath in the Qur'anic verse is made not only to pen but to *nun* as well (al-Tabari 12/177). Abu al-Qasim Jarullah al-Zamakhshari (538 h.), the Mu'tazili commentator of the Qur'an, claims that it would be wrong to imagine *nun* as a fish, inkpot or golden scripture. If it were a common or proper noun, it would be declined or would be definite or indefinite. "What about the oath?" wonders Zamakhshari. God swears here only by the pen. If He took an oath by the letter *nun*, the particle *wa* (*by*) would be placed before the *nun* (al-Zamakhshari 4/572–573). According to al-Fadl ibn al-Hasan al-Tabarsi (548 h.), *nun* was the whitest and sweetest river in paradise. God ordered it to become ink, then ordered the pen to write everything with this ink (29/22).

In Ibn al-Arabi's ontology, the Highest Pen (*al-qalam al-a'la*) is the Muhammadan Reality (*al-haqqiqah al-Muhammadiyyah*) and the Prime Intellect (*al-'aql al-awwal*) (*al-Futuhat* 73). When God created the Pen (*qalam*) and the Tablet (*Lawh*), He named the first, Intellect (*'aql*), and the second, Spirit (*ruh*) (*al-Futuhat* 107). Then, God ordered the Pen to write everything on the Tablet, and the Pen wrote what God had dictated, thus establishing the spiritual marriage established between Tablet and Pen (*al-Futuhat* 127). Such an erotic Sufi cosmogony is observable also in Ibn al-'Arabi's interpretations of the Mother of the Book, *Umm al-Kitab* (3:7; 13:39; 43:4), and the Scroll Unfolded, *Raqq Manshur* (29:3). Both were considered to be the feminine elements of universe. It is noteworthy that in Ibn al-'Arabi's ontology, the process of writing by the Pen is compared with the birth of Son (*al-Futuhat* 94). While interpreting the attached letter *nun*, Ibn al-'Arabi related that its element is earth which also is feminine (*al-Futuhat* 42). According to him, both *nun* and *qalam* are angels; Allah chose the Pen as an angel-scribe. In hierarchy, it comes after the angel *nun*. *Nun* is ink and it maintains all the divine decrees in condensed form, which are expounded by Pen (*al-Futuhat* 313). All these sayings served as a rich repository for multidimensional and multilayer Sufi symbolism and provided an inexhaustible source for poetic embellishment.

Nun's poetic image related, first of all, to its configuration as a letter. Its arched form contains the elements of a semicircle. Furthermore, there are seven basic letters in the Arabic alphabet,[16] two of which are contained in *nun*, so in addition to its arched form it maintained a dot which signified some mysterious meanings in Sufism.[17] The symbolism of the letter *nun* can be traced back to ancient Egyptian-Babylonian cosmogonical beliefs which were not alien to medieval Azeri authors since they lived in the cradle of these civilizations.[18] Another point is focused on *nun*'s Qur'anic connection with the prophet Yunus (*Sahib-u Nun*) (21:87; 68:48), who attained divine grace in the oceanic waters, in the well of fish

(Schimmel, *Letter symbolism* 416). It is noteworthy that, in both the mythological system and the sacred book, *nun* has been connected with the ocean. Tears created a very good basis for artistic illustrations. In Nasimi's poetry, the emergence of tears has been explained (*husn-i ta'lil*) by their being near to the eyebrows and lips. Eyebrows have been symbolized by *nun* which, as we have mentioned above, was a fish. Lips, however, have the symbolic meaning of life-giving water. These two letters compose *nam* which means "damp" and "moist": "My eyes are always moist [*nam*] for this love, / As your eyebrows are *nun* and your mouth is *mim*" (Nasimi 104). The same motif with minor variations has been depicted in Kishwari's poetry (Kishwari 44, 93).

There are some images in Azeri-Turkish poetry that are related to post–Qur'anic stories regarding *Qaf* and *'Anqa*. Kishwari, for example, compares the eyebrows with "wings of the bird of Majestic *Qaf*" (*Qafi qudrat*) (21) thus indicating *Simurq-'Anqa* which in Sufi literature was a symbol of the Ultimate and One Substance. According to al-Mas'udi, *'Anqa* was created in time immemorial.[19] In 'Ibn al-'Arabi's teachings, this is the spirit blown into bodies. By such a symbol, Sufis implicated that there is nothing like the Absolute Supreme Spirit (Kasanzan "*qaf*"). In general, the symbol of *'Anqa* was frequently used by Sufis in order to express spiritual ascent.[20] As an image of the eyebrows, *'Anqa* also embodies the nearness to divine presence.

In post–Qur'anic stories and Sufi tradition *'Anqa* is a symbol of the Sufi Shaykh who acts as a guide to union with God. This mysterious bird was "potentially existent but not existent, and no one has first-hand knowledge of it except for Solomon, the prophet of God" (Elmore, Notes). *'Anqa*'s mysterious abode is the mountain *Qaf*. There are different Sufi explanations for the Qur'anic *Qaf*, namely, the attached letter of the *Surah Qaf* (The Chapter of *Qaf*). First of all, it is considered to be a mountain and the abode of *Simurgh*. This mountain is so great that it almost surrounds the world (Lahici 229). Furthermore, *Qaf* is an alphabetical letter which resembles *nun* by its appearance. In other words, it contains the elements of a circle. According to some Muslim scholars, *Qaf* is a letter connected to the Divine throne (*'Arsh*). According to Ibn 'Abbas, it is one of the most beautiful names of God. According to Sahl Tustari, *Qaf* represents swearing by God's power and might (Kasanzan "*qaf*"). For Lahici, all divine names and attributes manifest themselves through *Qaf* (229). The mysterious *Qaf* is one of the most wide-spread images of eyebrows: "I have seen the face of the Compassionate [*Surahu Rahman*] on your face, / I have seen *Qaf* and Qur'an in your eyebrows" (Nasimi 168). In Kishwari's following distich, the feathers of the bird are utilized as an image of the eyebrows: "O Kishwari! Every arrow of sorrow [*tigh-i gham*] shot by that idol with the eyebrows as bow [*kamanabru sanam*], / Are the wings of the happy Hud-hud, which comes from Suleyman" (Kishwari 19). *Hud-hud* also is a frequently repeated image in Sufi literature. Its roots are traced back to ancient beliefs. Proceeding from the literal meaning of *Hud-hud*, which traces back to the Arabic root *hada* (lead to the right path), the ancient Arabs branded the hoopoe with the badge of the straight path. Subsequently, the hoopie came to personify the *Sufi Shaykh*—guide of *murids* (disciples)—in mystical Muslim literature (Bertels 342, 394).

Conclusion

As can be seen from the aforementioned poetic citations, images related to eyebrows as *qaba qawsayn*, *shaqq al-qamar*, *qalam*, *nun* etc. were repeated over and over again in Classical Azeri-Turkish poetry. In discussing the Qur'anic images of eyebrows, it is worthwhile to consider common images used alongside eyes and eyelashes. The well known symbolical meanings of the eyebrows, alongside with eyes and eyelashes as *fitnah* (temptation, delusion) and *sihr* (magic), have been grown on the soil of the Qur'anic stories as well; these are temptation of Adam (2:30; 7:11; 20:116), Babylonian magic (2:102), and occasionally Samiri's sorcery (20:85) which is found in Khata'i's poetry (Khata'i, i, 227). In the poetry of Qadi Burhanuddin, the unique image of the disciples of Jesus, the *hawariyyun*, is used as a common comparison for brows, cheeks, and eyes: "O Shah! Your pearl lips are Jesus ['Isa], / your cheeks, eyes, and brows [*hajib*] are apostles [*hawaris*]" (Qadi 477). A great number of examples could be provided because Azeri poetry is rich in this area. However, it would be appropriate here to limit our topic to the aforementioned due to the impossibility of covering such a voluminous subject within the bounds of a single study.

As evidenced in this study, mythopoesis related to the Qur'an represents one of the richest aspects of Medieval Azeri-Turkish poetry. Owing to its use of Qur'anic imagery as a repository, the depiction of beauty, particularly of the eyebrows, gained a profound mystical meaning and contributed to poetic embellishment. Furthermore, as it is seen from the aforementioned poetic examples, the poetic canon, which circulated around Qur'anic motifs, has not limited the artistic imagination; rather, it represented fertile ground for the emergence of new and unique images. This is simply one example in which a single image from the Qur'an represented a seed that spawned hundreds of other inspirational images.

Chapter Notes

1. The exact date of arrival of the first Turk-Oghuz tribes to Azerbaijan is still the subject of divergent opinions. It is noteworthy that medieval Arabian historians such as Ibn Jarir al-Tabari (839–923) and 'Izz al-Din Ibn al-Athir (1160–1233) claim that it took place during the rule of Tuban As'ad (IV CE), the semi-legendary Yemenite king of the Tubba'a dynasty. According to their records, Tuban As'ad led a military campaign in the northern lands. There, it is said that he encountered Turks in Azerbaijan and waged a battle against them. After the defeat of the Turks, the Yemenites took the defeated people's children back to Yemen as captives. Although the record's authenticity is doubtful, it deserves attention for illustrating the effort made by Arab historians to give a more archaic color to the Arab-Muslim invasions (al-Tabari 566–567; Ibn al-Athir 210).

2. Nasimi is one of the prominent figures of Sufi poetry. Being an exponent of hurufism, Nasimi is considered the founder of the mystical-philosophical poetry of *hurufiyyah*. He wrote *diwans* in the Azeri-Turkish and Persian languages.

3. Khata'i was the founder of the Safavid dynasty. He produced both lyrical and epic poetry. Khata'i wrote in both the classical and popular genres. His poem, *Dahname*, is a very original work that blends epic stories with lyrics and descriptions. He "was not only a fine poet in Turkish but wrote a good hand" (Schimmel, *Calligraphy* 64).

4. The famous Turkish poet, Muhammad Fuduli, wrote in three languages: Azeri-Turkish, Persian, and Arabic. Besides the *diwans* of *ghazals* and *qasidahs*, Fuduli produced epic poems, mathnawis, and philosophical treatises.

5. Even in the Qur'an, the metaphor is a frequently used figure. As R. Bell has noted, there are more than four hundred metaphors in the Qur'an (100).

6. According to *hurufi* teachings, the Divine Essence can never be reached without passing through God's Names and Attributes, reflected in the twenty-eight sacred Arabic letters and the thirty-two holy Persian letters.

7. By making use of the poetical figure *talmih*, the poet alludes to the Qur'anic story (38:34) concerning the theft of Sulayman's ring by a *jinn* on which, according to post–Qur'anic tradition, *al-ism al-'azam*, the greatest name of God, had been graved (38:34). See Gasimova 95–6.

8. Suleymanova supposes that Nizami, by this expression, noticed that the Prophet found himself inside the figure-eight trajectory of Sirius A and Sirius B, which in their circulation become nearest to each other every 49.9 years (303).

9. Arab poets used these weapons in declamation of their poems. Al-Jahiz points to the adherents of the *shu'ubiyyah* movement who, through misunderstanding their true meaning, criticized Arabs for using the staff, the bow, and the spear. According to al-Jahiz, however, the true sense of this use was much deeper. Thereby, he alluded to the mystical meaning of such attributes (5–14).

10. When the ancient Arabs concluded an alliance they took bows, placed them together, drew them, and then shot arrows in such a way. This act meant that they had common joy and anger (Akar 48). There was also another tradition: when Arab tribes wanted to end discord and to agree on an armistice, all of the male members of those tribes marshaled along the borders of their territory with bows in their hands (Akar 49).

11. Mirza Jahanshah Haqiqi (1397–1467) was one of the rulers of Qaraqoyunlu dynasty. He wrote poems in Azeri-Turkish and Persian. In poetry, he was a follower of Imaduddin Nasimi.

12. Ni'matullah Kishwari (XV-XVI), a follower of Fuduli's poetic tradition, is a prominent figure of Azeri-Turkish poetry. He is an author of diwans in Azeri-Turkish and Persian languages.

13. The first verse of the *Surah al-Qamar* has evoked controversial interpretations. According to I. Krachkovsky, the verse refers to eschatology. At the same time, it is a legend about the miracle of the the Prophet Muhammad who split the moon in two parts with the waving of his finger (Ibn Kathir, vol. 4, 279–281; Krachkovsky 603; Kutub 9/445–8).

14. Recording human destinies in sacred books traces back to the ancient times. In the poem of *Gilgamesh*, the goddess of the underworld Ereshkigal had a scrivener-woman, Lord of the Book of Destinies. In accordance with the ancient Sumerian-Acadian mythology, the deity of fate, Enlil, wrote the tables of destinies (http://www.sacred-texts.com/ane/sum/sum07.htm). According to Egyptian myths, the ibis-headed god Thoth was considered to be the patron deity of writing and scribes. According to Babylonian myths, Nabu — god of wisdom and writing — was the patron of the scribes and, to a certain extent, Lord of Human Fate (McCann web).

15. *Nun*'s roots traced back to ancient times, In Egyptian mythology it was the First Cause in the state of water. In both the Egyptian and Phoenician alphabet, *nun* is a spiral formed letter in the form of bowl. It referred to water, life, lightening, and reincarnation (Suleymanova 296–316). It seems the religious-mythological image of *nun* was not alien to pre–Islamic Arabs. The false prophet Tuleyha claimed that while being in trance, he received revelations from an angel named "Zun-Nun" (Piotrovsk, Prorocheskoye dvijenie 20–21).

16. They are *alif, sad, dal, nun,* beginning form of *sin,* crown of *waw* and *nuqta* (dot) (Kaziyev 65).

17. Accoprding to Hallaj, the Qur'an embraced the teaching of everything. The entire teaching of the Qur'an is condensed in the letters found at the start of some surahs. The meaning of these letters can be found in the letters *alif* and *lam* while the meanings of *alif* and *lam* can be found in a single dot (al-Hallaj 95). Furthermore, Muslim calligraphers believed that all the letters consist of dots (Kaziyev 58).

18. Fuduli was born, and lived, in Karbala, Iraq. Nasimi spent some years in Syria and was executed in Halab. He was very famous in Egypt as well. Khata'i's (the Safawid kingdom's) capital was Baghdad.

19. They existed until the time of Khalid ibn Sinan — the prophet of the tribe 'Abs, who was "one of the prophets who had been killed by their fellow tribesmen" as was called by the Prophet Muhammad. This bird had been destroyed by the invocation of Khalid (Boyko 150–2).

20. Bistami describes his union with God in the following termes: "when I reached *wahdat* (union) with Him, I realized that I had turned into a bird. My body was He, and my wings were the depths of Eternity" (Bertels 33).

Works Cited

Akar, Metin. *Turk Edebiyati'nda Manzum Mi'rac-nameler.* Ankara: Kultur ve Turizm Bakanligi, 1987.

'Alibayli, Shafaq. "*Badan Mulku* (Fuzulinin farsca divaninda badan uzvlerinin adlari) / The Reign of Body, (The Names of the Body Organs in the Persian *diwan* of *Fuduli*"). *Issues of Oriental Philology* (2005): 387–415.

Bertels, Yevgeniy E. "Kniqa o Solove (Bulbulname) Faridaddina 'Attara." *Izbanniye Sohineniya, Sufizm i Sufiyskaya Literatura.* Moscow: Nauka, 1965. 340–354.

_____. "Zametki po Poeticheskoy Terminologii Persidskix Sufiev." *Izbanniye Sochineniya, Sufizm I Sufiyskaya Literatura.* Moscow: Nauka, 1965. 109–126.

Boyko, Konstantine A. *Arabskaya Istoricheskaya Literatura v Eqipte* (VII-IX vv.) Moscow: Nauka, 1983.

Elmore, Gerald. *Ibn al-'Arabi's* Book on the Fabulous Gryphon (*Anqa Mughrib*). Internet: www.ibnara-bisociety.org/articles/anqamughrib.htm

Ernst, Carl W. "Sufism and the Aesthetics of Penmanship in Siraj al-Shirazi's *Tuhfat al- Muhibbin*" (1454). *Journal of the American Oriental Society* 129.3 (2009): 431–442.

Fuduli, Muhammad. "Sahhat ve Marad." *Selected Works*. Vol. 5. Trans. M.M. Asgerli. Baku, "Sharq-Qarb," 2005.

_____. *Works (Ghazals)*, vol.1 (In Azeri-Turkish), Baku: Publishing House of the Academy of Sciences Azerbaijan, 1958.

Gasimova, Aida. *Fuzuli Yaradiciliginda Qur'an Revayetleri*. Baku: Baku State University, 1995.

Goyushov, Nasib. *Tasavvuf anlamlari ve dervishlik ramzlari*. Baku: Tural, 2001.

Hallaj, al-. *Kitab Akhbar al- Hallaj*. Ed. Louis Massignon. Paris: Larose, 1936.

Ibn al-'Arabi, Muhyi al-Din. *al-Futuhat al-Makkiyyah*. Internet: www.al-mostafa.com

_____. *The Tarjuman al-ashwaq / A Collection of Mystical Odes*. Trans. Reynold A. Nicholson. London: Royal Asiatic Society, 1911.

Ibn al-Athir, 'Izz al-Din. *al-Kamil fi al-tarikh*. Bayrut: Dar al-Kutub al-'Ilmiyyah, 1415 h.

Ibn al-Nadim, Abu al-Faraj Muhammad ibn Ishaq. *al-Fihrist*. Bayrut: Dar al-Ma'rifah, 1994.

Ibn Hisham. *al-Sirah al-nabawiyya*. al-Qahirah, 1936.

Ibn Kathir, Abu al-Fida. *Tafsir al-Qur'an al-'azim*. Bayrut: Dar al-Ma'rifah, 1987.

Jahiz. Abu 'Uthman al-. *al-Bayan wa al-tabyin*. Tahqiq wa Sharh 'Abd al-Salam Muhammad Harun. Bayrut: al-Majma' al-'Ilmi al-'Arabi al-Islami, n.d.

Kasanzan, Muhammad 'Abd al-Karim al-, *al-Mawsu'ah al-Sufiyyah*. Internet: www.dahsha.com/old/view article.php?id=9324

Kaziyev, 'Ali Y. *Khudojestvennoye Oformleine Azerbaydjanskoy Rukopisnoy Kniqi XIII-XVII vekov*. Moscow: Kniqa, 1977.

Khata'i, Shah Isma'il. *Poems*. Vol. 2. Baku: n.p., 1976.

Kishwari, Ni'matullah. *Poems*. Baku : Yazichi, 1984

Köpruluzade, Mehmet Fuat. *Azeri Adabiyyatina aid Tadqiqlar*. Baku: Sabah, 1996.

Krachkovsky, Ignatiy Y. *Kommentarii k perevodu Korana*. Moscow: Izdatel'stvo Vostochnoy Literaturi, 1963. 501–647

Kutub, Seyyid. *Fi Zilalil-Kuran*. Trans. Salih Uchan and Vahdettin Ince. Istanbul: Dunya Yayincilik, 1991.

Lahiji, Shamsuddin Muhammad. *Sharh Gulshan-i Raz*, (Shaykh Muhammad Shabistari).Trans. N. Goyushov. Baku: Adiloglu, 2008.

McCann, David. *Mercury in Myth and Occult Philosophy*. Internet: www.skyscript.co.uk/mercurymyth.html

Muslim ibn al-Hajjaj al-Qushayri al-Nisaburi. *Sahih Muslim*. Riyadh: Dar al-Mughni, 1998.

Nasimi, Imaduddin. *Poems*. Ed. Arasli Hamid. Baku: Elm, 1985.

Nizami Ganjewi, *Sharafname*. Trans. Qaliyev. Baku: Elm, 1983.

Perry, John R. "Persian in the Safavid Period: Sketch for an *État de Langue*." *Safavid Persia, The History and Politics of an Islamic Society*. London / New-York: I.B.Tauris, 1996. 269–284.

Piotrovsky, Mikhail B. "Prorocheskoye dvijenie v Aravii." *Islam, Reliqiya, Obshestvo, Qosudarstvo*. Moscow: Nauka, 1984. 19–28.

Qadi Burhanuddin. *Diwan*. Baku: Azernashr, 1988.

Qahramanov, J., ed. *XIII-XVI Asrlar Azerbaycan Sheri*. Baku: Elm, 1984.

Qurtubi, Shamsuddin al-. *al-Jami' li al-Ahkam al-Qur'an*. Riyadh: Dar 'Alam al-Kutub, 2003.

Qushayri al-. *al-Risalah al-Qushayriyya fi 'ilmi al-tasawwuf*. Trans. Alexander Knysh. Garnet Publishing, 2007.

Razi, Fahrutdin Er-. *Tefsir-i Kebir, Mefatihul-Gayb*. Terc. Prof. Dr. Suat Yildirim, Prof. Dr. Lutf Celebi. Ankara: Basin yayin Kazarlama. vol. 23.

Richard.Bell, William M. Watt. *Introduction to the Qur'an*. Trans. S.A. Jdanov, B.V.Norik and M.Q.Romanov. Moscow / Saint-Petersburg: Dilya, 2005.

Sam'ani, Abu al- Muzaffar al-. *Tafsir*. Riyadh: Dar al-Watan, 1997.

Schimmel, Annemarie. *Calligraphy and Islamic Culture*. New York: New York University Press, 1984.

_____. "Letter Symbolism in Sufi Literature." *Mystical Dimensions of Islam*. Lahor: Sang-e-Meel publications, 2003. Appendix 1.

_____. *Mystical Dimensions of Islam*, Lahore: Sang-e-Meel publications, 2003.

Seferçioglu, Mustafa N. *Nevi Divaninin Tahlili*. Ankara: Kultur Bakanlari, 1990.

Seyidov, Mirali. *Azerbaycan Mifik Dushuncesinin Qaynaqlari*. Baku: Yazichi, 1983.

Spense, Lewis. *Tainstvo Egipta: Obryadi, Traditsii, Rituali. The Mysteries of Egypt: Secret Rites and Traditions*. Trans. by Kalashnikova L.A. Moscow: Izdatel'stvo "Centrpoligraf," 2007.

Stebleva, Inna V. "K Voprosu Formirovaniya Obraznoy Sistemi liriki v Klassicheskoy tyurkoyazichnoy Poezii" in *Problemi Istoricheskoy Poetiki Literature Vostoka*. Moscow: Izdatel'stvo "Nauka," 1988. 176–188

Suleymanova, Sevda. "Sirius-Shira v Islame i v Poveryax Narodov Azii i Kavkaza." *Elmi Arashdirmalar*. Baku: Elm, 2006. 296–317.

Tabari, Ibn Jarir al-. *Jami' al-bayan fi ta'wil al-Qur'an*. Bayrut: Dar al-Kutub al-'Ilmiyyah, n.d.
_____. *Tarikh al-Rusul wa al-Muluk*, Misr: Dar al- Ma'arif, 1967. vol. 1.
Tabarsi, al-Fadl ibn al-Hasan al-. *Majma' al-bayan fi tafsir al-Qur'an*. Bayrut: Dar Maktaba al-Hayat, n.d.
Usluer, Fatih. *Hurufilik Ilk Elden Kaynaklara Do'u'udan itibaren*. Istanbul: Kabalci Yayinevi, 2009.
Zamakhshari, Abu al-Qasim Jarullah al-. *al-Kashshaf an haqa'iq ghawamid al-tanzil*. Vol. 4. Bayrut: Dar al-Kutub al-'Ilmiyyah, n.d.

The Camel

Mohamed Elkouche

"Do they not look at the camels, how they are made?" (Qur'an 88:17)

Introduction

The figurative idea concerning the (im)possibility for a camel to pass through the eye of a needle occurs in the Qur'an as well as in the Bible. In both Islamic and Judeo-Christian cultures, this image or metaphorical expression has been subject to a great deal of debate and controversy regarding its exact meaning and symbolic implications. Besides attempting to shed some light on this problematic issue, this study aims generally at revealing some aspects of Islamic and Qur'anic imagery.

Between the Bible and the Qur'an

In the Qur'an we read:

> To those who reject Our signs and treat them with arrogance, no opening will there be of the gates of heaven, nor will they enter the garden, until the camel can pass through the eye of the needle: such is Our reward for those in sin [7:40].

This same verse is — perhaps better — translated by Mawdudi as follows:

> Believe it that the doors of heaven will not be opened for those who have treated Our revelations as false and have shown pride in regard to them: their admission into paradise is as impossible as the passing of the camel through the eye of the needle, so do We recompense the guilty ones [7:40].

In the Bible, one can find the same image, but the context of its occurrence is clearly different:

> And Jesus said unto his disciples, "Verily, I say unto you: It is hard for a rich man to enter into the kingdom of heaven. And again I say unto you: It is easier for a camel to go through a needle's eye, than for a rich man to enter into the kingdom of God" [19:23–24].

One can easily notice that while the Qur'anic verse speaks generally about all disbelievers, who proudly disregard and disdain Allah's signs or revelations, the passage from the Bible refers specifically to the category of the rich. In both cases, one can see that such people will certainly find it (almost?) impossible to gain access to paradise, since the condition for this possibility is that a camel can pass through the needle's eye — a matter which is logically and practically impossible.

Nevertheless, there exist interpretations of both the Bible and the Qur'an that insist that the word "camel" should not be taken literally to mean the large land mammal this term commonly designates; in fact, according to some authorities, it refers to some sort of rope. Moreover, some Biblical interpretations assert that the image is not meant to express the impossibility but rather the difficulty of entering paradise by rich people. In the following pages, the arguments of both Biblical and Qur'anic commentators will be presented. The implicit contrast between the views of both sides can broadly serve as a vivid illustration of how the image of the camel and the needle's eye is conceived of and conceptualized in both Islamic and Western (Judeo-Christian) traditions.

In their interpretation of the above-cited statement of Jesus Christ, Biblical commentators are divided among those who believe that the image under discussion implies the impossibility that the rich could enter paradise and those who see that it refers just to the difficulty of this entrance. On the one hand, some commentators hold the view that Jesus was just speaking figuratively to warn rich people against getting engrossed in their riches and forgetting about their duties to God and fellow humans. He wanted to teach people that those who do so can never go to paradise, except if such an impossible thing as the passing of a camel through the needle's eye could really happen. As one scholar confirms, people at that time actually employed such figures of speech, and Jesus himself frequently used them in his discourses: "It was common for them to use exaggerated language, or hyperbole, and paradoxes to teach a lesson. Of course, Jesus also loved to use hyperbole to make his points (e.g. "remove the plank in your eye," "cut off your right hand," and "gouge out your eyes if they cause you to sin")."[1] These examples prove clearly that Jesus was intentionally using the exaggerated image of a real camel disproportionately placed vis-à-vis a needle's eye to convey the idea that it can never pass through it. This implies that it is quite impossible for the type of people to whom he was referring to enter paradise. On the other hand, some other interpreters of the latter image maintain that Jesus had a real geographical place in mind while delivering his discourse and that he wanted to express the notion of difficulty, rather than that of impossibility. In their view, as John Andrew Morrow has explained,

> "the eye of the needle" was a narrow gate in Jerusalem where it was very difficult for a camel to pass. The camel had to be unloaded in order to pass. Otherwise, it needed to pass through on its knees. If this is correct, then the expression does not mean that it is impossible to enter heaven. Rather, it means that it is very difficult to enter heaven [Morrow, Note 251].

Some critics, however, point out that there is no concrete proof concerning the actual existence of any narrow gate in Jerusalem that bore such a name. G. Stimpson, for instance, states that "There is no positive evidence to support this theory and it is apparently without foundation, although many students of the Scriptures accept it." He asserts that he "has been unable to find a particle of evidence that such a gate was called 'the eye of a needle' or 'the needle's eye' in the time of Jesus." On his part, Robert Sheaffer sees the notion of this gate as a mere story invented by Christian fundamentalists to resolve the contradiction between their love for money or wealth and their fear that they will be denied access to paradise. For if a camel can somehow pass through the narrow gate, regardless of how much difficult or laborious that might be, paradise may still remains accessible to the rich. Sheaffer quotes the *Jerome Biblical Commentary* that underscores the idea that "the figure of the camel and the eye of the needle means exactly what is said; it does not refer to a cable or a small gate of Jerusalem."

The above-mentioned "cable" has to do with a debatable theory which some Biblical scholars and commentators have advanced in their attempt to find a convincing interpretation of the image of the camel and the needle's eye. This theory presumes that the word camel in Jesus' statement does not refer to the animal in question but rather to a cable or rope. This view is based on the assumption that the Greek term *kamilos,* which means rope, has been erroneously translated into Latin as *kamelos,* which means "camel" (Morrow, note 251). Some scholars have even attempted to seek for such linguistic explanation in Aramaic, Jesus' original language in which most — if not all — gospels are written, according to them. George Lamsa, for instance; has noted that:

> The Aramaic word *gamla* means camel, a large rope, and a beam. The meaning of the word is determined by its context. If the word riding or burden occurs then *gamla* means a camel, but when the eye of a needle is mentioned *gamla* more correctly means a rope. There is no connection anywhere in Aramaic speech or literature between camel and needle, but there is a definite connection between rope and needle.[2]

Nonetheless, this theory is far from being unquestionably plausible or enlightening as it fails to provide a convincing answer to the question of whether Jesus' statement means that the rich can enter heaven, or the opposite. As a matter of fact, this theory has been paradoxically cited to argue both for and against this possibility. Although most scholars and commentators assert that Jesus wanted to express the notion of impossibility, as it is quite evident that a rope cannot be squeezed through the eye of a needle, some other ones still see a hint of possibility in his statement. They argue that, at least in comparison with the camel, a rope can be conceivably visualized to pass through the eye of a needle — especially if the latter's size is unusually huge and the rope is very thin.[3]

Yet, the prevalent view among Biblical scholars and commentators is that Jesus was simply using a figurative and proverbial expression to allude to something that is impossible. One is, in fact, eventually inclined to say that if neither a real camel nor a rope can penetrate through the needle's eye, and if the narrow gate of Jerusalem never existed, as several scholars confirm, Jesus' message cannot but be understood as implying that the rich cannot go to heaven. Nevertheless, the subsequent verses to the one under discussion seem to problematize such a logical conclusion owing to their paradoxical implications: "And when the disciples heard it, they were astonished exceedingly, saying, 'Who then can be saved?' And Jesus looking upon *them* said to them, 'With men this is impossible; but with God all things are possible'" (Mathew 19: 25–26). While the response of Jesus' disciples reveals that themselves construed his first judgment as meaning "impossibility," his last utterance in the above quotation seems to open up some room for the possibility that even rich people can go to heaven; obviously, if they know how to win God's grace.

As concerns the interpretation of the image of the camel and the eye of the needle, the consensus of Qur'anic commentators is that it refers to the impossibility that unbelievers will enter paradise. Of the hundred or so commentaries that were consulted — all of them from authentic sources or *tafasir* written by both major and minor Qur'anic commentators belonging to different Islamic schools, periods and countries — none of them has even hinted that the Qur'an means anything other than impossible. None of them have made the slightest reference to the presumable existence of that gate of Jerusalem or the story of the camels passing through it with difficulty. What is more, all of them assume unquestioningly that that Qur'anic image is an original and authentic Arabo-Islamic one. Only two of them — namely, Muhammad Husayn Fadlullah and al-Shirazi — mention very briefly that the same image also occurs in the Bible. While al-Shirazi comments by stating that this fact proves that the image was commonly used by different peoples/nations ever since antiquity, Fadlullah glosses over the Biblical statement by conceding that the rich really find it hard to adapt themselves to the path of faith and piety that lead to paradise. He notes that richness actually opens widely the doors of deviation and impiety for humans (see CD).

The reason why all Islamic commentators confirm that the image of the camel and the needle's eye indicates "impossibility" rather than "difficulty" is most probably due to the context in which it occurs in the Qur'anic verse. This latter speaks unambiguously about the disbelievers, "who reject [Allah's] Signs and treat them with arrogance" and it is quite clear that it means that it is impossible for such people to go to paradise. This verse — 7:40 — is, in fact, preceded by a similar verse that stresses the same fact as it states that "those who reject Our signs and treat them with arrogance, — they are companions of the Fire, to dwell therein (for ever)" (7:36). Many other verses from the same *surah* as well as from the whole Qur'an reiterate the same judgment, which evidently signifies that hell is the only "reward" for such radical sinners.

In addition to this, several commentators, as already mentioned, see that that image is of Arab origin and is by no means alien to the Arabo-Islamic socio-cultural context. They say that the camel is a very well-known animal for Arabs; it is, in fact, the biggest animal related to their life and environment. That is why they often take it as an example of huge bodily size, as in this idiomatic expression: "the body of camels and the dreams of birds." And since the eye of a needle is also considered for them as the smallest eye or hole, they couple it in that image with the camel to refer to something which they view as being completely impossible. In other words, they invoke the queer idea of a tremendous animal passing through a minute hole to express the impossibility of some fact or event. As al-Muraghi, for instance, explains:

> To express what cannot be possible, the Arabs often cite such examples/images as: I will not do it "until the raven gets white-haired," or "until tarmac becomes white," or "until the camel passes through the needle's eye"; and by this they want to mean that they will never do that. So [with reference to the verse] the meaning is that they will never enter paradise [Trans. from CD].

This view is corroborated by most other commentators; al-Shanqiti, for example, says:

> The camel can never pass through a needle's eye, so they will never enter paradise. This is, in fact, a well-known Arabic style; they predicate some thing on what cannot happen, and this implies that this thing is impossible.... This is a familiar trope in Arab speech [Trans. from CD].

It can be thus confirmed that the Qur'anic commentators differ from the Biblical ones in their interpretation of the image of the camel and the needle's eye. While the former always associate this image with the notion of impossibility, the latter argue that the image also refers to what is possible, albeit probably very difficult, to materialize.

Yet, in spite of this difference, there is a striking resemblance in their interpretation of the word "camel." As already pointed out, some Biblical commentators see that the latter word does not necessarily refer to the animal called "camel" but to some kind of rope. Those who hold this view base this argument on some linguistic facts and problems of translation. Most Islamic commentators also consider the possibility that the Arabic word *jamal* may refer to "rope" in addition to "camel" as animal. This argument is also linguistically based, as the interpretation here depends on the way the word *jamal* is inflected in Arabic language. In *Lisan al-'arab*, Ibn Manzur explains, in detail, these nuances of meaning depending on the inflection of this word. The most relevant point to our current discussion — a point which most Qur'anic commentators take into consideration — consists in reading *jamal* as *jummal*. Ibn 'Abbas is famously reported to be one who used the latter word in his reading of the Qur'an, instead of the commonly used word *jamal*. It is this reading that gave rise to the controversy of whether the Qur'an means *jamal* (the animal) or *jummal* which is a plural noun that means a set of ropes knit together to form one huge rope whereby ships or boats are moored (see CD & *Lisan al-'arab*).

The reason for Ibn 'Abbas' preference to speak about a rope rather than a real camel is due, as some commentators point out, to his belief that there is a strong and logical correspondence between the idea of rope (or thread of any form) and the needle's eye. On the contrary, he finds it as something absurd to speak about a camel and a needle's eye, as there is no semantic correspondence between them. In his view, Allah is too wise to make such a figurative mismatch (see CD, e.g. al-Zamakhshari and Ibn 'Adil).

Nevertheless, the majority of Islamic commentators are content with the word *jamal* (i.e. camel rather than rope). As mentioned before, they conceptualize the Qur'anic image in terms of the correspondence that exists between the camel as one of the biggest animals and the needle's eye, as one of the narrowest "doors" or openings through which an object can enter. Some famous Islamic figures have even found it absurd, if not really ridiculous, to think of anything other than the real camel. For instance, when asked about the meaning of the word *jamal* in the verse under discussion, Ibn Ma'sud answered that it is *zawj al-naqah*—literally, "the husband of a she-camel." Likewise, al-Hasan al-Basri answered when asked the same question: "It is the offspring of a she-camel, standing with its four legs in the stable" (al-Zamakhshari and Atfish: CD). Of course, underlying both answers is a strong irony or even sarcasm which is meant to imply that the word *jamal* should not be seen as meaning anything other than "camel."

In support of the latter view, one can say that there are good reasons for believing that the camel referred to by the Qur'anic verse is the real animal called by this name. One of these reasons consists in the fact that there are other verses in the Qur'an wherein this particular creature is taken by Allah as an example or symbol. The people of Thamud, for instance, were sent a she-camel that was evidently meant as a sign whereby Allah wanted to test them, as the following statement of Prophet Salih to these folks makes clear:

O my people! Worship God; ye have no other god but Him. Now had come unto you a clear (sign) from your Lord! This she-camel of God is a Sign unto you: So leave her to graze in God's earth, and let her come to no harm, or ye shall be seized with a grievous punishment [7:73].

When those haughty people disregarded Salih's heavenly warning and slew the she-camel—Allah's symbolic material sign—the result was utterly catastrophic: a tremendous earthquake overtook them and wreaked havoc with their apparently great and advanced civilization, burying them in the process under the wreckage of their homes.

In addition to this example, which recurs in different words in some other parts of the Qur'an, the following verses make reference to the camel—among other huge things or signs—to draw attention to the existence and greatness of the Almighty Creator:

Do they not look at the camels, how they are made?—and at the Sky, how it is raised high?—and at the mountains, how they are fixed firm?—and at the earth, how it is spread out? Therefore do thou give admonition, for thou art one to admonish [88:17–21].

Since the camel is associated here with three other things that are all characterized by their ample or massive size—namely, the sky, the mountains and the earth—one can say that in relation with the tiny eye of a needle, this same huge-bodied animal is figuratively evoked to convey the idea that it is impossible for the disbelievers to enter paradise (just as it is impossible for the camel to pass through the needle's eye).

This stylistic feature of taking as examples or symbols either huge or very small things — or both at the same time, as in the metaphorical expression under discussion — is not uncommon in the Qur'an. As a matter of fact, in one *surah*, Allah has even referred to the minutest particle on earth — namely the atom — to show His absolute justice on the Day of Judgment, when "anyone who has done an atom's weight of good [shall] see it! And anyone who has done an atom's weight of evil, shall see it" (99:7–8). In another *surah*, we are told clearly that

> God disdains not to use the similitude of things, lowest as well as highest.[4] Those who believe know that it is truth from their Lord; but those who reject Faith say: "What means God by this similitude?" By it He causes many to stray, and many He leads into the right path; but He causes not to stray, except those who forsake (the path)... [2:26].

And just as Allah uses the similitude of such tiny creatures as a gnat, a fly, and a spider,[5] he equally uses that of His massive creations like the sky, the earth, and the mountains. For instance, the latter element (i.e., mountain) is repeatedly spoken about in Qur'anic discourse in manners that well indicate that it is one of Allah's greatest signs or symbols, as the following verse illustrates:

> Had We sent down this Qur'an on a mountain, verily, thou wouldst have seen it humble itself and cleave asunder for fear of God. Such are the similitudes which We propound on men, that they may reflect [59:21].

Despite the very solid and tremendously bulky make-up of the inanimate mountain, it still can behave so humbly and so "sensitively" out of fear of Allah and veneration of His revealed book. On the Day of Judgment as well, the mountains will (be made to) behave in manners that are utterly and miraculously incompatible with their huge and bulky constitution. This particular time is described by the Qur'an as "a Day whereon men will be like moths scattered about, and the mountains will be like carded wool" (101:4–5). In another verse, Allah says that, on that Day, "Thou seest the mountains and thinkest them firmly fixed: But they shall pass away as the clouds pass away: (such is) the artistry of God, who disposes of all things in perfect order" (27:88).

In the Arabic language, the mountain is called *jabal*, while *jamal* is the common name for the camel. Besides such phonetic proximity of these two Arabic nouns, one can say that the mountain and the camel share at least two important characteristics — namely, huge size and wonderful constitution.[1] It is certainly because of the fact that such features also bespeak "the artistry of God" that the Latter chooses to take them in many verses as eloquent Signs and very instructive metaphors.

And just as there is "artistry" and beauty in the ways in which mountains and camels are created, there is also art and aesthetic wonder in the style they are spoken about in the Qur'an. If we call again to mind that verse that refers panoramically to the camels, the sky, the mountains and the earth, we shall not fail to perceive such artistic touches and aesthetic value. As Sayyid Qutb has commented, this panoramic view includes the vast sky above and the extensive earth below. On this spacious stage, we can see huge erect mountains as well as big upright camels, composing thus two vertical lines that harmoniously contrast with the two horizontal lines formed by the Sky and the earth. This is, in fact, a well-wrought painting that addresses people's religious sense with the language of artistic beauty in such a way as to make them feel and appreciate the greatness of God and the sublimity of His created universe (Qutb 3899). Sayyid Qutb's view is corroborated by Ibn Kathir, who states that such a scene or painting is designed for the (Arab) Bedouin to prompt him to recognize Allah's existence and appreciate His greatness and artistry deductively from what he sees as he rides his camel and watches the Sky above him, the earth below and the mountains in front of him (Ibn Kathir 645).

In the camel-and-needle's-eye metaphor, this sense of artistic beauty is not lacking. As already pointed out, the very fact of bringing the huge camel side by side with the tiny needle eye is artistically expressive in the sense that their incompatibility and lack of correspondence convey quite beautifully the connotation of impossibility which the image is essentially meant to express. This is what Ibn 'Adil has confirmed while noting that the image used in that Qur'anic verse is of the utmost beauty (see CD).

Before bringing this argument to a close, it is worth clarifying one important point that concerns the occurrence of the image of the camel and the needle's eye in both the Bible and the Qur'an. Some non–Muslim commentators and ideologues maintain that since this image existed first in the Bible, several centuries before the birth of Muhammad and the rise of Islam, so the Qur'an's citation of the same image means that this Prophet has plagiarized it from scriptural sources. What is more, such a "fact" proves that the Qur'an was just written or "invented" by Muhammad, rather than being a revealed religion.

This allegation is, of course, untenable, especially when looked at from a sound religious or Islamic perspective. Indeed, given that the Bible and the Qur'an issued from the same source — God Almighty — it is no surprise if some similar ideas, expressions, or tropes are found in both texts as there is unity and much similarity between Allah's Revelations to His different messengers and prophets. Accusing the Prophet of plagiarism and having invented the Qur'an amounts to disbelieving Muhammad's prophethood and ridiculing the sacred messages revealed to him by God. Those who do this obviously run the risk of being among the ones "who reject [Allah's] Signs and treat them with arrogance — ones whose "admission into paradise is as impossible as the passing of the camel through the eye of the needle."

Conclusion

In conclusion, it may be confirmed that even though both the Qur'an and the Bible have made use of the figurative expression "the camel and the needle's eye," the ways this latter has been interpreted and conceptualized by Muslim and Christian commentators differ quite noticeably. For while there is a sort of consensus in Islamic culture concerning the idea that the Qur'anic use of this expression refers unambiguously to something that is impossible, the opinions of the Biblical scholars and commentators remain divided over the question of whether Jesus meant the impossibility or just the difficulty that the rich could enter heaven. This difference of the attitudes of Muslims as opposed to Christians is basically due to the difference of contexts wherein that image is deployed in each of the two religious texts.

Although the story of the narrow gate of Jerusalem is frequently discussed by Biblical scholars and interpreters, their Muslim counterparts make no mention of it. On the contrary, both sides consider seriously the question of whether the word "camel" in their respective texts refers to a camel or to a rope. That such a connection between these two words — i.e., camel and rope — should exist in both the Qur'an and the Bible is a surprising coincidence because the Arabic linguistic repertoire upon which the Qur'anic interpreters rely is quite different from that of their Biblical counterparts.

Yet it seems less surprising, at least from an Islamic perspective, that the Qur'an should use a similar metaphorical expression that has already been used in a previously revealed book. In fact, the unique divine source of revelation and the oneness or unity of religion account for this kind of religious intertextuality. And if it is true or "probable that the saying about the camel and the needle's eye was proverbial already in the time of Jesus," as G. Stimpson notes — which suggests that Jesus himself was drawing upon an expression or image that was commonly used at that time — the Qur'an's use of it is justified by the fact that this Book does not shy away from addressing its Arabic audience in the language and imagery they have been accustomed to. Like the Bible, the Qur'an often uses hyperboles and striking images or symbols to transmit its religious messages in a powerful and efficiently instructive manner. That is why, in order to stress and make it quite clear that the disbelievers can never set foot in heaven, this Book has appropriately cited the compelling image of the camel and the needle's eye.

Chapter Notes

1. Blogger under the pseudonym of SoulRiderGirl, http://www.godmammon.com/2007/10/camel-in-eye-of-needle.html.

2. Quoted in "The Eye of the Needle," http://www. eyeofthe needle.net/Church%20Traditions/eye_of_a_needle.htm.

3. One scholar mentions that "Jesus could be describing a rope (made of a camel's hair) passing through a large wooden needle (used for 1st century industrial projects)." http://www.godmammon.com/2007/10/camel-in-eye-of-needle.html.

4. The translator has dropped here the Qur'an's direct use of the word "gnat," but he adds a note in which he explains that: "The word for 'the lowest' in the original Arabic means a gnat, a byword in the Arabic language for the weakest of creatures" (Yusuf 'Ali, Note 45). Maududi translates the first sentence of this verse as follows: "Allah is not ashamed to cite the similitude of a gnat or of something even more insignificant than this."

5. About the fly Allah says: "O men! Here is a parable set forth! On whom, besides God, ye call, cannot create (even) a fly, if they all met together for the purpose! And if the fly should snatch away anything from them, they would not have power to release it from the fly. Feeble are those who petition and those whom they petition" (22:73). And about the spider He says: "The parable of those who take protectors other than God is that of the Spider, who builds (to itself) a house; but truly the flimsiest of houses is the Spider's house; if they but knew" (441).

6. Yusuf 'Ali describes the camel in the following words: "what a wonderful structure has this Ship of the Desert! He can store water in his stomach for days. He can live on dry and thorny desert shrubs. His limbs are adapted to his life. He can carry men and goods. His flesh can be eaten. Camel's hair can be used in weaving. And withal, he is so gentle! Who can sing his praises enough?" (Note 103).

Works Cited

'Ali, 'Abdullah Yusuf, trans. *The Glorious Qur'an*. Bayrut: Dar al-Fikr, 1937.

al-Jami' al-tarikhi li tafsir al-Qur'an al-Karim. Fez: Institute of Research and Scientific Studies, 2011. CD.

Ibn Kathir, Isma'il ibn 'Umar. *Tafsir al-qur'an al-'azim*. al-Qahirah: Dar al-Bayan al-'Arabi, 2006.

Ibn Manzur. *Lisan al-'arab*. Vol. 2. al-Qahirah: Dar al-Hadith, 2002: 206–207.

Lamsa, George. "Church Traditions." Internet: http://www.eyeoftheneedle.net/Church%20Traditions/church_traditions.htm.

Matthew. *The Gospel According to St. Matthew*. Internet: www.earlychristianwritings.com/text/matthew-asv.html.

Mawdudi, Abul A'la. *Meaning of the Qur'an*. Vol. 4. Lahore: Islamic Publications, 1993.

Morrow, John Andrew, ed. *Kitab al-Tawhid* (The Book of Divine Unity). Trans. Sayyid 'Ali Raza Rizvi. Ed. John Andrew Morrow and Barbara Castleton. London: Savior's Foundation, 2010.

Sheafer, Robert. "The Camel and the Needle's Eye." Internet: texts/needleyehtml.SoulRiderGirl; Internet: www.godmammon.com/2007/10/camel-in-eye-of-needle.html.

Stimpson, G. "What Did Jesus Mean by 'The Eye of a Needle?" Internet: www.ensignmessage.com/archives/needle.html.

Qutb, Sayyid. *Fi zilal al-Qur'an*. al-Qahirah: Dar al-Shuruq, 1992.

THE SOCIETAL

Center[1]

Hamza Zeghlache

"I do call witness this city." (Qur'an 90:1)

Introduction

The human use of space and the values with which society imbues spatial relations involve a collective representation of the world. In his book, *The Sacred and the Profane*, Mircea Eliade states that "[i]f the world is to be lived in, it must be founded" (22). To understand how a society founds its world is to understand the cultural process governing the system of ideas that a society has of itself and the universe outside. An exploration of the representation of the world as an image must begin with grasping clusters of governing ideas which are developments from long historical and textual tradition, and are deeply rooted within society. At the core of such clusters there is a coherent, integral, world image. Its form and meaning has a collective origin which is the result of the investment of society's prescriptive configuration of ideal purposes, values, and beliefs. This configuration is an organizing principle which is at work in everyday life as acknowledged social convention and gets absorbed into the realm of social values thereafter. These social values are consciously or unconsciously codified in elaborate rituals which influence ways of thinking, perceiving and categorizing experiences.

The world image as conceived by the Islamic cultural tradition involves traditional worldview (or ideology); the complex of ideas that humanity possesses; and the relationship that it shares with nature, society, and cosmos; its relation with mundane things and forces, as well as with mystical beings and forces; and its ultimate reality. Characterized by the interrelatedness of the universe and the world, this worldview forms a complex construct. Consisting of a complex system of symbolic classification of apparently unrelated elements (non-social things), this integral system of beliefs in the traditional world is interwoven with and communicated to the people of the cities. This process makes things resonate symbolically as they become associated with the social values of a society, achieved by society's attempts to create a starting point, the center of the world. Thus a "spatial" configuration, as characterized by a central element, is used as an organizing principle of mental and moral dispositions for future spiritual and physical orientation. Such mental and moral dispositions comprise the components of a society's images and constitute its inner world." For such images, they reappear implicitly (or explicitly) in the way man reassures himself when feeling adrift" (Kakar 15).

The Concept of the Center of the World

The way society conceptualizes and perceives space is a projection of the image of itself into spatial arrangement. People interpret this system in religious terms and project images of the integral components of the world derived from religious teaching. The most basic of these projected images usually revolves around such conception as earth, heaven, and under-world or, what Eliade calls, the "system of the world." Such logical classifications of reli-gious-primordial concepts are made in order to bring life activities and spatial arrangements into harmony with the universe. In order to structure the world, human beings use a process in which they project their inner vision of the world onto the outside world through various idiosyncratic and cultural symbols. "Everywhere the visible seemed to reflect the invisible," or as Von Simson puts it, "It is this process by which the symbolic instinct transformed vision into architectural form" (xviii).

As a result of this process, a communication between human beings and space develops in a form of resonance resembling musical polyphony. An audible musical melody requires at least two different strings of notes performed synchronically together (Wagner). By analogy, the resonance or the "complicity between man and space" requires at least two elements — the space in its physical shell, on the one hand, and the meaning that the human being gives to it, on the other. This resonance includes the cosmological symbolism that humanity uses in constructing on earth a reduced version of his encompassing universe. This process brings into association and harmony the natural and supernatural world: "Visible and audible har-monies are actually imitations of that harmony and proportion which the blessed will enjoy in the world to come" (Simson 24). This association is achieved by starting at a point with which the human being participates in the symbolism of the center of the world. According to Eliade, this process of human beings' imitation of the celestial archetype is as a repetition of the paradigmatic work of gods on earth, and this resemblance is seen as a sacred experience. As Wheatley puts it, "only the sacred was 'real'... Reality was achieved through the imitation of celestial archetype, by giving material expression of that parallelism between macrocosms and microcosms without which there could be no prosperity in the world of man" (9–10).

Symbolism of the Center in Islam

In elaborating the parallelism between this idea of macrocosm and microcosms, Robert Heine-Gelderm states that

> humanity is constantly under the influence of forces emanating from the direction of compass and from stars and planets. These forces may produce welfare and prosperity or work havoc, according to whether or not individuals and social groups, above all the states, succeed in bringing their lives and activities in harmony with the universe [15].

According to a widespread conception of the ancient Semitic world, the world consists of a central element as a starting ontological point around which units are ordered and organized. The world consists of a circular central continent surrounded by seven annular oceans and seven annular continents. Beyond the last ocean, the seventh, the world is closed in by an enormous mountain range:

> some of the ancients have alleged that the earth is surrounded by water, and the water is surrounded by fire, and fire is surrounded by the lowest heaven, which in turn is surrounded by the second

heaven ... and so on, to the seventh [heaven] and the latter is surrounded by the sphere of fixed stares... [Jwaideh 33].

According to Yaqut, who reported the narratives of thirteenth century Muslim story-tellers in Egypt, the earth is the central continent and from its central point raises the mountain *Qaf*, which in Muslim mythology is the mountain range which encircles the world. According to popular belief, all mountains branch out from it and connect with it by subterranean branches and veins. Furthermore, it has been said that the mountain *Qaf* originated from the green corundum which serves as the support for the angel who holds the earth on his shoulders. Yaqut added that the stability of the system is secured by animals such as the bull and the fish which in their turn are held by a sterile wind which is fastened to the Throne: e.g. the king. In this literature of cosmological symbolism, the mountain is a magical center as an axis, at the top, middle, and the bottom of which were respectively placed the divine, human, and nether worlds. Thus the mountain is an *axis mundi*, as Eliade has called it.

In the ancient Semitic world many places were considered, depending on cultural tradition, an *axis mundi*: "[o]ne of these was Golgotha, in the folklore of the Eastern Christians conceived as summit of the cosmic mountain upon which Adam had been both created and buried" (Wheatley 15). In the Semitic world, one of the most dramatic examples of the cosmological center is Jerusalem,

> the very omphalos of the world ... and it was this symbolism which was subsequently transferred by Muslim hadith to Mecca, a point which had been in existence according to a tradition preserved by Azraqi on the authority of one of Muhammad's contemporaries, the converted Jew Ka'b al-Ahbar, for "forty years before Allah created heavens and the earth" [Wheatley 15].

This point, the Ka'bah, is not only the central point of Mecca but also the symbol of the navel of the earth. Its ontological point is the Mount Abu Qubays where "never a repentant sinner had climbed it without being heard" (Wheatley 16). At this mountain top, as a referential point of Mecca, communication between human beings and their Creator is to be held. Mecca is the holy city of the Muslim world in which millions of Muslims meet annually and to which one fifth of human beings orient their prayers five times a day.

The central idea here is that a configuration of the concept of the center is manifested at different levels of life by means of evocation in order to make orientation possible. In essence, the manifestations of the center of the world are various, as Eliade mentioned, "Whether that space appears in a form of a sacred precinct, a ceremonial house, a city, a world, we everywhere find the symbolism of the center of the world" (37). In the Islamic cultural tradition, the center is based on an organizing principle which turns multiplicity into unity. As Seyyed Hossein Nasr puts it, "the sacred traditions, although outwardly different, are inwardly united into a center which transcends all forms" (qtd. Critchow 6).

The Developmental Process of the City of the Prophet

As to the conception of the city in the Islamic cultural tradition, we will attempt, in the following section, a brief exposition of the Prophet's Medina which is considered to be the first settlement following the consecration of the holy city of Mecca.

During the decade of the Prophet's life in the Medina, the city expanded enormously. The *Muhajirun* (Emigrants), the people who accompanied the Prophet from Mecca, settled around the Prophet's Mosque, which later formed the center of the city. Consequently, life, in its social, economic, religious, and political aspects, was ordered around this central mosque.

The traditional oral formulation states that when the Prophet traveled to Medina in order to dwell there, he did not want to locate by himself the site of his future dwelling, and he therefore left it to his she-camel to decide. From then on, it seems that the area, designated as the dwelling and the main Mosque, became the center of the city (Hadhloul 30). This process is seen as an end to relativity and confusion. As Eliade puts it,

> something that does not belong to this world has manifested itself apodictically and in so doing has indicated an orientation or determined a course of conduct... This amounts to an evocation of sacred forms or figures for the immediate purpose of establishing an orientation in the homogeneity of space [27].

In essence, the she-camel has played the role of mediator between the divine and the human world. A widespread literature of the ancient world deals with the participation of animals in the sacrality of space.

The Prophet's Mosque and his dwelling were the starting point to make the territories surrounding them become habitable and hence become "the world." In other words, the Mosque is seen as the sacred central pole by means of which communication with other worlds is ensured. This pole, therefore, was the ultimate reference for organizing the layout of the city.

Subsequently, the territories were consecrated by the Prophet who distributed them in the form of fiefs to people. These territories were known as the *khittahs*. As Guest explains,

> from its root, the term *khittah* seems to convey the idea of marking out with a line; its general meaning is ground occupied for the first time, a "pitch" a holding; hence it comes to mean a site of any sort. In connection with Fustat (the old city of Cairo), as with other towns rounded by the Arabs, the sense is often connected spatially with a foundation. Thus, when a mosque is described as *Khitti*, the meaning is that the original construction dated back till then [57].

Khittah also denotes the quarter in the city. Al-Baladhuri (d. 892 CE) stated that following the erection of the mosque in Medina, the *Ansar* (Helpers) gave to the Prophet whatever extra land they had within their own *khittah* (quarter). Yaqut (d. 1229 CE), in an account of the fiefs granted by the Prophet, gives the impression that the Prophet assumed chief responsibility for distributing land and settling people in Medina (El-Hadhloul 31):

> When the Prophet arrived at Medina he granted the *dur* (house plot) and quarter to people. Thus, he marked a *khittah* for Bani Zahra in a part of the place behind the mosque ... and granted 'Abd Allah and Utbah the sons of Ma'sud al-Hudhali their well known Khattah near the mosque, and granted Talha ibn 'Ubayd Allah the site of his *dur*, and for Abi Bakr al-Siddiq the site of his *dar* (house) near the mosque. And granted each of 'Uthman ibn 'Affan, Khalid ibn al-Walid, and al-Miqdad and others the sites of their *dur* [31].

As to the layout of areas for commercial streets, the *suq*, the Prophet spatially arranged them to be within the city. The Prophet ordered that the *suq* should be close to the mosque.

Ibn Shabbah (d. 876) reports that the Prophet choose Baqi al-Zubayr as the site of the *suq* but was forced to move it to its present location as he wanted it to be close to the mosque (Hadhloul 33). One of the principal commercial streets was also branched off so that it would lead to the mosque. The market of Medina was developed into specialized areas devoted to "date sellers, fruit sellers, bakers, dryers, tailors, leather merchants, sellers of copper utensils, and smiths" (Hadhloul 34). As to Medina's fortification, a wall surrounding it was erected following the formative period of the city. This wall was rebuilt by the governor of the city Muhammad Ibn Ishaq in 850 CE. The wall was rebuilt again in 1145 CE by the Sultan of Mosul, and Nur al-Din ordered an outer wall to be erected in 1161 CE. In 1183 CE, Ibn Jubayr noted that Medina was double walled and had four gates one facing the other on opposite walls (Jairazbhov 57).

Medina was conceived as an organizing circle divided into smaller circles; a reminder of the divine city as conceptualized in pre–Islamic time. The central circle consisted of the Prophet's house or the "Mosque of his Deity." The mosque with its gate of *Rahmah* denotes, within the city, the heaven from which the cosmological force (consecrated goods) of the universe overflowed into the city and the entire region through the city gates. By being the dwelling of the Prophet and the spatial center of the layout of the city, the mosque was considered the abode of the divine microcosm on earth. In other words, it was the locus of the *axis mundi* that united the city with the divine macrocosm. The Prophet was considered the "Lord of the World," *Khalifat Allah*, God's vice regent on earth. According to Nasr, "[i]t is because man is the vicegerent of the Creator that things in this world are ordered on his behalf, and he is given power over them" (50). During the period following the Prophet's reign, the heads of government of Medina and other cities bore the title of "Caliph," and to the people they were the successors of Muhammad.

All the cities which came after Medina were built in varying degrees of approximation to this ideal city. They were conceived as microcosms of the divine cosmos. Numerous cities were founded during the territorial expansion of Islam. Different locations were used for the foundation of these cities. Some of these locations were known as *mawaqit* (plural of *miqah*). The term *mawaqit* is used to denote the stations which pilgrims visit to assure themselves a state of ritual consecration. These locations define the nature of cities as places of pilgrims and visitors, domiciles of the companions and followers of the Prophet, tomb-shrines of the saints and the pious, sites of expeditions, and territories conquered by the imams and orthodox caliphs (Jwaideh 4).

Conclusion

By founding these cities, the caliphs or imams were mediators between the human and divine worlds. The process of lying out and building the city started with the first two elements, the mosque and the palace of the ruler or the king. It was the ruler's task to facilitate worship by constructing religious buildings. This was also conceived as spiritually producing good results. The benefits to the city and kingdom took visible form in the demarcation of fortifications such as armories, ramparts, moats, and gateways. The capital, protected by fortifications, was conceived to be located at the center of the kingdom and was the territory of effective contact between the ruler or the king and the kingdom. Moreover, the city, as capital, played a central role in the kingdom like the sun's central role in the universe. According to the principles of astrology expounded upon by the *Ikhwan al-Safa*, "God has placed the Sun at the center of the universe just as the capital of a country is placed in its middle and the ruler's palace at the center of the city" (Nasr 77). In short, the center of the city is the image of the Divine in earthly architecture.

Chapter Note

1. This article is part of an interdisciplinary research project on architecture and anthropology that has received financial support from the Wenner Gren Foundation for Anthropological Research, Inc., New

York, and the Department of Anthropology of the University of Virginia, USA. I am very grateful for this support.

Works Cited

Critchow, Keith, ed. *Islamic Patterns, and Analytical and Cosmological Approach.* London: Thames and Hudson, 1976.

Eliade, Mircea. *The Sacred and the Profane: The Nature of Religion.* Trans. Willard R. Trask, New York: Harcourt, Brace and World, 1959.

Guest, A.R. "The Foundation of Fustat and its *Khittahs* of that Town." *Journal of the Royal Asiatic Society of Great Britain and Ireland* (January 1907): 49–83.

Hathloul, Salah al-. "Tradition, Continuity and Change in the Physical Environment: The Arab-Muslim City." Cambridge, MA: Harvard University, 1975. (Dissertation)

Jairazbhoy, R.A., *Art and Cities of Islam.* Bombay: Asia Publishing House, 1964.

Jwaideh, Wadie. *The Introductory Chapter of Yakut's* Mu'jam al-buldan. Trans. Waidie Jwaideh. Leiden: E.J. Brill, 1959.

Kakar, Sudhir. *The Inner World.* Oxford: Oxford University Press, 1978.

Nasr, Hossein Seyyed. *An Introduction to the Islamic Cosmological Doctrines.* London: Thames and Hudson, 1978.

Wagner, Roy. *The Liminal Dynamo: Culture as the Tension of Neocortical Expansion.* AAA National Meetings. Denver, Colorado, Nov. 1984.

Wheatley, Paul. *The City as Symbol: An Inaugural Lecture Delivered at University College London, Nov. 1967.* London: H.K. Lewis & Co.Ldt., 1967.

Ijtihad

SAYYED HASSAN VAHDATI SHOBEIRI

"Why should not a group from every section of the believers go forth and become learned in religion; and to warn their people when they return to them, that they may become aware?" (9:122)

Introduction

Ijtihad can be defined as "deducing religious rules on various issues using religious evidence," which establishes the dynamism of Islamic jurisprudence. In this regard, Shi'ite jurisprudence, unlike Sunnite jurisprudence, does not deem necessary to use *qiyyas* (analogy) and *ijtihad bi-ra'i* (deduction by personal opinion) when inferring religious rulings. One can infer the religious rulings on new issues in various legal, economic, political, and ritual fields through traditions transmitted from *ahl al-bayt* (the Prophet's Household) based on definitive religious evidence.

Among the privileges that make *Imamiyyah* jurisprudence distinctive from other Islamic sects is the absolute openness of reasoning (*ijtihad*) in all places and all times. The revivalist jurist, Imam Khomeini, stressed the belief that the method of *ijtihad* in the modern age is the same as the traditional method of *Jawahir al-Kalam* (the book written by the great jurist, Shaykh Muhammad Hasan Najafi), but *ijtihad* must always have its doors open, and the jurist must infer the religious ruling for every issue based on religious evidence, considering the demands of place and time.

According to Usuli Shi'ites, Islamic rules must be extracted from specific sources and by specific people called *mujtahids*. This process is not an easy task and is called *ijtihad* and must be carried out by qualified people. The topic of this study is "The Image of *Ijtihad*"; the emphasis, however, is on the openness of the doors of *ijtihad* and its influence on the dynamism of Islamic Jurisprudence in the *Ja'fari Shi'ite* School. This study will also refer to the rulings of Imam Khomeini, the famous *faqih*. This study will cover the following topics: the importance of *ijtihad*; the concept of *ijtihad*; the prerequisites of *ijtihad*; the methodology of *ijtihad*; the role of time in *ijtihad*; the role of place in *ijtihad*; the openness of the doors of *ijtihad*; as well as the role of modem developments in *ijtihad*.

The Importance of Ijtihad

Ijtihad and its related issues have recently been thought and written about by great jurists as one new subject (Hakim 541). After the Islamic Revolution of Iran, and new industrial and technological developments in the world, this issue has presented many challenging questions for both the layman and the scholar. As a matter of fact, Muslim jurists have not used one similar approach towards *ijtihad* throughout history.

Seemingly, the importance of *ijtihad* can be summarized in three parts: the first, and most important of all, is the obligation to practice Islamic religious duties by all Muslims, namely, abiding by the divine rulings identified by means of *ijtihad*. Thus, one of the most sacred branches of knowledge, *fiqh* (jurisprudence), deals with these rulings. If the correct method of *ijtihad* is not followed we would be entrapped in *'iftira* (fabrication) which is disapproved by the verse of the Qur'an: "Hath Allah indeed permitted you, or do ye invent (things) to attribute to Allah?" (10:59).

Second, *ijtihad* covers all aspects of human life by having a viewpoint on all issues. Thus, it reveals the diversity of Islamic views in all dimensions of human life. Today, Muslim society faces many judicial questions in economy, politics, and so on, which can only be resolved through collective consultation between Muslim jurists and authorized *ijtihad*.

Third, Muslim scholars did not have one identical approach towards *ijtihad*. Some regarded *ijtihad* as *Qiyyas* (analogy) and deduction of personal opinion (Hakim 546). Later on, the deduction of *shari'ah* rulings from the suitable sources in one way or another was embraced as *ijtihad* (Mutahhari 77) Sometime later, because *ijtihad* was being misused, the doors on *ijtihad* were closed (87).

However in the *Ja'fari* Shi'ite view, *ijtihad* was known to be broad throughout history. More decisively today, we are in an acute need of *ijtihad*, because Islam is being attacked by its different enemies who attempt by all means to cast doubts on the sanctity and competence of Islam. They have gone as far as saying that Islam is a religion of radicalism, animosity, terrorism, while Islam is free from such unfair accusations (Mutahhari 79). Today, Muslims are expected to join hands, strengthen their force, and stand in one line against the attackers. They are to prove that the Islamic ideology is well-founded and based on justice, freedom, peaceful coexistence, and sympathy for all human beings who are equal and not prioritized except in *taqwa* (piety). *Ijtihad* and Islamic doctrines shall be revived once again to allow Muslims to navigate through cross-cultural exchanges and allow them to advance along with modern technological and scientific developments; namely, the developments that have taken all nations into "one global village" which has challenged not only the social and cultural dimensions, but also the spiritual and ideological ones. It is, therefore, necessary to study *ijtihad* which requires ceaseless effort and a godly mind, to determine its clear-cut concept and domain in order to prevent any kinds of extremism or impartiality affecting the way of Allah.

The Concept of Ijtihad

In its etymology, *ijtihad* is derived from the root *jahd* which means "to make effort to reach a goal" (*Wizarat-i Awqaf* 316). In the technical meaning of jurisprudence, Muslim jurists have proposed different meanings one of which is "a jurist makes all the efforts possible in order to deduce the proof on the rulings of *shari'ah* whether primary or secondary, real or apparent, from appropriate source" (Hakim 289).

During the early centuries of Islam, from the first to the fifth century after the Hegira, *ijtihad* was synonymous with *qiyyas* (analogy). *Qiyyas* is rejected by Twelver Shi'ites if the ruling is not well-founded or based on a categorical rationale. A jurist may attribute the ruling of one particular case (which is *asl*) to another similar (which is *far'a* only if the rationale behind the former is mentioned in the holy texts or the jurist is absolutely certain about it. For this reason, Shi'ites used to reject *ijtihad* as it was synonymous with *qiyyas*. However, when the sense of *ijtihad* changed, namely, during the fifth and sixth centuries AH, they embraced it.

It is noteworthy that the word *ijtihad* only became popular among Shi'ite jurists after the 5th and 6th centuries after the Hegira. Since the very beginning of Islam, the process of *ijtihad*, namely, deducing *shari'ah* rulings from the Book and the *Sunnah*, acknowledged by Imam Ja'far al-Sadiq and Imam Muhammad al-Baqir, among others, was being practiced. The Holy Imams taught their students how to deduce the rulings from the Qur'an. For example, when Imam Sadiq was asked how somebody who had a bandage on his feet could wipe them during the ritual ablution, he responded that "Issues like this can be extracted from the Qur'an" because "He has not placed for you any obstacle in religion" (22:78). As such, the Imam instructed that he should "Wipe the dressing." Following their Imams, Shi'ite jurists base themselves on the Qur'an and the *Sunnah* of the Prophet. They also regard the traditions narrated from the Imams as the continuation of the *Sunnah* of the Holy Prophet (Hakim 315).

The Prerequisites of Ijtihad

To study and contemplate on the sources of the *shari'ah* to deduce laws, *ijtihad* requires mastering many branches of knowledge helping the *mujtahid* to succeed. These branches are: Arabic morphology and grammar, literature, logic, Qur'anic studies and exegesis, *hadith* studies, '*ilm al-rijal* (biography of those appearing in the chain of transmitters of *hadith*), '*ilm usul al-fiqh* (methodology of jurisprudence), history of the Islamic schools and the like (Mutahhari 81). To become a qualified and expert jurist, one is to master at least *ayat al-ahkam* (those verses of the Qur'an that deal with the *shari'ah* rulings), *al-nasikh wa al-mansukh* (the abrogating or abrogated verses), *al-muhkam wa al-mutashabih* (the clear-cut meaning verses and the verses whose meaning becomes clear only through the former), and to master recognizing accepted *hadith* from the rejected ones and to be able to resolve the inconsistency and conflict among *hadiths*; all these require a great deal of effort and practice so much so that they will take the entire life time of the jurist (Mutahhari 82).

Imam Khomeini regards all the above as insufficient for a *faqih* (jurist) and anticipates that this field requires knowledge of certain legal subjects particularly those pertaining to all aspects of social relations in the world today in order to be able to apply the correct rulings of the *shari'ah* to them (Khomeini 295). In spite of the fact that a *faqih* is not to be an expert on every case, he needs to know every case fully in order to be able to assign the right ruling of *shari'ah* to the case. This is because one case can be an instance of different concepts which requires its due ruling (Khomeini 295)

According to the above, we ought to divide *ijtihad* into two categories: authorized and unauthorized. The former is that of a jurist having all the above-mentioned prerequisites puts all his efforts to obtain the rulings concerning the issues of the past and present from the Book and the *Sunnah*, and if not there from the definite intellectual or definitive reason ('*aql qat'i*). The latter, however, is when somebody having mastered not the related branches of knowledge embarks on issuing *fatwas* (legal opinions).

As a matter of fact, Islam, through its long history, has suffered many blows from the amateurs who by learning only one or two branches of knowledge supposed themselves qualified to give opinions on Islam and issue *fatwas* from the Qur'an. Impressed by foreign cultures, these unskilled amateurs have introduced strange ideas and opinions not only bizzare in Islam, but also contrary to the established teachings of Islam and the Qur'an. Therefore, we should not allow those who are illiterate in fiqh trifle with the Qur'an and marginalize it.

The Methodology of Ijtihad

Generally, the *shari'ah* can be divided into two parts: *'ibadat* (acts of worship) and *mu'amalat* (transactions) (Zarqa 56). The accuracy of the former section depends on intention. The servant must intend to obey Allah when performing acts of worship; only in this way can he perform Allah's command in order to win His satisfaction. Acts of worship are known to be *tawqifi* (defined by *shari'ah*) which means we do not need to know the wisdom and reason behind Allah's command to perform acts of worship in a particular way. Why do we, for example, perform *fajr* prayers in two *rak'ahs* (units) rather than three or four? Why do we perform *hajj* as we do and only during the period of pilgrimage? And so on. This is because when we perform acts of worship, we may not be expected to know what will happen in our life hereafter. We are then expected to exactly follow the commands of Allah and perform acts of worship exactly as described in the *shari'ah* law with all the details.

However, the case is different in transactions which broadly cover all social, political, and economic relations, as well as all human rights (private, social, civil or penal). We do not need the divine legislator to describe the rulings of transactions in detail because as human beings endowed with reason and common sense; we know the reason and wisdom beyond the rulings of transactions. He, accordingly and contrary to the former, has confined Himself to describe only the general rules. There are a very few cases, however, in which He has prescribed something which differs from common practice.

According to intellectual conducts, transactions are merely known to be confirmed by the Divine Legislator rather than to be founded by Him. As a result, the method of *ijtihad* in acts of worship differs from that in transactions. With the former, a *faqih* confines him or herself to the limits set by the holy texts of *shari'ah*. The concepts of acts of worship are fixed and may not change through history. Thus, what a jurist requires is to master the holy texts of the *shari'ah* and sometimes resolve the inconsistencies and conflict in the traditions. With the latter, however, the case is different. The concept of social issues in transactions may change as life changes day by day with the advances in industry and technology.

Imam Khomeini, along with other clear-sighted jurists, conceived that an issue that had a simple ruling in the past will have a different ruling in the multifaceted social and political times of today (297). As an example, cultivating and restoring a piece of barren land at the time of holy Prophet of Islam would give the right of ownership to the restorer under the condition that his intention of the job is ownership (Tusi 658). However, the instrumentation today allows one person to restore large portions of barren lands limiting the ownership of others. In today's world, where facilities are limited, but people are many and political issues have mixed with economics, it is not possible to apply the previous ruling as it was. Today private ownership and freedom have been restricted for public rights and collective interests by some governments.

Jurisprudence, in Imam Khomeini's view, aims to manage the life of human beings from birth to death. Thus, the subject matter of jurisprudence is to be defined accordingly. When a jurist tries to manage the lives of human beings today, he or she should be familiar with the requirements of his time and environment. He believes that a jurist who is not fully aware of the complicated social situation of the time is not qualified to issue a fatwa regarding modern human rights, politics or economics (Khomeini, vol. 21, 289).

The Role of Time in Ijtihad

Not only should a jurist know the sources of the *shari'ah*, he must also master how to apply the law in practical cases. Time, accordingly, and place, may have a crucial role in *ijtihad*. This, of course, does not mean that we leave out the blessed rulings of Islam for new developments of the time. Knowing the world of today is necessary for understanding the concept of each subject matter involved in each event. However, the doors of *ijtihad* in the Ja'fari school of jurisprudence are not closed and Shi'ite jurists at all times have the right to freely scrutinize the views of preceding jurists and, sometimes, even cast doubts upon them. This is not particular to our time and has been practiced by the Ja'fari school of jurisprudence since its earliest days. Our jurists have been changing their views of the *shari'ah* in accordance with time and customs. For example, knowing the view of the various Sunni schools of thought over history is important. Only with such an understanding can we comprehend the intention of the Imams when they made certain statements. This is called *jahat al-sudur* (i.e. by what intention Imam issued a tradition)

In our time, there are also cases of *jahat al-sudur*. We have some traditions which jurists treat as preliminary legislative rulings which are definitive until the end of times. However, after the introduction of legislative subjects and issues, it became clear that such rulings are not the real primary ones, but merely secondary political rulings intended to help run the Islamic administration and manage regulations among Muslims. If that is the case, then these rulings can change as circumstances change. Examples of such cases include the prohibition of private water ownership or rules preventing ranchers from acquiring further pasture. This is perhaps the reason why, in the views of the majority of Ja'fari Shi'ite jurists, people are not allowed to follow the *fatwas* of a dead jurist (Mutahhari 97). This reveals the vital role of time in *ijtihad* and how jurisprudence is constantly developing day by day. There are many new cases or events that the jurist of a hundred or a thousand years ago was not qualified to rule upon no matter how knowledgeable he was at the time.

The Role of Place (Geographical Location) in Ijtihad

Place, as well as time, has a decisive role in deducing the *shari'ah*. The fact that a certain jurist wrote *Jurisprudence for Westerners* suggests the role of place in *ijtihad*. A jurist who is not well acquainted with the West or who has never lived there is not qualified to issue the proper *fatwas* for Westerners.

The Shi'ites, however, were few in the past and each region had their own jurist to follow. Nevertheless, today they live all over the world which multiplies the burden of *ijtihad* for the jurists having to know the various situations in different regions. This can be done through continuous communication among jurists in different countries. Great jurists such as Imam Khomeini have, for the longest of time, encouraged cooperation and communication between the leading jurists in different continents. Such cooperation depends on welcoming friendly negotiation by Muslim jurists. As Imam 'Ali said, "Behold, those endowed with Allah's knowledge preserve His secrets and keep open the springs of knowledge for the people. They have friendly relations with one another, meet one another warmly and sincerely, and share their knowledge with one another" (*Nahj al-Balaghah,* Sermon 212).

As a matter of fact, the practice of Islam in predominantly Shi'ite regions is bound to differ from its practice where Shi'ites are the minority or where they suffer under an anti-religious establishment. Many *fatwas* were being issued when there was no Islamic government, such as the prohibition of maintaining Friday Prayer (Tabataba'i 190) or the prohibition of imposing the *hudud,* namely, the fixed punishment for grave sins such as robbery, adultery, and so forth (Ibn Idris 432) some of which are based on the traditions of our Imams ('Amili 12). Before the Islamic Revolution of Iran, Imam Khomeini cast some doubts on the legitimacy of Friday Prayer during the Major Occultation of Imam Mahdi (Khomeini, vol. 1, 295). However, after the triumph of the revolution, and the establishment of an Islamic State, he changed his fatwa.[2] Another instance is the playing of chess which could be allowed, he says, in cultural contexts where it is not associated with gambling (Khomeini, vol. 21, 151). It is noteworthy that in all such cases what has changed is not the Divine Law but rather the concept of the issues involved. What is prohibited is not "chess" per se but rather the "means of gambling." Hence, the importance of all Muslim communities, regardless of where they are located around the world, to send students to be trained in the religious sciences, thus enabling them to issue qualified edicts regarding their respective realities. As Almighty Allah asks in the Holy Qur'an, "Why should not a group from every section of the believers go forth and become learned in religion; and to warn their people when they return to them, that they may become aware?" (9:122). The wisdom behind this verse is that the jurist from a specific society is familiar with the conditions and culture of his people and the environment for each society has its own peculiarities.

The Openness of the Way of Ijtihad

Since the process of *ijtihad* consists of deducing Islamic rules on the basis of religious sources, successors, much like their predecessors, have every right and obligation to become jurists. As such, every qualified jurist may deduce divine rulings from the book and the *Sunnah* and then follow them. In fact, he or she is not allowed to follow the *fatwas* of another jurist, especially when they draw contrary *fatwas* based on different understandings. This is because one jurist, by his own process of *ijtihad,* may consider the fatwa of another jurist to be incorrect and ill-founded. How, then, could he or she dare to follow an ill-informed and unsound edict?

Referring, for example, to the verse: "or ye have been in contact with women" (5:6), Imam Shafi'i believes that touching a woman would cause violation of *wudu'* (minor ablution). Supposing that today a jurist researches the meaning of "touching a woman" in the Qur'an. Referring to the verse i.e. "There is no blame on you if ye divorce women before consummation or the fixation of their dower" (2:236) which suggests that if you divorce your wife before sexual intercourse it is all right, he says that "touching a woman" in Qur'anic terminology means "to sleep with her" rather than touching her hand, for example, which is an apparent meaning. This jurist thus refutes the fatwa and understanding of Imam

Shafi'i. It would accordingly be *haram* (forbidden) for him to follow Imam Shafi'i's fatwa, for he supposedly knows that Shafi'i's understanding of the term was incorrect.

In this day and age, *ijtihad* is that which is most needed for it is a dynamic mechanism that ensures an ever-evolving interpretating and implementation of Islamic principles. In Shi'ism, *ijtihad* is what prevents Islam from becoming rigid and frozen in time. It grants Islam flexibility and makes it applicable in all circumstances. Since it is rooted in eternal and immutable principles, as opposed to time-bound cultural convention, *ijtihad* is able to answer any questions that arise in different times and places.

Muslim jurists, with no exception, have spared no effort to promote Islamic jurisprudence. They have cultivated a tree that can bear fruit at any time. As such, a campaign of scholarly cooperation, sympathy, and solidarity, be launched between the Ja'fari and Sunni schools of jurisprudence. It has been said, from times of old, that "trust is the fruit of discussion." Bringing two minds together is like the positive and negative wires brought together to produce light. Hence, Ja'fari jurisprudence should be taught alongside other schools in the various jurisprudencial centers. After all, Ja'fari jurisprudence receives its legitimacy from the Qur'an and the Prophetic traditions passed down through the Imams of *ahl al-bayt* who are respected by all believing Muslims as the saintly offspring of the Holy Prophet. If Shi'ite scholars should study Sunni *fiqh*, so should Sunni scholars study Shi'ite *fiqh*. Rather than divide, such efforts could help promote Islamic Unity.

Since they maintain the religion of Islam, Muslim jurists are all lanterns of light that guide towards eternal salvation and happiness. They, be they dead or alive, have a very high position with the Almighty Lord. However, due to the fact that "those who are present can see what those who are absent cannot," a living jurist can be mindful of the context of time and place in such a way that a deceased jurist cannot. In fact, were the deceased jurist living at the moment, he would not hesitate to change his *fatwa* according to current conditions. Hence, while a few scholars have recently opined that it is permissible to emulate deceased jurists, even those who lived over one thousand years ago, it remains recommended, if not obligatory, to follow the most knowledgeable living jurist to ensure the most current, up-to-date, and accurate guidance. In fact, following a living jurist is more concordant with human nature.

Closing the doors of *ijtihad* means to close the gateway of mental thought, thus eliminating living thoughts. In reality, the fruit of such a tree would be bitter rather than sweet. As Imam 'Ali said, "The learned survive the test of time." As such, there is no doubt that the scholarly contributions and legacy of preceding jurists and scholars lives on. However, this does not imply that we, ourselves, should make no contribution to their efforts and continue their great work. The same applies to all other branches of knowledge: one should respect the effort of those who came before us and then embark on contributing one's own ideas to human knowledge. In other words, each generation of scholars and scientists builds upon the work of the authorities who preceded them. Early physicians, for example, are alive through their valuable works, which however does not imply closing medical schools feeling satisfied with the previous ideas in medicine. Such an approach only leads to scholarly and scientific stagnation. To respect predecessors and admire their works is one thing. However, to close the gateway of the mind thinking, making no contribution at all, is another. There may be classics of the past; however, nothing prevents us from creating classics of the present. The process of absolute *ijtihad* does not entail the rejection of previous ideas and starting everything anew. Having made, however, use of the valuable heritage of the past, later jurists are expected to improve and enrich the field of jurisprudence by making their own contribution about which there is no anxiety. What creates anxiety, however, is when jurists practice *ijtihad* without any established methodology.

The Role of Modern Developments in Ijtihad

Jurisprudence can undoubtedly not be indifferent towards the constantly increasing modern developments which not only influence human life and the progress of science, but also the process of *ijtihad*. Within itself, *Ja'fari* school of jurisprudence has the necessary dynamism and mechanisms to develop and be developed. There are, however, some modern developments which can contribute to the field of *ijtihad*. The following, at first sight, may be proposed: (1) subjects of Islamic rulings; (2) the *shari'ah*, rather than the concept of case law; (3) the methods of *ijtihad*; (4) the principles and rules of jurisprudence; and (5) the sources of jurisprudence.

Now, what is not acceptable, according to any criteria, is changing the divine rulings of *al-halal and al-haram* (the permissible and the prohibited) which are applicable and immutable until the end of time.[3] Fornication and adultery are and always will be outlawed according to the law of Allah and no wordly authority has the right to legalize them. Intoxicants are prohibited and no elected or unelected official has any right to declare them permissible. The same applies to the majority of religious doctrines and revelation which will not, and cannot change, due to the passage of time.

The method of *ijtihad*, in Imam Khomeini's view, is the so-called *ijtihad Jawahiri*, namely, the method practiced by the preceding great jurists such as Shaykh Hasan al-Najafi, the author of *Jawahir al-kalam*.[4] Having recognized the conventional method of understanding the holy texts as standard, Imam Khomeini adds: "The extent of understanding the verses of the Qur'an and apparent meaning of the words is public customs and common sense, rather than scientific analysis, and we follow common sense [in the process of understanding]. If a jurist wanted to insert scientific scrutiny [in the process of *ijtihad*], he might unwillingly give up many issues" (Khomeini 115).

Seemingly, modern developments cannot have an effect on number 4. What is left, then, for the influence of modern developments is number 1. In this regard, Imam Khomeini says: "Time and place are the two decisive factors in the process of *ijtihad*. Something that had a particular ruling in the past may have a new ruling in the socio-political or economic relations of today. That is to say, something that apparently remains the same may, in the profound understanding of socio-political or economic circumstances [of today], transform into another thing that naturally requires a different ruling" (Khomeini, vol. 21, 153).

Business, in today's world, has changed from local, regional, and national, into a complicated international reality, resulting in the complex networks of the world economy. Stock markets and exchanges, electronic banking, artificial insemination, organ transplantation, complex political and economic relations with different countries all over the world, and many other findings of human modern knowledge which have transformed the life today require jurists to double their efforts to accurately understand them in order to to issue the proper and correct fatwa in each case so that people suppose no sort of inconsistency or conflict between tradition and modernity nor between faith and science (Khomeini, vol. 21, 154).

Conclusions

As a result of their expertise, jurists can play their role as the drivers of the engine of Islamic jurisprudence and hence harmonize Islam with the requirements of the time. New medical issues such as organ donation and transplantation, dissection, artificial insemination, cloning, newfound judicial issues such as spiritual ownership, electronic banking and trading, and so on, newfangled issues in politics such as modern democracy, elections, legislative assemblies, the organization of government, and new questions in acts of worship such as prayer and fasting in the north or south poles or when traveling to space, performance of the rituals of *hajj* when it is overcrowded, and the like; all such questions can be resolved in the light of dynamic *ijtihad*.

Rules such as the obligation of maintenance of social security, the obligation of the prerequisites of what is obligatory, secondary titles such as emergency and non-damage, prioritizing during dilemmas — for example, we can only have a choice of one, the principle of *al-maysur* (abiding by the *shari'ah* based on the extent of ability) or the principle of *al-'usr wa al-haraj* (distress and constriction) — and the like, are the mechanisms of *ijtihad* that help jurists resolve the above mentioned questions. The authority given to Muslim governors, where the administration is an Islamic one, is one such mechanism that permits Islamic law to run the affairs of society.

As a result of its long tradition of *ijtihad*, the followers of Ja'fari jurisprudence feel no vacuity in the law. By the grace of the guardianship of *ahl al-bayt*, no deadlock or vacuity has been left in the practical law. It is, as demanded by the *hadith* of *Thaqalayn*, suggested that Sunni jurists also refer, in the process of their *ijtihad*, to the traditions narrated from *ahl al-bayt* which are accessible, not only to Shi'ites, but to the entire Muslim community. In so doing, they can help revive, redress, and redirect their *ijtihad*, thus preventing deadlocks or vacuity of law at all in their future. Considering that the Qur'an calls upon Muslims to think nearly one thousand times, the process of *ijtihad*, namely, that of critical thought, remains one of the most critically important features of Islam. As Imam 'Ali warned, if you have a choice between faith and intellect, always opt for the intellect for the intellect will always lead you to faith. For far too long, intellectually mortified Muslims have relied on faith and a frozen interpretation of Islam. The result was the downfall of Islamic culture and civilization and all the problems that currently face the Muslim ummah. It is only with a revival of *ijtihad* that the primary principles, morals, and values of Islam will help Muslim to rise up and regain their stature and status in the modern world.

Chapter Notes

1. After the establishment of Islamic government in 1979, the Friday prayers were held in most Iranian cities. Imam Khomeini would nominate the leaders of the Friday prayer personally. The first Friday prayer in Tehran was led by Ayatollah Taliqani.

2 Imam Sadiq says, "What Muhammad has proclaimed as allowed is allowed until the Judgment Day, and what he has proclaimed as forbidden is forbidden until then" (Kulayni 58)

3. Sheikh Muhammad Hasan Najafi (1200–1266 AH), known as Sahib Jawahir, was one of the prominent Shi'ite jurists. He is the author of *Jawahir al-Kalam* on jurisprudence, which may be well called as the most comprehensive encyclopaedia of Shi'ite jurisprudence (Mutahhari, vol. 3, 100).

Works Cited

Hakim, Sayyid Muhammad Taqi. *al-'Usul al-'amma li al-fiqh al-muqarin*. Qum: Ahl al-Bayt Global Assembly, 1427 AH.

Hilli, Muhammad ibn Idris. *al-Sara'ir.* Qum: al-Nashr al-Islami Publications, 1417 AH.

Hurr 'Amili, Muhammad ibn Hasan. *Wasa'il al-shi'ah.* Vol. 5. Bayrut: Dar al-Ihya al-Turath al-'Arabi, 1399 AH.

Khomeini, Ruhullah. *Sahifay-i Imam.* Vol. 21. Tehran: Institute for Compilation and Publication of Imam Khomeini's Works, 1378 SH.

_____. *Tahrir al-wasilah.* Vol. 1. Qom: Mu'asisat al-Nashr al-Islami, 1420 AH.

_____. *Wilayat-i Faqih.* Tehran: Institute for Compilation and Publication of Imam Khomeini's Works, 1376 SH.

Kulayni, Muhammad ibn Ya'qub. *'Usul al-kafi.* Vol. 1. Tehran: Dar al-Kutub al-Islamiyyah, 1339 SH.

Mutahhari, Murtada. *Ashna'i ba 'ulum-i Islami.* Vol. 3. Qum: Sadra Publications, 1370 SH.

_____. *Dah Guftar.* Qum: Sadra Publications, 1364 SH.

Tabataba'i Ha'iri, Sayyid 'Ali. *Riyad al-masa'il.* Qum: Al-ul Bayt Institute, 1418 AH.

Tusi, Muhammad ibn Hasan. *Tahdhib al-ahkam.* Tehran: Saduq Publications, 1376 SH.

Wizarat al-Awqaf wa Shu'un al-Islamiyyah. *al-Mawsu'at al-fiqhiyyah al-Kuwaytiyyah.* Kuwait: Kuwaiti State, 1381 AH.

Zarqa, Mustafa Ahmad. *al-Madkhal al-fiqhi al-'Am.* Dimashq: al-Dar al-Shami li al-Tiba'a wa al-Nashr, n.d.

Governance

ZAHUR AHMED CHOUDHRI *and*
ZAHID SHAHAB AHMED

"Obey Allah, and obey the Messenger, and those charged with authority among you."
(Qur'an 4:59)

Introduction

Islamic governance is grounded on several foundational aspects, such as justice (*al-'adl*), honesty, equality, freedom, rule of law, as well as accountability to maintain an order and balance in society that is grounded in the spiritual teachings of Islam. Allah has created this world with a balance (*al-mizan*) and wise governance is needed to maintain this delicate equilibrium in all aspects of life on earth (Brockwell online). In the two main branches of Islam, comprising Sunnis and Shi'ites, there are no differences on the issue of divine governance and that a leader on earth is responsible to have the abilities to do justice and manage society (Tomita 3).

Islam and the State

More than 1400 years ago, the Holy Qur'an narrated with elaboration the basic principles, characteristics and attitudes that set the governance standards for both rulers and individual members of the society. The prominent theories of government in Islam were formulated between the 11th and 14th centuries, beginning from the treatises of Mawardi (d. 1058) to those of Ibn Taymiyya (d. 1328). Owing to the dominant perception among Islamic political thinkers that the *ummah* (Muslim world) was the basic collective religio-political unit, the concept of the state was not well delineated until Ibn Khaldun articulated his idea of the state in the 14th century.

Sayyid Qutb stressed that the Islamic state must be based on the Qur'anic principle of consultation. He believed that the *shari'ah*, so complete as a legal and moral system, does not require further legislation. Therefore, Islamic scholars believe that *shari'ah* is based on the fundamental values, morals, and ethical foundations of Islam (Hashem 66). In 1982, Shaykh Muhammad Mutawwali al-Sha'rawi, a popular religious leader, created controversy by suggesting that Islam and democracy were incompatible and that *shura* does not mean simple domination of the majority (NYU online).

A third line of argument, advanced by Abu al-'Ala Mawdudi, founder of the Jama'ate-Islami (a major Islamic party with chapters in Pakistan, India, and Bangladesh), contains both of the preceding perspectives and yet differs subtly from them. Like the first school of thought, this line of argument holds that Islam constitutes its own form of democracy but, like the second, concentrates on the relationship between divine and popular sovereignty. Arguing that democracy, as commonly understood, is based solely on the sovereignty of the people, he concluded that Islam is "the very antithesis of secular Western democracy" (Donohus and Esposito 253–254). It is for this reason that some have called Mawdudi an "absolutist" or "doctrinal" purist (Ahmed 205). Yet, he went on to argue that if democracy is conceived as a limited form of popular sovereignty, restricted and directed by God's law, there is no incompatibility at all. The term that he used to describe this alternate view is theo-democracy.

Some Islamic activists of today invoke the term *hakimiyyah*—a term that has a range of meanings, including divine sovereignty and that ultimate authority belongs to God. When invoked without qualifications, the terms "democracy" and *hakimiyyah* remain vague and Muslims ascribe different meanings to them. Dr. Hassan al-Turabi, a well-known Islamic leader, tried to solve the problem of defining *hakimiyyah* by announcing that *hakimiyyah* belongs to God, and political authority belongs to people. As noted before, the problem associated with the use of the term democracy may be easily solved by using it within a specific context or by coupling it with qualifiers: "democratic means" or "means of representation and political participation" (Hashem 68).

The main characteristic of the Islamic system of governance is the propagation and dissemination of knowledge to bring a positive, attitudinal change in the members of the *ummah* to make them functional in this world and the hereafter. Islam, for this, demands constant conscientious effort for continuous self-appraisal, corporeal and incorporeal improvement, as well as development, which also is deemed as *jihad* (holy struggle):

> Those who listen to the Word [good advice *La ilaha illa Allah* (none has the right to be worshipped but Allah) and Islamic Monotheism, etc.] and follow the best thereof (i.e. worship Allah Alone, repent to Him and avoid *Taghut*, etc.) those are (the ones) whom Allah has guided and those are men of understanding [39:18].

The Holy Prophet was always careful not to dictate any of his personal teaching. His mission was limited to conveying God's message and doing his best to implement it. This is evident from the fact that the Prophet Muhammad, on migrating from Mecca to Medina, entered into numerous treaties with Jews, Christians, pagans and idol-worshippers. The *Charter of Medina*, for example, "enunciated the principles of the civic equality unqualified freedom and worship, tolerance and equity" (Ahmad 140).

Islamic governance inherited its origin from the practices adopted by the Holy Prophet and later on followed by his early four Caliphs. On this matter, there is a major difference between Sunnis and Shi'ites, because the latter believe that Imams are the successors of Prophet Muhammad. In the light of the teachings in Holy Qur'an, Islam is the universal *din* or way of life, the only straight path leading to salvation. It shuns all human-made isms, concepts and "religions" that exploit creatures. It is Allah's favorite *din* since He created His own '*abd*' (servant, slave, and devotee), who has explicitly negated all forms of false ideas. The Holy Qur'an says:

> Say (O Muhammad SAW): "If the Most Beneficent (Allah) had a son (or children as you pretend), then I am the first of Allah's worshippers [who deny and refute this claim of yours (and the first to believe in Allah Alone and testify that He has no children)]." Glorified be the Lord of the

heavens and the earth, the Lord of the Throne! Exalted be He from all that they ascribe (to Him). So leave them (alone) to speak nonsense and play until they meet the Day of theirs, which they have been promised. It is He (Allah) Who is the only *Ilah* (God to be worshipped) in the heaven and the only Ilah (God to be worshipped) on the earth. And He is the All-Wise, the All-Knower [43: 81–84].

In Islam, Allah has made every individual personally responsible for the well-being and the welfare of others. The divine law of justice (*'adl*) rules out the acceptance of social injustices in any form/shade or degree even as a pretext for economic and social progress. As Caliph 'Umar once said to the governor of Egypt: "Since when have you made your slaves? Their mothers have given them birth as free men." The Holy Qur'an has used the terms *musrifin* (the exploiters, snatchers, squanderers) and *mustakbirin* (presumptive, vain-glorious) for the exploiters whom Allah shuns, while the disadvantaged deprived ones are termed as *mustad'afin* (those who have been slighted and rendered powerless, who are made weak through exploitation). This indicates that it is human beings who exploit fellow humans; thus, it is their own doing and not Allah's, who has made man in His own image. Throughout the ages, the arrogant powers of the *musrifin* and *mustakbirin* have tried to control the destinies of the masses for their own vested interests, and have tried to maintain the status-quo. Anyone who tried to bring change to alleviate the conditions of the disadvantaged, including the prophets and the pious ones, was harassed and tortured by these tormenters of humanity, as has been acknowledged in the Holy Qur'an.

The holy and the virtuous preached that all human beings were equal before Allah and that we are all the progeny of one man, Adam, and one woman, Eve. The core issue of all the guidance and preaching of these pious ones is the unity of all humankind and community economics in which everyone supports the other as it is to be based on equity and justice. It is not the destiny of human beings to be born poor for long-lasting marginalization or for persons to be born rich with all the freedoms of life. Everyone has to face the reckoning on the Day of Judgment. The Holy Qur'an says:

> Did you think that we had created you in play (without any purpose), and that you would not be brought back to us? [23:115].
>
> We have fastened every man's deeds to his neck, and on the Day of Resurrection, We shall bring out for him a book which he will find wide open. (It will be said to him): "Read your book. You yourself are sufficient as a reckoner against you this Day" [17:13–14].

Almighty Allah, for their own progress, welfare and well-being, has asked the people for complete adoption of His directions and guidance given in Qur'an, which is complete in all respects for this world and hereafter. "We have neglected nothing in the Book" (6:38); hence, "Allah burdens not a person beyond his scope. He gets reward for that (good) which he has earned, and he is punished for that (evil) which he has earned" (2:286); "Say: "Shall I seek a lord other than Allah, while He is the Lord of all things? No person earns any (sin) except against himself (only), and no bearer of burdens shall bear the burden of another" (6:164).

As for those who serve the *ummah* as its leaders, they must be more careful, as they will answer not only for themselves due to their greater responsibilities. In the words of the Qur'an: "They will bear their own burdens in full on the Day of Resurrection, and also of the burdens of those whom they misled without knowledge" (16:25). Therefore, Nazir Ahmad (151) is of the view that the Qur'an does not explicitly talk about the form of government. The author further argues that "the Qur'an and the written constitution of a pluralistic state left by the Holy Prophet prescribe civic equality and guarantee, equal protection to the religious and cultural sensibilities of all components of state" (Ahmad 151). In Islam, it is more about responsibilities and a prescribed code of conduct in socio-economic and other matters than a full sketch of governance. However, as per the teachings of Islam, it has to be ensured that all individuals and special interest groups, particularly minorities and other vulnerable sections of the population, are ensured an effective say in all matters, which affect them directly, or indirectly (Ahmad 145).

Governance is about the way a state should be run, a subject on which the Prophet Muhammad and the Four Caliphs have provided plenty of directions. Caliph 'Ali, for example, provided the following advice:

> Avoid showing obligation to your people for having done to them or extolling of your actions or making promises and then breaking them because showing obligations destroys the good, extolling takes away the light of truth and breaking of promises earns hatred of Allah and the people. Allah says: "Most hateful it is with Allah that you say that which you do not do" [61:3].

This allows the right to whomsoever it is due, whether or not the individual is near you. In this matter, you should be enduring and watchful even though it may involve your relations and favorites. This is also one of the principles of Islamic governance.

In Islam, all belongs to God Almighty, the Creator of everything. He knows the aptitude, strength, shortcomings, and weaknesses of His creation. He decreed that human beings would act as His vicegerent on earth (Qur'an 2:30). Thus, human beings were granted knowledge and wisdom to discharge their duty. Almighty God gave them guidance through the Qur'an. Allah is the Knower of what was, what is, and what will be. As far as Muslims are concerned, the Holy Qur'an is, beyond doubt, the Word of God sent through His messenger Jibra'il (Gabriel) to Muhammad, the Seal of the Prophets.

Allah has sent tens of thousands of prophets and messengers to humanity in order to guide them. The message of the Qur'an contains essentially the same teachings that God sent to previous prophets. As such, it is a confirmation of all the revelations and scriptures that were sent before. The commonality of all religious fundamentals, themes, substance, and spirit is so complete that the Qur'an describes all Abrahamic religions as *Islam*, namely, submission to God. The difference between Judaism, Christianity, and Islam, revolves mainly around peripheral and ritualistic matters. The central belief of all religions is oneness of God (*tawhid*). Islam, like all other religions, preaches virtues like mercy, forgiveness, compassion, equality, justice and righteousness as the very essence of its teachings. It believes in duality of spirit and matter, personal accountability, reward and punishment. It believes in the triumph of truth over evil, dignity of the individual, as well as the power of the spirit over the mind.

All creation is equal before Allah and there is no favorite race, nation, class or group. No label — religious, ethnic, gender or genetic — matters whatsoever. In Islam, what matters is the extent of implementation of the prescribed Divine agenda at individual and collective levels for the good of the society and without discrimination. Based on this, the righteous person stands a greater chance of Allah's forgiveness in the life hereafter. All religions, which received their inspirations from Allah, are described as *Islam* or submission, and all of their followers are described as *Muslims* or submitters. Followers of all religions are described to be one *ummah*: "And verily, this ummah of yours is single ummah and I am your Lord" (23:52). The mission assigned to Muhammad, the last of the Prophets, is summed up in the Qur'an in the following words: "We sent thee not but as a mercy for all creatures" (21:107). Islam is thus meant to be an instrument of achieving well-being and peace for humanity at large and, indeed, all other forms of life. To this end, it offers to humankind optimally the most bountiful and practicable way of life for all times to come" (Ahmad 1).

The Islamic ideology, therefore, is addressed to all humankind, not a particular caste, class, community or group. According to Islam, there is no god-ordained blue-blooded superior class to rule over or subjugate Allah's creatures. All are equal before Him. The Holy Qur'an says,

> O humankind! We have created you from a male and a female, and made you into nations and tribes, that you may know one another. Verily, the most honorable of you with Allah is that (believer) who has *al-taqwah* [i.e., one of the *Muttaqun* (pious — see V.2:2)]. Verily, Allah is All-Knowing, All-Aware [49:13].

To ensure good governance in Islam, the role of a leader is very important. According to Naqvi et al (10990), Islamic governance rests on the shoulders of leaders and therefore could be measured through the leadership capabilities of a person in command. Therefore, there are certain qualifications to be an Islamic leader. As it is written in the Qur'an,

> This is the Book; in it is guidance sure, without doubt, to those who fear Allah. Who believe in the Unseen, are steadfast in prayer, and spend out of what We have provided for them; And who believe in the Revelation sent to thee, and sent before thy time, and (in their hearts) have the assurance of the Hereafter. They are on (true) guidance, from their Lord, and it is these who will prosper [2:2–5].

The above description is a criterion for judging a good Muslim and only such a person qualifies to take the command of Muslim nation. On this matter, the Qur'an further tells:

> Allah has promised, to those among you who believe and work righteous deeds, that He will, of a surety, grant them in the land, inheritance (of power), as He granted it to those before them; that He will establish in authority their religion — the one which He has chosen for them; and that He will change (their state), after the fear in which they (lived), to one of security and peace: "They will worship Me (alone) and not associate aught with Me. If any do reject Faith after this, they are rebellious and wicked" [24:55].

There are several other qualities that are required by Muslim leaders and officials and which have been sorely lacking since the general demise of Islam in the world. According to Rai, however, "the principles of honesty enunciated by the Prophet were strictly adhered to by his four successors in organizing and administrating the affairs of the state" (1). 'Umar, the Second Caliph, who administered an effective and efficient government, set high ethical standards for public servants. Civil and military officers found guilty of corruption were always subjected to severe reprimand, and very often given exemplary punishment. In 17 A.H. 'Umar dismissed Khalid ibn al-Walid on charges of bribery. In his dismissal order, he wrote that corruption in any form was a naked tyranny. In another letter to 'Amr bin al-'As, Governor of Egypt, the Caliph 'Umar made serious inquiries about the ways and means by which 'As had accumulated wealth and property which he did not possess before his appointment as Governor. In an official circular addressed to all governors, 'Umar forbade them to accept gifts of any kind.

The Islamic system of governance is not merely for material benefits, it strives for complete material and spiritual well-being for all times — present and future. As Saionji observed,

> All human beings, without exception, have no choice but to go forward. Even the so-called, rational thinkers, who have denied or laughed at the idea of an invisible realm — a world where life continues after death — will face a moment when they, too, must recognize and step into that realm [Saionji 168].

The theoretical aspects of governance were described in the Qur'an and important Islamic values were manifested through the teachings of Prophet Muhammad. According to the *Sirah of* Ibn Hisham, the Holy Prophet told Mu'adh ibn Jabal:

> Make things easy for the people; do not make them difficult; win their hearts by telling them pleasing things; do not scare them away; and when you offer prayers with them, your prayers should suit the weakest of them [qtd. Mutahhari iii].

The pioneers of Islam, as true disciples of the Holy Prophet, educated, trained, and organized people for the common good since human-management and leadership are the art of better mobilization, better organization, better control and better employment of human forces. As for managing other people, the modern age believes in its importance so much that Dr. Abu Talib speaks of our age as "the age of management" (Mutahhari 6). This importance given to management is based on several considerations.

This idea of Islamic governance could be further understood by exploring the system established during the Caliphate of 'Umar ibn al-Khattab, the distinguishing features of which were summarized by al-Qudsy as follows:

> There will be no such thing as governance if it is carried out in a bad and immoral manner. His governance concentrated on the practice of accountability (al-Amanah) and responsibility, respect, carefulness and a high regard for his people. Many reformations and innovations in governing were introduced during his period and he is well known as a father of reformation [622].

The process in which governance is taking place can also be learned from the practice of *al-shura* where multiple entities are involved in decision-making. As a result, the people gained economic, social, and political benefits as well as prosperity with the faith to God. 'Umar focused on the well-being of the people (*maslahah 'ammah*), in particular, those poor and underprivileged people, as this group constitutes the bulk of any community. The idea of Government to Citizens (G2C), which has become a major theme for effective governance, was practiced, long ago, during the rule of 'Umar ibn al-Khattab. For example, to ensure that nobody slept hungry in his empire, he used to walk through the streets almost every night to help needy people, such as the poor and the sick. Hence, he earned the title *al-Faruq* (The one who distinguishes between good and bad) and his house as *Dar al-'adl* (house of justice). Also, 'Umar was the first Caliph to be called *Amir al-Mu'minin* or Commander of the Faithful. In the words of al-Qudsy, "It is, therefore, strongly suggested that this concept and practice can provide good guidance in practicing effective governance" (622).

A judicial system and its integrity largely depend upon the morality of the people. It will not be truly Islamic unless the people develop an Islamic character. In the time of the Holy Prophet and the rightly guided Caliphs the moral sense among the people was developed to such an extent that if a person committed a wrong he/she had the courage to confess his/her fault of his/her own accord, and seek punishment. In Islam, justice is not the exclusive concern of the courts: every individual, as the vicegerent of God, is under an obligation to be fair and just to others. It is, therefore, inevitable that the administrative set-up must be based on people of character. In an Islamic state, institutional arrangements through education will have to be made to help develop an Islamic character among the people, thereby avoiding unnecessary litigation.

Almighty Allah has designated the human being as the vicegerent of His attribute *Rab* (The Sustainer and Preserver). By its very nature, the concept of vicegerency indicates that the human being is only a trustee. Actual power and ownership rests with Allah. Whether they are heads of state or simple servants, human beings are all equally accountable for their actions. In fact, it is this very faith in the hereafter that regulates both the thought and action of believing human beings. The person of faith finds that he or she is not only answerable to Almighty Allah on the Day of Judgment, he is face to face with Him all the time in this world. The Holy Qur'an, the book of knowledge and action, has enjoined human beings to follow Allah's guidance in all fields of his life. This requires acquisition of proper knowledge as it brings sanity, namely, the ability of the mind to adjust to the reality of this world and the hereafter. In Islam, there is no Brahmanism to pronounce the first and last word as "[t]here is no compulsion in religion" (2:256). Consequently, there is no concept of an ordained clergy, a savior or original sin. If Islam has a central concept, it must surely be accountability. Labels or any other categorization shall be of any avail. On the Day of Judgment, every one shall be judged in terms of deeds.

Islam, being a complete and total way of life, is concerned with all fields of human existence. Its main concern is the well-being of Allah's creatures in this world and the hereafter through reform and reconstruction of human life. The Holy Qur'an enjoins human beings to enter the fold of Islam, without any reservation, and to follow Allah's guidance in all fields of life. This requires the acquisition of knowledge for the purification of the self (*nafs*) and to do well in this world. The Holy Qur'an, which is "the guidance sure, without doubt, to those who fear Allah; who believe in the unseen" (2:2) has clearly spelled out the concept of accountability as it has clearly defined the functions and responsibilities of the human beings. It has asked to ponder and contemplate on its content, which is full of wisdom:

> Indeed We have sent Our Messengers with clear proofs, and revealed with them the Scripture and the Balance (justice) that humankind may keep up justice. And We brought forth iron wherein is mighty power (in matters of war), as well as many benefits for humankind, that Allah may test who it is that will help Him (His religion), and His messengers in the unseen. Verily, Allah is All-Strong, All-Mighty [57:25].

Islam demands complete obedience to Allah by complete acceptance and adherence to His laws, not in piece-meal or adulterated fashion with personal likes and dislikes, whims and notions. The two basic elements of humanity, according to Islam, are knowledge and faith. Knowledge gives light and power while faith gives us love, hope, compassion, and worth. Both knowledge and faith give humans security. The first gives protection from worldly calamities and outer insecurities while the second provides security against restlessness, loneliness, sense of insecurity, and base thoughts. Knowledge harmonizes the world with human beings while faith harmonizes human beings with themselves. The increase in knowledge enriches one's faith. The importance of acquiring knowledge can be gauged from the frequency of the use of word '*ilm* (knowledge) in the Holy Qur'an. Tellingly, it is the second most frequently employed after *Allah*. The Muslim history of culture is divided into the period of advancement of knowledge and faith, and the period in which they declined. In the enlightened period (up to 12th century CE), Muslim students and scholars were pioneers and trendsetters in many disciplines of knowledge and sciences. They were torch-bearers of scholarship while the West lived in the darkness of poverty, ignorance, superstition, and prejudice.

Since Islamic rule is the rule of law, it provides equity and justice for all, without any consideration of caste, color, creed or affluence. Islam acts as a great unifier and transforms everyone under its rule into a member of a united *ummah*. Its unifying factors are divine unity, prophecy, and the Day of Judgment. According to Kettani,

> The fact of the matter is that by ideal Islamic standards, the *ummah* finds itself completely disorganized in the twentieth century. This lack of organization is acutely felt by most of the thinkers of the *ummah*. And the effort to go back to the ideal, consciously or otherwise, is indeed the

driving force behind political and social forces requiring an improvement of the situation of the ummah [259].

While the Qur'an does not specify a particular form of government, it does provide relevant social and political values that can be used positively to promote effective governance in modern times. That, however, requires the translation of the relevant values from mere ideals into pragmatic policies that can contribute effectively to the realization of good governance in our time. The initial search for new paradigms to improve modern state governance poses a challenge to Islam as a religion, civilization, and culture. In order to make possible contributions in that regard, Muslims must turn to traditional Islamic sources in order to meet that challenge pragmatically. Islam requires people to be civilized and enlightened which is why literacy and proper education are considered of prime importance, as well as the most powerful indicators.

During the Prophet Muhammad's lifetime, the small Muslim state was governed, like most desert tribes through *shura* (consultation) and *ijma'* (consensus) and held together by the moral authority of one man — Muhammad — who was both leader and conduit for a dialogue between individual Muslims and Allah. For the first thirty odd years after Muhammad's death (632 CE), the problem of how Muslims were to govern themselves was fudged. Kettani observed that

> The deviation from the ideal model of reorganization of the Muslim *ummah* started early in the Islamic history. The first deviation occurred when the governor of Syria defied the order of the elected head of the state (the fourth Caliph 'Ali) and was able to overthrow the legitimate government by force [259–260].

The influential Pakistani thinker Mawlana Mawdudi (d. 1979) expressed little interest in Western theories of democracy. Mawdudi rejected the idea that the *ummah* can ever be sovereign. He was categorical: the very idea of popular sovereignty was blasphemous. It was a usurpation of God's will. Mawdudi argued that the only purpose of an Islamic state was to promote Islam and only those who truly believe in Islam can exercise power in God's name. A consultative assembly can only advise and consent; not exercise sovereignty or ultimate political control. In Iran, Ayatullah Khomeini updated and amplified the traditional Shi'ite doctrine of *Velayat-i-faqih*, the Guardian who stands in for God, protecting the realm of faith, of *Dar al-Islam* against *Dar al-Harb*, the outside threat.

In Islam, knowledge is power and not mere ornamentation. It has been accorded the highest honor and dignity, as acquiring and applying it in everyday life improves the quality of individual and community conditions. Iqbal says:

> A society based on such a conception of reality must reconcile, in its life, to the categories of permanence and change. It must possess eternal principles to regulate its collective life because eternity gives us a foot-hold in the world of perpetual change. But eternal principles, when they are understood to exclude all possibilities of change which, according to the Holy Qur'an, is one of the greatest signs of Allah, tend to immobilize what is essentially mobile in nature. The failure of Europe in political and social science illustrates the former principles. The immobility of Islam during the last 500 years illustrates the later ['Allamah online].

As the Holy Qur'an teaches, "There is no compulsion in religion" (2:256). Islam, being the complete way of life, is concerned with all fields of human existence. Its main concern is the well-being of Allah's creatures through reform and reconstruction of human life in this world and hereafter. The mere fact of having faith in the hereafter impacts both the thought and action of human beings. The upholder of this faith finds that he or she faces

Almighty Allah at all times and places and seeks to please Him. The Holy Qur'an enjoins human beings to enter the fold of Islam without any reservation and to follow Allah's guidance in all fields of life. The Qur'an describes itself as a "reminder" which grants good "advice" and urges readers and listeners to contemplate its meaning carefully (4:82). As Almighty Allah instructs the Prophet to say, "Are the blind and the one who sees equal? Will you no then take thought?" (6:50).

Conclusion

Islamic law is simple for everyone to apply in order to organize life based on mutual love and support. It provides for the promotion and growth of innate qualities and abilities which contribute to progress in all spheres of human life, improvement of resources, and better occupations. Islam strives for perfection; for it, constant conscientious efforts for continuous corporeal and incorporeal development and improvements are required. It is a progressive creed covering all times — past, present and future — and requires a definite and positive attitude and approach of its adherents. Based on this study, it could be said that governance in Islam has many images, but most of all it relates to justice and equality, and therefore is commonly depicted as balance or *mizan*. Thus, governance, as depicted in Islamic literature, is about maintaining order in society by implementing the Islamic code of conduct of differential responsibilities.

Works Cited

Ahmad, Khurshid, and Zafar Ishaq Ansari, eds. *Islamic Perspectives: Studies in Honour of Maulana Syed Abul 'Ala Maududi.* Leicester: Islamic Foundation, 1979.

Ahmad, Nazir. *Qur'anic and Non-Qur'anic Islam.* Lahore: Vanguard Books, 1987.

Ahmed, Ishtiaq. *The Concept of an Islamic State: An Analysis of the Ideological Controversy in Pakistan.* London: Frances Printer, 1987.

Brockwell, Joshua. "Islam and earth Day." *New York Times* (April 7, 2011). Internet: islam.about.com/od/activism/a/earth_day.htm.

Bucaille, Maurice. "The Qur'an and Modern Science." (1995). Internet: www.sultan.org/articles/QScience.html

Donohue, John J, and John L Esposito. *Islam in Transition: Muslim Perspectives.* New York: Oxford University Press, 2006.

Hashem, Mazen. "Islamic Roots of Good Governance." *Arab Insight* 1 1 (2007): 63–71.

Iqbal, Allama. "Finality of Prophethood." *Najaf* (2010). Internet: www.najaf.org/ english/book/19/17.htm.

"Islam and Elections." New York University. January 4, 2012. Internet: islamuswest.org/publications_islam_and_the_West/Islam_And_Elections/Islam/And Elections_17.html.

Kettani, M 'Ali. *Muslim Minorities in the World Today.* Rawalpindi: Services Book Club, 1990.

Mutahhari, Ayatullah Shaheed. *Man and Universe; Man and Faith.* Lahore: Islamic Seminary Publications, 1990.

Naqvi, Imran Haider, et al. "The Model of Good Governance in Islam." *African Journal of Business Management* 2.27 (2011): 10984–92.

Noor, Abdun. "Ethnic, Religion and Good Governance." *Journal of Administration & Governance* 3 2 (2008): 62–77.

Qudsy, Sharifah Hayaati Syed Ismail al-. "Effective Governance in the Era of Caliphate 'Umar Ibn al-Khattab (634–644)." *European Journal of Social Sciences* 18.4 (2011): 612–24.

Rai, Rai Hamid A K. "Qualities of Public Servant in an Islamic State." *Pakistan Times* 26 (June 1980).

Saionji, Masami. *Vision for the 21st Century: A Rebirth in Individual Responsibilities and Values.* Tokyo: Byakko Press, 2005.

Tomita, Kenji. "Islamic Governance and Democracy: Intersection and Separation." *Journal of Interdisciplinary Study of Monotheistic Religions* 3.1 (2007): 1–17.

Otherness

MOHAMED ELKOUCHE

"The parable of those who take protectors other than God is that of the Spider, who builds (to itself) a house; but truly the flimsiest of houses is the Spider's house; if they but knew."
(Qur'an 29:41)

Introduction

The question of Otherness is so predominant in the Qur'an that one can find it expressed, whether explicitly or implicitly, in nearly all of its chapters. Yet one cannot easily define who or what the Qur'an's Other(s) is (are) exactly because the latter concept applies to different things, creatures, individuals and communities, depending on the particular themes discussed or events referred to by particular Qur'anic verses. This point can be well illustrated by considering briefly a couple of citations from different parts of the Qur'an. In the opening *surah*, named *al-Fatihah*, which is recited up to twenty times in daily ritual prayers by Muslims, Allah is addressed in the following words: "Thee do we worship, and Thine aid we seek. Show us the straight way, the way of those on whom Thou hast bestowed Thy Grace, those whose (portion) is not wrath, and who go not astray" (1:5–7). The last phrases refer to two categories of people who are clearly opposed to Muslims: those who have incurred Allah's wrath and those who have strayed away from "the straight way." According to Ibn Kathir, the first category implies the Jews and the second one the Christians (Ibn Kathir 43). Both are symbolically represented as Muslims' Others who have, in different ways, lost Allah's grace and guidance.

The Other can even be an inanimate object as in the case of the idols to which the following verse from the middle of the Qur'an makes reference: "Take not with God another object of worship; or thou (O man!) wilt sit in disgrace and destitution" (17:22). Here, the opposition is between the real God and any false god(s) of whatever kind that may be worshipped besides or instead of the former. Those who engage in such a practice are heathens and idolaters who stand as Others not only to Muslims but also to all monotheists. The Qur'an represents this category as the worst and the most radical Others because Allah is ready to pardon any sin, no matter how grave, except that of idolatry or polytheism.[1] Another type of radical Other is mentioned in the following verses:

> Behold! We said to the angels, "Bow down to Adam": they bowed except Iblis. He was one of the jinns, and he broke the Command of his Lord. Will ye then take him and his progeny as protectors rather than Me? And they are enemies to you! [18:50]

Unlike the angels, Iblis has openly disobeyed his Creator and rejected His order to bow down to Adam. By so doing, he incurs Allah's curse and becomes His enemy as well as that of humanity. Consequently, all those who choose Iblis' protection or patronage instead of Allah's are doomed to the harshest divine punishment.

The very last *surah* of the Qur'an reads as follows: "Say: I seek refuge with the Lord and Cherisher of Mankind ... from the mischief of the Whisperer (of Evil) ... who whispers into the hearts of Mankind,—among Jinns and among Men" (114:1, 4–6). The Whisperer here stands metaphorically for Satan, who has vowed to tempt humankind into evil-doing, as it will be soon illustrated. But along with the demonic Jinns embodied in Iblis and his progeny, the last phrase implies that there also exist human beings who can be symbolically considered as "human devils."[2] Both categories are evil Others from whom true believers must seek refuge in Allah so as to win His grace and paradise.

All the preceding quotations help to provide a glimpse at how the Qur'an speaks about Others and to show how the latter are so diverse. The Qur'anic discourse deals quite repeatedly with these and many other types of Others, like the disbelievers and the hypocrites,[3] but the image it reflects about each category changes according to the context of each verse and the texture of each *surah*. Sometimes, one can find different degrees of Otherness within the same category, as in the case of the People of the Book, which means Jews and Christians. In fact, the images of both are far from being the same; moreover, the Christians themselves are at times divided into those who are "close" to Muslims and "antagonistic" ones. The Otherness of the idolaters or pagans and the disbelievers too is sometimes depicted differently depending on whether they are at war or at peace with Muslims.

The Image of the Other in Chapter Seven of the Qur'an

In order to explore the image of the Other in the Qur'an with some depth and concentration, this study focuses on a single Qur'anic *surah*—namely, chapter VII, entitled *al-A'raf* (The Heights). It consists of an interpretive study that aims both to reveal the attitude(s) of Islam to its Others and to shed some light on the rich imagery and symbols the Qur'an deploys in its articulation of this question of religious Otherness. As the discussion will thus cover both some thematic and artistic aspects of the above-mentioned Qur'anic text, it is worth starting by pointing out that the Qur'an as a whole often utilizes art to express its discourses. As a matter of fact, even though this Book is primarily concerned with the transmission of religious thoughts and didactic messages, it also makes a considerable use of art to bring about this objective in a very effective manner. Thus diverse artistic modes and stylistic devices like description, story-telling, imagery, contrast and symbolism are deployed to help convey these messages and meanings in such a way as to impress them upon the reader or listener.

In this connection, Sayyid Qutb has argued in his book *al-Taswir al-fanni fi al-Qur'an* (*Artistic Imagery in the Qur'an*) that imagery is the favorite and the most important tool by means of which the Qur'an gives expression to its ideas and achieves its desired aesthetic and didactic effects. On the one hand, Qur'anic images and figures of speech usually serve as compelling illustrations that render abstract meanings concrete and draw vivid and visualized pictures that contribute to the artistic and aesthetic appeal of the whole discourse. On the other hand, this imagery is aimed to function, at the same time, as a means to an end — namely, moral instruction and the inculcation of Islamic doctrine. Indeed, the Qur'an itself makes frequent references to this instructive and didactic role of its imagery, as it can be well understood from the following verses: "Such are the similitudes which We propound to men, that they may reflect" (59:21) and "We have put forth for men, in this Qur'an every kind of Parable, in order that they may receive admonition" (39:27).

As the term "Parable" in this last verse suggests, the Qur'an often uses story-telling as an essential part of its imaginative and symbolic make-up. Indeed, this Book contains a remarkable number of stories, most of which tell about what actually happened to some ancient nations or relate various events and experiences in the real lives of prophets and messengers like Adam, Nuh (Noah), Ibrahim (Abraham), Hud, Musa (Moses), 'Isa (Jesus) and Muhammad. Here, again, the chief objective of recounting these stories consists in instructing people, as this statement at the end of *Surah Yusuf* (The Chapter of Joseph) makes clear: "There is, in their stories, instruction for men endued with understanding. It is not a tale invented, but a confirmation ,f what went before it,—a detailed exposition of all things, and a Guide and a Mercy to any such as believe" (13:111). Yet along with this instructive goal, these stories play a major role in enhancing the artistic and aesthetic dimension of the Qur'an thanks to the latter's deployment of the diverse techniques and strategies that are normally used in pure or imaginative narrative art.

The Image of Iblis

In the light of the preceding background ideas, we can now proceed to see how Chapter VII of the Qur'an reflects its theme of Otherness via the use of story, imagery, juxtaposition and other artistic and rhetorical elements. From the beginning, one is struck by the fact that this *surah* recounts not just a single story but a series of brief ones that combine to transmit the same religious message. But the essential story in this *surah* is that of Adam with Iblis, which took place right at the beginning of God's creation of Man. The story opens as follows:

> It is We who created you and gave you shape; then We bade the angels, "Bow down to Adam," and they bowed down; not so Iblis; he refused to be of those who bow down. (God) said: "What prevented thee from bowing down when I commanded thee?" He said: "I am better than he: Thou didst create me from fire, and him from clay." (God) said: "Get thee down from this: it is not for thee to be arrogant here: get out, for thou art of the meanest (of creatures)" [7:10–13].

Besides depicting vividly how Iblis is openly challenging and disobeying Allah, this scene reveals that Iblis is "othering" Adam—and all humankind, by implication—in the sense that he considers him as inferior, given the fact that he is created just of clay while he himself is created of fire. Moreover, his sense of superiority and self-importance prompts him to separate himself from the angels, who all readily and obediently execute Allah's command. His refusal to be one of those who bow down indicates that he despises not only humans but also the angels because of their prostration before Adam. This suggests that the angels too are somehow "othered" by Iblis.

Ironically enough, Iblis himself is rejected as a mere despicable Other; for Allah immediately dismisses him from his high status among the angels in paradise, and he stigmatizes him as "the meanest" of His creatures. This stigma of meanness and malignity is to remain a constant trait in Iblis' character and a salient marker of his evil Otherness for when Allah accepts to give him respite till Judgment Day, Iblis vows to do his best to take revenge on human beings and to deviate them from the straight path:

> He said: "Because thou hast thrown me out of the Way, lo! I will lie in wait for them on Thy Straight Way: then will I assault them from before them and behind them, from their right and

their left: nor wilt Thou find, in most of them, gratitude (for Thy mercies)." (God) said: "Get out from this, disgraced and expelled. If any of them follow thee,— hell will I fill with you all" [7:16–18].

Iblis' words confirm his whole-hearted determination to spare no time or energy to seduce human beings into doing evil and disobeying their Creator. In return, Allah's statement confirms Iblis' irrevocable dismissal and loss of His grace. It condemns him to perpetual malediction and warns that the punishment of all those who follow his evil instructions and seductions is hell. This warning means clearly that Iblis' followers are equally considered as Others, as it will be soon argued.

Soon after his repudiation from paradise, Iblis starts to carry out his devilish stratagem against Adam, whom he apparently regards as the cause of that disdainful expulsion. He thus begins "to whisper suggestions" (7:20) to him and his wife so as to tempt them to eat from the tree which Allah has warned them not to touch. His subtle machinations prove to be successful as they eventually lead to their Fall:

> And he swore to them both, that he was their sincere adviser. So by deceit he brought about their fall: when they tasted of the tree, their shame became manifest to them, and they began to sew together the leaves of the garden over their bodies. And their Lord called unto them: "Did I not forbid you that tree, and tell you that Satan was an avowed enemy unto you?" [7:21–22]

The last clause in the above passage is highly indicative of the fact that Iblis or Satan is an enemy and Other, not only to Allah, whom he has defied and disobeyed, but also to humans, whom he has duped and seduced away from the heavenly domain. This idea is further stressed in this subsequent verse which confirms that the antagonism between Satan and humanity is doomed to remain deep-seated and everlasting: "Get ye down, with enmity between yourselves. On earth will be your dwelling-place and your means of livelihood — for a time" (7:24).

By now, all the major constituents of Iblis' image as Other have been pointed out in the preceding citations from the *surah* under discussion. These features can be sketched out as follows: open disobedience and defiance of Allah, excessive arrogance and self-conceit, meanness and deceit, jealousy and vindictiveness towards humankind, and avowed commitment to lead people astray. The Qur'an has skillfully presented all these traits through a narrative form and style that superbly succeed in delineating a vivid picture wherein Iblis appears as evil incarnate and the symbol of rebellion against Allah and strong enmity to human beings. By contrast, the angels are represented as symbolizing absolute submission and obedience to Allah; whereas Adam is the embodiment of human nature, with all its inherent weakness, contradictions and fluctuation between vice and virtue (Qutb, *Fi zilal al-Qur'an* 1266).

The manner in which Iblis' image as Other is portrayed is highly artistic indeed. The story itself is mediated through a number of techniques that makes it appear as a piece of drama enfolding before our eyes. For example, dialogue helps to give a great deal of immediacy to the scenes presented, besides reflecting many aspects of Iblis' personality. Likewise, the implicit juxtaposition of Iblis with the angels helps to throw the former's vile personality and Otherness into sharp relief.

Yet, as already pointed out, such Qur'anic artistic uses are only a means to some didactic and religious ends: here the lesson has to do with revealing to people the true nature of Iblis and warning them against his devilish wiles and whisperings. Since all human beings are constantly liable to repeat Adam's mistakes in different ways, the Qur'an is thus teaching them how to seek Allah's Guidance and avoid Iblis' mischievous manipulations.

But lest this important lesson could be missed, the Qur'an soon stresses it didactically in these direct and more explicit terms:

O ye Children of Adam! Let not Satan seduce you in the same manner as he got your parents out of the garden, stripping them of their raiment, to expose their shame: for he and his tribe watch you from a position where ye cannot see them: We made the Evil ones friends (only) to those without Faith [7:27].

Here, the Qur'an spells out its religious message and reveals the secret of recounting the story of Adam with Iblis as it contains a crucial warning, consisting in the fact that people must be extremely cautious of the subtle strategies and imperceptible machinations of Iblis and his mysterious helpers. For it is true, as the preceding verse underscores, that Iblis has a whole tribe or "party" of invisible agents who are tirelessly endeavoring to seduce people into wrong-doing. So people must be on the alert; otherwise, they risk to be duped and become this party's disciples and allies.

This leads us to the important and pertinent idea that all Iblis' friends and followers are Others, according to the Qur'an. As a matter of fact, there are numerous Qur'anic verses that attest to the existence of this "other" party of Satan — one which is diametrically opposed to God's party. For instance, right at the beginning of the *surah* under discussion, Allah says: "Follow (O men!) the revelation given unto you from your Lord, and follow not, as friends or protectors, *other than Him*" (7:3, italics added). Another verse defines clearly those who follow Allah's Straight Path as being "the Party of God that will achieve felicity" (58:22); whereas those who fail to do so are "the Party of the Evil One that will perish!" (58:19). Likewise, the following verse succinctly draws a clear-cut distinction between these two opposite groups:

God is the Protector of those who have faith: from the depth of darkness He will lead them forth into light. Of those who reject faith the patrons are the evil ones: from light they will lead them forth into the depths of darkness. They will be companions of the Fire, to dwell therein (for ever) [2:257].

Here, believers are symbolically associated with light and ultimately with God, whereas non-believers are associated with darkness and ultimately with Satan. Such rich symbolism informs both implicitly and explicitly, most of the Qur'anic discourse, and Chapter VII under discussion is a good case in point.

Indeed, underlying the latter *surah* is an extended implicit contrast between the antithetical parties of God and Satan — a symbolic contrast that helps to highlight the image of Satan and its followers as Others. This contrast manifests itself in a number of significant binary oppositions that can be presented as follows:

God/Angels	vs.	Iblis (Satan, Devil)
Adam (humankind)	vs.	Iblis (and his tribe)
Believers	vs.	Non-believers/Idolaters
Good (Right)	vs.	Evil (Wrong)
Paradise (garden)	vs.	hell (Fire)

As already mentioned, besides being opposed indirectly to both God and the angels, Iblis is explicitly categorized as the enemy of Adam and Eve. Yet it is worth noting that even if Iblis succeeds in seducing this couple away from the garden, they soon repent and ask God's forgiveness, whereas Iblis arrogantly vows to persist in his devilish manipulation till the very end. People are subsequently judged according to whether they, metaphorically, subscribe to the Party of God (= Good: faith, obedience, repentance etc) or the Party of the Devil (= Evil: *Kufr*, disobedience, sins etc). Those who accept and follow Allah's guidance are certainly the victorious partisans whose reward is paradise, while those who are misguided by Satan are the damned Others, with whom Allah has promised to fill hell.

The wretched fate of these Others is depicted in much detail by different verses of the *surah*. For instance, the certainty of their being condemned to hell and their complete loss of Allah's grace and mercy are expressed in the following figurative manner: "To those who reject Our signs and treat them with arrogance, no opening will there be of the gates of heaven, nor will they enter the garden, until the camel can pass through the eye of the needle: such is Our reward for those in sin" (7:40). Just as it is impossible and quite inconceivable that a camel, with its enormous size, could penetrate through the tiny eye of a needle, so it is absolutely impossible that those Others could win Allah's favor or gain access to paradise.[4] The metaphors used in this verse help to reflect the gravity of the ultimate situation of those partisans of Satan and the amount of Allah's wrath against them. The subsequent verse makes it clear that Allah will requite these disbelievers' deeds with "hell, as a couch (below) and folds and folds of covering above" (7:41). The words "couch" and "covering" are used here as further apt metaphors that enhance the idea of severe and merciless infernal retribution. Both words in this context are strongly indicative of the fact that such sinful Others will be completely surrounded and enveloped by the fire of hell owing to their vain pride and rejection of Allah's revelations.

Another image of those Others is portrayed as follows: "Many are the Jinns and men We have made for hell: they have hearts wherewith they understand not, eyes wherewith they see not, and ears wherewith they hear not. They are like cattle — nay more misguided: for they are heedless (of warning)" (7:179). The Others here are metaphorically described as ones whose senses and perceptive faculties are utterly inoperative, not because of any "physical" harm or deficiency but rather because of their religious blindness and spiritual bankruptcy. They are thus likened to cattle, or even worse than cattle, because they see and hear Allah's signs but fail to take heed of them or they reject them disdainfully. They have missed Allah's guidance and are consequently doomed to hell.

In the same vein, the Qur'an cites the parable of the man who was endowed with the knowledge and intelligence to read and comprehend Allah's signs; unfortunately, he shed these faculties stupidly and failed to use them properly in such a way that he could win God's Favor and Guidance. He let Satan lead him astray and he consequently became like a wretched panting dog: "His similitude is that of a dog: if you attack him, he lolls out his tongue, or if you leave him alone, he (still) lolls out his tongue. That is the similitude of those who reject Our signs; so relate the story; perchance they may reflect" (7:176). The use of animal imagery in the last two quotations is deliberately meant to debase those who do not heed God's Signs and follow Satan instead. It thus contributes to making the image of the Other uglier and much more negative.

The Qur'an also uses the technique of juxtaposition to expose in a vivid manner the ugly face of such damned Others and the unenviable fate they are doomed to. In a revealing dramatic scene, these Others are brought side by side with the true believers who are granted access to paradise while the former are already suffering in hell. They insistently solicit the help and benevolence of these lucky believers, but all their requests are utterly vain and fruitless: "The companions of the fire will call the companions of the garden: 'Pour down to us water or anything that God doth provide for your sustenance.' They will say: 'Both these things had God forbidden to those who rejected Him'" (7:50). Both contrast and dialogue help to reveal the agony and horror of these inmates of hell. As Sayyid Qutb has commented in *Fi zilal al-Qur'an* (1288), this is one of the scenes of resurrection and the Last Judgment which are so frequent in the Qur'an and which are often characterized by their power to make the reader or listener visualize the events as if they are being witnessed directly. Such scenes are not conveyed through simple and inert descriptions but rather portrayed in vivid and sensuous terms that make them throb with movement and emotional significance. This artistic use has again the aim of keeping alive in people's minds these scenes of paradisiacal bliss and infernal anguish so as to beware in making their choices.

This scene is preceded by a long passage which also depicts the scene of resurrection and the Last Judgment. Those who have been following Allah's straight way go to paradise while Satan's followers go to hell. The direct contrast between the situations of these two groups helps to reveal the bliss of the inmates of paradise and the aguish and horror of the inmates of fire. To warn against the unenviable fate of the latter group, the *surah* cites a series of brief stories that happened to some messengers of God with their peoples. What is striking about these stories is that they all tend to be similar in both theme and structure. In each one, the Messenger calls his people to worship God alone, and those who disobey him are soon visited upon by some severe Divine punishment. Here is one representative case:

> We sent Noah to his people. He said: "O my people! Worship God! Ye have no other God but Him. I fear for you the Punishment of a dreadful Day!" ... But they rejected him, and We delivered him, and those with him, in the Ark: But We overwhelmed in the Flood those who rejected Our signs. They were indeed a blind people! [7:59–64].

The last phrase — which also applies to the disbelievers among the peoples of Hud, Thamud, Lut, Shuayb and certainly those of many other Prophets and Messengers — corroborates to the image of the Other as morally and spiritually blind.

The repetition of the same message by different Prophet — "O my people! Worship God! Ye have no other God but Him" — is significant in more than one respect. On the one hand, it serves as a kind of leitmotif that helps to highlight and stress the *surah*'s main theme. This latter consists in the invitation of people to acknowledge Allah alone as their Guide and warning them against turning to anyone other than Him for guidance (Mawdudi 8–9). On the other hand, that repetition reflects the unity of religion by showing how the missions of all the Prophets revolved around the question of the Oneness of God.

In connection with this notion of "unity of religion," it is also significant that the *surah* starts with the story of Adam, the first Messenger, and ends by making a lot of references to Muhammad, the last Prophet. For example one verse reads:

> Say: "O men! I am sent unto you all, as the Apostle of God, to whom belongeth the dominion of the heavens and the earth: there is no god but He: it is He that giveth both life and death. So believe in God and His apostle, the unlettered Prophet, who believed in God and His words: follow him that (so) ye may be guided" [7:158].

This quotation makes it clear that Muhammad is a prophet who was sent to all humankind, whereas each of the previous prophets and messengers was sent to a specific group or nation. Such a universalist self-image of Islam has much to do with the issue of religious and cultural Otherness as it forcefully raises the question of Islam's relation with the other religions, be they heavenly or pagan.

The Image of the Unbeliever

As regards this relation, one can generally notice that Islam distinguishes between two major categories of Others: the People of the Book, on the one hand, and both pagans and disbelievers, on the other hand.[5] While the latter category concerns those whom Islam considers as mere *kuffar* (unbelievers) and *mushrikin* (polytheists), whose irreligious or heathen beliefs and practices oppose them sharply to Muslim believers and lead to hell, as has been illustrated, the former category concerns essentially Jews and Christians, who share with Muslims the property of having each a heavenly and monotheistic religion. The true believers of all these religions are looked at quite favorably by Islam, as the following verse indicates:

> Surely those who believe (in the Qur'an), and those who follow the Jewish (scriptures), and the Christians and the Sabians,—any who believes in God and the Last Day, and work righteousness shall have their reward with their Lord: on them shall be no fear, nor shall they grieve [2: 62].

This does not however mean that the image of the Jewish and Christian Others is always positive in Islam. In fact, the nature of this image depends on whether these Others are close or faraway from the Right Path, to which the Qur'an invites all people.

In the *surah* under discussion, for instance, the Israelites who refused to follow Musa (Moses) are rewarded as follows: "So We sent (plagues) on them: wholesale death, locusts, lice, frogs, and blood: signs openly self-explained: but they were steeped in arrogance,—a people given to sin" (7:133). On the contrary, some other Israelites are depicted positively as follows: "Of the people of Moses there is a section who guide and do justice in the light of truth" (7:159). Similarly, one can cite many verses from the Qur'an that speak either positively or negatively about Christians. The following one opposes the disbelievers and the believers among the people of 'Isa al-Masih (Jesus Christ): "When Jesus found unbelief on their part he said: 'Who will be my helpers to (the work of) God?' Said the Disciples: 'We are God's helpers: we believe in God and do thou bear witness that we are Muslims'" (3: 52). The word "Muslims" here is used in the sense that "Islam" means literally bowing and submitting to the Will of God. In this sense, Islam is supposed to be the one Religion of God which all messengers from Adam up to Muhammad embraced and called their peoples to embrace ('Abd al-Wahhab 13–15).[6] It is probably the presence of such believers among Christians that makes the Qur'an look at the latter as being closer to actual Muslims than the Jews are: "Strongest among men in enmity to the Believers wilt thou find the Jews and Pagans; and nearest among them in love to the believers wilt thou find those who say 'We are Christians'" (5:85).[7]

Both here, and in the rest of its numerous and diverse images about religious and cultural Others, the Qur'anic discourse issues from Islam's self-image as the last and perfect religion that came to supersede its predecessors (i.e. Judaism and Christianity). When Allah asks his last Prophet Muhammad to say: "O men! I am sent unto you all, as the Apostle of God... So believe in God and His apostle... [F]ollow him that (so) ye may be guided" (7:158), it is clear that Islam is meant as the ultimate revealed religion and the supreme Divine Message to all humankind. This is supported by several statements and verses in the Qur'an like: "The Religion before God is Islam" (3:19), and "If any one desires a religion other than Islam (submission to God), never will it be accepted of him" (3:85).

Yet, in spite of this universalist claim of Islam, this latter still believes in diversity, religious freedom and tolerance. It also stresses that Islamic faith and jurisprudence should not be imposed by force on any individual, group or nation as "there [is] no compulsion in religion" (2:256). What is more, Islam extends a friendly invitation to both Jews and Christians to promote peaceful relations and fruitful mutual understanding on the basis of the unity of religion and the Oneness of God: "Say: 'O People of the Book! Come to common terms as between us and you: that we worship none but God; that we associate no partners with Him; that we erect not, from among ourselves, lords and patrons other than God'" (3:64).

From all that has been discussed in this study, it can be concluded that Chapter VII of the Qur'an or *Surah al-A'raf* (The Chapter of the Heights) is highly illustrative of a number of important aspects pertaining to the question of Otherness in the Qur'anic discourse as a whole. Throughout this discussion much focus has been laid on showing how Iblis figures as a major Other owing to his open disobedience of God and avowed enmity to humankind. It has been then argued that all those who follow Iblis and join his party, instead of seeking God's Guidance and abiding by His rules and instructions, are similarly Others. The latter include such categories as the pagans, the disbelievers and all those who disregarded or rejected the Divine Messages propagated by the different apostles and prophets.

If Iblis and his followers among the above-mentioned categories are viewed by Islam as its radical Others, the People of the Book obviously occupy a different position of Otherness. One can say that their degree of Otherness is generally milder and less extreme owing to the common religious denominators they have with Muslims. That is why there is a number of positive images and statements about them (especially Christians) in the Qur'anic discourse. Nevertheless, it is also true that this discourse frequently portrays both Jews and Christians in ways that indicate that they are also enemies to Muslims and that some of their beliefs and practices have made them lapse into heresy and polytheism.[8]

Given that the Qur'an includes both negative and positive images about the People of the Book, its discourse about them tends to be rather ambivalent and paradoxical. This quality makes it quite difficult to know what its final attitude towards this category of Others is exactly. To achieve an approximate full understanding about this attitude, it is necessary, as has been hinted at, that one should take into consideration the textual context of each verse (or group of verses) as well as the reasons and chronological order of its (their) revelation (what is known in Islamic culture as *asbab al-nuzul;* that is to say, the causes and circumstances that necessitated that some verse(s) should be revealed at a specific time or historical conjuncture.)[9]

Besides the aforementioned problem of the ambivalence of Qur'anic discourse, one can say that the whole concept of Otherness in Islam is highly complex and problematic due to the fact that some Muslims themselves are categorized as Others in this discourse.[10] A case in point is the group of Muslims whose allegiance to the Prophet Muhammad was insincere or characterized by much indecision or deceit, especially at the time of wars. This group is openly stigmatized as "Hypocrites" in verses such as "God hath promised the Hypocrites men and women, and the rejecters of Faith, the fire of hell: therein shall they dwell..." (9:68), and "O Prophet! Strive hard against the Unbelievers and the Hypocrites, and be firm against them. Their abode is hell, — an evil refuge indeed" (9:73). In both instances this category of "bad" Muslims is put side by side with unbelievers or radical Others because they evidently embody what might be called "recognizable" hypocrites. Yet the problem arises when one takes into account the existence of another type of hypocrites — those who were not "frank" or recognizable hypocrites, in the sense that they honestly aligned themselves with Muslims but failed to be true followers of the Prophet due to some psychological flaws like fear, doubt or selfishness. This category, of course, cannot be equated with those Hypocrites who pretended to be Muslims while they practically hated Islam and tried to undermine it. The Qur'an itself mentions that they may not be punished as their sins and failures were mitigated or counterbalanced by their good and honest pious deeds: "Others (there are who) have acknowledged their wrong-doings: they have mixed an act that was good with another that was evil. Perhaps God will turn unto them (in mercy): for

God is Oft-forgiving, Most merciful" (9:102). The use of the word "perhaps" in this verse is very revealing; it actually shows that the fate of these hypocrite Others depends on the Will and Mercy of God. Hence the difficulty of classifying them either as "good" or "evil" Others since only God knows about their real personalities and identities.

Conclusion

All in all, it can be generally said that, with the exception of few verses that refer to some categories of people — like the People of the Book — in a relatively positive way, the image of the Other in the Qur'an is essentially negative. Indeed, this Other is most often described and portrayed in terms and images that expose him as an ignoble and accursed creature, who resembles a mindless animal and who will soon be severely punished in hell. In drawing and reflecting this negative and dreary image of the Other, the Qur'anic discourse makes use of a multiplicity of narrative techniques and stylistic devices that help to convey its meanings and achieve its instructive effects in a very effective manner. Thus, elements like imagery, description, dialogue, contrast and stories (both real and parabolic) all co-operate and work in unison to render the text highly symbolic and pregnant with didactic meanings and instructions. These technical and artistic tools are not just means to an end but they are valuable in themselves as they help to infuse the Qur'anic text with both aesthetic and didactic appeal.

Chapter Notes

1. One Qur'anic verse, in fact, makes it clear that: "God forgiveth not (the sin of) joining other gods with Him; but He forgiveth whom He pleased other sins than this: one who joins Other gods with God, had strayed far, far away (from the Right)" (4:116).

2. The Qur'an actually makes reference to *shayatin al-jinn* and *shayatin al-ins*.

3. One chapter of the Qur'an is entitled literally *al-Kafirun* (The Disbelievers) and another one *al-Munafiqun* (The Hypocrites).

4. It may be worth mentioning here that a similar figurative idea concerning the (im)possibility for a camel to pass through the eye of a needle occurs also in the Bible. "Again I tell you," Jesus said, "it is easier for a camel to go through the eye of a needle than for a rich man to enter the kingdom of God" (Matthew 19: 23–24). As John Andrew Morrow has noted, Biblical commentators are divided among those who believe that this image implies the *impossibility* that such people could enter paradise and those who think it refers to the *difficulty* of this entrance (Morrow, *The Book of Divine Unity*, note 251). On the contrary, Islamic commentators on the Qur'anic verse under discussion unanimously agree that the image is meant to express the idea of impossibility. I have, in fact, read dozens of interpretations made by well-known commentators and none of them suggested that the image might be meant to express the notion of difficulty rather than that of impossibility. This unanimity is most probably due to the fact that the image is applied to a category which the Qur'an repeatedly and unambiguously represents as being doomed to hell — namely, the disbelievers, "who reject [Allah's] signs and treat them with arrogance." By contrast, the Biblical passage speaks specifically about the category of the rich; and since there is logically no reason why some members of this category can be devout people who deserve to go to paradise, the image thus obviously lends itself to being interpreted as implying difficulty rather than impossibility.

5. See Asghar Ali Engineer's "The Concept of the Other in Islam."

6. See also Yusuf 'Ali footnote 392.

7. Yusuf 'Ali comments on this verse: "The meaning is not that they merely call themselves Christians, but that they are such sincere Christians that they appreciate Muslim virtues, as did the Abyssinians to whom Muslim refugees went during persecution in Mecca. They would say: 'It is true we are Christians, but we understand your point of view, and we know you are good men.' They are Muslims at heart, whatever their label may be" (p. 268 note 789).

8. One verse of the Qur'an reads: "The Jews call 'Uzayr a son of God, and the Christians call Christ

the Son of God. That is a saying from their mouth; (in this) they but imitate what the unbelievers of old used to say. God's curse be on them: How they are deluded away from the Truth!" (9:30)

9. See, Muhammad 'Abed al-Jabri, 72–76.

10. It is worth mentioning here that the Qur'an never uses the term "other" as a noun, but it often uses it as an adjective that means "except" or "additional" as in "lords and patrons other than God."

Works Cited

'Abd al-Wahhab, Ahmad. *al-Islam wa al-adyan al-ukhra*. al-Qahirah: Maktabat Wahibah, 1998.

'Ali, 'Abdullah Yusuf, trans. *The Glorious Qur'an*. Bayrut: Dar al-Fikr, 1937.

Engineer, Asghar 'Ali. "The Concept of the Other in Islam." Internet:www.just-international.org/index. php?option=com_content&view=article&id=46 92%3Aaugust-commentary &catid=3%3Anewsflash& Itemid=150.

Ibn Kathir, Isma'il ibn 'Umar. *Tafsir al-Qur'an al-'Azim*. al-Qahirah: Dar al-Bayan al-'Arabi, 2006.

Jabri, Muhammad 'Abed al-. *Mawaqif*. Series No. 62. Casablanca: Apress, 2007.

Mawdudi, Abu al-'Ala. *Meaning of the Qur'an*. Vol. 4. Lahore: Islamic Publications (Pvt) Ltd, 1993.

Morrow, John Andrew, Sayyid 'Ali Raza Rizvi, Barbara Castleton, eds. *Kitab al-Tawhid / The Book of Divine Unity*. Trans. Sayyid 'Ali Raza Rizvi. London: Savior's Foundation, 2010.

Qutb, Sayyid. *al-Taswir al-fanni fi al-Qur'an*. al-Qahirah: Dar al-Shuruq, 1988.

_____. *Fi zilal al-Qur'an*. al-Qahirah: Dar al-Shuruq, 1992.

Ashura[1]

MUHAMMAD-REZA FAKHR-ROHANI

"My followers, who will befriend my ahl al-bayt, will mourn for Husayn and commemorate his martyrdom each year in every century." (Prophet Muhammad)

Introduction

The Arabic word *'Ashura'* is derived from the Syriac word *'Asiroya* (Mashkour, vol. 2, 567) or *Asora* (*SOED*, s.v. *Ashura*), and ultimately from the Hebrew word *'Asor* (Bowker, s.v. Ashura). In Arabic, Ashura means "the tenth day [of the month Muharram]" (*al-Munjid*, s.v. *'A-Sh-R*; Lane, Bk 1, Pt. 5: 2053; Steingass, s.v. Ashura). That the 10th day of Muharram has had a particular name, especially since "[f]ew nouns of the measure *fa'ula* have been heard" (Lane, loc. cit.) signifies that Ashura must have been a special day even in pre–Islamic history of the Arabs, and perhaps it might be the same with other Semitic peoples, cultures, and civilizations. In the Islamic world, the significance of Ashura lies in the fact that on such a day in the year 61 AH/ 680, the third Imam, al-Husayn (b. 4 AH/ 626), and over one hundred of his mostly male companions were martyred in an imposed war. This bloodbath took place at the command of Umayyad generals in the month of Muharram, an Arabic month in which fighting was forbidden even in the pre–Islamic period of *Jahiliyyah*, the Age of Ignorance, which is still generally "used as a byword for ungodliness and immortality" (Silverstein 129).[2] In Islamic history, the memory of Ashura has been associated mainly with the Battle of Karbala of 61 AH/ 680. On such a day, the agents of the Umayyad regime, under 'Umar ibn Sa'd, initiated an unparalleled, imposed battle, unto the small band of Imam al-Husayn and his companions. In consequence of this military confrontation, almost all of the male companions of Imam al-Husayn were martyred, a moment that marked the definitive split of the Muslim community into the Sunnis, who continued to follow the Caliphs in spite of their crimes, and the Shi'ites, who sided solely with the Imams from the Household of the Prophet.

The Battle of Karbala

One of the terms included in the peace treaty signed on 15 Jamadi I 41 AH/ 660 between the second Imam, al-Hasan al-Mujtaba (3–49 AH/ 625–669), and Mu'awiyyah (c. 605, r. 661–680) was that the latter was not entitled to introduce anybody as his successor (Majlisi 435; al-Yasin 620; Jafri 151). However, as expected, Mu'awiyyah nominated his son Yazid (c. 642, r. 680–683) as his successor and obtained allegiance of the people by force. Imam al-

Husayn never consented to this gesture. After the death of Mu'awiyyah on 15 Rajab 60 AH/ March 680, Yazid declared himself as the next Umayyad ruler and forced his agent at Medina, viz., al-Walid ibn 'Utbah, to get, inter alia, Imam al-Husayn's consent by force. If the Imam refused, he was to be beheaded right away (Majlisi 593; al-Tabasi 84; Ibn A'tham 822).

After Imam al-Husayn was invited to the Government House at Medina, al-Walid ibn 'Utba informed him of the death of Mu'awiyyah and asked his pledge of allegiance (bay'a) in favor of Yazid. The Imam never succumbed to such an imposed allegiance. Rather, he declared that since he belonged to the Household of the Prophet Muhammad, he was the most deserving person for leading the Muslim community. In contrast, Yazid was a notorious profligate and an open-sinner. Hence, he was utterly unfit to serve as the ruler of the Muslim ummah (community) (Ibn A'tham 823).

Considering the increasing pressure placed upon him by Yazid, Imam al-Husayn decided to leave Medina after twelve days for Mecca in the late afternoon of 28 Rajab of the same year. Due to the sanctity of the Ka'bah (the House of Allah) at Mecca, it had long been considered a place of safety, security, and asylum; hence, a true divine sanctum. Consequently, no conceivable threat was expected to emerge thereat. Imam al-Husayn reached Mecca on his birth anniversary, that is, on 3rd Sha'ban 60 AH/ 680 (al-Mufid 430; Ibn A'tham 836). He remained at Mecca for about four months and ten days (Mohaddethi 35). During his stay at Mecca, he received approximately 12,000 letters of invitation from the inhabitants of al-Kufah, Iraq. They claimed to want him as their leader. To weigh the political situation of al-Kufah, Imam al-Husayn dispatched his cousin and brother-in-law, Muslim ibn 'Aqil ibn Abi Talib (d. 9 Dhu al-Hijja 60 AH/ 11 September 680), as his envoy. Later on, a great majority of those who had welcomed Muslim betrayed him owing to the threat of mass execution by 'Ubayd Allah ibn Ziyad (d. 686). In consequence, he was arrested and martyred.

As the pilgrimage season approached, Yazid sent a secret band of his agents to assassinate Imam al-Husayn during the hajj rituals (Majlisi 624). Since such an assassination would certainly infringe the divine security and sanctity of Mecca, Imam al-Husayn was forced to leave Mecca on the 8th Dhu al-Hijja. Since the Umayyads no longer treated Mecca as an inviolable sanctuary of safety, Imam al-Husayn decided to leave there lest no insult, however trivial, would be done toward the Divine sanctity of Mecca. That Imam al-Husayn left Mecca precisely during the pilgrimage was cause for curiosity for everybody was rushing into the region for the hajj rituals. His forced departure therefrom, especially by the Tan'im station just outside Mecca, made it a loud and peaceful voice of dissidence, for it was by Tan'im that the prospective hajjis enter the sanctum of Mecca. Without causing any harsh confrontation, his mere departure thereat, and particularly on the last day of entering Mecca for performing hajj, made everybody cognizant of the real face of Umayyad rule.

Imam al-Husayn and his entourage moved toward al-Kufah, Iraq, and after 25 days, reached the region of Karbala on 2 Muharram 61 AH/ 2 October 680 (Muhammadi-Reyshahri, Shahadatnameh 351). There he encountered a military band dispatched by 'Ubayd Allah ibn Ziyad, the newly-appointed Umayyad governor of al-Kufah. Al-Hurr ibn Yazid al-Riyahi (d. 61 AH/ 680) was the commander of the military band whose mission was to block Imam al-Husayn's progression toward al-Kufah. Since the enemy forces were then exhausted and already suffering from exhaustion and thirst, Imam al-Husayn ordered his male companions to distribute among them the limited quantity of water they had gathered for themselves (Muhammadi-Reyshahri, Daneshnameh 5: 220–221). Imam al-Husayn intended to help them survive, all out of his tenderness for humankind.

Time and again, Imam al-Husayn informed the enemy forces that he intended to correct the prevailing un–Islamic atmosphere. He explained that he was responding to many letters of invitation he had received and delegations that had contacted him (Jafri 186). In his lectures and sermons, Imam al-Husayn tried to direct the enemy forces to the Right Path (Majlisi 599). Several days passed in this way. During those days more and more enemy forces reached the plain of Karbala. Although the accounts differ, some reports state that the number of enemy forces reached approximately 30,000 soldiers (Majlisi 654).

From the 7th day of Muharram, the Umayyad forces never let any of the companions of Imam al-Husayn have easy access to water, although the whole region was very close to the river Euphrates. In consequence of this sanction, many men, women, and children on Imam al-Husayn's side had to bear intense thirst. The objective of this psychological and physical pressure was to oblige Imam al-Husayn to succumb to the whims of Yazid through recognition and allegiance.

By the evening of 9th Muharram, Imam al-Husayn had a dialog with 'Umar ibn Sa'd, the chief commander of the Umayyad forces. Imam al-Husayn tried to direct him to the straight path, and suggested him to compensate his losses for 'Umar ibn Sa'd was frightened of having his house and garden confiscated by the Umayyad agents in response to refraining from fighting Imam al-Husayn. Imam al-Husayn wanted to prevent him from initiating the battle for two reasons: (1) He was concerned about the destiny of 'Umar ibn Sa'd and his eternal damnation; and (2) because Imam al-Husayn loathed the commencement of hostilities.

In the late afternoon of the ninth day of Muharram, the Umayyad army under 'Umar ibn Sa'd made a move to start attacking Imam al-Husayn's encampment. Imam al-Husayn dispatched his standard-bearer and step-brother al-'Abbas ibn 'Ali (26–61 AH/ 647–680) to them to take that night as respite, for Imam al-Husayn intended to spend the last night of his life reciting the Holy Qur'an and performing ritual prayers. During that very eve of Ashura, Imam al-Husayn gave his companions the freedom to leave him. This was because he knew very well that he was the only person that was targeted. However, none of his staunch and steadfast companions left him.

The ensuing day witnessed one of the most heart-wrenching massacres the world has ever known. Although it lasted less than a day, its memory has been permanently preserved in the hearts and minds of the Shi'ites of *ahl al-bayt*. In the morning of Ashura, when the two parties stood ready for the battle against each other, Imam al-Husayn prohibited his companions from commencing hostilities (Majlisi 657). Even when an enemy soldier abused Imam al-Husayn and Muslim ibn 'Awsaja (d. 61 AH/ 680) intended to answer the affront, the Imam prevented him from igniting the flame of the battle (Majlisi 657).

In reality, one cannot even speak of an army when referring to Imam Husayn's band of approximately one hundred saintly souls. In military terms, it can only be compared to a troop. The Ummayad forces, however, consisted of four thousand to forty thousand soldiers, representing a veritable army. Instead of a *bona fide* battle, what occurred in Karbala was the slaughter of a small band of ill-equipped and poorly armed men, women, and children, by a large, professional, military force. It was a war crime of the highest order committed against a noble band of believers who posed no military threat to the powerful Ummayad edifice.

Although Imam al-Husayn was already a renowned personality, he introduced himself, expounded upon his lofty aims, and explained why he refused to pledge allegiance in favor of Yazid (Majlisi 658–660). At last, 'Umar ibn Sa'd shot the first arrow toward Imam al-

Husayn's encampment and in this way the Battle of Karbala started (Majlisi 662). Before heading the call of martyrdom, a large number of Imam Husayn's companions recited some *rajaz*es or battlefield poems in which they expressed their sublime goals.[3] On the other hand, few *rajaz*es have been recorded from the Umayyad horde whose shameful actions went down in infamy.

In consequence of Imam al-Husayn's illuminating speeches on the morning of Ashura, some enemy forces deserted the Umayyads in order to side with him. Most notable among the forces who left the Umayyad horde and joined Imam al-Husayn was al-Hurr ibn Yazid al-Riyahi who had earlier blocked his way toward al-Kufah (al-Mufid 504). Having joined Imam al-Husayn, al-Hurr received the warm welcome and appreciation of Imam al-Husayn. As such, al-Hurr has since symbolized last-minute repentance and the attainment of eternal felicity.

On the day of Ashura, almost all the male combatants on Imam al-Husayn's front were put to the sword. Among the slain dignitaries were such renowned figures like 'Ali al-Akbar (33–61 AH/ 652–680), Imam al-Husayn's eldest son who was a true lookalike of the Prophet Muhammad (al-Mufid 510), Habib ibn Mazahir al-Asadi (BH 14–61 AH/ 605–680), who had been a companion of the Prophet Muhammad and the first Imam, 'Ali ibn Abi Talib, along with several other faithful friends. Amongst the Hashimids martyred, there was Imam al-Husayn's step-brother al-'Abbas ibn 'Ali, who was martyred while attempting to bring a limited quantity of water for the thirsty women and children. It is reported that eighteen martyrs belonged to the House of Abu Talib, many of whom were either Imam al-Husayn's step-brothers or his cousins. (For a study on the matchless Ashura companions of Imam al-Husayn, the books developed by the following scholars are helpful: al-Samawi, as a pioneering work; and Hadizadeh-Kashani, for listing them in 17 phases of the Battle of Karbala.) There was at least one baby amongst the Ashura martyrs, as well. In the last minutes of his life, Imam al-Husayn went to the encampment and asked for his baby. No sooner had he lifted the baby in the air, in the hope of eliciting empathy from his opponents, than the innocent child was killed by a three-pronged arrow shot by Harmala ibn Kahil al-Asadi, pinning the lifeless infant to the Imam's arm (al-Mufid 512). According to a recent study on the basis of authentic *ziyarat* texts, Imam al-Husayn appears to have lost three of his little children by arrows shot by the foes (see Soleymani-Boroujerdi).

Despite all the afflictions that Imam al-Husayn endured on Ashura, he strived to guide the enemy forces to the Right Path and called them to repentance. In his last speeches, he reminded his foes that he was the grandson of the Prophet Muhammad and repeated the motives of his movement (Majlisi 657–660; Najmi, *Sokhanan* 232–244). He also pointed out that he had received a vast number of invitations, some of which had been sent by individuals such as Shabath ibn Rib'i, who were standing in the lines of the enemy forces (Najmi, *Sokhanan* 242).

Fearing that his forces would be influenced by Imam al-Husayn's speeches, 'Umar ibn Sa'd ordered his horde to attack him (Majlisi 685–686). At this moment, the enemy forces launched their final offensive against the grossly outnumbered Imam. In spite of all of his suffering, the intensive thirst he was subjected to, and the wholesale massacres of his sons, step-brothers, relatives, and companions, Imam al-Husayn put up a valiant defense. After he had received over 320 wounds, an enemy soldier threw a piece of rock at his forehead and a gush of blood poured out.[4] Trying to wipe the blood off of his forehead, Imam al-Husayn received another arrow in the chest (Majlisi 688–689). Bloodied, battered, and brutalized, Imam al-Husayn dropped to the ground. At that moment, Imam al-Husayn offered a sincere prayer and supplication to Allah (Majlisi 354–356). Finally, 'Umar ibn Sa'd commanded his hordes to slay Imam al-Husayn (Ibn al-A'tham 910–911). Although several members of the enemy forces ran out to kill him, it was reportedly Shimr who beheaded Imam al-Husayn.[5] To add insult to injury, and abomination to infamy, Imam al-Husayn's beheaded body was trampled upon by nearly a dozen cavalry forces (al-Mufid 518).

Soon after slaying Imam al-Husayn in the late afternoon of Ashura, the enemy forces severed the heads of the martyrs so that they could be taken back as trophies to 'Ubayd Allah ibn Ziyad at al-Kufah (al-Mufid 518). After that, the enemy soldiers attacked the encampment and started looting the limited belongings available in the tents (Majlisi 714). They cowardly chased the women and orphaned children across the desert in violation of both Islamic and Arab practice (Majlisi 692–693). The survivors were taken as prisoners of war first to al-Kufah and then to Damascus, the capital of the Umayyad empire (Majlisi 705).

The Impact of Ashura

Imam al-Husayn's movement is synonymous with martyrdom. Ashura has been, *inter alia*, an outstanding symbol of martyrdom. Since over one hundred of Imam al-Husayn's companions were murdered on Ashura, all subsequent martyrs have been compared to them. Evidently, not all of the martyrs of Karbala were slain on the day of Ashura. As such, they can be classified into pre–Ashura, Ashura, and post–Ashura martyrs. The pre–Ashura martyrs of Imam al-Husayn's movement were those who were martyred in the cause of Imam al-Husayn before the day of Ashura. An outstanding personality in this regard was the aforementioned Muslim ibn 'Aqil. While most of the Ashura martyrs were buried at Karbala, some of the post–Ashura martyrs were buried at other places. For example, Imam al-Husayn's daughter Fatimah, commonly known as Ruqayyah, is buried in Damascus, Syria.[6]

Ashura has been regarded as a paradigm. Granted that there were some movements to take revenge on those who committed the crime of slaying Imam al-Husayn and his companions,[7] in recent time, Ashura has proven to be an effective paradigm for liberation movements and revolutions.[8] The Islamic Revolution of Iran (1979) and especially the movement started and led by the late Imam Khomeini (d. 1989) have shown the efficiency of the Ashura paradigm in the present world. Quite repeatedly, the Lebanese resistance leader Sayyid Hasan Nasrallah has expressed that it is the Ashura paradigm which inspires the Shi'ites of Lebanon to struggle against Zionism.

The Battle of Karbala has been packed with numerous lessons for both Muslims and non–Muslims. Since the Umayyad forces treated Imam al-Husayn's front in such an inhuman fashion, the image of Ashura makes every rational individual feel upset and gloomy. There is no justification for slaying an infant in his father's arms; nobody accepts denying women and children access to water. In a nutshell, Ashura has been a manifestation of tyranny and savageness against humanity. Ashura has proved to be a unending lesson: steadfastness in the cause of Allah; being kind to humankind, even to one's enemies; trying to guide others, again even one's enemies, to the right path; and being staunchly loyal to Islam to one's last breath, just to mention some. (For some lessons deduced from the Battle of Karbala, see the books written by Najmi, *Payam-e* Ashura; Delshad-Tehrani; and Qa'emi.)

Literary Expressions of Ashura

As a result of Ashura, and the triumphant martyrdom of Imam al-Husayn and his companions, a large body of literature has been produced. Known in Arabic and Persian as *ziyarat* literature, it includes eulogistical-cum-supplicational texts in Classical Arabic that pilgrims are recommended to read in order to pay homage to Imam al-Husayn.[9] Imam al-Husayn has inspired the most varied types of *ziyarat* texts, both short and long, and both general and time-specific. The fifth Imam, Muhammad al-Baqir (57–114 AH/ 676–733), who was the grandson of Imam al-Husayn, produced many such *ziyarat* text based on his eye-witness account of the tragedy of Karbala. The sixth Imam, Ja'far al-Sadiq (83–148 AH/ 702–765), also produced and promoted eulogies about the tragic death of Imam al-Husayn and his band of brothers. Parenthetically, it must be clarified that no *ziyarat* text has been related from the fourth Imam, 'Ali Zayn al-'Abidin al-Sajjad (33–95 AH/ 653–712), who was one of the sole male survivors of the Battle of Karbala. This was owing to the political pressure the Umayyad and Marwanid tyrants imposed on him and the fact that they are constantly checked and oversaw all his relations and contacts. For more on the subject, scholars and students can refer to my synoptic account of such literature in "The Ziyarat Texts."

Granted that a *ziyarat* performer or pilgrim may read out any such *ziyarat* text in favor of Imam al-Husayn, there are some, commonly-known as *ziyarat* texts for Ashura. As such, the title of *ziyarat* texts for Ashura pertains to those *ziyarat* texts which are recommended to be read during Ashura, although they may also be read at any other times as well.[10] Some comprehensive collections of *ziyarat* texts contain four or five Ashura *ziyarat* texts.[11] Despite this variety, the designation *ziyarat-e Ashura* (for Shi'is) signifies the Ashura *ziyarat* text anthologized in the late Shaykh 'Abbas Qummi's Shi'i prayer compendium *Mafatih al-Jinan* (*Keys to the Gardens of Paradise*). An older version of the same text is available in *Kamil al-Ziyarat* of Ja'far ibn Muhammad ibn Qulawayh al-Qummi.[12] It deserves mention that *ziyarat-e Ashura* was ultimately issued by Allah the Almighty; however, it was first issued for the public by Imam Muhammad al-Baqir. (For some studies in this regard, see Karimi-Qomi; al-Sobhani; Heydarifar; and Tabrizi, *Ziyarat*.)

As a public day of mourning and lamentation, Ashura has produced many forms of commemoration rites and rituals. Throughout history, the day of Ashura has been commemorated across the Muslim world, particularly in Shi'ite communities. The earliest forms of reviving and commemorating Ashura consisted of mourning, shedding tears, and reciting or composing mournful poems. This was the practice of the survivors of the Battle of Karbala. Such was the case of Zaynab al-Kubra, the sister of Imam Husayn. Such was also the case with Rabab bint Imra' al-Qays, one of the wives of Imam Husayn, who was also present at Karbala. Moreover, the sixth Imam, Ja'far al-Sadiq, used to invite poets to his home where he would ask them to compose and/or recite mournful poems —*marthiya*s (elegies)— in commemoration of the martyrdom of Imam al-Husayn. He also explicated the ample and awe-inspiring rewards for performing *ziyarat* for Imam al-Husayn and for shedding tears for the afflictions imposed on him on Ashura. He strongly recommended Muslims to take *ziyarat* trips to Karbala. Moreover, to eternalize Ashura in the Shi'is' historical memory, he instructed one of his companions by the name of Dawud ibn Kathir al-Riqqi, hence by extension all Muslims, to offer salaams to Imam al-Husayn and to invoke the divine curse on the slayers of Imam al-Husayn after each and every instance of drinking water.[13] Therefore, the memory of Imam al-Husayn constantly gets refreshed and revived as many times as any person drinks water. Another *modus operandi* utilized by the Imams was their insistence that Shi'ites perform prostration in ritual prayer on a piece of clay prepared from the soil of Karbala. (For some studies in this regard, see al-Shahristani; al-Musawi al-Khirsan; al-Darwish; and Ja'fari-Shandizi.)

With the gradual decline of the 'Abbasid dynasty in Baghdad, the originally Persian Shi'i Buyid rulers announced Ashura as a public holiday for the first time. It was in the reign of the Buyids in 352 AH/ 963 that the central bazaar of Baghdad was closed on Ashura (Rizvi, *Socio-Intellectual History* 2: 288; al-Shahristani, *Tarikh* 200; Faghihi 30). Perhaps this was due to the practice of closing bazaars on religious occasions. It may also have been inspired by a *hadith* by the eight Imam, 'Ali al-Rida (148–203 AH/ 765–818), which encourages Muslims to desist from working for monetary gain on the day of Ashura (al-Saduq, *'Uyun* 1: 262, hadith No. 53).

Religious and Cultural Commemorations of Ashura

Muslim nations hold various kinds of ceremonies to commemorate Imam al-Husayn's martyrdom. With its culmination on Ashura, Muslims of different cultural background in diverse geographical areas have developed various types of commemorations. Not only are the local dishes served, but also the type of preaching and lamentations differ across the Muslim lands. For example, in the sacred shrine cities of Iraq, such as Karbala and Najaf, well-to-do families serve cooked rice and *qaymah*, while low-income people may offer only strong, sweet tea, yet those of even less financial capacity may welcome the mourners with a glass of water. At the same commemorations held in northern Iran, the mourners will be served *tahchin polo* or cooked rice with chicken. Moreover, it seems to be a common practice, not only among Muslims, but also among some non–Muslims, to serve and consume special dishes on Ashura so as to receive divine grace through such consecrated food. Such Shi'ite-inspired practices are found as far away as Turkey, Albania, Morocco, Indonesia, and China (Seidel).

The commemoration of Ashura is not limited to Muslims. In Muslim countries, there are some followers of other religions, such as Christianity and Zoroastrianism, who take part and/or hold commemorative gatherings in favor of Imam al-Husayn. Examples of such cooperation can be seen in Iran, Iraq, and Lebanon. Even Hindus hold their own rites in India.[14]

To recapitulate, Ashura ceremonies are characterized by lamentation, tears, and recounting the afflictions of the victims of the Battle of Karbala. Regardless of the language or dialect used, ceremonies held in commemoration of Imam al-Husayn may commonly contain some brief biographical accounts, explication of fragments of the Holy Qur'an, with or without interpreting a few *hadiths*, mostly relevant to Ashura and/or Imam al-Husayn, some moral teachings, and recounting the afflictions of Ashura. At the end, either the preacher or another eulogizer who has a moving voice recites some mournful, often heart-rending, poems, viz., *marthiyas* and *nawhas*. This is followed by offering some prayers for the needy and sick people. This is done to make the audience shed tears for the victims of the Battle of Karbala.

The Various Forms of Ashura Literature

The image of Ashura has left a profound and tremendous impact on literature. Here, Ashura literature can roughly be divided into *ziyarat* texts, both *hadith*-based and non-

hadith-based, with the former being either general or occasion or time-specific. *Ziyarat* texts that pertain to the Ashura martyrs may focus either on a single personality (e.g., the *ziyarat* text in favor of Imam al-Husayn's step-brother, al-'Abbas ibn 'Ali) or on a group of martyrs (e.g., the Warith *ziyarat* text). Among the non-*hadith* based *ziyarat* texs, the following can be mentioned: the *ziyarat* text produced by Ibrahim ibn Abi al-Bilad that received the approval of the seventh Imam, Musa al-Kazim (128–183 AH/ 745–799), hence mentioned as the fifth type of general *ziyarat* text in the late 'Abbas al-Qummi's *Mafatih al-jinan*.

Other than the *ziyarat* texts that deserve a separate contribution, there are other types of Ashura literature. In Muslim communities, a prominent form of Ashura literature is poetry. This type of Ashura-oriented literature may be (i) place-oriented, e.g., focusing on the Karbala tragedies, or the Damascus events; (ii) time-oriented, e.g., the events of the eve and day of Ashura, the night of Ashura or even the time the survivors passed across and at al-Kufah or detained at Damascus as captives; or (iii) personality-oriented, that is, the tragic fate of an Ashura martyr may be the hard-core of a poem.[15]

There have been some outstanding poets whose Ashura-oriented works brought them fame. Although it is next to impossible to come up with an exhaustive collection of Ashura poems in such (predominantly Muslim) languages as Arabic, Persian, Turkish, Kurdish, and Urdu, there have been both several collections of Ashura-oriented poems in Persian and Arabic, and quite a great number of individual poems that have appeared (and continue to appear) either in anthologies or in the press. There are also so many individual poems that may be kept as a personal work, without being published, by the poet. Thematically, both Ashura and Ashura-oriented poems deal with the afflictions of Imam al-Husayn and his companions as well as the hardships and denigrations imposed on the survivors of the Ashura tragedy.

Parenthetically, Ashura-oriented literature, in its broadest sense, can, and must, include research literature. In addition to poems, there have been an enormous number of biographies, *maqtals*,[16] political analyses, explications of *ziyarat* texts, and merits that concern paying *ziyarat* to Imam al-Husayn and his companions. In addition to the above, there have been a considerable number of *hadiths* that shed light on the religio-moral issues concerned and have an educative function.

Ashura Literature in Arabic

Ashura-oriented literature in Arabic has the longest history. Included in this category one can find Imam al-Husayn's discourses, the poetry recited by his partisans, as well as the *rajaz*es, the *nawha*s (dirges) and *marthiya*s (elegies) composed by the survivors of the Ashura tragedy, the *ziyarat* texts issued in favor of Imam al-Husayn as well as those of his companions and the survivors who passed away after the Ashura tragedy, and the lamentations composed by Muslims as well as non–Muslims. Lamentations over the afflictions of Imam al-Husayn had been composed long before he was born (Majlisi, Ch. 7; al-Awhadi, Ch. 4). Such lamentations must be included in the wide spectrum of Ashura-oriented literature. Hence, Ashura-oriented literature can be divided into those composed before Ashura, on Ashura, and those that appeared after Ashura.

There have been several anthologies of Ashura-oriented poems in Arabic, both in Classical Arabic and in Iraqi Arabic. Perhaps the most comprehensive of such anthologies is J.

Shubbar's *Adab al-Taff*, divided by century. Other works give various periodizations, e.g., al-'Ashshash divides the Shi'i poetry up to the 3rd/9th century into five periods, of which the third one deals specifically with the Ashura tragedy. Muhammadzadeh divided Arabic poetry on Ashura into five periods, all with the exception of the earliest *marthiya*-composers who were the relations of Imam al-Husayn (Muhammadzadeh, vol. 1). The Lebanese Shi'i scholar Muhammad Mahdi Shams al-Din provides seven locations for lamentations, e.g., Karbala, Damascus, Medina, and so on, plus a four-period division of holding commemorative sessions, namely, the first period received the encouragement of the fifth Imam, Muhammad al-Baqir, and the sixth Imam, Ja'far al-Sadiq, both of whom encouraged people to pay *ziyarat* unto Imam al-Husayn's tomb and shrine, issued *ziyarat* texts, recounted some tragic scenes of the Ashura tragedy, and encouraged poets to compose poems, mainly *marthiya*s. While the first period tried to portray the tragic scenes, the second period sought to inspire people and to stir their sentiments, hence an emotive language is prevalent, with poetic and rhyming prose as its stylistic marker. The third period has witnessed the emergence of *maqtal* books whose concentration has been on the martyrdom account of Imam al-Husayn, a religio-literary-cum-historical phenomenon that has never finished (Shams al-Din, *Rokhdad-e Karbala* 229–274).

Christian Arabs also contributed to Ashura scholarship. Granted that a great majority of them live in Muslim countries and experience no language barrier, they have been active in composing mournful poems and developing books that portray their sincere devotion to Imam al-Husayn. Bolous Salama, Anton Bara, and Sulayman Kattani are just a few to mention. Since the story of Imam Husayn is so tragic and filled with pathos, it has shown great universal appeal to Christian poets and prose writers who consider the third Imam as a tragic, Christ-like figure, who stood for social justice and died in a dignified act of defiance.

Ashura Literature in Persian

Next to Arabic, Persian literature has had several outstanding instances of Ashura-oriented literature. Perhaps the earliest Persian elegy on Imam al-Husayn was the poem composed by Abu al-Hasan Majd al-Din Kasayi Marvazi (341–394 AH/ 952–1003). Of course, one may guess that Ashura-oriented literature must have a background in Persian much older than the time of Kasayi Marvazi; however, the prevailing non–Shi'i political atmosphere might have prevented Shi'is from expressing their intense grief and lamentation. Kasayi Marvazi was the earliest Persian-speaking Twelver Shi'i poet who is credited with having composed a *marthiya* in Persian (Riyahi 35). His *marthiya*, composed in the *musammat* rhythm, is the earliest religious lamentation and obituary (devoted unto Imam al-Husayn) in Persian. (Riyahi 37) Also, his *musammat marthiya* contains the earliest recorded use of the word *maqtal* in Persian, hence suggestive that reciting *maqtal* texts must then be in vogue in Shi'i communities.

Not only Shi'i poets, but also Sunni poets, as well, expressed their grief and sorrow in Persian-poems. Among ancient Sunni poets who composed *marthiya*s, the following can be named: Jalal al-Din Rumi (604–672 AH/ 1207–1273) and Seyf Farghani (d. *ca*. 749 AH/1348) both of whom were Sunni Muslims. Orami displays Sunni Kurdish-speaking poets' works in favor of Imam al-Husayn. This proves that the Ashura tragedy cannot be confined to the Shi'i denomination.

As expected, Persian literature is honoured to have outstanding examples of Ashura literature. Kamal al-Din Ali Muhtasham Kashani's (905–996 AH/ 1499–1587) 12-*band* (12-strophes) poem has proven to exert a profound influence on both Persian and Arabic Ashura-oriented poetry. Kamal al-Din Muhtasham Kashani produced a 12-*band* (12-strophes) poem on the Ashura tragedy that has since proven to be the most widely-quoted *marthiya* in Persian. It has been a truly over-anthologized *marthiya* in Persian; furthermore, over twenty other poets either followed his style or incorporated his lines in their own *marthiya*s. Moreover, in Arabic, the late Sayyid Mahdi Bahr al-'Ulum (1155–1212 AH/ 1742–1797), an outstandingly original Iranian *mujtahid* and Shi'i scholar of Najaf, emulated him, and composed a similar *marthiya* in Classical Arabic that is still regarded as a literary masterpiece, as well. Muhtasham Kashani's *marthiya* has also received several explications. Up to the 13th /19th century, there have appeared at least six explications and commentaries on Muhtasham Kashani's *marthiya* (Mojahedi 87).[17]

The prevailing Shi'i atmosphere in Iran has contributed greatly to Ashura-oriented literature and scholarship. Generally speaking, Ashura-oriented literature in Persian is as old as Persian poetry and no other Persian poetry genre can match it (Mojahedi 13). According to Kafi, Ashura-oriented poetry in Persian can be divided into four periods, namely, the first period, starting from the earliest time to the Safavid era, that is from the 4th/ 10th century to the 10th/ 16th century; the second period, that is the Safavid era (1501–1723), is just when a great number of Shi'i works appeared. The Persian-speaking Husayni poet laureate, the aforementioned Muhtasham Kashani belongs to this era. The Safavid era was significant because the Shi'ah denomination was declared the state denomination, hence it made a much-awaited cradle for Shi'i literature and scholarship. It was in this period that such poets as Baba Faghani Shirazi (d. 925 AH/ 1519), Nezam Estarabadi (d. 970 AH/ 1562), Fayyaz Lahiji (d. 1052AH/ 1642), and Muhammad-Ali Sa'eb Tabrizi (1016–1081 AH/ 1607–1670) flourished. The third period concerns the dynastic eras concerned with Afasharids (1736–1796), Zandids (1750–1794), and Qajarids (1785–1925). The third period reached its pinnacle in the time of the Qajar dynasty who were zealous and attentive to donating money to the sacred shrine cities of Iraq, especially Karbala and Najaf. Some of the renowned Ashura-oriented poets of this period are as follows: Muhammad-Ali Hazin Lahiji (1103–1181 AH/ 1594–1767), 'Asheq Isfahani (1111–1181 AH/ 1699–1767), Sabahi Bidgoli (d. 1207 AH/ 1792), Fat'h Ali Khan Saba (1179–1238 AH/ 1765–1822), the Qajar monarch Fat'h Ali Shah (1185–1250 AH/ 1771–1834), Asif al-Dawlah of India (1188–1212 AH/ 1774–1797), Mirza Mahmoud Fadayi Mazandarani (1200–1282 AH/ 1785–1865), Mirza Asadullah Ghalib Dihlavi (1212–1285 AH/ 1797–1869),[18] Muhammad Ishraq-Asefi (1219–1280 AH/ 1804–1863), Mirza Habibullah Qa'ani Shirazi (1222–1270 AH/ 1807–1853) whose dialog-like *marthiya* is still very famous and widely anthologized,[19] Nowruz Ali Fazel Bastami (1237–1309 AH/ 1821–1891), Mirza Muhammad-Taqi Nayyer Tabrizi (1247–1312 AH/ 1831–1894) whose fame rests on his Persian poetic *maqtal*, generally known as *Ateshkadeh*; Dr. Muhammad Iqbal (1252–1317 Sh/ 1873–1938), and Iraj Mirza (1291–1344 AH/ 1874–1925). The fourth period, our contemporary period, has started from 1300 Sh/ *ca.* 1920 onward, for in 1304 Sh/ 1925 the Qajar dynasty collapsed and the Pahlavi regime got on the scene. It is, of course, within this fourth period that the Islamic Revolution of Iran of 1357 Sh/ 1979 gave a much greater impetus to the current of Ashura-oriented poetry in Iran. In the post–Revolutionary period, the eight years of the Iraqi imposed war against Iran (1360–1368 Sh/ 1980–1988) proved more significant by far in making use of the Ashura movement and the Battle of Karbala as an active and effective motivator to encourage Iranian combatants to resist against the oppressions imposed on Iran.[20]

Parenthetically, *ta'ziyeh* is a dramatic form developed in Iran heavily influenced by and symbolizing a selection of some tragic scenes of the Battle of Karbala over the centuries. Although drama has since been regarded as a major literary form in the Graeco-Roman-based Western culture, it has seldom been regarded thus in Iran. Its popularity in Iran comes from its connection with the Battle of Karbala. However, a number of works have been developed on *ta'ziyeh*, e.g., Chelkowski.

At this point, it is also worthwhile to make mention of some poetic *maqtal*s or martyrdom accounts. Although *maqtal*s are expected to be mainly in prose, with some mournful poems inserted here and there, some Persian-speaking poets depicted the whole Karbala tragedy all in verse form. Examples of such poetic *maqtal*s are the works produced by the following: Jajarmi, Keyvan-Kashani, Sabouni, and Shams-Ansari.

Ashura Literature in Urdu

Marthiya, also recorded as *marsiyah* and *marsiya*, is a hallmark of the impact of Ashura on Urdu literature. In Urdu literature, the genre of *marthiya* has become synonymous with the names of Mir Babr Ali, better known as Mir Anis (*ca.* 1801–1874),[21] and Mirza Salamat Ali, better known as Mirza Dabir (1803–1875). The roots of *marthiya* in the Indian Subcontinent trace back to the Deccan region, with its pioneer being Muzaffar Husain Zamir, better known as Mir Zamir (1771–1888) (Abbas 40). It must be emphasized that it was the Shi'i Adil Shahis at Bijapur in 1489 and quite shortly Qutub Shahis at Golkonda who established a Shi'i state where *marthiya* witnessed its heyday as an elaborate Shi'i ritual genre (Bayat 23; Zaidi, *History*, Ch. 10; Naqvi, *Muslim Religious Institutions* 203–218).

The Urdu *marthiya* is, in some respects, different from Persian and Arabic *marthiya*s. Whereas in Arabic and Persian *marthiya*s are relatively short — so as to keep the audience interested and eager to listen more, typically Urdu *marthiya*s are rather long: they sometimes amount to 300 sixtains (Abbas 40). On the other hand, Urdu *marthiya*s contain nine parts or constituents (Abbas 41). Essentially laments, the Deccani *marthiya*s were those of Sharaf, Imami, Riza, Ghulami, Sayyid Qadir, Hashim 'Ali, and others (Sadiq 204). The Urdu *marthiya*s are characterized by their "naivety, brevity, restraint, and lyricism" (204).

Marthiya-writing has exerted a profound literary-cum-linguistic impact on Urdu. It has broadened the linguistic scope of Urdu and introduced more Arabic and Persian words into it. From a literary point of view, *marthiya* "enriched the style" (Sadiq 212). Despite raising some seemingly-serious criticisms against *marthiya*s, Sadiq maintains that "their most remarkable feature is their universal appeal and intense humanity" (206).

Marthiya also found a home in northern India. The genre *marthiya*, due to its flourishing in the Lucknow region, came to be so highly regarded that it was said that "there is nothing so admirable in Urdu poetry as the *marsiya*" (Bailey 61; Kazimi's ed., 59). It can be expected that composing *marthiya* was in vogue before Mir Anis and Mirza Dabir; Mir Mustahsan Khaliq (1774–1804) was, in fact, already a famous *marthiya* composer. Nevertheless, it was due to the literary contributions of Mir Anis and Mirza Dabir that *marthiya* reached its apex and was honored to be regarded as "the highest form of Urdu verse" (Bailey, 67; Kazimi's ed., 65). Mir Anis and Mirza Dabir were both similar and different. Although both of them were credited to be *marthiya*-composers, Mir Anis was more straightforward, lucid, and picturesque. On the other hand, Mirza Dabir sounded more scholarly and, at times, heavy for the public due mainly to his abiding by the scholarly traditions of his time (Zaidi, *History* 167–168; Trivedi 171).

The impact of Mir Anis never remained confined to Urdu. Granted that Mir Anis proves hard "to manage in English translation" (Zaidi, *Mir Anis* 9), he was lucky to have appeared in English translation. Moreover, several studies have been made on him and his poetry (Zaidi, *Mir Anis* 108–109). It seems to be almost impossible to come up with an exhaustive collection of Mir Anis's *marthiyas*. Such a poet who composed poems in favor of Imam al-Husayn and his companions day and night must have produced a really great number of *marthiyas*. Hence, any collection of his *marthiyas* can and must present just a portion of his poetic output, for his whole work is expected "to contain over 250,000 distiches" (Saksena 128). He also proved to have established a school in Urdu.

Ashura Literature in Sindhi and Balti

Next to Urdu, one may mention Ashura-oriented poems in such languages as Sindhi (Abbas 123–151; Sorley 338–343) and Balti (Sohnen-Thieme, "Six Balti Marsiyas"). Here, it is in order to mention that there have been a number of poets who composed poems in languages that were neither their mother tongues nor a state language. Of those who composed *marthiyas* in Persian, some were residents in Arabic-speaking countries like Iraq. Fuzuli Baghdadi (d. 970 AH/ 1562) composed his Ashura-oriented poems in Arabic, Persian, and Turkish (Kiyani; Mazioglu). In this category, mention must be made that due to the long historical ties between Iranian Shi'is and the sacred shrine cities of Iraq, especially Karbala and Najaf, a number of Iranian and/or Persian-speaking merchants and '*ulama*' have long visited and resided there. They also contributed to the Ashura-oriented literary legacy in Arabic, all in addition to their mother tongues, e.g., Persian. Examples of such poets include the aforementioned Sayyid Mahdi Bahr al-'Ulum, and Ayatullah Muhammad-Husayn Gharawi-Isfahani (1296–1361 AH/ 1879–1942), who was originally Iranian. To adduce but one example, in a recent *ziyarat* (pilgrimage) to Karbala, a Karbala'yi Arab friend gave the present writer an Arabic booklet that contained a four-distich Persian elegy in honor of Imam al-Husayn's sister Zaynab al-Kubra (al-Hallaq al-Ha'iri 19).

Inter-Asiatically and eastward, the Indian Subcontinent proved a cradle for devout Shi'i Ashura-oriented literature. This is no doubt that this was due to the presence of the Persian language there as the court language, especially in the time of the originally Iranian and Shi'i dynasties in the Indian Subcontinent. It must also be mentioned that there have been several Persian-composing poets. Some such poets are as follows: Mirza Asadullah Khan Ghalib (1797–1869), Mirza Salamat Ali "Mirza Dabir" (1803–1875/6), and Dr. Muhammad Iqbal (1873/7–1938), to mention just a few.

Ashura Literature in Spanish

Following in the footsteps of Ibn al-'Abbar (1199–1260), the Andalusian author of *Durar al-simt fi khabar al-sibt*, an Arabic work which chronicles the suffering of *ahl al-bayt* and which includes a *maqtal* of Imam al-Husayn, the Moriscos used to recite Spanish-language Ashura literature. The *Crónica y relación de la esclarecida descendencia xarifa* or *Chronicle and Relation of the Purified Sharifian Descendants* was translated from Arabic into Spanish, using the Latin script, in 1639 CE, supposedly by Ibrahim Taybili, a Morisco living in Tunis. Since one can hardly imagine Umayyad-style Sunnis gathering together to mourn the martyrdom of Imam Husayn, the presence of such works among the Moriscos suggests that a Shi'ite minority had existed in the Iberian Peninsula.

Ashura Literature in Albanian

The Bektashi Order, which is a synthesis of Twelver Shi'ism and Sufism, is found predominantly in Anatolia and the Balkans. Founded in the 13th century by the Persian saint Hajji Bektashi Veli, the *tariqah* places a great deal of importance on the commemoration of Ashura. In Albania, Kosovo, and other parts of the world, the Bektashis recite dirges, poetry, elegies, and eulogies in honor of Imam al-Husayn and his companions. The national poet of Albania, Naim Frashëri (d. 1900), is particularly famous for having authored a moving *qasidah* about the tragedy of Karbala entitled "Qerbelaja." Besides having produced a body of Ashura literature in Albanian, the Bektashis recite prayers and litanies about al-Husayn in the Arabic language.

Ashura Literature in Turkish

In Turkey, the Alevis, who combine Twelver Shi'ism and Sufism, have also produced a body of Ashura literature. Like the Bektashis from Albania, the Alevi Turks mourn with calmness and serenity. Besides collectively praying for the martyrs of Karbala, they listen to a *mersiye* or mournful poem, which is interspersed with poems in praise of the Prophet and Qur'anic recitation. The commemoration of Ashura in Turkey is particularly moving and devoid of extremist elements such as self-mutilation which are found in places like southern Lebanon, Iraq, Pakistan, and India. In Turkey, Ashura is somber and moving, never bloody or violent.

Ashura Literature in Chinese

The Muslim Chinese also commemorate *Ahshula* or 'Ashura as it is pronounced in Arabic, the tenth day of the Islamic month of *Muharram*. Unlike other Sunnis who celebrate Ashura as some sacred day in the lives of prophets such as Adam, Noah, Abraham, and Moses, the Hui Muslims of China actually commemorate the martyrdom of Houssainiyuce or Husayn. Consequently, their imams recite litanies in Mandarin recalling the Battle of Karbala.' The fact that Islam was spread to China by Zaydi Shi'ites and Persian Sufis explains, in part, the commemoration of the martyrdom of Imam Husayn in this particular part of the world.

Ashura Literature in Mazandarani

Usually classified as a Caspian dialect, Mazandarani is typologically a language, with a vast number of Persian words in it, and spoken in northern Iran, just below the Caspian

Sea. With its geographical distribution stretching from around the south of the Caspian Sea to the city of Gorgan, Mazandarani has long been used as a vernacular, and largely unwritten, among the inhabitants of the above region. The present writer has had access to a few Ashura-oriented poems in Mazandarani; however, most of such poems are anthologized in volumes containing Persian *marthiyas* composed by Mazandarani-speaking poets. Mashmouli-Saravi (15: 68–71; 16: 43–44) and Golbabapour are Mazandarani-speaking poets who produced such poems. Unfortunately, it is very hard to come up with a collection of *marthiyas* published entirely in Mazandarani.

Ashura Literature in English

Ashura-oriented literature in English is a different story. It deserves mention that the impact of Ashura on English can be viewed on two planes: linguistic and literary. Linguistically, the word 'Ashura has not been included in such outstanding English dictionaries as Skeat's *Etymological Dictionary* (1910), *The Oxford English Dictionary* (2nd ed., 1989), and Wyld's *Universal Dictionary of the English Language* (1961). It has been absent from Onion's *Dictionary of English Etymology* (1966), Speake's *Dictionary of Foreign Words and Phrases* (1997), and Stevenson and Waite's *Concise Oxford English Dictionary* (12th ed., 2011). It was only in *The New Shorter Oxford English Dictionary* (4th ed., ed. L. Brown [1993]) that the word Ashura has appeared (perhaps for the first time).[22] This being so, *The Oxford English Dictionary* (1933) records three citations for the word "Muharram," the earliest of which is William Bedwell's volume *The Arabian Trudgman* (1615). On the other hand, within the Oxford family of dictionaries, Lewis in his dictionary, *Sahibs*, (s.v. "Moharram") mentions Ashura as 'Ashura-a'.

On the basis of the "semantic field" notion in semantics, one may rightly expect to find at least a single instance of the use of Ashura in the works of those English-speaking merchants, tourists, envoys, and diplomats who visited Karbala, or witnessed the ardently-held Muharram ceremonies in Muslim, and particularly Shi'i, communities. This much is sufficient for mostly general-purpose English dictionaries chiefly published by Oxford University Press. Amongst notable English specialized dictionaries, "Ashura" is recorded in Hughes's *Dictionary of Islam* (1885), Bowker's *Oxford Dictionary of World Religions* (1997), and Esposito's *Oxford Dictionary of Islam* (2003). The word Ashura appears elsewhere, as well. It deserves mention that there is a list of selected 29 words related to Muharram, used in Pakistani English newspapers published between 1987–1991 (Baumgardner, Kennedy, and Shamim 197).

As for Ashura-oriented literature in English, it appears that India must be considered its cradle. On the basis of the existing evidence, the earliest instances of Ashura-oriented literature were the works of Europeans and Britishers who visited or stayed in the Indian Subcontinent. (See, for example, Kidwai, *The Crescent and the Cross*, and Ali, *Observations*.) This is due to two factors. English started to be used "for literary purposes" in the Indian Subcontinent since the 18th century (Shamsie 72) where it was used mainly as a "supra-language" (Mehrotra, "Introduction" 18). With the establishment of English for use in "cultural-written-formal" contexts in India (Mehrotra, "Introduction" 18), it made a good juncture of the English language and literature on the one hand, and Ashura culture on the other hand.[23]

Although no chronology or documented bibliography of Ashura literature has ever been worked out,[24] the English poems on Ashura, especially those composed by India-residing Britishers, reveal the impact of Ashura on them. Then come those non–Muslim Indians who composed a few Ashura-oriented poems, e.g., Sarojini Naidu (1879–1949). Granted that one of the major incentives behind imposing English on the people of the Indian Subcontinent was to force them to succumb to the British rule (Paranjape, "Introduction" ii), later on globalization of the English language has proved to be an asset for internationalization of Ashura-oriented literature. It seems that it has been within the Indian Subcontinent context that the earliest pieces of Ashura-oriented literature emerged.

Ashura-oriented literature in English seems to be as old as the 17th century. The earliest mentions of the word *Ashura* can be traced back to 1600 when the earliest European delegations visited Muslim lands and encountered the Ashura ceremonies. To give an instance, the German scholar Adam Olearius (1599–1671) mentions Ashura as *Aschur* in his book *The Travel of Olarius in Seventeenth-Century Persia.*[25]

Observations indicate that the earliest instances of Ashura-oriented poems in English were simply the reflections of non–Muslims on the whole tragic event. In this capacity, such laments or elegies were merely mournful reflections, bearing little indications of the poet's knowledge of Islamic articles of faith and early Islamic history. For example, the late Sarojini Naidu was born and raised at Hyderabad, India, had a relatively good grasp of Islamic history. According to Naravene, Naidu "had a particularly close rapport with Islam" (89) and was informed of Muharram (33, 87). Singh wrote that Naidu "imbibed the best of the Hindu and Muslim cultures" (*Six Women Poets* 57) while Paranjape said that "[h]er special interest was Islamic culture and thought" (Paranjape, *Sarojini Naidu* xxvii). Paranjape explains that Naidu wrote about "[t]he torch light procession of the Moharram" in one of her letters dated 8 June 1911 (*Sarojini Naidu* 53). Naidu composed two poems: "The Imam Bara (Of Lucknow)" (*The Sceptred Flute* 152–153; Fakhr-Rohani, ed. Ashura *Poems in English* 1: 41–42) and "The Night of Martyrdom" (Naidu, *The Feather of the Dawn* 6; also available in Lallijee, ed., *The Martyrdom of Imam Husayn* 59–60; Fakhr-Rohani, ed., Ashura *Poems in English* 1: 40; Khurshed, *Imam Husayn* 155).

Unfortunately, Naidu's explanatory footnote to her poem "Imam Bara" is defective. Muslims "of the Shi'ah Community" never "celebrate," but commemorate, "the tragic martyrdom of 'Ali, Hassan ... during the mourning month of Moharram" (Naidu, *The Sceptred Flute* 153). Mourning commemorations for the First Shi'i Imam, 'Ali ibn Abi Talib, are held on 19–23 Ramadan, not in Muharram. Furthermore, such lamentation ceremonies for the second Shi'i Imam al-Hasan are held by the end of the Arabic month Safar. Naidu's poem "The Night of Martyrdom" has a footnote that relates the event and scene described to "the ninth of the mourning month of Moharram" (Naidu, *The Feather of the Dawn* 6). This is not true. The scene depicted pertains to the situation of Imam al-Husayn's camp on the eve of the 11th of Muharram, namely, the evening of Ashura', precisely when the Umayyad horde had attacked, looted, and burnt Imam al-Husayn's front and encampment. The military clashes took place all on Ashura, the 10th of Muharram, not on the "ninth" day.

There is also another type of Ashura-oriented literature that can be categorized as instances of such literature in English translation. In this category, one may find English translations of *marthiyas*[26] *ziyarat* texts,[27] and *maqtal*-texts.[28] Besides the above category of Ashura-oriented literature in English translation, there is a category of such literature produced originally in English. Included in this category, there are all sorts of materials that have something to do with Ashura, Imam al-Husayn, and the Battle of Karbala, provided that they are written originally in English. Included in such a category, there are graduate-level works, both MA theses and PhD dissertations,[29] biographies,[30] analytical reflections,[31] journal articles,[32] encyclopedic articles,[33] and dictionary entries.[34] To the above, lamentation poems must be added, composed by both Muslims[35] and non–Muslims.[36] No doubt, such lamentations may be episode-specific[37] or an overall reflection.[38] Rather than merely repeating poems produced by poets of the past in their original languages or reciting translations of such works, Ashura literature remains a living tradition of religious expression. An interesting phenomenon is the rise of more modern forms of Ashura literature produced by Muslim converts from the West such as the epic poetry of Shaykh 'Ali Abu Talib, an African American revert to Shi'ism. If the Shaykh creates Ashura poetry with hip-hop influences; other authors and artists like Malik Shahid and XXX have produced Ashura-infused rap songs both with and without music. Increasingly, youtube.com serves as a repository of chants, songs, and elegies on the subject of Ashura and its protagonists.

Conclusions

The above sketch indicates the uniqueness and universality of Ashura-oriented poetry. As stated elsewhere, Ashura poetry can be composed by any devout poet and can appear in any language.[39] There are still some shortcomings about Ashura literary scholarship. It has not had any international academic forum particularly in the format of a research journal in English, and there has seldom been any literary and/or critical theory suitable for Ashura and Ashura-oriented literature. Moreover, despite the merits of Ashura-oriented literature, it has seldom been subject of comparative literary scholarship. It still lacks a comprehensive literary history (Hakimi 32). It is strange, if neither a question nor a pity, that Ashura literature in English has not been recognized as a type of literature in countries where English has become the dominant language.[40] Granted that Ashura-oriented literature, particularly in its genre of *ziyarat* texts, contains all the features of great world classics, it has seldom been so regarded, let alone its specifications being laid down or dissected. Considering the impact that it has had on history, literature, and culture, Ashura represents one of the most powerful images in Islam. Although Imam al-Husayn was martyred, his memory has never died. Since, for many Shi'ites, every day is Ashura and every place is Karbala, the image of Ashura forms part of the living legacy of Islam.

Chapter Notes

1. I express my gratitude to the following for their help while this chapter was in gestation: Morteza Vafi, Abdol-Hoseyn Taleie, Morteza Haerizadeh, Abolfazl Hafeziyan, Haydar al-Mankoushi, and Behdad Harsini. I am grateful to Dr. John Andrew Morrow for his insightful and educative comments, additions, and suggestions. Needless to say, my family, particularly my wife, deserve my most sincere thanks for making home a fitting environment to develop this contribution. No doubt, words fail to express my gratitude to them all.

2. For a chapter-length treatment of *Jahiliyyah*, see Armstrong, *Muhammad*, Ch. 2. The citation in question is found in a tradition from the Eighth Imam, 'Ali al-Rida, when he addressed al-Rayyan ibn Shabib on the first day of Muharram. The *hadith* is quoted in Shaykh al-Saduq's [d. 381 AH/991] *al-Amali* 206, pertaining to the sermon No. 27, *hadith* No. 5, al-Saduq recounted on Friday 1 Muharram 368 AH/978. The same *hadith* is quoted in al-Saduq's *'Uyun akhbar al-Rida* 1: 262, *hadith* No. 54.

3. A great majority of books devoted to Imam al-Husayn and the Battle of Karbala contain the *rajazes* vociferated by the martyrs of Imam al-Husayn's front. For a collection and analysis of such *rajazes*, see Foadiyan and Hasanlouyi, *Sharh va Tahlil-e Rajazha*, and Effati, *Rajazha-ye Qahramanan-e 'Ashura.'*

4. This is on the basis of a piece of *hadith* related from the Fifth Imam, Muhammad al-Baqir, qtd. in Majlisi, *Jala al-'Uyun* 687.

5. It is also reported that Khawli ibn Yazid al-Asbahi committed this most horrible crime; see Ibn al-A'tham, *al-Futuh* 911; and Majlisi, *Jala al-'Uyun* 689.

6. Most of the books on the Battle of Karbala render a list of the Ashura martyrs. However, more information in this regard can be found in the following sources: al-Samawi, *Ibsar al-'Ayn fi Ansar al-Husayn*; al-Qurayshi, *al-Balighun al-Fath fi Karbala'*; Shams al-Din, *Yaran-e Husayn 'Alayh al-Salam*; Amini, *Yaran-e Paydar-e Imam Husayn*; and Musawi, *Shohada-ye Enqelab-e Karbala'*.

7. The Penitents' (*Tawwabun*'s) movement is a case in point for which Jafri's *Origins* is a good read in English.

8. Throughout history, tyrants were watchful and scared of the lessons inferable from Imam al-Husayn's movement; hence, rulers such as the Umayyads, Marwanids, 'Abbasids, and recently the Baath Party of Iraq, and particularly Saddam Husayn, were profoundly anxious about any practical lesson to be taken from the case of the Battle of Karbala. For this reason, Imam al-Husayn's Sacred Sanctuary was devastated in the past by the 'Abbasid rulers Harun al-Rashid (b. 766, r. 786–890) and al-Mutawakkil (b. 822, r. 847–861) and, in recent time, by Saddam Husayn in 1990.

9. The word *ziarat* (as recorded in the *OED* [2d. ed., 1989] and in *SOED* [6th ed., 2007]) is used as a noun. The *OED* indicates no part of speech for it, however. It is spelled as *ziyarat* in Bowker's *Oxford Dictionary of World Religions* (1997) and as *ziyarah* in Esposito's *Oxford Dictionary of Islam* (2003). Although an act of *ziyarat* is expected to be performed *in situ*, it can be achieved *in absentia* or by proxy.

10. The *ziyarat* texts issued in favor of the twelve Imams and, in the present case, those that concern the Third Imam, al-Husayn, may receive various classifications. One such classification is to classify them as general (*mutlaqah*) vs. occasion- or time-specific (*mu'aqqatah*). Whereas the general *ziyarat* texts can be read out at any given time, the occasion-specific ones have their own, most recommended, time for being read out. The '*Ashura*' *ziyarat* text belongs to the second category, although the Fifth Imam, Muhammad al-Baqir, recommended one of his companions by the name of 'Alqama ibn Muhammad al-Hadrami to read out the '*Ashura*' *ziyarat* text each and every day, if possible (See Majlisi, *Tuhfa al-Za'ir* 426).

11. Al-Turbati al-Karbala'yi lists nine *Ashura ziyarat* texts divided into five categories. It seems that there must be several occasion-specific *ziyarat* texts whose most recommended time of being read out is Ashura.

12. The '*Ashura*' *ziyarat* text has received a number of explications. Three such explications are as follows: Abu al-Ma'ali Sharif ibn Muhammad Ibrahim, *Ziyarat-e 'Ashura'*; Abu al-Fazl Tehrani, *Shafa al-sudur fi sharh ziyara al-ashur*; and Tabrizi, *Barrasi-ye sanad-e ziyarat-e 'Ashura'*, to mention only a few. It seems that Abu al-Fazl Tehrani's explication is the best one ever published.

13. Al-Majlisi, ed., *Bihar al-anwar* 10: 303, *hadith* No. 16; Ibn Qulawayh al-Qummi, *Kamil al-ziyarat*, Najaf ed. 106, *hadith* No. 1.

14. Examples of such inter-faith Ashura-oriented rituals and commemoration can be found in Zaman 138; Fruzzetti, 106; Rizvi, *Socio-Intellectual History* 2: 334; and Naqvi and Kishan Rao, eds., in which the entire book is devoted to five examples in this regard. Ahmad, *Studies in Islamic Culture* 157–158, indicates the Hindus' veneration for Imam al-Husayn.

15. It seems appropriate to make a distinction, however rough, between Ashura literature vs. Ashura-oriented literature. While the former is expected to deal exclusively with the events of the day of Ashura, the latter may take in whatever has anything to do with Imam al-Husayn's movement, both before and after Ashura. See Fakhr-Rohani's papers, "Ashura Literature" and "Reflections on Ashura-Oriented Literature."

16. For a study of the *maqtal* texts, see Fakhr-Rohani, "The *Maqtal* Genre."

17. For the influence of Muhtasham Kashani, see Dargahi, Anvari and Tale'i, *Shuresh dar Khalq-e 'Alam*. K. G. Ruffle's MA thesis is also devoted to Muhtasham Kashani.

18. For a life and career of Ghalib, see Russel, ed., *The Oxford India Ghalib*; for an anthology of Ghalib's poems in Persian, see Kiyani, ed., *Divan-e Ghaleb-e Dehlavi*, where the *marthiyas* can be found on pp. 436–438.

19. For its English translation, see Browne, *A Literary History of Persia* 4: 177–181. Browne's translation has some mistakes, entirely unexpected of him because of his knowledge of Persian literature.

20. Most modern, and especially recent, anthologies of Persian Ashura-oriented poems contain pieces that reveal the impression of Ashura on post-revolutionary and war-time attitudes; see, for example, Kafi 666–716. Azar roughly divides Persian Ashura-oriented poetry into three phrases or stages, without any more elaboration (*Shokuh-e Eshq* 15–16).

21. On the life of Mir Anis, see Zaidi, *Mir Anis*.

22. In mid–2009, I received an email from Dr. John Simpson, the esteemed chief editor of the forthcoming *Oxford English Dictionary*, 3d. ed., to contribute a definition of Ashura; I did so with alacrity.

23. It was on this premise that I chose India for collecting data and instances of Ashura literature in English.

24. I am delighted to have made a pioneering effort in the brand new field of Ashura literature in English. A portion of the materials I have gathered and edited can be found in Fakhr-Rohani, ed., '*Ashura*' *Poems in English, Explained and Annotated* (2007; 2d. ed., 2011). However, one of the problems is that some poems lack a date and there is hardly any reliable biography for some poets.

25. The word Ashura appears near footnote 27 in the same text. I am grateful to Dr. Lance Jenott for his explanations by email.

26. For example, Browne's translations of some fragments of Muhtasham Kashani's *marthiya* as well as that of Qaani in his *Literary History of Persia* 4: 175–177, and 180–181; D. Matthews's *Battle of Karbala'*, 34–86, includes a selection of Mir Anis's *marthiyas*; Abbas, *The Immortal Poetry and Mir Anis*; and Sohnen-Thieme, "Six Balti Marsiyas."

27. Unlike Qur'an translations into English, English translations of the *ziyarat* texts in favor of Imam al-Husayn and/or his martyred companions seem to be a recent phenomenon. While the Holy Qur'an has been translated into English by some non–Muslim translators (e.g., Arberry, Nicholson, and Palmer), the translators of the *ziyarat* texts seem to be exclusively Shi'i Muslims. Some such translations are as follows: Ibn Qulawayh, *Kamilal-ziyarat*, trans. Al-Husayni al-Milani; al-Qummi, *Mafatih al-jinan*, trans. B. Shahin, both of which contain such *ziyarat* texts in English translation.

28. *Maqtal* means, *inter alia*, a martyrdom account. By extension, it has come to be applied to the case of the martyrdom accounts of the Ashura martyrs. Some *maqtal* texts in English translation are as follows: Abu Mikhnaf, *Kitab maqtal al-Husayn*; Howarth, *The Twelver Shi'ah as a Muslim Minoriy in India*, contains several *maqtal* fragments as presented in some Shi'i preachings delivered at Hyderabed, A. P., India; and 'Abdal-Razzaq al-Muqarram, *Maqtal al-Husain: Martyrdom Epic of Imam Husain*, www.shiabooks.org/urdn/maqtal-al-Husain.pdf.

29. There have been several theses and dissertations that deal with the Ashura Battle of Karbala, e.g., Hylen, *Husayn, the Mediator*; S. Akber Hyder, *Reliving Karbala* (originally a Ph.D. dissertation); Ruffle, "Verses Dripping the Blood"; and Ayoub, *Redemptive Suffering in Islam*.

30. Although it sometimes proves very different to make a distinction between a *maqtal* and a biography of Imam al-Husayn, a *maqtal* seems to focus on tragic scenes, while a biography tends to give an overall picture of the life and career of Imam al-Husayn. Some biographies are as follows: Mir Ahmed Ali, *Husain: The Saviour of Islam*; Ali, *Life of Imam Husain: The Saviour*; Mazahir, '*Ashura': The Martyrdom of Imam Husayn*; and al-Qarashi, *The Life of Imam Husain*.

31. Such analytical reflections can be divided broadly in to two categories: (1) those written by (chiefly Shi'i) Muslims that have an insider's view, e.g., Jafri, *The Origins and Early Development of Shi'a Islam* (1979/2000); Kazimi, *The Blood of Husayn* (2011); Aghaie, *The Martyrs of Karbala'* (2004); Ayati, *Barrasi-ye Tarikh-e 'Ashura'* and its English version, *A Probe in to the History of 'Ashura'* (1984); al-Badri, *al-Husayn* (2009); Rizvi, *Undrestanding Karbala'* and *Four Californian Lectures*; and (2) those written by non–Muslims, Howarth, *The Twelver Shi'ah as a Muslim Minority in India*; and Hylen, *Husayn, the Mediator*.

32. See, for example, Aghaie, "The Karbala Narrative;" Ruffle, "May Fatimah Gather Our Tears"; and Nakash, "An Attempt to Trace the Origin of the Rituals of 'Ashura'."

33. See, for example, the article "'Ashura'" in *Shorter Encyclopaedia of Islam* which depicts Ashura from a purely non–Shi'i perspective, without making even a single reference to the Battle of Karbala and Imam al-Husayn.

34. Such dictionary articles can be divided according to those that portray a fairly acceptable view, e.g., "'Ashura'" in *The Oxford Dictionary of World Religions*, edited by Bowker (1997), and those that are flawed for not giving a Shi'i perspective, e.g., "'Ashura'" in *Dictionary of Islam*, by Hughes (1885/1999).

35. Examples of (chiefly) Muslim lamentations are as follows: A. Khorasanee's poem "Husain of Karbala,'" cited in Lalljee, *The Martyrdom of Husain* (1977); Tyro's poems in *The Manifestations of the Light Pristine* (1996); and Taki's *The Epitome of Sacrifice* (2010).

36. Examples of such poems are those composed by Hari Kumar, Russel, and Wells, anthologized in Fakhr-Rohani, ed., '*Ashura' Poems in English*, 1 (2011).

37. For example, Tyro's poem, "Hurr's Repentence" in his anthology *The Manifestations* 34–35; and A. J. Chapman's "Ali-Asghar," anthologized in Khurshed, ed., *Imam Husain* 143–152, and quoted with annotations in Fakhr-Rohani, ed., '*Ashura' Poems in English* 1: 88–97.

38. For example, A. D. Russel's poem "The Martyr of Karbala'," anthologized in Khurshed's *Imam Husain* 136–140; and quoted with annotations in Fakhr-Rohani, ed., '*Ashura' Poems in English* 1: 55–59.

39. For characteristics of Ashura-oriented literature, see Shams al-Din, *Rukhdad-e Karbala'*; Kazimi, *The Blood of Husayn*, Ch. 16; Muhammadzadeh, ed., *Daneshnameh* 1: 32–33; id., "She'r-e Hoseyni dar

Masir-e Tarikh" 432, 439, and 452; and Fakhr-Rohani, ed., *'Ashura' Poems in English* 1: 28–31; id., "Some Traits of 'Ashura' Literature"; id., "'Ashura' Literature"; id., "Reflections on 'Ashura'-Oriented Literature"; and Mohaddethi, *Adab-e Al Allah* 72–83, and 114–142.

40. See, for example, Paranjape (ed.), *English Studies, Indian Perspective*; Mehrotra (ed.), *An Illustrated History of Indian Literature*; Patke, *Postcolonial Poetry in English*; Boehmer, *Colonial and Postcolonial Literature*; and de Souza, ed., *Early Indian Poetry in English*, where there is no mention of Islamic, let alone Ashura, literature.

Works Cited and Consulted

Abbas, Syed Ghulam. *The Immortal Poetry and Mir Anis*. Karachi: Majlis-e-Milli, 1983.

'Abedi, Syed Taghi, ed. *Mushaf-e-farsi of Mirza Dabir*. New Delhi: Shahid, 2005.

Abu al-Ma'ali Sharif ibn Muhammad Ibrahim. *Ziyarat-e 'Ashura'*. Trans. Sayyid Muhammad-Reza Ghiyathi-Kermani. Qom: Daftar-e Entesharat-e Islami, 2008.

Abu Mikhnaf, Lut ibn Yahya ibn Sa'id. *Kitab maqtal al-Husayn: Narrative of the Martyrdom of al-Husayn*. Trans. Hamid Mavani. Montreal, Canada: Privately Printed, 2002.

Aghaie, Kamran Scott. "The Karbala' Narrative: Shi'i Political Discourse in Modern Iran in the 1960s and 1970s." *Journal of Islamic Studies* 12:2 (2001): 151–176.

_____. *The Martyrs of Karbala'*. Seattle: University of Washington Press, 2004.

Ahmad, Azia. *Studies in Islamic Culture in the Indian Environment*. Oxford: Oxford University Press, 1964.

Ahmad, Imtiaz, ed. *Ritual and Religion among Muslims in India*. New Delhi: Manohar, 1981.

Ali, Gulam Abbas. *Life of Imam Husain: The Saviour*. 1931. Rpt. Mumbai: Haidery Kutub Khana, n.d.

Ali, Meer Hasan. *Observation on the Mussulmauns of India*. London: Parbury, Allen, 1832.

Amini, al-Najafi, 'Abd al-Husayn al-. *Siratuna wa Sunnatuna*. Tehran: Haydariyyeh, 1965.

Amini, Muhammad-Hadi. *Yaran-e paydar-e Imam Husayn*. Tehran: Sa'eed, 1982.

Araki, 'Abd al-Nabi. *Mabahethi Piramoun-e Ziyarat-e 'Ashura'*. Ed. Naser Baqeri-Bidhendi, Qom: Jamkaran Mosque, 2010.

Armstrong, Karen. *Muhammad: Prophet of Our Time*. London: Harper Perennial, 2006.

Ashshash, al-Tayyib al-. *al-Shi'r al-tashayyu' ila al-qarn al-thahith al-tasi'*. Bayrut: Dar al-Gharb al-Islami, 1997.

Awhadi, Amin al-. *Hazin al-dama' 'ala qatil al-'abara*. Tehran: Tour-e Tehran, 2011.

Ayati, Muhammad-Ibrahim. *Barresi-ye tarikh-e 'Ashura'*. Tehran: Saduq, 2003.

_____. *A Probe into the History of 'Ashura'*. Trans. Amir Ali Aini. Karachi: Islamic Seminary Publications, 1984.

Ayoub, Mahmoud. *Redemptive Suffering in Islam*. The Hague: Mouton, 1978.

Azar, Amir Esma'il, ed. *Shokouh-e 'eshq: tarikh va she're 'Ashura'*. Tehran: Sokhan, 2010.

Badri, Sayyid Sami al-. *al-Husayn fi muwajaha al-dilal al-umawi*. 2d. ed. Baghdad: Dar Tur Sinin, 2009.

Bailey, Thomas Graham. *A History of Urdu Literature*. Calcutta: Asia, 1932.

_____. *A History of Urdu Literature*. 1932. Rpt. Ed. Muhammad Reza Kazimi. Karachi: Oxford University Press, 2008.

Bara, Anton. *al-Husayn fi al-fikr al-masihi*. 5th ed. Bayrut: Dar al-'Ulum, 2009.

Baumgardner, Robert J., ed. *The English Language in Pakistan*. Karachi: Oxford University Press, 1993.

_____, Audrey E. H. Kennedy, and Fauzia Shamim, "The Urduization of English in Pakistan." *The English Language in Pakistan*. Ed. Robert J. Baumgardner. 83–203.

Bayat, Ali. "Barrasi-ye now'-e adabi-ye marsiyeh dar zaban-e urdu." *Pazhouhesh-e Adabiyat-e Moaser-e Jahan* 60 (Winter 2011): 21–39.

Boehmer, Elleke. *Colonial and Postcolonial Literature: Migrant Metaphors*. 2d. ed. Oxford: Oxford University Press, 2005.

Bowker, John, ed. *The Oxford Dictionary of World Religions*. Oxford: Oxford University Press, 1997.

Browne, Edward G. *A Literary History of Persia*. Vol. 4. Cambridge: Cambridge University Press, 1924.

Chelkowski, Peter, ed. *Ta'ziyeh: Ritual and Drama in Iran*. New York: New York University Press, 1979.

Crónica y relación de la esclarecida descendencia xarifa: un maqtal chií en castellano escrito por un morisco exiliado del siglo XVII. Ed. José Francisco Cutillas Ferrer. Alicante: Universidad de Alicante, 1998.

Dargahi, Husayn, Muhammad-Jawad Anwari, and Abul-Hoseyn Tale'i. *Shuresh dar khalq-e 'alam*. Tehran: Ershad, 1994.

Darwish, Amin Habib al-. *Turbah al-Husayn*. Bayrut: Dar al-Mahajjah al-Bayda', 2009.

Delshad-Tehrani, Mustafa. *Madraseh-ye Hoseyni*. 31st ed. Tehran: Darya, 2008.

De Souza, Eunice, ed. *Early Indian Poetry in English: An Anthology: 1829–1947*. New Delhi: Oxford University Press, 2005.

De Tassy, Garcin. *Muslim Festivals in India and Other Essays*. Trans. and ed. M. Waseem. Delhi: Oxford University Press, 1995. (French orig., 1831.)

Effati, Qodrat. *Rajazha-ye qahramanan-e 'Ashura'* . Qom: Jam-e Javan, 2012.

Esposito, John L., ed. *The Oxford Dictionary of Islam*. New York: Oxford University Press, 2003.

Faghihi, Ali-Asghar. *Tarikh-e al-e Buyeh / The History of the Buyids*. Tehran: SAMT, 1999.

Fakhr-Rohani, Muhammad-Reza. "*'Ashura'* Literature: Its Status amongst the World Literatures and for Comparative Studies." *Hussein Revivalism* 8 (2011): 32.

_____. "The *Maqtal* Genre: A Preliminary Inquiry and Typology." *Payam-e Mehr*, 1.2 (October–December 2009): 114–130.

_____. "Reflection on *'Ashura'*-Oriented Literature." *Message of Thaqalayn* 12.3 (Autumn 2011): 95–101.

_____. Rev. of *al-Maqtal al-Husayni al-m'thur* by M.-J. al-Tabasi. *Third Frame: Language, Culture and Society* 2.3 (2009): 207–210.

_____. "Some Traits of *'Ashura'* Literature." *Hussein Revivalism* 6 (2011): 30–31.

_____. "The *Ziyarat* Texts Issued in Favor of Imam al-Husayn." *Hussein Revivalism* 9 (2012): 12.

_____, ed. *'Ashura' Poems in English, Explained and Annotated*. Karbala': Imam al-Husayn's Sacred Sanctuary, 2007.

_____, ed. *'Ashura' Poems in English, Explained and Annotated*. 2d. ed. 2 vols. Karbala': Imam al-Husayn's Sacred Sanctuary; Qom: al-Mustafa International University, 2011.

Foadiyan, Hoseyn, and Fatemeh Hasanlouyi. *Sharh wa tahlil-e rajazha*. 2d. ed. Tehran: Azhang, 1389 Sh/ 2011.

Fruzzetti, Lina M. "Muslim Rituals: The Household Rites vs. the Public Festivals in Rural India." *Ritual and Religion among Muslims in India*. Ed. Imtiaz Ahmad. 91–112.

Gibb, H. A. R., and J. H. Kramers, eds. *Shorter Encyclopedia of Islam*. Leiden: E. J. Brill, 1953.

Golbabapour, Muhammad-Kazem. *Mourinomeh*. n.p., 1970.

Guenther, Sebastian. "*Maqatil*-Literature in Medieval Islam." *Journal of Arabic Literature* 25 (1994): 192–212.

Hadizadeh-Kashani, Muhammad-Reza. *Shohada-ye Karbala'*. Tehran: Faraz-e Andisheh-ye Sabz, 2010.

Ha'eri-Tehrani, 'Abbas. *Masa'il al-turbatiyyah*. Ed. Sayyid Husayn Razawi-Ha'eri. Qom: Tuba-ye Mohabbat, 2010.

Hakimi, Muhammad-Reza. "Hemasehha-ye maktabi." *Kheimeh* 62 (March 2010): 32–33.

Halm, Heinz. *Shi'ism*. 2d. ed. New York: Columbia University Press, 2004.

Heydarfar, Majid. *Manshur-e Neynawa: Sharh wa Tafsiri bar Ziyarat-e 'Ashura'*. Qom: Jamkaran Mosque, 1998.

Howarth, T. M. *The Twelver Shi'ah as a Muslim Minority in India: The Pulpit of Tears*. London: Routledge, 2005.

Hughes, Thomas P. *A Dictionary of Islam*. London: W.H. Allen, 1885. Rpt. New Delhi: Munshiram Manoharlal, 1999.

Hyder, Syed Akbar. *Reliving Karbala': Martyrdom in South Asian Memory*. New York: Oxford University Press, 2006.

Hylen, Torsten. *Husayn, the Mediator*. Uppsala: Uppsala Universitet, 2007.

Ibn A'tham al-Kufi, Ahmad ibn Ali. *al-Futuh*. Trans. Muhammad ibn Ahmad Mostowfi Herawi. Ed. Ghulam-Reza Tabatabaie-Majd, 2001. Rpt. Tehran: Elmi-Farhangi, 2008.

Ibn Qulawayh al-Qummi, Ja'far ibn Muhammad. *Kamil al-ziyarat*. Ed. 'Abd al-Husayn al-Amini al-Tabrizi. Najaf: al-Murtadawiya, 1935.

_____. *Kamil al-ziyarat*. English Trans. Sayyid Mohsen al-Husayni al-Milani. Miami: Shiabooks.ca, 2008.

Ibn Manzur al-Afriqi, Muhammad. *Lisan al-'arab*. 2 vols. Bayrut: al-A'lami, 2005.

Jafri, Syed Husain Mohammad. *The Origins and Early Development of Shi'a Islam*. Karachi: Oxford University Press, 2000.

Jajarmi, Isma'il. *Setareh-ye Sevvom*. Gorgan: Peyk-e Reyhan. 2005.

Kafi, Ghulam-Reza. *Sharh-e manzumeh-ye zohr*. Tehran: Mojtama' Farhangi-ye 'Ashura', 2008.

Kattani, Sulayman. *al-Imam al-Husayn fi hullah al-barfir*. Qom: Dar al-Kitab al-Islami, 1990.

Karimi-Qomi, Hoseyn. *I'tebar-e Ziyarat-e Ashura wa Raf'-e Barkhi az Shobahat*. Qom: Markaz-e Feqhi-ye A'immeh-ye At'har, 2008.

Kazimi, Muhammad Reza. *The Blood of Husayn*. Karachi: Literama, 2011.

Keyvan-Kashani, Mahdi. *Divan-e Keyvan-e Kashani*. Kashan: Hamgam ba Hasti, 2004.

Khazali, Ensiyeh. *Taswir-e 'asr-e jaheli dar Qur'an*. Tehran: Amir Kabir, 2010.

Khurshed, M. H., ed. *Imam Husayn: The Leader of the Entire Humanity.* 2d. ed. Mumbai: World Islamic Network, 2003.

Kidwai, Abdul Rahim. *The Crescent and the Cross: Image of the Orient in English Literature up to 1832.* Aligarh: Aligarh Muslim University Press, 1997.

King, Bruce. *Modern Indian Poetry in English.* Rev. ed. New Delhi: Oxford University Press, 2001.

Kiyani, Mahmoud, ed. *Divan-e ghaleb-e dehlavi.* Tehran: Rowzaneh, 1998.

Lalljee, Yusuf, ed. *The Martyrdom of Imam Husain: Grandson of the Holy Prophet.* Bombay: Author, 1977.

Lane, Edward W. *An Arabic-English Lexicon.* London, 1874. Rpt. Bayrut: Librairie du Liban, 1980.

Lewis, Ivor. *Sahibs, Nabobs, and Boxwallas: A Dictionary of the Words of Anglo-India.* Delhi: Oxford University Press, 1991.

Majlisi, Muhammad-Baqir. *Jala al-'uyun: tarikh-e chaharda ma'sum.* Tehran: Andishe-ye Sabz, 2008.

Majlisi, Muhammad-Baqir al-, ed. *Bihar al-anwar.* 110 vols. Ed. Muhammad-Baqir Behboudi. Tehran: al-Maktabah al-Islamiyyah, n.d.

Majlisi, Muhammad-Baqir. *Tuhfa al-za'ir.* Qom: Imam al-Hadi Institute, 2007.

Malik, Hafeez, and Yuri V. Gankovsky, eds. *The Encyclopedia of Pakistan.* Karachi: Oxford University Press, 2006.

Mashkour, Muhammad-Jawad. *A Comparative Dictionary of Arabic, Persian, and the Semitic Languages.* 2 vols. Tehran: Bonyad-e Farhang-e Iran, 1978.

Mashmouli-Saravi, Ahmad. *Asrar-e Hoseyn.* Vol. 15. Sari: Mazandaran, 1995.

_____. *Asrar-e Hoseyn.* Vol. 16. Sari: Mazandaran, 1995.

Matthews, David, trans. *The Battle of Karbala': A Marsiya of Anis.* New Delhi: Rupa, 1994.

Mazahir. *'Ashura': The Martyrdom of Imam Husayn: A Historical Perspective.* Mombasa, Kenya: Bilal Muslim Mission of Kenya, n.d.

Mazioglu, Hasibeh, ed. *Divan-e Farsi-ye Fuzuli.* Ankara, 1962. Rpt. Tehran: Ershad-e Islami, 1999.

Mehrotra, Arvind Krishna. "Introduction." *An Illustrated History of Indian Literature in English.* Ed. Arvind Krishna Mehrotra. 1–26.

_____, ed. *An Illustrated History of Indian Literature in English.* Delhi: Permanent Black, 2003.

Mir Ahmad Ali, A. V. *Husain: The Saviour of Islam.* 1964. Rpt. Qom: Ansariyan, 2005.

Mirjahani-Tabatabayi, Sayyid Hasan. *al-Buka' li al-Husayn.* Ed. Ruh Allah 'Abbasi. Qom: Resalat, 2006.

Misri, Hussein Mojeib al-. *Karbala' bayn shu'ara al-shu'ub al-islamiyyah.* Cairo: al-Dar al-Thaqqafiyyah, 2000.

Mohaddethi, J. *Adab-e Al Allah,* Qom: Za'er, 2008.

_____. *Darsha-yi az Ziyarat-e Ashura.* 2d. ed. Qom: Boustan-e Ketab, 2005.

_____. *Farhang-e 'Ashura'.* 8th ed. Qom: Ma'ruf, 2006.

Mojahedi, Muhammad-Ali. *Shokouh-e she'r-e 'Ashura' dar zaban-e farsi.* Qom: Markaz-e Tahqiqat-e Islami-Sepah, 2001.

Mufid, Muhammad ibn Muhammad al-. *Kitab al-irshad.* 2000. Rpt. Qom: Tahdhib, 2011.

Muhammadi-Reyshahri, Muhammad, ed. *Daneshnameh-ye Imam Husayn.* 2d ed. 14 vols. Qom: Dar al-Hadith, 2010.

_____, ed. *Shahadat nameh-ye Imam Husayn.* Qom: Dar al-Hadith, 2011.

Muhammadzadeh, Marziyeh. *Daneshnameh-ye Sh'r-e 'Ashura' yi.* 2 vols. Tehran: Irshad, 2008.

_____. "She'r-e hoseyni dar masir-e tarikh." *Otarod-e Danesh.* Ed. Tale'ie. 429–457. *Munjid al-.* 38th ed. Bayrut: Dar al-Mashreq, 2000.

Musawi al-Khirsan, Sayyid Muhammad-Mahdi. *al-Sujud 'ala al-turbah al-husayniyyah.* Karbala': Imam al-Husayn's Sacred Sanctuary, 2005.

Musawi al-Muqarram, Sayyid 'Abd al-Razzaq al-. *al-'Abbas.* 1948. Rpt. Ed. Muhammad al-Hassoun. Karbala': al-'Ataba al-'Abbasiya, 2006.

_____. *'Ali al-Akbar.* 2d. ed. Najaf: al-Haydariyyah, 1947.

Naidu, Sarojini. *The Feather of the Dawn.* London: Asia, 1961.

_____. *The Sceptred Flute: Song of India.* Allahabad: Kitabistan, 1943.

Najmi, Muhammad-Sadiq. *From Medina to Karbala in the Words of Imam al-Husayn.* Trans. Muhammad-Reza Fakhr-Rohani. Birmingham: Sun Behind the Cloud, 2012.

_____. *Payam-e Ashura.* 2d. ed. Qom: Daftar Intesharat Islami, 2004.

_____, ed. and trans. *Sokhanan-e Husayn ibn 'Ali az Madineh ta Karbala'.* 3d. ed. Qom: Boustan-e Ketab, 1387 Sh/ 2009.

Nakash, Yitzhak. "An Attempt to Trace the Origin of the Rituals of 'Ashura" *Die Welt des Islams* 33.2 (1993): 161–181.

Naqvi, Syed Sadiq. *Muslim Religious Institutions and their Role under the Qutb Shahs*. 2d. ed. Hyderabad, A. P.: Bab-ul-Ilm Society, 2006.

_____, and V. Kishan Rao, eds. *The Muharram Ceremonies Among the Non-Muslims of Andhra Pradesh*. Hyderabad, A. P.: Bab-ul-Ilm, 2004.

Naravane, V. S. *Sarojini Naidu: Her Life, Work, and Poetry*. Hyderabad, A. P.: Orient Longman, 1980.

OED, The Oxford English Dictionary. 2d. ed. 20 vols. Ed. John Simpson, and Edmund Weiner. Oxford: Oxford University Press, 1989.

Onions, C. T. *The Oxford Dictionary of English Etymology*. Oxford: Oxford University Press, 1966.

Orami, Shahrokh. *Sho'a'-e mehr-e Hoseyn dar adab-e kord-e ahl-e sonnat*. 2d. ed. Tehran: Taqrib-e Madhaheb-e Islami, 2007.

Paranjape, Makarand, ed. *English Studies, Indian Perspectives*. New Delhi: Mantra Books, 2003.

_____, ed. *Sarojini Naidu: Selected Letters, 1890s to 1940s*. New Delhi: Kali for Women, 1996.

Patke, Rajeev S. *Postcolonial Poetry in English*. Oxford: Oxford University Press, 2006.

Pouramini, Muhammad-Baqir. *Chehreha dar Hemaseh-ye Karbala'*. Qom: Boustan-e Ketab, 2003.

Qa'emi, Abu al-Qasem. *Hemaseh-ye 'Ashura: Anguizehha, Ahdaf, Natayej*. Qom: Majlesi, 2011.

Qarashi, Baqir Sharif al-. *al-'Abbas ibn 'Ali*. Ed. Mahdi Baqir al-Qarashi. Karbala': al-'Ataba al-'Abbasiyah, 2009.

_____. *Hayat al-Imam al-Husayn*. 10th ed. 3 vols. Qom: al-Mu'assasah al-Islamiyyah, 2006.

_____. *The Life of Imam Husain*. Trans. Syed Athar Husain Rizvi. Qom: Ansariyan, 2007.

Qasir, Sayyid 'Ali al-. *Hayat Hayb ibn Mazahir al-Asadi*. Karbala': al-'Atabah al-Husayniyyah, 2011.

Qummi, 'Abbas, ed. *Mafatih al-jinan*. Various editions.

_____. *Mafatih al-jinan / The Keys to the Gardens of Paradise*. English Trans. Badr Shahin. Qom: Ansariyan, 2009.

_____. *Muntaha al-amal*. Various editions.

_____. *Nafas al-mahmoum*. Ed. Reza Ostadi. Qom: Basirati, 1974.

_____. *Nafas al-mahmoum*. Persian Trans. Abu al-Hasan Sha'rani. Tehran: 'Ilmiyyeh Islamiyyeh, 1953. Rpt. Qom: Hejrat, 2004.

_____. *Nafasul mahmoom*. English Trans. Aejaz Ali Bhujwala (al-Husainee). Qom: Ansariyan, 2005.

Qurayshi, 'Abd al-Amir al-. *al-Balighun al-fat'h fi Karbala'*. Bayrut: Dar al-'Ilm li al-Nabihin, 2008.

Riyahi, Muhammad-Amin. *Kasayi marwazi: zendegui, andisheh, va she'r'u*. 12th ed. Tehran: Elmi, 2008.

Rizvi, Syed Saeed Akhtar. *Four Californian Lectures*. Dar es Salaam: Bilal Muslim Mission of Tanzania, 1989.

_____. *Understanding Karbala'*. Trans. Syed Athar Husain Rizvi. Qom: Ansariyan, 2006.

Rizvi, Saiyid Athar Abbas. *A Socio-Intellectual History of the Isna Ashari Shi'is of India*. 2 vols. Canberra: Ma'rifah, and New Delhi: Munshiram Manoharlal, 1986.

Ruffle, Karen G. "May Fatimah Gather our Tears: The Mystical and Intercessory Powers of Fatimah al-Zahra in Indo-Persian, Shi'i Devotional Literature and Performance." *Comparative Studies of South Asia, Africa, and the Middle East* 30.3 (2010): 386–397.

_____. "'Verses Dripping Blood': A Study of Muhtasham Kashani's Karbala'-Namah." MA thesis, University of North Carolina, Chapel Hill, 2001.

Russell, Ralph, ed. *The Oxford Indian Ghalib Life, Letters and Ghazals*. New Delhi: Oxford University Press, 2003.

Sabouni, Muhammad-Karim. *Chekameh-ye 'Eshq*. 2d. ed. Tehran: Ershad-e Islami, 2006.

Sadiq, Muhammad. *A History of Urdu Literature*. 2d. ed., rev. and enl. Delhi: Oxford University Press, 1984.

Saduq, Muhammad al. *al-Amali*. Qom: Tahdhib, 2008.

_____. *'Uyun akhbar al-Rida*. 2 vols. Qom: Payam-e Alamdar, 2011.

Saksena, Ram Babu. *History of Urdu Literature*. Allahabad: Ram Narian Lal, 1927.

Samawi, Muhammad Tahir al-. *Ibsar al-'ayn fi ansar al-Husayn*. Najaf: al-Haydariyyah, 1920. Rpt. Ed. Muhammad-Ja'far al-Tabasi. Qom: Zamzam, 2006.

Sarkissian, Sebouh. "The Event of Karbala': A Survey of Some Classical Sources: al-Ya'qubi, al-Tabari, and al-Mas'udi." PhD dissertation. Birmingham: University of Birmingham, n.d.

Sayyid, Kamal al-. *Bolous salama: sha'ir al-Ghadir wa Karbala' fi al-zaman al-akhir*. Bayrut: al-Ghadir, 2004.

Schubel, Vernon James. *Religious Performance in Contemporary Islam: Shi'i Devotional Rituals in South Asia*. Columbia, SC: University of South Carolina Press, 1993.

Seidel, Kathleen. *Serving the Guest: Food for Remembrance*. Internet: superluminal.com/cookbook/

Sengupta, Padmini. *Sarojini Naidu*. New Delhi: Sahity Akademi, 1974.

Shahristani, Sayyid 'Abd al-Rida al-. *al-Sujud 'ala al-turbah al-husayniyyah*. Ed. Haydar al-Jidd. Karbala': Imam al-Husayn's Sacred Sanctuary, 2010.

Shahristani, Sayyid Salih al-. *Tarikh al-Niyaha 'ala al-Imam al-Shahid al-Husayn ibn 'Ali*. Vol. 1 Tehran: Jama'ah al-Nashr wa al-'Alaqat al-Islamiyyah, 1973.

Shams al-Din, Muhammad Mahdi. *Rokhdad-e Karbala' dar nahad-e toudehha*. Trans. Muhammad-Jawad Ma'muri. Qom: Dar al-Kitab al-Islami, 2008.

_____. *Yaran-e Husayn 'alayh al-salam*. Trans. A.-B. Ma'muri, n. p.: Kalima al-Haqq, 2006.

Shams-Ansari, Sa'id. *Hoseyn Khoda-ye Hemasehha*. Tehran: Daftar-e Nashr-e Farhang-e Islami, 2004.

Shamsie, M. "English Literature." *The Encyclopedia of Pakistan*. Ed. Hafeez Malik, and Yuri V. Gankovsky. 72–25.

Shoja'i, Muhammad. *Neynawa*. Qom: Zohour-e Shafaq, 2005.

Shubbar, Jawad, ed. *Adab al-Taff*. 10 vols. Bayrut: Dar al-Murtada, 1988.

Siddiqui, M. A., ed. *Common Heritage*. Karachi: Oxford University Press, 1997.

Silverstein, Adam J. *Islamic History: A Very Short Introduction*. Oxford: Oxford University Press, 2010.

Singh, Iqbal. *The Ardent Pilgrim: An Introduction to the Life and Work of Muhammad Iqbal*. London: Longmans, Green, 1951. Rpt. Delhi: Oxford University Press, 1971.

Singh, Mina Surjit. *Six Women Poets: A Cross-Cultural Study*. New Delhi: Prestige Books, 2003.

Skeat, Walter W. *An Etymological Dictionary of the English Language*. 4th ed. Rev. enl. and reset Oxford: Clarendon-Oxford University Press, 1910.

Sobhani, Ja'far al-. *Ziyarat 'Ashura Sanadan wa Makanatan*. Qom: Mu'assisah al-Imam al- Sadiq, 2010.

SOED, Shorter Oxford English Dictionary. 6th ed. 2 vols. Ed. A. Stevenson. Oxford: Oxford University Press, 2007.

Sohnen-Thieme, Renate. "Six Balti Marsiyas." *Dimensions of South Asian Religion*. SOAS Working Papers in the Study of Religions. London: University of London, 2007. 35–65.

Soleymani-Boroujerdi, Mirza 'Ali. *Tahqiqi Jame' Piramoun-e Seh Tefl-e Shahid-e Sayyed al-Shuhada dar Karbala': 'Ali Asghar, 'Abd Allah al-Radi', 'Ali-ye Radi'*. Qom: Dar al- Tafsir, 2010.

Speake, Jennifer. *Dictionary of Foreign Words and Phrases*. Oxford: Oxford University Press, 1997.

Steingass, F. *A Learner's Arabic-English Dictionary*. London, 1884. Rpt. Bayrut: Librairie du Liban, 1989.

Stevenson, Angus, and Maurice Waite, eds. *Concise Oxford English Dictionary*. 12th ed. Oxford: Oxford University Press, 2011.

Tabasi, Muhammad-Jawad al-. *al-Maqtal al-Husayni al-ma'thur*. 2d. ed. Tehran: Dar al-Sami, 2007.

Tabrizi, Ja'far. *Barrasi-ye sanad-e ziyarat-e 'Ashura'* . Qom: Neynawa, 2011.

Tabrizi, Jawad. *Ziyarat 'Ashura Fawq al-Shubahat*. Qom: Dar al-Siddiqah al-Shahidah, 2005.

Taki, Sakina. *The Epitome of Sacrifice*. Nairobi: ABSN, 2010.

Tale'ie, 'Abd al-Hoseyn, ed. *Otarod-e Danesh*. Tehran: Library of Islamic Majlis, 2011.

Tehrani, Abu al-Fazl. *Shafa al-sudur fi sharh ziyarat al-'ashur*. 2 vols. Ed. Sayyid 'Ali Mowahhed Abtahi. Qom: n.p., 1991.

Trivedi, Madhu. "Appropriating an Iranian Literary Tradition: *Marsiya* in the Indian Context." *Journal of the Indian Musicological Society* 36–37 (2006): 149–172.

Tu'mah, Sayyid Salman Hadi al-. *Turath Karbala'*. 2d. ed. Bayrut: al-'Alami, 1983.

Turbati al-Karbala'yi, Haydar al-. *Ziayarat dhabih al-i Muhammad al-'ashura'iyyah*. Tehran: Farsad, 2008.

Tyro, Nawab Syed Mahmoud Ali Khan. *The Manifestation of the Light Pristine, or the Story of the Faith Divine: An Apopee and Other Poems*. Hyderabad, A. P.: Master Plus DTP, 1960.

Van Donzel, E. *Islamic Desk Reference Compiled from The Encyclopedia of Islam*. Leiden: E. J. Brill, 1994.

Wyld, Henry C. *Universal Dictionary of the English Language*. London: Routledge and Kegan Paul, 1961.

Zaidi, Ali Jawad. *A History of Urdu Literature*. New Delhi: Sahitya Akademi, 1993.

_____. *Mir Anis*. New Delhi: Sahitya Akademi, 1986.

Zakeri-Shandizi, Sayyed Mojtaba. *Sajdeh bar Torbat-e Imam Hoseyn wa Gueristan bar an Hazrat*. 3d. ed. Tehran: Farhang-e Sabz, 1384.

Zaman, Muhammad. "Hindu-Muslim Cultural Relations before Partition." *Common Heritage*. Ed. Siddiqui. Karachi: Oxford University Press, 1997. 129–145.

Arabic

JOHN ANDREW MORROW

"(It is) a Qur'an in Arabic." (Qur'an 39:28)

Introduction

As highly developed and cultivated as it may have been in pre–Islamic times, the Arabic language was perceived as the insignificant language of an insignificant people. The fate of the Arabic language, and its speakers, the Arab people, would be forever changed as a result of an event that occurred in the cave of Hira', on the Mountain of Light, on the auspicious night of August 10, 610 CE. The revelation of the Qur'an, as offered to the Prophet Muhammad, would produce one of the most powerful socio-cultural, linguistic, economic, political, and religious revolutions the world had ever seen. Within the twinkle of an eye, an obscure, self-destructive, and primarily polytheistic band of brigands, thieves, warlords and outlaws were suddenly subjected to collective illumination and enlightenment, inspiring a complete and total cultural transformation. Without warning, the waning superpowers of the period were soon overwhelmed by the missionary zeal of a menacing monotheistic movement. Wherever they went, these highly motivated Muslims spread the message of Islam and conquered hearts with the Qur'an. Though merely a humble linguistic conduit, one through which Gabriel conveyed divine revelation to the Prophet Muhammad, the Arabic language soon assumed a central role as the liturgical and scholarly language of Islam.

The Arabic Language in the Qur'an

Although many religions have sacred or liturgical languages, such as Sanskrit in Hinduism, Hebrew in Judaism, as well as Latin and Greek in Catholicism, the scriptures of these various faiths, however, simply do not stress the importance of their respective languages of revelation, composition or compilation. In contrast, the Qur'an repeatedly emphasizes that it is an Arabic Qur'an: "We have sent it down as an Arabic Qur'an" (12:2); "We revealed it to be a judgment of authority in Arabic" (13:37); "We sent this down — an Arabic Qur'an" (20:113); "We sent by inspiration to thee an Arabic Qur'an (42:7); and "We have made it a Qur'an in Arabic" (43:3).

Since the Vedas do not stipulate that "these are Sanskrit Vedas," the Old Testament does not speak of "this Hebrew Torah," and the New Testament never emphasizes that "this is a Greek gospel," why, then, does the Author of the Qur'an stress that it is an Arabic recital? The reason is more historical than metahistorical. Although the Islamic tradition teaches that God sent 124,000 prophets and messengers to humankind, most of the known prophets of the Abrahamic faiths were of Jewish extraction. While the Jews of Arabia were expecting the arrival of a final prophet and messenger prior to the return of the Messiah, they were completely convinced that he would belong to the line of Ishaq (Isaac). Although the *sirah* (biography) of the Prophet mentions cases of Jewish people who acknowledged that Muhammad, the son of 'Abd Allah, was indeed the long awaited one, they ultimately rejected him because he belonged to the wrong branch of the family.

If the Qur'an stresses its Arabic origin, it was in response to its Judeo-Christian detractors. As Almighty Allah reveals regarding Muhammad: "We know indeed that they say, 'It is a man that teaches him'" (16:103). Responding to such allegations, the Divine Author points out that "The tongue of him they wickedly point to is notably foreign, while this is Arabic, pure and clear" (16:103). According to Jalal al-Din al-Mahalli (d. 1459) and Jalal al-Din al-Suyuti (d. 1505), the individual alluded to in this verse was a Christian blacksmith to whom the Prophet used to give his custom. The claim was that the Qur'an was composed on the basis of Christian Aramaic sources. According to the *Tanwir al-miqbas*, attributed variously to 'Abd Allah ibn 'Abbas (d. 687) and to Muhammad ibn Ya'qub al-Firuzabadi (d. 1414), "the man that teaches him" refers to Jabr and Yasar who spoke Hebrew, while the Qur'an was in distinctly Arabic speech. 'Ali ibn Ahmad al-Wahidi (d. 1075) is even more precise in his identification of the individual(s) who supposedly taught the Prophet. In his *Asbab al-nuzul*, Wahidi relates a tradition on the authority of 'Abd Allah ibn Muslim who said:

> We owned two Christian youths from the people of 'Ayn Tamr, one called Yasar and the other Jabr. Their trade was making swords but they also could read the Scriptures in their own tongue. The Messenger of Allah, Allah bless him and give him peace, used to pass by them and listen to their reading. As a result, the idolaters used to say: "He is being taught by them!" To give them the lie, Allah, exalted is He, revealed (The speech of him at whom they falsely hint is outlandish, and this is clear Arabic speech).

While this version of events is perfectly plausible, it appears that allegations were also made that Waraqa ibn Nawfal was the originator of the Qur'an. According to a tradition on the authority of 'A'ishah, Waraqa, the uncle of the Khadijah, the Prophet's first and favorite wife, reportedly converted to Christianity during the pre–Islamic period. Not only did he become a Christian, he is said to have translated the Gospels into Arabic (Bukhari; Muslim). The allegation in this instance would be that the Qur'an was inspired on the basis of Christian Aramaic sources which had been translated into Arabic by a person closely connected to the Prophet.

Finally, the Qur'anic emphasis on the Arabic nature of the revelation appears to come as a response to repeated provocations on the part of some Medinan Jews. According to several companions of the Prophet, "The People of the Book used to recite the Torah in Hebrew and used to explain it in Arabic to the Muslims" (Bukhari). Their intent was obvious: seek to cause doubt and dissent among the Muslims through scriptural fault-finding. The Prophet adopted a diplomatic solution. "Do not believe the People of the Book or disbelieve them" he instructed, "but say: 'We believe in Allah and what is revealed to us'" (2:136). While the Qur'an was in Arabic, it stressed that it was a confirmation of previous scriptures: "And before this, was the Book of Moses as a guide and a mercy: And this Book confirms (it) in the Arabic tongue; to admonish the unjust, and as Glad Tidings to those who do right" (46:12).

Almighty Allah also revealed that "(It is) a Qur'an in Arabic, without any crookedness (therein): in order that they may guard against Evil" (39:28). The verse is interesting since *qur'anan 'arabiyyan* is a circumstantial qualifier of emphasis. According to the two Jalals, however, the verse refers to the Qur'an itself. In other words, "It is an Arabic Qur'an without any deviation, that is, [without] any contradiction or variance." According to the Qur'anic commentary attributed to Ibn 'Abbas, the words "without any crookedness" means that it contains nothing "contradicting the Torah, the Gospel, the Psalms, or any other divinely inspired Scripture in terms of the affirmation of Allah's divine Oneness, some legal rulings and punishments."

The importance of Arabic in the Qur'an revolves partly around this battle of the holy books. As the Muslim scripture insists, the Qur'an was revealed in Arabic for Arabs in departure from previous prophetic practice. The Arabs were thus the intended audience. As the Qur'an explains, it would have been preposterous for an Arab prophet to preach to his people in a foreign language. As Almighty Allah explains:

> Had We sent this as a Qur'an (in the language) other than Arabic, they would have said: "Why are not its verses explained in detail? What! (a Book) not in Arabic and (a Messenger an Arab?" Say: "It is a Guide and a Healing to those who believe; and for those who believe not, there is a deafness in their ears, and it is blindness in their (eyes): They are (as it were) being called from a place far distant!" [41:44]

Consequently, the Prophet preached to the people "[i]n the perspicuous Arabic tongue" (26:195), which, according to the *tafsir* (commentary) attributed to Ibn 'Abbas means: "Inform them, O Muhammad, using their own language." Almighty Allah also described the Muslim scripture as "A Book, whereof the verses are explained in detail; a Qur'an in Arabic, for people who understand" (41:3). Although the term "people of understanding" has many meanings, the *Tafsir Jalalayn* explains that "they are the Arabs."

The fact that the Qur'an was revealed in Arabic was evidently not an exclusivist claim. The Prophet was simply following the tradition of speaking to the people in the language of the people. As Almighty Allah explains, "We sent not an apostle except (to teach) in the language of his (own) people, in order to make (things) clear to them" (14:4). The early Arabs did not assume ownership over Arabic, the Qur'an or Islam. They realized that it was incumbent upon them, as Arabs, to spread the final word of God to the rest of the world:

> Thus have We sent by inspiration to thee an Arabic Qur'an: that thou mayest warn the Mother of Cities and all around her, and warn (them) of the Day of Assembly, of which there is no doubt: (when) some will be in the garden, and some in the Blazing Fire [42:7].

Finally, and most importantly, if the Qur'an references its linguistic origin, it is because the Prophet's major miracle was the revelation he received. As the Qur'an conveys, each and every time the Messenger of Allah was asked for a miracle from the Jews, Christians, and polytheists (6:109; 7:203; 13:38; 20:133; 21:5; 29:50; 40:78), he pointed to the Qur'an.

Besides being accused of concocting a Judeo-Christian forgery, the Prophet was also accused of being a poet: "'Nay,' they say, '(these are) medleys of dream!—Nay, He forged it!—Nay, He is (but) a poet! Let him then bring us a Sign like the ones that were sent to (Prophets) of old!'" (21:5). The Composer of the Qur'an then challenged any mere mortal to come up with a comparable composition:

> Say: "If the whole of humankind and Jinns were to gather together to produce the like of this Qur'an, they could not produce the like thereof, even if they backed up each other with help and support" [17:88].

And if ye are in doubt as to what We have revealed from time to time to Our servant, then produce a Surah like thereunto; and call your witnesses or helpers (If there are any) besides Allah, if your (doubts) are true [2:23].

This Qur'an is not such as can be produced by other than Allah. On the contrary it is a confirmation of (revelations) that went before it, and a fuller explanation of the Book — wherein there is no doubt — from the Lord of the worlds. Or do they say, "He forged it?" Say: "Bring then a Surah like unto it, and call (to your aid) anyone you can besides Allah, if it be ye speak the truth!" [10:37–38].

Or they may say, "He forged it," Say, "Bring ye then ten suras forged, like unto it, and call (to your aid) whomsoever ye can, other than Allah. — If ye speak the truth!" [11:13]

Or do they say, "He fabricated the (Message)?" Nay, they have no faith! Let them then produce a recital like unto it, — If (it be) they speak the truth! [52:33–34]

Despite defiantly determined efforts over the ages, not a single poet or prose-writer in the Arabic language has ever been able to match the eloquence of the Qur'an. Universally acknowledged by Arabs as the masterpiece of Arabic literature, the literary value of the Qur'an has also been expounded upon by a long line of non–Muslim Arabists and Orientalists. E.H. Palmer grudgingly acknowledged that "the best of Arab writers has never succeeded in producing anything equal in merit to the Qur'an" (lv). Even Hamilton Gibb admitted that,

> As a literary monument the Koran thus stands by itself, a production unique to the Arabic literature, having neither forerunners nor successors in its own idiom. Muslims of all ages are united in proclaiming the inimitability not only of its contents but also of its style ... and in forcing the High Arabic idiom into the expression of new ranges of thought the Koran develops a bold and strikingly effective rhetorical prose in which all the resources of syntactical modulation are exploited with great freedom and originality [36].

The Arabic Language in the Sunnah

If the word "Arabic" is repeated eleven times in the Qur'an, it is rarely mentioned as a subject in the *Sunnah*. The Prophet is reported to have instructed Muslims to "Love the Arabs for three reasons: because I am an Arab, because the Qur'an is in Arabic, and because the language of the people of paradise is Arabic" (Tabrizi 6006; Tabarsi; Hakim; Bayhaqi; Ibn Manzur, qtd. Chejne). While many early Muslim authorities believed that Arabic was the language of Adam, the "mother of all languages," and that even its script was a God-given gift (Chejne, *The Arabic Language 10*), Ibn al-Jawzi, al-Dhahabi, and al-Albani have all asserted that the tradition in question is fabricated. Although this is a spurious saying, which has been falsely attributed to the Prophet by Arab chauvinists, nationalists or supremacists, it shows the efforts made by some Arabs to encourage the Arabization of Islamized populations. These were the same silly people who spread sayings stipulating that if Arabic was the language of paradise then Persian was the language of hell. There is a tradition, however, attributed to the Prophet, which states that Arabic is a language like any other. It says, "O men! There is only one God, and all men have only one ancestor. The true religion is one. The Arabic language is neither the father nor the mother or any one of you; it is just a language. Thus, whoever speaks Arabic is an Arab" (qtd. Chejne, The Arabic Language, 183, note 63). This more sobre attitude towards the language was also echoed by Imam Ja'far al-Sadiq who instructed his Shi'ites to "Learn Arabic, the language of the final word of Allah" (qtd. in Pooya Yazdi 765). The reason, of course, is practical and does not imply ideas of linguistic superiority.

The Impact of the Arabic Language

As Islam spread throughout the world, so did the Arabic language. The first wave of expansion, which took place during the lifetime of the Prophet from 622 to 632 CE, consolidated Classical Arabic's hold on the Arabian Peninsula. The second wave, which took place during the Rashidun Caliphate from 632 to 661, spread the Arabic language throughout the Levant and the Near East. The third wave of expansion, spearheaded by the Umayyads from 661 to 750, spread the Prophet's Semitic tongue into North Africa and al-Andalus in the West and well into the lands of the Indus Valley in the East.

While the process of Arabization was slow, typically taking centuries in Egypt, North Africa, and Islamic Spain, it was, nonetheless, facilitated by the establishment of an Islamic educational system, namely, a network of *madrasahs*, which imparted Arabic language instruction, as well as institutions of higher learning that attracted the brightest minds of the period. Intermarriage between Arab men and indigenous women throughout these areas also augmented the process of Arabization. Although Muslims were less than 10 percent of the population in Iraq, Syria, Egypt, Tunisia, and Spain towards the end of the Umayyad period (Hourani 41–48), and bilingualism or trilingualism was the norm rather than the exception, most of the subjects of the Islamic empire were drawn towards the Arabic language as it represented the language of power, culture, civilization, science, and progress. While it took time, and many local languages continued to co-exist with Arabic, the language of the Qur'an eventually came to dominate religious, political, and educational life.

For Muslims, both Arabs and non–Arabs, the Arabic language had even greater significance as it was the spiritual language of Islam. In the case of converts, the use of the Arabic script even became a religious-identity marker. Muhammad Hamidullah explains how Arabic is the spiritual mother-tongue of all Muslims (183). Consequently, it is their duty to learn it, even if their knowledge might only be an understanding of its alphabet. The goal, however, is to read the Qur'an in the original (183). "Since all time," Hamidullah observes, "converts have attached so great an importance to it, that they have even adopted the Arabic script in their local languages. Such is the case with Persian, Turkish, Urdu, Malay, Pashto, Kurdish, Spanish, Lithuanian, Afrikaans, etc." (183). For many Muslims, knowledge of the Arabic script connected them to the Qur'an. This explains why the Moriscos, despite having lost use of the Arabic language, maintained the Arabic script as much as possible. The result was the production of a diverse body of literary works in *aljamiado*, specifically, Spanish written with the Arabic alphabet. Like most Muslims, the Moriscos revered the Arabic language as it was the earthly recipient of *Kalam Allah* or the Word of God.

Arabic: The Language of Allah?

Although *kalam* or speech is one of Allah's attributes, it does not refer to language or sound and does not resemble human language in any way. To claim that Allah speaks a human language like Arabic or Hebrew is to claim that Allah has a body for, in order to speak, one needs a mouth, a tongue, teeth, glottis, and nasal cavity. However, according to the teachings of Islam-original, Almighty Allah does not have a body. Since *kalam* refers to action and not essence, it is not an eternal attribute. As Imam Ja'far al-Sadiq explained, "Speech is an accidental [*muhdathah*] attribute and not sempiternal [*azaliyyah*]. Allah, the Mighty and High, existed when no speakers existed" (qtd. Saduq 266). Furthermore, since

Allah is eternal, and the Arabic language evolved from early Semitic languages, it cannot be said that Arabic is the language of Allah. Since all languages are limited, and Almighty Allah is limitless, no mundane mode of communication could completely capture and convey the expansive thoughts of the Primal Intellect. The divine language of the Creator and Sustainer of the Universe must necessarily predate and supersede human speech. Any communication between the spiritual and earthly realm is compelled to pass through a series of emanations. Unveiled, the Word of God would completely shatter mountains and vaporize oceans. Since speech is vocalized human communication, which requires the tongue, lips, jaw, and other organs in order to make sounds, it would be silly to suppose that spiritual beings would express themselves in the same fashion as corporeal creatures. The claim that Arabic is the language of paradise is thus simply unsustainable. Likewise, the claim that the Arabic alphabet was revealed by Allah (Chejne, *The Arabic* 180, note 22), and introduced by the Prophet, is patently false (Morrow, *Kitab al-tawhid*, note 493 & 497). As I explain in *Kitab al-tawhid*, "The Arabic alphabet developed around 400 C.E. It evolved from Proto-Canaanite > Phoenician > Aramaic > Nabataean or Syriac into the Arabic *abjad*" (note 503). Furthermore, as I observe in "The Pre and Early Islamic Period" found in *A Cultural History of Reading*), "[t]he first recorded text in the Arabic alphabet was written in 512 C.E., and consists of a trilingual dedication in Greek, Syriac, and Arabic. It is only one of five pre-Islamic Arabic inscriptions known for certain" (525). Although claims that Arabic is the language of paradise have been categorically debunked by *hadith* scholars, many Muslims maintain a belief in the monogenesis of languages, mistakenly believing that all languages evolved from Arabic, the primal paradisiacal language.

Arabic: The Language of Islam

Although Arabic is not the literal language of Allah, and Arabic is not the language of paradise, Arabic is very much the scholarly and liturgical language of Islam. It is the language of the Qur'an, the language of the *hadith*, the language of the *shari'ah*, and the language of a large body of critically important early Islamic scholarship. As Tibi explains,

> The language of Islam is Arabic because the Koran is revealed in it. Arabic is also the language of Islamic law. Numerous verses of the Koran emphasize its Arabic character. Non-Arab Muslims must say their prayers and similarly recite the Koran in Arabic, for which reason the language used in non–Arab Koranic schools is also Arabic. All Islamic jurists are educated in Arabic. Pious Muslims also have Arabic names, even if they are not Arabs [156].

The author, however, errs by asserting that this attachment to Arabic "is an indication of a mostly accepted Arabocentrism" (156). He is equally mistaken when he asserts that "Sacred law is brought to expression by means of the sacred language of the Koran" (156). It is essential to stress that it is the Qur'an, and not the Arabic language, to which Muslims are attached. Had the Qur'an been revealed in Zulu, then Muslims would have revered the Zulu language. Without the Qur'an, the Arabic language would be of little significance to Muslims. So, more than being Arabic centered, Muslims are Qur'an centered. Arabic is merely the means of reaching the Message. After all, it is the Qur'an which is sacred; not the Arabic language. The sacredness of the Arabic language is very much limited to the Arabic content of the Qur'an. While one can touch the Arabic script while in a state of ceremonial impurity, it is prohibited to touch the name of Allah or the verses of the Qur'an without being in a state of ritual purity.

Although the Arabic language is not sacred per se, and is only spoken by 10 percent of Muslims, it remains of central importance to the followers of the Islamic faith. In Imam Shafiʿi's view, all Muslims should learn Arabic at least to the point that they can make the act of testimony (*shahadah*), recite the Qurʾan, and invoke the name of Allah (Hourani 68). While complete proficiency is enviable, religious scholars are only required to have reading comprehension of Arabic: namely, the ability to read and use an Arabic dictionary. As all intelligent Muslims are well-aware, Islamic knowledge is not confined to the Arabic language and Arabs do not have a monopoly over truth and wisdom.

Besides being the language of the Qurʾan, the *Sunnah*, and the *shariʿah*, Arabic has been a language of communication between Muslims. While Arabic has always been the maternal language of a minority of the Islamic ummah, it has nevertheless acted as a *lingua franca* among the one billion Muslims around the world. It was a language of culture, class, education, and commerce. When spoken as a second language, it enabled Muslims to communicate with their brethren in Europe, Africa, the Middle East, and Asia. Since Muslims have traditionally been united on the basis of faith and language, the enemies of Islam set out to undermine the ummah by eroding its linguistic foundation.

The Decline of Classical Arabic

Since Arabic functions as a powerful unifying factor, it comes as no surprise that various conniving European conquerors and colonizers made a determined effort to eradicate the Arabic language, suppressing the use of Classical Arabic, and encouraging the spread of Colloquial Arabic in its mutually unintelligible forms. When the invaders arrived, most Arab Muslims were literate and could communicate with each other in Qurʾanic Arabic. By the time the outsiders were ousted during different periods in history, the literacy of the majority of Arab Muslims had devolved and they could no longer communicate with fellow Arabs outside their regional frontiers. The Arabic-speaking Muslim world effectively disintegrated and it was divvied up on the basis of politically-contrived national identities. As Iqbal Siddiqui has explained, the loss of political power resulted not only in political fragmentation, it produced intellectual degradation.

While it is true that assorted dialects of Arabic existed during the time of the Prophet, the production of the Qurʾan fourteen centuries ago, and the dissemination of Islam resulted in a leveling of those dialects (Bassiouney 120). Despite the fact that Classical Arabic's waning coincides with the decline of the ʿAbbasid Caliphate in the late tenth century, and a recognition that the Ottomans virtually forced *fushah* into oblivion by propagating Turkish and encouraging the use of the Arabic vernacular (Chejne, *The Arabic* 83–84, 107), it cannot be denied that the process of dialectical divergence increased as a result of the policies of Western powers in more recent times. In the words of Darwish al-Jundi,

> The imperialists were aware of the influence of the Arabic language drawing the Arabs together, in binding their past to their present, and in consolidating Arab nationalism. They fought it and tried to replace it with their own languages. They also attempted to develop colloquial and regional dialects, hoping thereby to stamp out classical Arabic, tear the links between Arabs, and weaken Arab sentiment, which is everywhere nourished by the language [qtd. Laffin 67–68].

The French, for example, closed Qurʾanic schools, imposed their own language on a foreign people, while simultaneously promoting the use of Colloquial Arabic. Machiavelli could not have initiated a more devious plan.

By imposing French as the official language in all public spheres, including education, public life, and administration, France attempted to eradicate Standard Arabic from all of its North African holdings (Bassiouney 212). In Algeria, which was occupied from 1830 to 1962, "France tried ruthlessly and meticulously to eradicate Standard Arabic there" (213). Bassiouney describes the French strategy in the following fashion:

> To achieve their aim of eradicating Standard Arabic, the French took hold of the religious endow-ments which provide the financial base for education and closed all Qur'anic schools, allowing education only in French ones. Education was related to religion and usually run by Muslim reli-gious institutions in which one of the means of learning Standard Arabic for children was mem-orizing the Qur'an. Thus the old education system in Algeria collapsed [214].

Besides killing off one third of the Algerian population between 1830 and 1872, the French were committed to culling the Arabic language and culture as well. By 1938, the suppression of the Arabic language had succeeded to such a point that it was officially decreed a foreign language (Bassiouney 215). If 40 to 50 percent of Algerians were literate in Arabic at the onset of colonization, 90 percent of them were illiterate in both Arabic and French by the time the French left (214). While most Algerians could speak Colloquial Algerian Arabic, which had now become a combination of French, Arabic, and Berber, only 10 percent of them were proficient in Standard Arabic, namely, 300,000 out of 30 million (216). In short, "French policy helped eradicate [Standard] Arabic" (215). Not only was French imposed on Algeria, it was then used to play the Arabs against the Berbers (203). The effects of this policy can be felt to this day pitting secularized French-speaking Berbers against Arabic-speaking Muslims.

In Morocco, which had the misfortune of being a French protectorate from 1912 to 1956, "French was ... imposed as the medium of instruction in schools, government, administration, and the media" (221). "Standard Arabic," however, "was used only in religious and traditional activities" (221). The French, of course, "had neither the intention of educating the whole population nor that of modernizing them" (221). In 1946, Resident General Labonne admitted that "Après quarante ans de protectorat, il y a dans ce pays 95 percent d'analphabètes" (After forty years of protectorate, 95 percent of people in this country are illiterate) (Azizi and Le Braz). Ten years later, when independence finally arrived, the situation was scarcely any better: 89 percent of Moroccans remained illiterate (Moscoso García 17). By 1960, only 6 percent of Moroccans were literate in French; and only 12 percent were literate in Arabic (Bassiouney 222). By 1978, the literacy rate was still only 15 percent (Nydell, 2002: 150).

Although the French were only briefly in Egypt, from 1798–1801, they attempted to appropriate Arabic as a tool of imperialism. As explained in "The Future of the French Lan-guage in Light of French Anti-Islamism,"

> Napoleon, with great cunning, identified his interests as those of the Egyptians. When he invaded Egypt in 1798, he told them that he had arrived to implement the *shari'ah*, namely, the Islamic legal system. He used to read the Qur'an, and even wrote that "There is no god but Allah" in his personal copy. He covered Cairo with flyers that said that Allah is the Greatest and that he had come to liberate the Muslim people from the Mamelukes. In Cairo, during a meeting with dig-nitaries and religious leaders at the University of al-Azhar in July of 1798, he publicly professed to be a Muslim. After embracing Islam, he adopted the Muslim name 'Ali. Napoleon's conversion to Islam was featured in page 61 of *Le Moniteur*, the official French newspaper of the period. Acting as a Muslim, he prohibited French officers from drinking alcohol in public; he prohibited them from harassing women; and forbade them to enter mosques. All of the decrees made by French administrators commenced with the words, "There is no god but Allah and Muhammad

is the Messenger of Allah." His council even passed a *fatwa* (or religious edict) declaring that Napoleon was the Mahdi, the Awaited Savior, and affirmed that there were twenty Qur'anic verses which referred implicitly to him [Morrow].

As Edward Said has summarizes: "Napoleon tried everywhere to prove that he was fighting *for* Islam; everything he said was translated into Koranic Arabic, just as the French army was urged by its command always to remember the Islamic sensibility" (170). Although many Muslims were dupped by Napoleon's duplicity, traditional scholars of Islam denounced his strategy as an effort to subvert Islam.

Although they were not as intent as the French on imposing their language, the British also did a great deal of damage in Egypt and the Sudan. During their occupation, which lasted from 1882 to 1952,

> The British administration aimed to weaken [Standard] Arabic from the beginning of the occupation. To do so they first introduced English and French as the required languages in the education system. Second, they elevated the status of Egyptian Colloquial Arabic rather than Standard Arabic by emphasizing the distinctiveness of the Egyptian identity as opposed to the Arab identity [Bassiouney 237].

Key figures in the British administration called for replacing Classical Arabic with Egyptian Colloquial Arabic as the official language (238). As always, Orientalists were eager to serve the cause of imperialism and commenced a scholarly campaign to cultivate the various forms of Colloquial Arabic (238). By 1917, only 6.8 percent of the Egyptian population was literate (Fahmy 6). Among these, only a minute fraction was able to effortlessly code-switch any significant Classical vocabulary into Colloquial speech (6).

Whether it was the French or the British, European imperialists imposed language policies with precise long-term objectives. The results of British language policy can be felt to this day. In the Sudan,

> The British ... tried to stop the spread of Arabic in the south by attempting a southern policy / closed district policy in 1930–46. Under this policy Britain claimed that the Negroid Africans of the south were culturally and racially different from the northerners, who claim to be Arab. As a result, the southerners could either be separated from the northerners or be integrated into what was then British East Africa [246].

The conflict between north and south Sudan was created by the British over eighty years ago in order to slow the spread of Arabic and Islam. Had the Arabic language and culture been allowed to expand freely in the Sudan, the country would have been united culturally, religiously, and linguistically. *Divide et impera* was the motto. To a large extent, the challenges faced by Arabs and Muslims are a legacy of the colonial past and form part of a larger neo-imperial agenda in which language played an important role.

While most Arab nations embarked on ambitious Arabization programs upon attaining their independence, they have all universally failed in their attempts to restore Classical or Modern Standard Arabic as the dominant language of their lands. After a century of meddling in Morocco and Algeria, the French had effectively eradicated speakers of Classical or Standard Arabic. Although Arab nationalists were eager to re-impose Standard Arabic across the Arab world, some even striving to suppress Colloquial Arabic dialects, they simply could not find enough competent teachers to fulfill such an ambitious task (202–203). Ironically, the Algerians were obliged to ask the French to send them teachers of Standard Arabic. The Algerians also brought scores of Egyptian instructors; however, the colloquial in which they taught was almost completely incomprehensible to North Africans.

To make matters worse, students schooled in Arabic could not find jobs nor could they succeed in university studies since French had become the dominant language of higher education, business, and administration (Bassiouney 216–217). With the exception of Syria, virtually all Arab countries have abandoned their efforts to completely Arabize their educational systems and most have opted to universalize them, offering education in English and French. While Classical or Modern Standard Arabic remains the official language of Arab countries, the *de facto* official language is the Colloquial variety of the country or, in some cases, English or French. If they were responsible for suppressing Standard Arabic, Western imperialists continue their campaign to promote the Colloquial Dialects over the Classical language. Besides their attempts to secularize the Arabic language, removing religious expressions which form an essential part of etiquette (Morrow 2007), the French decided in the year 2000 that they would only teach Colloquial Moroccan Arabic in their secondary schools (Bassiouney 266).

As case studies have shown, once a language is lost, it cannot be recovered. Attempts to revive Gaelic in Ireland, Euskadi in the Basque country, Galician in Galicia, and countless indigenous languages in the Americas, have all failed miserably. Only languages in positions of power have been able to be revived. If French has survived in Canada, it is because it was always the language of the majority in Québec. If it has been preserved in other parts of the country, it is because of legal protection and rights to education in the French language. Once a language ceases to have native speakers it is dead for all intents and purposes.

As sad as it may be to state, there are no native speakers of Classical Arabic or Modern Standard Arabic. Classical Arabic has long been in a coma. It is a dead language which has been artificially maintained for religious reasons. The small number of Arabs who speak *fushah* speak it as a second language. From a dominant language of culture, civilization, religion and science, High Arabic has been relegated to the role of a written literary language. The few Arabs who speak *fushah* are Arabic language teachers and religious scholars. If given the option to communicate with non–Arabs in Classical Arabic as opposed to English or French, the Arabs almost invariably opt for the easier Western language. If even the French, with their systematic language policy, have been unable to slow the encroachment of the English language (Bassiouney 268), how will the Arabs — as utterly divided, unorganized, and unresourceful as they are — do anything to protect Arabic from the ravages of linguistic imperialism? English, in the eyes of Fishman (4) and Skutnabb-Kangas, is very much a "killer language." Ahmad al-Issa warns that if the current trend towards English continues in the United Arab Emirates, "people will continue to speak Arabic, but fluent Classical or Modern Standard Arabic (MSA) will become a language of the past." If it took executive and legislative action to eliminate Arabic speech in Spain over the course of three generations after 1492, with laws passed in 1501, 1511, 1526, and again in 1566 (Ostler 100), all it takes now is television.

As Arab Muslims soon learned after independence, the mere fact that the foreigners were forced out did not mean the end of foreign meddling in domestic affairs. If imperialism was physical in nature throughout the past, requiring expensive and permanent military occupation and colonization, neo-imperialism has focused on conquering minds by means of the mass media and popular culture. As a result of dialectical dominance, the Colloquial varieties have triumphed over the Classical idiom. Iqbal Siddiqui's analysis is sobering:

> [T]he reality is that Arabic no longer has the importance it once did in the Muslim world. It remains central to Islamic religiosity, as the language of the Book of Allah (swt) and of the canonical works of *hadith* and *fiqh*, but in other spheres of intellectual work it is English rather than Arabic

that is crucial. Some misguided Muslims have even welcomed English as the new lingua franca of the ummah, an attitude encouraged by the arrogance of some Arabs who have tried to claim a privileged position in the ummah because of their language. But the deeper reality is that, like the Turks after Mustafa Kemal, generations of Muslims have been cut off from their Islamic heritage as a result of losing their knowledge of Arabic.

Although Islamic civilization has always demonstrated the greatest appreciation for linguistic diversity and Muslims have a long history of learning new languages in order to expand their learning as well as to spread the message of Islam, Muslims were then operating from a position of power. Muslims have been marginalized since the fall of their respective empires and the subsequent rise of Imperial Europe, and the linguistic tables have been turned. While Iqbal Siddiqui recognizes the practical reasons for the emphasis on English and other Western languages, he stresses the importance of understanding the implications that this phenomenon has on Muslim societies:

> One is that the links of other languages are fragmenting the ummah by turning Muslim attention from the heartlands of Islam, which were once the core of a united ummah, towards various intellectual centers of the West, be they Washington, London, Paris or Moscow. The other is that other languages, English in particular, have become tools for the marginalization of Islamic perspectives, and conduits for the wholesale adulteration of Muslim discourse by Western ideas and attitudes.

As Siddiqui admits, "[t]here are no easy solutions to this problem." Among his proposals, however, is that "Muslims learn Arabic if at all possible, and certainly ensure that their children are taught Arabic so that they can feel at home anywhere in the Muslim world in the future." Considering the complexity of the Classical Arabic language, and the time it takes to master, the idea that Muslims should all head to university for ten years of full-time study will certainly fall on deaf ears. Since only a minuscule minority of educated Arabs master Classical Arabic, the Arabs would first need to Arabize themselves.

With twenty-five different dialects, the most divergent of which are mutually-incomprehensible to each other, the Arabs cannot even communicate with one another. As Bassiouney puts it, "someone who knows only a dialect of spoken Arabic will be likely not to understand an educated speaker of another dialect or be able to make herself or himself understood" (2). The reasons revolve around major differences in grammar, pronunciation, and vocabulary. According to Nydell, "more than 50 percent of the words are different from the local dialect in some countries" (1996: 116; 2002: 118). In a study conducted on 6-year-old Tunisian children in the early 1970s, it was found that 70 percent of their words differed from those found in Classical Arabic (Nydell, 1996: 124, note 3; 2002: 118 fn). Understandably, most Arabs have difficulty speaking and writing in Classical Arabic. Consequently, most Arabs with high school or college level educations cannot maintain a conversation in the Classical idiom.

Ostler claims, without providing any proof whatsoever, that out of 205 million Arabs, about 100 million of them know Classical Arabic (527). This makes no statistical sense since approximately 60 percent of Arabs are illiterate (Hammoud 3). It goes without saying that one cannot be illiterate and proficient in Literary Arabic at the same time. According to studies conducted by Dilworth Parkinson, most urban Egyptians with a high school education are "abominably fluent" in *fushah* while the average Egyptian with a college education is competent in Modern Standard Arabic (69). Although 30 percent of Egyptians go to university, only 15 percent of them graduate. Hence, the proficiency rate in Standard Arabic could not conceivably surpass 15 percent of the population of the country. If fluency in *fushah* is associated with university education, then the percentage of college graduates in various countries could serve as an indicator of linguistic proficiency. If, according to the UNESCO Institute for Statistics, 22 percent of people in the Arab world attend university, proficiency in Standard Arabic could not top that number. However, considering that drop-out is approximately 50 percent, this number falls to 11 percent. Considering that most fields such as mathematics, science, and engineering are taught in English, with MSA being used mainly in the fields of Arabic and Islamic Studies, it would not be inconceivable that people fluent in *fushah* number above 5 percent of the population. Since most Arabs are not competent in Classical Arabic, and 60 percent of Muslims as a whole cannot read or write, the focus should be on basic literacy in their own languages and not some unattainable goal of Arabizing the entire Islamic world.

With the exception of religiously motivated Muslims and non–Muslims seeking to serve the cause of Western imperialism, there are few reasons for foreigners to study the Arabic language. As Bassiouney has explained, the success of any language depends on economic factors as well as prestige (269). "In our age," writes Ostler, "Arabic is for foreign learners the language of the Koran, English the language of modern business and global popular culture" (521). How many times have language learners been confronted by Arabs incapable of comprehending why anyone would want to study Arabic? As one Arabic professor explained to me, "Ibn Khaldun wrote that people learn the language of power. You should not be learning our language. Our time has past. We Arabs should be learning your languages." And they are. In fact, "the use of foreign languages, French and English specifically, is still prevalent in the Arab world, even more so than at the time of colonization" (Bassiouney 210). The words of the broken man from Bou'arfa, Morocco, embody the broken spirit of a broken people. As proud as many Arabs may be, they are only proud of their past glories. In point of fact, most of them have resigned themselves to their role as subaltern subjects. Consequently, they cannot be relied upon to revive Arabic or Islam. If Islam will ever become the world culture that it once was, its torchbearers will be Western converts who combine the zeal of the ancient Orient with the advances of the modern Occident.

The idea that all Muslims should master Arabic is manifestly mistaken. "Although Arabic is associated with Islam," argued Bassiouney, "the Islamic nation is a universal one where kinship, language and territory are surpassed" (Bassiouney 209). Although "[t]he Arabic language spread together with Islam" (Hourani 48), it never took root in regions which did not have a Semitic or Hamito-Semitic substrate (Ostler 97–99). In areas with Indo-European language roots, such as Spain and Iran, the Arabic language never established a permanent presence (Ostler 97; 554). If the overwhelming majority of Muslims never adopted Arabic during over one thousand years of Islamic domination, it is delusional to believe that they could ever do so when they are disempowered and dispossessed.

It was only as a written language, as the language of religion, that Arabic found no frontier within the world of Islam (Hourani 48; Ostler 96). The Arabic script, as opposed to the language itself, was much more universally attractive (Ostler 97). Despite its serious phonetic shortcomings and defects, it was adopted as the alphabet for Persian, Turkish, Kashmiri, Berber, Uighur, Somali, Housa, Swahili, Malay, as well as Spanish and Bosnian (Ostler 97). As Ostler explains, the success of the Arabic script was due to the fact that "literacy in Muslim countries finds its alpha and its omega in the sacred text of the Qur'an in Arabic script; so any other writing system can only be an extra complication" (Ostler 97).

As important as Arabic may be, it is not the only Islamic language: any language spoken by Muslims is an Islamic language. As Ayatullah Mutahari has stated, "In the eyes of Islam, which is a universal religion, all alphabets are equal" (76). He also made it explicitly clear that "In the eyes of Islam, the English, Japanese, and Persian languages are all of equal value" (77). Persian, in particular, has played an important role in the spread of Islam in Iran, Azerbaijan, Tajikistan, as well as Uzbekistan, Turkey, and Afghanistan (Ostler 99). Although the Shi'ite Seminary in Qum was founded by Arabs, Persian has long been the dominant language of instruction and scholarship in this sacred city. In the Indian subcontinent, the Urdu language is intimately associated with Islam. As Tariq Rahman explains,

> Except for Arabic, there is no special language of Islam. However, a language used by a community of Muslims can become the language of Islam and of Muslim identity in a specific time period and region. With the advent of modernity, Urdu, a language of North Indian origin, became such a language with political, social, educational, economic and cultural consequences. It became part of [*ashraf*] Muslim identity replacing Persian which occupied that position earlier. It became a symbol of the Muslim political identity next only to Islam itself during the struggle for the creation of Pakistan out of British India. Then, in Pakistan, it became a part of the Pakistani (as opposed to the ethno-nationalist) and Muslim (as opposed to secular and Westernized) identity [115].

Siddiqui's second suggestion is sounder and would call upon Islamic institutions to establish a policy to promote Arabic as the language of Islamic discourse, re-establishing intellectual links with the heartlands of Islam, and re-connecting with the Islamic movements in those heartlands, even when it is easier and more practical to work only with English-speaking Muslims in Western countries or non–Arab Muslim countries. However, as Olivier Roy has explained, it is English, and not Arabic, which is the *lingua franca* of the Muslim movement. Since the advent of the Islamic Revolution of Iran, there are more Islamic books published in Persian than there are in Arabic. In fact, there are now more than twice as many books on Islam in English than there are in Arabic.

While Arabs often boast that Arabic is the third or the fifth most spoken language in the world, they refer to Arabic as if it were a single language when, in fact, it consists of over twenty-five distinct dialects which, for most linguists, should be categorized as individual languages. Without the mythic bond of Classical Arabic and the imaginary diglossia which is alleged to exist in the Arab world, Arabic does not even make it into the list of the thirty most important languages on earth. If educational and political policies properly promote Standard Arabic, the Arab world may remain a linguistic bloc. Considering the high birth rates across Arabic-speaking countries, Arabic dialects are in no danger of disappearing any time soon. Unfortunately, "there is no trend towards a unified standard outside elite usage" (Ostler 530). On the contrary, Arabic dialects are flourishing around the Arab world while knowledge of Standard Arabic is declining. If Imams used to give their sermons in Classical Arabic, many of them have turned to a combination of Classical and Colloquial while others make exclusive use of the vernacular. If there was once hope that satellite television would help standardize the Arabic language through broadcasting in Classical Arabic, the opposite has been the case. If cartoons, soap operas, and newcasts were always in Modern Standard Arabic, they are increasingly being produced in Arabic dialects, thus reducing exposure to the High language. As such, the vernacular is not giving way to the classical, as Mahmdu Taymur has hoped (qtd. Chejne 201, note 94). The dialects have become even more firmly embedded and their development accelerated.

Although Arabs view *'amiyyah* or *darijah* as dialects devoid of prestige, they should certainly not be destroyed. All languages are valuable and should be valued. While it cannot be denied that "[t]he literacy problem in the Arab World stems significantly from the difficulty of Classical Arabic" (Nydell 116), replacing Classical Arabic with Colloquial Arabic is not the solution. It should be recalled that Classical Arabic was the medium through which literacy was obtained in the past. It is no wonder that the North African Arabic word for school-teacher is *faqih* or jurist for it was the *fuqaha'*, the *'ulama'*, who imparted education in traditional Muslim societies. Prior to colonial times, however, knowledge of Arabic script was accompanied with knowledge of Standard Arabic. Learning to read and write had a point and a purpose. Since virtually all Arabs can only comprehend Colloquial Arabic, literacy is a dead end road. What benefit does one draw from learning to read and write in a language one cannot comprehend? As Nydell explains,

> Even people who can read and write are still functionally illiterate (unable to use the written language for more than rudimentary needs, such as signing one's name or reading signs) if they have had only five or six years of schooling [116].

If Arabic dialects were accepted as written languages, illiterate individuals might be motivated to alphabetize themselves. Literacy would serve a practical purpose. The solution is not to officially replace Standard Arabic with Colloquial Arabic. As Nydell has synthesized,

> Classical Arabic is a cultural force which unites all Arabs. To discard it, many fear, would lead to a linguistic fragmentation which would exacerbate the tendencies toward political and psychological fragmentation already present [116–117].

The solution is to provide instruction in Colloquial Arabic while teaching Classical Arabic as a second language. As recent studies have shown, literary Arabic is expressed in the brain of Arabic speakers as a second language and not as a mother tongue (University of Haifa). According to researcher Raphiq Ibrahim,

> The cognitive disparity between the two languages is similar to the difference between a native and a second language. This offers an explanation for the objective and day-to-day difficulties that confront Arabic-speaking students when attempting to learn to read the non-spoken language

As native speakers of Colloquial Arabic, Arab students face the added difficulty of being taught to read and write in a second language: Classical Arabic. As Ibrahim explains,

> the results of this study indicate that linguistic structures of MSA that constitute the basis for reading acquisition are likely to be unfamiliar to the Arabic-speaking child when beginning to learn to read in first grade. This makes learning to read in Arabic a double mission, whereby children are expected to acquire in parallel an auditory linguistic system as well as a complex orthographic-visual language system.

As it currently stands, the method employed in teaching Classical Arabic can have a negative effect on the development of reading skills, potentially compromising achievements at more advanced levels, particularly for less skilled students. This dichotomy between the Colloquial and the Classical explains the high rate of illiteracy in the Arab world along with its abysmal drop-out rate. Ibrahim's study suggests that Modern Standard Arabic should be taught with techniques typically employed for the instruction of second languages. Arab children are sorely lacking auditory exposure to High or Literary Arabic at an early age. Ideally, then, Arabs should complete high school with a mastery of both Colloquial and Classical Arabic. Currently, this is not the case. With the exception of experts in Arabic and Islam, graduates in all other fields master only Colloquial Arabic along with the Western language in which they completed their advanced studies.

Considering the dire state of affairs, the call to save Classical Arabic is heard at regular intervals in the Arab world. In 2007, the Arab League held a special conference in order to discuss the future of Standard Arabic and ways in which it could be taught to children (Bassiouney 198). Works such as *Arabic, Islam, and the Allah Lexicon: How Language Shapes our Conception of God*, as well as *Global English and Arabic: Issues of Language, Culture, and Identity*, have warned of the demise of Classical Arabic. The situation is alarming to Arab unity for, as Darwish al-Jundi, wrote: "The Arabic language is the strongest foundation of Arab nationalism" (qtd. Laffin 67). It is also alarming to Muslims as a whole for to weaken Arabic is to weaken Islam. According to Bassiouney's forecasts,

> In a hypothetical world, if each Arab country started using its own colloquial in domains in which Standard Arabic was used, then in fifty years, all Arab countries would be detached from Standard Arabic, and the common Standard Arabic literature which was read by all Arabs would be incomprehensible for a young generation trained only in colloquial. Whether Arabs would still understand each other is difficult to predict [266].

As critically important as they may be, increased connections between Muslims, and the encouragement of Arabic in Islamic discourse will by no means slow or stem the tide or erosion of proficiency. If the Arabs themselves have lost the Classical Arabic language, how can one expect non–Arabs to somehow save it? Will *al-lughah al-'arabiyyah al-fushah*, the most eloquent Arabic language, go the way of Biblical Hebrew and Latin, becoming merely a liturgical as opposed to a living language? It may already have. Still, the issue is of unparalleled urgency for, as Ostler has expressed, "Islam is unthinkable without Arabic" (537). While many strategies have been attempted, and many policies have been put into place, they have all fundamentally failed in reviving Classical Arabic. If many Arabists are pessimistic about the fate of *fushah*, Bassiouney hopes that "the mission to preserve Standard Arabic and the struggle to save it are just at their onset" (270). While the manner in which this can be done is unclear, Bassiouney believes that "[r]eligion has a vast role to play in the survival of Standard Arabic" (269). Students and scholars of Islam should thus rise to the occasion as effective action is long overdue.

Conclusions

The Classical Arabic language is a linguistic treasure which has produced some of the most magnificent literary masterpieces in existence, the magnum opus of which is none other than the Glorious Qur'an. Since Almighty Allah's first command to the Prophet was "Read!" (96:1), all Muslims were henceforth obliged to read the Qur'an, ensuring that the entire population of the Islamic community had an elementary level of literacy. The love of the Qur'an produced love for the language in which it was written. For many Muslims, the Arabic language became, not only the liturgical, literary, cultural, artistic, scientific, and educational language of Islam, it became viewed as the language of Allah, the language of paradise, and the source of all other languages. Consequently, most Arabs are convinced of the superiority of their own language. Although Islamic scholars and linguists have rejected assertions that Arabic is a divine, heavenly language, from which all other languages originated, all Muslims love the Qur'an and the miraculous mode in which it was written. One of the greatest expressions of such love is the Muslim cultivation of Arabic-Islamic calligraphy based on the most beautiful depictions of the names of God and Qur'anic verses. For these, and many other reasons, Islamic jurist Subh al-Salih rightly concluded that "Arabic is the symbol of Islam" (122).

Works Cited

Albani, Muhammad Nasir al-Din al-. *Silsilah al-ahadith al-da'ifah wa al-mawdu'ah.* al-Riyad: Maktabat al-Ma'arif li al-Nashr wa-al-Tawzi', 2009.

Azizi, Abdellatif El-, and Eric Le Braz. "Protectorat: Cent ans sans solitude."*Actuel* 123 (6 janvier 2012). Internet: www.actuel.ma/Dossier/ProtectoratCent_ans_sans_solitude/863.html

Bassiouney, Reem. *Arabic Sociolinguistics: Topics in Diglossia, Gender, Identity, and Politics.* Washington, DC: Georgetown University Press, 2009.

Bayhaqi, Ahmad ibn al-Husayn. *Shu'ab al-'iman.* al-Riyad: Maktabat al-Rushd, 2003.

Chejne, Anwar G. *The Arabic Language: Its Role in History.* Minneapolis: University of Minnesota Press, 1969.

Fahmy, Ziad. *Ordinary Egyptians: Creating the Modern Nation through Popular Culture.* Stanford: Stanford University Press, 2011.

Fishman, Joshua. "Endangered Minority Languages: Prospects for Sociolinguistic Research." *International Journal on Multicultural Societies* 4.2 (2002). Internet: www. unesco.org/most/vl4n2fishman.pdf

Gibb, HAR. *Arabic Literature: An Introduction.* Oxford: Clarendon Press, 1963.

Hakim al-Nisaburi, Muhammad ibn 'Abd Allah. *Mustadrak 'ala al-sahihayn.* 'Amman: al-Dar al-'Uthmaniyyah, 2007.

Hamidullah, Muhammad. *Introduction to Islam.* Paris: Centre Culturel Islamique, 1969.

Hammoud, Hassan. *Illiteracy in the Arab World.* Paper commissioned for the *EFA Global Monitoring Report 2006, Literacy for Life.* Internet: unesdoc.unesco.org/images/0014/001462/146282e.pdf

Hourani, Albert. *A History of the Arab Peoples.* Cambridge: The Belknap Press of Harvard University Press, 1991.

Ibn Taymiyah, Ahmad ibn 'Abd al-Halim. *Iqtida' al-sirat al-mustaqim.* al-Qahirah: Matba'at al-Sunnah al-Muhammadiyyah, 1950.

Issa, Ahmad al-. "Arabic Must be the Focus in Pursuit of 'True' Bilingualism in the UAE: Why a Serious Language Policy is Needed." *Arabizi* (February 19, 2012). Internet: arabizi.wordpress.com/tag/modern-standard-arabic/

Issa, Ahmad al-, and Laila S. Dahan, eds. *Global English and Arabic: Issues of Language, Culture, and Identity.* Peter Lang: Oxford, Bern, Berlin, Bruxelles, Frankfurt am Main, New York, Wien, 2011.

Laffin, John. *Rhetoric and Reality: The Arab Mind Considered.* New York: Taplinger Publishing Company, 1978.

Morrow, John Andrew. "Arabic Instruction in France: Pedagogy or Politics?" *The International Journal of the Humanities* 4:6 (2007): 17–24.

_____. "The Future of the French Language in Light of French Anti-Islamism." *Islamic Insights: Writings and Reviews.* Qum: Ansariyan, 2012. 21–25.

_____. "The Pre and Early Islamic Period." *A Cultural History of Reading.* Ed. Gabrielle Watling. Westport, CT: Greenwood Press, 2008. 521–540.

_____, ed. *Kitab al-Tawhid / Divine Unity.* Shaykh al-Saduq. Trans. Sayyid 'Ali Rizvi. Qum: The Saviour Foundation, 2010.

_____, and Barbara Castleton. *Arabic, Islam, and the Allah Lexicon: How Language Shapes our Conception of God.* Lewiston: Edwin Mellen Press, 2006.

Moscoso García, Francisco. "Situación lingüística en Marruecos: árabe marroquí, bereber, árabe estándar, lenguas europeas." BIBLID [1133–8571] 10 (2002–2003): 153–166. Internet: www.arabemarroqui.es/Recursos/Situacion%20linguistica%20Marruecos.pdf

Motaheri, Morteza. *Los derechos de la mujer en el islam.* Teheran: Organización de Propagación Islámica, 1985.

Nydell, Margaret K. *Understanding Arabs: A Guide for Westerners.* Yarmouth, Maine: Intercultural Press, 2002.

_____. *Understanding Arabs: A Guide for Westerners.* Yarmouth, Maine: Intercultural Press, 1996.

Ostler, Nicholas. *Empires of the World: A Language History of the World.* New York: HarperCollins, 2005.

Palmer, Edward Henry, trans. *The Qur'an.* Oxford: The Clarendon Press, 1900.

Pooya Yazdi, Ayatullah Agha Hajji Mirza Mahdi, Ed. *The Holy Qur'an.* Trans. S.V. Mir Ahmed 'Ali. Elmhurst: Tahrike Tarsile Qur'an, 1988.

Parkinson, Dilworth. "Knowing Standard Arabic: Testing Egyptians' MSA Abilities." *Perspectives on Arabic Linguistics.* Ed. Mushira Eid and Clive Holes. Amsterdam: John Benjamins Publishing Company, 1993: 47–74.

Rahman, Tariq. "Urdu as an Islamic Language." *Annual of Urdu Studies* 21 (2006): 101–119. Internet: www.urdustudies.com/pdf/21/06Rahman.pdf

Roy, O. Interview with Olivier Roy: Author of *Globalized Islam: the Search for a New ummah*. Internet: cup.columbia.edu/static/Interview-roy-olivier-globalized

Saduq, Shaykh al-. *Kitab al-Tawhid / Divine Unity*. Trans. Sayyid 'Ali Rizvi. Edited by John Andrew Morrow, Sayyid 'Ali Rizvi, and Barbara Castleton. Annotated by John Andrew Morrow and Sayyid 'Ali Rizvi. Qum: The Saviour Foundation, 2010.

Said, Edward. "Orientalism: The Cultural Consequences of the French Preoccupation with Egypt." 'Abd al-Rahman Jabarti. *Napoleon in Egypt: al-Jabarti's Chronicle of the French Occupation, 1798*. Princeton: Markus Wiener Publishers, 2004

Salih, Subhi al-. *Ma'alim al-shari'ah al-islamiyyah*. Bayrut: Dar al-'ilm li al-Malayin, 1975.

Siddiqui, Iqbal. "Centrality of Arabic as a Unifying Factor in the Islamic Movement." *Crescent International* (2012). Internet: www.crescent-online.net/component/content/article/2514-centrality-of-arabic-as-a-unifying-factor-in-the-islamic-movement.html

Skutnabb-Kangas, Tove. *Linguistic Genocide in Education or Worldwide Diversity and Human Rights?* Mahwah, NJ & London, UK: Lawrence Erlbaum Associates, 2000.

Tabarani, Sulayman ibn Ahmad. *al-Mu'jam al-awsat*. al-Qahirah: Dar al-Haramayn, 1995. Qum: Kitab Khani Ayatullah al-Uzma Mar'ashi Najafi, 1982.

Tabarsi, Abu 'Ali al-Fadl ibn al-Hasan al-. *Tafsir majm'a al-bayan fi tafsir al-Qur'an*. Bayrut: Mu'assasat al-A'lami li al-Matbu'at, 1995.

Tabrizi. *Mishkat al-masabih*. Bayrut and Dimashq: al-Maktab al-Islami, 1985.

Tibi, Bassam. *Islam between Culture and Politics*. New York: Palgrave, 2001.

UNESCO. *Country and Regional Profiles*. Internet: stats.uis.unesco.org/unesco/TableViewer/document.aspx?ReportId=198

University of Haifa. "Literary Arabic Is Expressed in Brain of Arabic Speakers as a Second Language." *ScienceDaily* (November 4, 2009). Internet: www.sciencedaily.com/releases/2009/11/091104091724.htm

Zogby, James. *Arab Voices: What They Are Saying to Us and Why It Matters*. New York: Palgrave MacMillan, 2010.

About the Contributors

Zahid Shahab **Ahmed** received his Ph.D. in political and international studies from the University of New England, Australia, and is an assistant professor of peace and conflict studies at the National University of Science and Technology in Pakistan. He has published and presented on a wide range of issues, including Islam, human rights, peace and conflict, regionalism, and regional security.

Bridget **Blomfield** received her Ph.D. from Claremont Graduate University where she specialized in Islamic studies and women in religion. An assistant professor of religious studies at the University of Nebraska, Omaha, she teaches "Women in Islam," "Muslims in America," and "Sufism," and is also the director of the Islamic Studies Program.

Zahur Ahmed **Choudhri** is a Pakistan-based scholar of Islamic studies whose major areas of interest are development and good governance. From 1989 to 2006, he served as the director of research at the Akhtar Hameed Khan National Centre for Rural Development in Islamabad. He is the president of the South Asia Centre for Peace.

Mohamed **Elkouche** is a Senior Lecturer of English language and literature at the University Mohamed I in Oujda, Morocco. He obtained his Ph.D. in American Literature in 2005. He has published several articles in both Arabic and English; many of his contributions pertain to the question of Otherness and the complex relationships between the West and the Islamic world.

Muhammad-Reza **Fakhr-Rohani** received a Ph.D. in linguistics from the University of Tehran and teaches at the University of Qom, Iran. His publications focus primarily on Ashura literature in English, and his current interest is the impact of Ashura on English language and literature since the 17th century.

Aida Shahlar **Gasimova** is a professor of Arabic literature in the Department of Oriental Studies at Baku State University. She holds two doctoral degrees from the Institute of Oriental Studies of the Russian Academy of Sciences and the Institute of Azerbaijani Literature. Her research interests include classical Arabic literature, Qur'anic stories and mental-spiritual life in pre–Islamic Arabia.

Naglaa Saad M. **Hassan** is an assistant professor of English and cultural studies at Fayoum University, Egypt. She received her B.A. and M.A. from Cairo University and was a Fulbright Scholar in Residence at Bridgewater State University. She has published articles on Arab and Muslim writers, and has a column page on Examiner.com where she tackles pertinent controversial issues.

Matthew **Long** received his M.A. in religion from the University of Georgia specializing in Islamic studies. He teaches religion courses at Chatfield College. Among his publications are entries for such works as *The Princeton Encyclopedia of Islamic Political Thought* and Oxford's *Encyclopedia of Islam and Women*.

Anna Maria **Martelli** received her doctoral degree from the University of Modern Languages of Milan where she specialized in English and French. She studied oriental languages at the University of Venice where she specialized in Islamic studies. She is a member of the Italian Institute for Africa and Orient (Is.I.A.O.) and the editor of *Quaderni Asiatici*.

Said **Mentak** teaches English at Mohammed I University in Morocco. He wrote his doctoral dissertation on aspects of postmodernism in American fiction with a specific focus on Kurt Vonnegut. He has published many articles and participated in conferences about cultural studies, media and Islam and was a visiting lecturer at Jacksonville State University in Alabama in 2006.

John Andrew **Morrow** received his Ph.D. from the University of Toronto. He is a specialist in Hispanic, Native, and Islamic studies, and has taught at numerous institutions, including the University of Toronto, Park University, Northern State University and Eastern New Mexico University. He has published a large body of articles in peer-reviewed journals and numerous books.

Mustapha **Naoui Kheir** received his third cycle doctorate in Chomskyan generative grammar from the University of Fez (Morocco) and has been teaching at the University of Meknes since 1989, where he is an assistant professor. One of his main interests is the language of the Qur'an and Qur'anic stylistics.

Hisham M. **Ramadan** received a doctor of juridical science degree from the University of Wisconsin where he specialized in Islamic law, criminal law, and human rights. He teaches at Kwantlen Polytechnic University, Canada. He has authored and co-authored numerous publications on criminal law, Islamic law, and comparative law.

Amar **Sellam** obtained his Ph.D. in contrastive rhetoric from Mohamed I University in Oujda, Morocco, and an M.A. in English language and linguistics from the University of York, England. He is engaged with a team translating into Arabic various English books for the benefit of the Centre for Studies & Research in Human Sciences (CERHSO) in Oujda, Morocco.

Mahdi **Tourage** completed his Ph.D. at the University of Toronto and is an associate professor at King's University College at the University of Western Ontario. He is also the book review editor of the *American Journal of Islamic Social Sciences* (AJISS). His areas of interest are Islamic religious thought and Sufism, classical Persian literature, gender and sexuality, and postmodern theories.

Sayyed Hassan **Vahdati Shobeiri** received a doctorate in law from Tarbiat Modares University in Tehran, Iran. He has published several articles and books, including the 2012 Iranian Book of the Year in jurisprudence and principles, *Contract Rights in Imami Jurisprudence*, co-edited with Seyed Mostafa Mohaghegh Damad, Jalil Ghanavati and Ebrahim Abdipoor Fard.

Cyrus Ali **Zargar** received a doctorate in Near Eastern Studies from the University of California, Berkeley, and is an assistant professor of religion at Augustana College in Rock Island, Illinois. He has published several articles and a book, *Sufi Aesthetics: Beauty, Love, and the Human Form in the Writings of Ibn 'Arabi and 'Iraqi*.

Hamza **Zeghlache** received both his master's and doctoral degrees from the University of Virginia and is a professor of Islamic architecture at the University of Setif, Algeria. He has published and presented in French, Arabic and English all over the world. His research interests include the textual representation of space in the Islamic cultural tradition.

Index